PETRUS ROMANUS

The FINAL Pope Is Here.

PETRUS ROMANUS

THOMAS HORN & CRIS PUTNAM

Defender

Crane, MO

Petrus Romanus: The Final Pope is Here
Defender
Crane, MO 65633
©2012 by Thomas Horn

A collaborative work by Thomas Horn and Cris Putnam.
All rights reserved. Published 2012.

Printed in the United States of America.

ISBN 13: 9780984825615

A CIP catalog record of this book is available from the Library of
Congress.

Cover illustration and design by Daniel Wright.

All Scripture quotations from the King James Version; in cases of
academic comparison, those instances are noted.

Acknowledgements

We wish to acknowledge the following people, without whose friendship, inspiration, assistance, and research this book would have been difficult to finish on time: our lovely wives Shelley Putnam and Nita Horn, Sue Bradley, Gary Stearman, J. R. Church, Christian Pinto, Mike Bennett, Mike Tatar Jr., Brian and Sonya Hedrick, Chris White, Majel Hyers, Pastor John MacArthur for his excellent teaching series on Roman Catholicism, and to Daniel Wright for a superior cover design. Of course editor, Donna Howell, must be shown gratitude for making us sound better than we are, and typesetter Pamela McGrew, whose world-class interior designs are constantly unparalleled. Finally, to the many thousands of friends who visit our websites and constantly express their love and support, please know how much your affection lifts us up in these critical times.

Contents

Preface

A book about a medieval prophecy is necessarily a book of history. The papacy is arguably the most ancient institution in existence today. While we seek to define the historical context of the matters at hand, the scope is enormous. Accordingly, we must paint in broad brush strokes and will inevitably fail to present events with a balance acceptable to all readers. First, we offer the big picture. The papacy is an outgrowth from the early Christian Church, which sprung up from the events of the first century centered on Jesus of Nazareth, as recorded in the ancient collection of documents known as the New Testament. There were certainly some great and godly men associated with Catholicism over the years, but we believe Rome became a juggernaut intoxicated by its own power. Our standard of truth is the Bible. Christianity is defined by the New Testament and all claimants to the title "Christian" are necessarily evaluated by it.

The formation of the New Testament cannon (rule of faith) was more organic that organized and largely in response to an onslaught of heretical books falsely attributed to the apostles. Scholars detect that the cannon was in evidence long before it was declared by any magisterial council. For instance, John Barton used data on the number of times the Early Church fathers quoted the various books and there is a clear distinction in frequency of usage between the New Testament books and the non-canonical works.[1] Also Christians adopted the codex instead of the scroll and the earliest examples predominantly attest to the same twenty-seven New Testament documents being bound together.[2] Hence, the argument that the formation of the cannon was a spiritual work of God by his providential authentication gains credence over the brute authority of magisterial councils.

Historically, the New Testament is an utterly unique and revolutionary collection of ancient documents. Unlike other so-called holy books, it explicitly claims divine inspiration: "All scripture is given by inspiration of God, and *is* profitable for doctrine, for reproof, for correction, for instruction in righteousness" (2 Ti 3:16). While some may wish to debate the intricacies of this, it is not the purpose of this book to argue that case, rather it is presupposed. Another revolutionary aspect of the New Testament which is often overlooked is its utterly unique socio-political worldview. Contrary to every other religious system, the New Testament documents present an inimitable picture of a composite society. We mean this in the sense that the world is defined as being made up of two groups of people as to the Gospel: believers and unbelievers. Believers are charged to do the work of ambassadors entering into hostile territory, peacefully appealing to the unbeliever to be reconciled to God (2 Corinthians 5:20). This is to be done by humble example and persuasion, never by threats or coercion. Jesus' greatest opponents were the religious leaders; you might even think of them as the popes, bishops, and cardinals of first-century Judaism.

Similarly, the church and state are considered separate and Christians are commanded to live peacefully even within hostile governments (cf. Rom 13). Consider that, prior to Jesus Christ, this concept of a composite society was unheard of in all of human experience. In all previous societies, religion and the state were a unified magisterium. Even in the Old Testament, the church and state were one as a theocratic and then monarchial system and priesthood. While there was a separation between the duties and rights of the priest and the king, the Jewish nation was a unified sacral society. The New Testament discarded the sequestered priesthood for the universal priesthood of the believer under Jesus Christ. Nowhere are church leaders called "priests." They are called elders or overseers and are encouraged by Peter to act, "Neither as being lords over God's heritage, but being ensamples to the flock" (1 Peter 5:3).

Today, Islam is an obvious illustration of a sacral system with its system of sharia law. In countries like Iran, Saudi Arabia, or Yemen, religious laws are enforced by the state and you risk your life if you accept the Gospel. Similarly, in China or North Korea, the atheistic state cult will jail, torture, and execute Christians as political dissidents. In Hinduism, the caste system mandates your position in society. This is the darkness of non-Christian religions. It also reveals the distinctiveness of the kingdom instituted by Christ. Jesus announced the "kingdom of God is at hand" (Mark 1:15), but simultaneously that this kingdom is "not of this world" (John 18:36). In addition, Satan's temptation of Christ involved a shortcut to possess all the kingdoms of this world which he rejected (cf. Mat 4:9). Accordingly, we believe that the separation of church and temporal power is essential to pure Christianity. The New Testament is the only religious book that endorses a composite society over a sacral society. Accordingly, there has never been a true "Christian nation" or "Christendom" and there will not be one until Christ returns. We believe this teaching is vigorously attacked and obfuscated by Satan. It was virtually lost for most of history and it took the Protestant reformation to begin bringing it back to light.

It is because of that reformation that America is also a composite society in that it advocates the separation of church and state. This was largely from the plight of Puritans and others who fled the state-mandated religions of England and Rome. Of course, in America it was originally conceived to keep churches free from the state more than keeping prayer out of schools and other such distortions. The original motivation was freedom *of* religion, not freedom *from* religion. That being said, what made America great was its Christian roots and New-Testament worldview. The Bible teaches us to be model citizens. It extols the virtues of hard work, loving your neighbor (even your enemies), and paying your taxes. Jesus illustrated the composite worldview perfectly when he taught, "Render therefore unto Caesar the things which are Caesar's; and unto God the things that are God's" (Mt 22:21). When considering the weight of that teaching, it is important to remember how utterly opposed to Christ the Roman government was. Even so, believers were taught to live in this church-state/world dichotomy as His ambassadors. However, there is a very real enemy working against us and we are in a state of war.

The New Testament also proclaims that "the whole world lieth in wickedness" (1 John 5:19); even the Roman Catholic translation confirms "the whole world is under the power of the evil one" (1 John 5:19). (Note however, for comparison, the NAB translation: "...is under the power of the evil one.").[3] Of course, we are talking about Satan who Jesus referred to as "the prince of this world" (John 12:31. 14:30). The apostle Paul called him "the ruler of the kingdom of the air" (Ephesians 2:2) and taught that "the god of this world hath blinded the minds of them which believe not, lest the light of the glorious gospel of Christ, who is the image of God, should shine unto them" (2 Co 4:4). So the whole evil world system is energized by Satan through a mystery of iniquity which is working around the clock opposing God (2 Thessalonians 2:7). The "world" system or *kosmos* is the evil sphere of influence through which Satan works. Accordingly, the Christian is taught to, "Love not the world, neither the things that are in the world" (1 John 2:15a). A major thesis of this book is that much of protestant Christianity as well as the Church of

Rome started well, but abandoned the New Testament bifurcation and has been absorbed into the world system. Accordingly, we are not attempting to present a balanced picture of institutionalized church history, but rather to provide evidence for our overarching thesis.

False religion invariably involves some sort of ritualistic system designed to appease the wrath of, or win the favor of, a deity. In this limited sense, true Christianity is not a religious system because it does not offer a means for people to approach God. Rather, in Christianity, God approaches man. Jesus made it clear that God makes the first move when He said, "No man can come to me, except the Father which hath sent me draw him: and I will raise him up at the last day" (Jn 6:44). In non-Christian systems, salvation is earned and maintained, but in the New Testament, grace through faith is offered as the means of salvation. Salvation is accomplished by God, not humans. Rather than a system, the New Testament presents a Savior and all that is required is faith in His atoning death and resurrection, the life-changing Gospel. As an example, we offer the introduction to Paul's letter to the Galatians:

> Paul, an apostle, (not of men, neither by man, but by Jesus Christ, and God the Father, who raised him from the dead;) And all the brethren which are with me, unto the churches of Galatia: Grace *be* to you and peace from God the Father, and *from* our Lord Jesus Christ, Who gave himself for our sins, that he might deliver us from this present evil world, according to the will of God and our Father: To whom *be* glory for ever and ever. Amen. (Galatians 1:1–5)

This brief passage contains seven essentials of Christian faith: 1) God as Father (v.1); 2) Jesus as Lord (vv.1, 3); 3) the resurrection (v. 1); 4) Grace from God the Father (v. 3); 5) Jesus uniquely gave Himself for our sins to deliver us from evil (v. 4); 6) Jesus' death was the Father's will (v. 4); 7) God alone is worthy of glory (v. 5).

It follows that any system which deviates from these essentials is no longer Christian. In the interest of transparency, we also affirm the five theological distinctives of the reformers: 1) *Sola scriptura* ("by Scripture alone"); 2) *Sola fide* ("by faith alone"); 3) *Sola gratia* ("by grace alone"); 4) *Solus Christus* ("through Christ alone"); and 5) *Soli Deo gloria* ("glory to God alone"). We offer this upfront as later argumentation is based on this presupposed foundation. Our hope is that the reader will leave religious rites and rituals behind to embrace the historic faith of the New Testament.

We believe God created humans in his image and likeness to live in relationship with Himself in community. Relationship entails connection and communication. Although this is how it began in the garden, the biblical record is clear that by rebellion man fell and compromised that relationship (Gen 3 ff.). In due course, God incarnated as a man in Christ to definitively provide the means of restoration for mankind. Jesus also came to bring meaning and purpose and to model the value system of heaven for us. Because of his redemptive sacrifice, God indwells believers by the Holy Spirit in intimate relationship. God makes His appeal to fallen men through redeemed believers by the power of the Holy Spirit. Believers are his ambassadors (2 Cor. 5:20) and the Spirit draws the unbeliever (Jn. 6:44). Only by justification and sanctification can man be restored to a right relationship with God. The ticket to the Kingdom is through the elegant simplicity of the Gospel:

> That if thou shalt confess with thy mouth the Lord Jesus, and shalt believe in thine heart that God hath raised him from the dead, thou shalt be saved. For with the heart man believeth unto righteousness; and with the mouth confession is made unto salvation. (Romans 10:9–10)

We want to extend this invitation to everyone including Roman Catholics. Accordingly, a few caveats are in order.

First, this book does not argue that all Roman Catholics are un-Christian. We affirm that Catholic Christians have accomplished some great things for God's Kingdom. However, we do believe certain dogma by Catholic, mainline protestant, and some evangelical churches represents a formidable stumbling block to the authentic Gospel. Thus, our intention is not to "Catholic bash" in a book about the Final Pope, but to sound a dire warning to all.

Second, we are not arguing exactly as the reformers, that the papacy is necessarily *the* Antichrist. Even so, we will demonstrate conclusively that up until a century ago, it was a definitive doctrine which has been quietly swept under the rug of history. We find the revisionism to be suspicious. Although we believe that there is substantial warrant for the classic protestant position, important qualifications and refinements are suggested herein.

Third, we are *not* setting dates for the tribulation or return of Christ. Let us phrase it more emphatically lest someone misunderstand: *We do not claim to know when the Lord will return.* Nevertheless, we are eager to discuss a remarkable conflation of prophecies, interpretations, and signs, principally the Prophecy of the Popes which is very near its end. The dates discussed are the product of research into the beliefs of various Christian and Catholic expositors. We make no claims to definite dates. Fourth, the Prophecy of the Popes has a somewhat dubious origin and the Vatican has a demonstrable track record of forgery and revisionist history. Even so, we are presenting a critical analysis which reveals remarkable chance defying evidence to support the prophecy of popes' accuracy. Our service to the reader is primarily one of "watchmen on the wall" (Ezekiel 3:17). We have simply investigated and followed the evidence where it led. This book is our submission of that research for your consideration.

Introduction: Timing is Everything

Things move at a glacial pace, until the time comes…

Author and publisher Tom Horn has repeatedly revealed a wonderful talent for discerning events that are ripe for disclosure. In combination with the scholarly research talents of Cris Putnam, they are now bringing a major development into the light of day. Working behind the scenes in a world characterized by swirling currents of challenging information, they have discovered that certain obscure documents now have a startling pertinence.

From these, they have distilled a clear stream of scholarship. A dark prophecy has now been illuminated as a real and present event on the verge of springing into reality. A great unveiling seems near.

As Solomon said in Ecclesiastes 3:1, "To every thing there is a season, and a time to every purpose under the heaven."

In the pages of this book, you will be challenged by the assertion that the timing of a long-awaited event is about to crystallize before the unbelieving eyes of the world.

Something of gigantic proportion is shifting in the landscape. Institutions worldwide are discovering that their foundations are turning to sand. Everything is changing. There is a mad scramble for ascendancy.

One of those organizations, the world's oldest continuing bureaucracy, the Roman Catholic Church, has reached a critical point…a crucial turn…that many among its ranks have quietly whispered about for centuries. The predicted time has arrived. Soon, as you read, you will find answers that have lain dormant for centuries.

By careful design, the Vatican stands as a monument to timelessness. Its theology nurtures thoughts of ushering in a Golden Age, in which the pontiff reigning in the end times welcomes Christ at His Second Coming and hands Him the keys to the Kingdom. Until that precise moment arrives, the Catholic hierarchy is obsessed with maintaining the status quo. It envisions itself as the guardian of the coming Millennium, and plans to be at the center of Christ's earthly reign from the rebuilt Royal City and the Third Temple.

It takes the role of this guardianship quite seriously, regarding the world outside as its enemy, the devil. It sees itself as the pure, strong preserver of the faith. Its traditions, though often self-generated and recent in origin, are deemed rock-solid. It has built what is perhaps the world's most convoluted, jurisdictional and bureaucratic barrier.

Its procession of popes, cardinals, and multileveled administrators extends back into the mists of the Dark Ages. Carefully, oh so carefully, it feels its way along as the centuries pass. Taught by the dramatic procession of passing eras, wars long and short, and delicate negotiations with the royal houses of Europe, its reflexes are finely tuned. It has perfected the art of camouflage, appearing as one thing while acting as another.

At the surface, it is a church with hundreds of traditions and beliefs. It is a teaching system with a global network of schools. Beneath that surface, it has a long history of manipulating power in ways that will accrue to its benefit.

Visually, the Vatican stands as an impassable monument to the religion of the Western world. Its labyrinthine archives are unequalled in historical scope. They are concealed beneath the layers of history... over a millennium and a half of history! Its libraries and laboratories are a maze of careful indexing and subterranean secrecy. It even maintains its own observatory, from which its directors issue occasional tantalizing announcements concerning the possibility that alien societies may soon visit Earth!

Viewed from the outside, the Vatican is implacable, inscrutable, and impenetrable. Those external to the faith see what the "Mother Church" wants them to see, and only that.

But on the inside, there are those who know. Institutionally, it is the originator of classified documentation, having invented the system that is known in our current parlance as "above top secret." The place is an amalgamation of vaults, rooms within rooms, and arcane traditions, stolid and self-righteous. It is the vision of quiet composure.

One is allowed to view its inner secrets only on a "need to know" basis. It is well known that the spoils of many wars are stored in its lower levels. They occupy many sites and secret locations, going back to the days of Vespasian's siege of Jerusalem, and the sacking of the Jewish Temple by his son Titus.

Near Capitoline Hill, and the Holy See of Vatican City, the Arch of Titus stands to this day as a memorial to the looting of Jerusalem in AD 70. Among other plundered items, it depicts the Temple Menorah in a triumphal parade through the streets of Rome. Illustrative of the Vatican's penchant for concealment is the following episode:

In 1996, during the tenure of Pope John Paul II, Shimon Shetreet, Israel's Minister of Religious Affairs drafted an official state letter, which was hand-delivered to the papal offices. In it, he asserted that he had uncovered clues in recent research from the University of Florence. He said that certain ancient documents had revealed that the Menorah and other valuable Temple artifacts were carefully and clandestinely stored in pristine condition, within the Vatican's underground vaults.

The mind reels in the attempt to imagine what might be in long-term Vatican storage. It's a certainty that there are scrolls from the first century, lying in nitrogen atmospheres where the temperature never varies by more than a fraction of a degree. Or, might there be cloth samples from robes once worn by the disciples? Paintings from the first century? Captured Hebrew scrolls that resided in Herod's Temple? Original New-Testament manuscripts?

Its traditions are deep and complex, often verging into breathtaking mystery, punctuated by deceptive "leaks" that point in the wrong direction. Recent motion pictures have publicized the dark and secret nature of this ancient institution. *The Da Vinci Code* and *Angels & Demons* have placed a strong suggestion in the public consciousness. Something is about to be exposed!

As self-protective as the Vatican can be, it somehow never dampened the ancient twelfth-century prophecy of St. Malachy that spoke of a great evil that would spring forth one day from the Papal Throne—the final pope would appear, and with him, the events of the last days.

The book you are about to read exists to throw a brighter light upon the famous prediction, along with captivating new information that makes sense in a chaotic world.

The future has arrived in a coalescing whirlwind of events which reveal a global background that seems aligned for the appearance of the prophesied pope. His mysterious figure appears on the brink of leaping full-blown into the modern world. When he does, he will be totally aware of the astonishing disclosures that are about to be laid wide open to the dumbfounded eyes of a naïve and deluded world.

Secrets from the vaults of history are about to erupt into a flood that flows through the streets of the world. Is this man of fundamental and solemn significance rising, even as the world is falling into moral, spiritual, and financial disorder? Some have called him "Peter, the Roman."

Who is he, really? Read on and discover his secret. His time seems to have arrived, and timing is everything.

—Gary Stearman
 Prophecy in the News

SECTION ONE

PROPHECY AT OUR DOORSTEP

1 | A Vision on Janiculum Hill

M alachy's head was spinning; he was short of breath, gasping, and a cold chill flushed his face. He wondered: was he about to meet the Lord or was he having another sorcerous vision?

He wanted rest. Bernard, oh where is Bernard? Then he remembered, confusion…so much confusion over the papacy. The words came fast and furious again. Phrases in liturgical Latin danced in his mind. Had the devil taken the papacy? *Schismaticus*, popes and antipopes, power-mad, political posturing in the house of God. The prophecies of the popes writhed in his feverish conscience; the dragon…oh no the dragon, *Draco depreffus* and then *Anguinus uir* was this to be a serpentine pope? Just last year, on the twenty-fifth of January, 1138, the antipope Anacletus had died, finally allowing the appointed Innocent II to ascend the Holy See. When the conspiring Cardinals had launched their coup, the opposed Innocent II fled Rome under his given name, Gregorio Papareschi, finding refuge with dear Bernard at the abbey. It was just this year Pope Innocent had reclaimed the Holy See prompting this pilgrimage from Ireland to Rome.

The fatigue began to fade and Malachy recalled what led him here to Janiculum Hill on this day. After his arduous journey from Ireland to Rome, only a brief respite at the Clairvaux Abbey in the Vallée d'Absinthe had given him hope. Yet, despite his fondness for Bernard, the bitterness of wormwood had infected his soul. He had requested permission from his holiness to end his days with his loyal friend Bernard in retreat at the abbey. Unfortunately, the Pontiff had only increased his responsibilities, making him Papal Legate for all of Ireland. But Malachy was weary of it all—so very tired. What was driving the Pope so hard? Had not Christ admonished His disciples, "but whosoever will be great among you, let him be your minister?" (Matthew 20:26 KJV). The beast was coming one day and Malachy knew it…*Bellua infatiabilis*. It was then that he knew the popes had taken the unspeakable bargain and there was no taking it back. After the fullness of time, *Petrus Romanus* would mark the end of *Mysterium Babylon magna*.

The Man Who Foresaw the Final Pope?

In the modest settlement of Armagh, in the beautiful, sweeping, emerald lands of Northern Ireland, in the year 1094, a nobleman and chief by the name of Lector Ua Morgair and his well-cultured wife celebrated the dawning of new life in their son, Máel Máedóc Ua Morgair. Neither of them could have known how the tiny boy they had just delivered would become a central figure in End-Times prophecy.

Little Máel Máedóc Ua Morgair (anglicized to the more modern "Malachy") lived his early, boyish days skipping amidst the comfortable sounds and familiar, candlelit ambiance of the Armagh Cathedral. He remained educated under the personal tutelage of his learned father, Lector of Armagh, until the fateful day of Lector's death in the year 1102. Malachy and his brother and sister were then raised by his mother alone, a woman who had been described as "A dutiful, Christian woman"[4] by St. Bernard de Clairvaux.

As the years progressed, Malachy continued his studies under the mentorship of Imar (also spelled "Imhar") O'Haglan: a man who focused his teachings on renouncing earthly pleasures to preserve the eternal soul. Following in O'Haglan's ascetical footsteps, Malachy showed astute perception within the walls of the cathedral and the shabby cell beneath where O'Haglan spent his days like a hermit. Despite the protests of his sister and school acquaintances when self-flagellation, penance, and other religious practices grew to be ultimately more important than becoming an inspired professor like his father before him, Malachy continued searching for opportunities to express his passion for the Church and the life he believed he was chosen to lead. Drawing everyday nearer to the effects of O'Haglan's authority and vision, Malachy soon introduced Gregorian chants into his regime, and a zeal for Church reform.

By the age of twenty-two, the archbishop Cellach of Armagh (also spelled "Ceollach" and "Celsus"), a good acquaintance to O'Haglan, found such promise and exception in the young man that he put aside canonical law and ordained the youth as a deacon three years prior to custom. In 1119, he declared Malachy vicar-general and entrusted him with the duty of reforming the diocese while he was away. The changes observed in the diocese were immediate and extraordinary. Malachy's sermons of penance ignited a passion in the common people and stirred the laity to respect canonical rules of the Church.

Eventually Malachy headed to Lismore to revise and sharpen his knowledge of the canon under the teaching and advice of well-known scholar Bishop Malchus. (St. Bernard writes that Bishop Malchus was "an old man, full of days and virtues, and the wisdom of God was in him."[5] He goes on to further explain that the bishop was later acknowledged as performing two miracles, one wherein he healed a young boy of a mental disorder who later became his porter, and another wherein "when the saint put his fingers into his ears on either side he perceived that two things like little pigs came out of them."[6] These distinctions of Bishop Malchus' reputation are of importance to St. Bernard, "that it may be known to all what sort of preceptor Malachy had in the knowledge of holy things."[7] Needless to say, Malachy worked and studied with associates whose names circulated within the Church as significant.)

Though his trip to Lismore was meant for a time of quiet learning, Malachy was not idle there, taking opportunities to speak out on current affairs within the Church that concerned him, and was often sent by Malchus himself "to preach the word of God to the people and to correct many evil practices which had developed over the years. He achieved notable success. To reform the clergy he instituted regulations concerning celibacy and other ecclesiastical discipline, and reinstituted the recitation of the canonical hours. Most importantly, he gave back the sacraments to the common people, sending good priests among them to instruct the ignorant. He returned to Armagh in 1123."[8]

This same year, Malachy was appointed Abbot of Bangor where he assisted in helping rebuild the abbey and establish a seminary. More importantly, from this time forward, a series of miracles and the gift of prophecy were attributed to him. One notable prophecy, especially hard to chalk up to pure coincidence, finds fulfillment in the twentieth century:

> Ireland will suffer English oppression for a week of centuries [700 years], but will preserve her fidelity to God and His Church. At the end of that time she will be delivered, and the English in turn must suffer severe chastisement. Ireland, however, will be instrumental in bringing back the English to the unity of Faith.
>
> Complete Anglo-Norman domination of Ireland was achieved a century after Malachy's prediction. Independence for the southern part of Ireland came 700 years later in the

early 20th century. If this utterance is not apocryphal, then it predates the schism between the Church of England and the Catholic faith by four centuries and implies that Anglicanism will falter sometime in our near future when the final pope finishes his reign.[9]

Yet, Yves DuPont argues this began in the twelfth century and ended after WW2. He says, "The liberation has come in stages: World War I, independence within the British Empire; World War II, complete independence. Thus, Ireland was under British rule for seven centuries."[10] However, it just as likely applies to the rampant secularism in England ultimately being conquered by Christianity.

At thirty years of age, Malachy became Bishop Malachy of Down and Connor. John Hogue says of Malachy's new position: "The bishopric was considered one of Ireland's blackest holes for the faith. Malachy would face a moratorium on church tithes, a shortage of priests and an even greater shortage of celibate clerics; he would wince at the improvised performances of the sacraments based on the rejection of canon law in favor of native and often semi-pagan Irish rituals."[11]

Never before had Malachy seen such lax cohesion to the laws of God within the walls of the Church. Discipline, offering, tithing, giving of the first-fruits, and going to confession were things of the past; marriages were made illegally. Christians behaved like pagans. "Never had he found men so shameless in regard of morals, so dead in regard of rites, so impious in regard of faith, so barbarous in regard of laws, so stubborn in regard of discipline, so unclean in regard of life."[12] Nevertheless, believing that he was a "shepherd and not a hireling,"[13] Malachy fought the issues head-on and in his enthusiasm, discovered followers who were willing to flock to his side to reestablish devotion to the rituals.

About this time according to legend, Malachy had a dream in which a woman appeared to him and revealed her identity as

Archbishop Cellach's wife. She handed Mallachy a pastoral staff, and then disappeared. He shared this with those in his company and it was esteemed important because for approximately fifteen generations by this time in Armagh, people high up in both secular politics and the Church had maintained office within family hierarchies. As a result, it was normal to nominate a successor to the seat of the archbishop by heritage instead of Church works. Archbishop Cellach, however, impressed by Malachy's ministry, rejected the expectations of his family in this regard. Hoping that Malachy could bring new life and hope to the Church, and wanting to put a stop to hereditary succession of the office, Cellach charged those under him with the task of spreading word that Malachy would be given his seat as Archbishop of Armagh. When the word reached Malachy, it came as no surprise after the dream he'd had, and just days after Cellach passed away, Malachy received Cellach's staff (the one from his dream), and a letter confirming the news of his latest promotion.

Cellach's family was outraged. Feeling usurped by his decision to appoint someone outside the family as archbishop, tension rose between them and Malachy. Cellach's cousin, Murtagh (also spelled " Murtough" and "Muirchetrach"), fancied himself worthy of the role, and his family stood behind him in his campaign to become archbishop, ready even to use force to claim the position if necessary. The people of the Church fell in support of Malachy, equally ready for the hereditary succession of the office to end.

Three years passed while Malachy remained at the monastery, not refusing the archbishopric but unwilling to participate in a war between Murtagh and the Church. The papal legate eventually became revolted enough by Murtagh's tyranny that the Church ordered Malachy, by threat of impending excommunication, to take his position. Malachy conceded and in response to the order, accepted his bishopric from a distance to avoid the mayhem of political/religious war. He made a deal with the legate that if the Church was ever fully restored to freedom in matters of succession, in return he wanted a leave from leadership so that he might find time to be alone in his studies and away from obligatory office. Remaining safely just outside the city, he maintained governance as the acknowledged Archbishop of Armagh, without immediately taking possession of his See.

When Murtagh passed away in 1134, he revealed that Niall, Cellach's brother, would be his successor. During this time, the people generally believed that anyone in possession of the crosier of St. Patrick (the Bachal Isu, or "Staff of Jesus") and the Book of Gospels (or Holy Book) was the true archbishop. In lieu of this, Niall saw and seized his opportunity to appear the legitimate and rightful archbishop by stealing these two artifacts from the cathedral of Armagh. Although history is cloudy when it comes to the issue of retrieving the stolen artifacts from Niall (most records point to a small war between the two sides, which was rumored to be brought to an end by diplomacy from Malachy, followed by his purchasing the artifacts back from Niall), Malachy did eventually get them back and take his place as primate in the cathedral city of Armagh. "In 1138, having broken the tradition of hereditary succession, rescued Armagh from oppression, restored ecclesiastical discipline, re-established Christian morals, and seeing all things tranquil, Malachy resigned his post as originally agreed."[14] Malachy retired to Bangor to live in rest for a time, among the camaraderie of his fellow monks, but with few demands on his schedule or solitary study.

Eventually Malachy felt the need to gain meeting with Pope Innocent II in Rome to officially recognize the archbishops (and the Sees) of Armagh and Cashel with a pallium, an official woolen cloak of authority, for each to signify the bishopric jurisdiction over the ecclesiastical provinces and to gain favor and blessing from the papal for the developments within the Church. In 1139, he gathered a few travelling companions and pack animals and headed to Rome through Scotland, England, and France. It was during his travels that he arrived at the Cisterian Abbey of Clairvaux, where he met the future-saint Bernard (who would later be his central biographer). Resting there for a short time, Malachy became enchanted with the Abbey and made a very close friendship with its abbot. Abbot Bernard was unusual in his approach to ministry. He maintained fitness of the body by practicing martial arts and kept those in his presence ready at all times to be counted upon for defending the Church at all costs. He proved to be such a wellspring of religious passion for Malachy that when the time came for him to leave the abbey and continue his pilgrimage to Rome, Malachy made a secret plan to ask for retirement in the seclusion of Clairvaux.

Sixteen months after the journey began Malachy finally arrived in Rome, his heart and mind lifted and hopeful. Quickly, he was brought to Pope Innocent II for official audience. Innocent approved Malachy's request for the pallia but with strict conditions: Malachy would take on new responsibilities. He was now the Papal Legate of Ireland with all of its ensuing political intricacies. This was not what he had wanted; he so desperately desired the peace and serenity of the Abbey. It was upon leaving the seven-hilled city so frustrated, framed by the breathtaking Western view from Janiculum Hill that it came upon him. Because of the impiety of the popes, Rome would burn.

As the legend goes, Malachy experienced what is today considered a famous vision commonly called "The Prophecy of the Popes." The prophecy is a list of Latin verses predicting each of the Roman Catholic popes from Pope Celestine II to the final pope, "Peter the Roman," whose reign would end in the destruction of Rome. According to this ancient prophecy, the very next pope (following Benedict XVI) will be the final pontiff, Petrus Romanus or Peter the Roman.

The final segment of the prophecy reads:

In persecutione extrema S. R. E. sedebit Petrus Romanus, qui pascet oves in multis tribulationibus: quibus transactis civitas septicollis deruetur et judex tremendus judicabit populum. Finis.[15]

Which is rendered:

In the extreme persecution of the Holy Roman Church, there will sit Peter the Roman, who will nourish the sheep in many tribulations; when they are finished, the City of Seven Hills will be destroyed, and the dreadful judge will judge his people. The End.[16]

The Good News and the Bad News

After studying the history of the Prophecy of the Popes and the surrounding scholarly literature, we have some good news and some bad news. What's that? You want the bad news first? Sure, no problem, let's get this unpleasantness out of the way.

The bad news is that part of the prophecy may be a forgery which was fabricated in the late sixteenth century. We say forgery meaning that over half of the prophecies, the first seventy or so predictions, could be *vaticinia ex eventu* (prophecy from the event). It seems likely that someone irrevocably altered the original medieval document and the original is either hidden away or lost to history. According to Vatican insiders, there is ample evidence that the original twelfth-century manuscript was discovered in 1556 by a Vatican librarian. Even so, the first known publication of the "Malachy Prophecy of the Popes" was in Arnold de Wion's massive eighteen-hundred-page volume entitled *Lignum Vitae* (Tree of Life), which was published in 1595. That text will be presented and examined below. Even though we have good reason to believe a much older document is still visible, we must accept that the earliest instance of the prophecy surfaced nearly four hundred years *after* its alleged origin in 1139. Despite the legend which pleads it was locked away in a musty Vatican vault those four hundred years, the skeptics still have valid points. Even so, it very well could be the work of Saint Malachy coarsely corrupted by a forger. Of course, this would fall neatly in line with the Roman Catholic practice demonstrated by the *Donation of Constantine* and *Pseudo–Isidorian Decretals*. Alternatively, some have suggested it was partially the work of Nostradamus cleverly disguised to protect his identity. While the identity of the actual prophet remains unclear, the author was a prophet whether he knew or not.

The exciting news is that the Prophecy of the Popes, although tainted, is still a genuine prophecy. Despite the superficial insincerity detectable in the first section of "prophecies," the post publication predictions show astonishing fulfillments. We have no critical analysis to explain away the sometimes jaw-dropping, post-1595 fulfillments. Indeed, we are currently at 111 out of 112 and believers argue they seem to have increased in precision over time. However, we shall deal with the bad news first. As we shall demonstrate, the Vatican's penchant for propaganda is undisputed in the record of history. In Rome's tradition of the altering of ancient documents for political expediency, the Prophecy of the Popes was allegedly used as propaganda for Cardinal Girolamo Simoncelli's papal ambitions. Nevertheless, if it happened, it was a ploy which did not work as Simoncelli lost to Gregory XIV, Innocent IX, and Clement VIII. While textual evidence for this conspiracy is provided, we suggest the reader remain objective and patient in lieu of the more astounding findings.

In recent history, the most popular and exhaustive handling of the Prophecy of the Popes is arguably the book, *The Last Pope*, by author and self-proclaimed "prophet" John Hogue. Hogue is a regular guest on the *Coast to Coast* radio show with a pretty impressive bio, and we have availed ourselves of his scholarship. While his own predictions do not typically fare so well, he is a well-respected figure in Nostradamus studies. Hogue has done some interesting work on the Malachy prophecy, but we promise that you have yet to learn the greatest parts of the untold story. For instance, in his 2000 best seller, Hogue laments that one of the oldest sources concerning the Malachy prophecy, an extremely rare Italian work, was forever lost to history: "There was once a work entitled *La Profezia de'Sommi Pontefici Romani* published in Ferrara in 1794 by an anonymous author. It claimed to trace back to the original paper trail to the time before Wion and Ciaconnius discovered St. Malachy's original manu-script. Unfortunately the last copy of *Profezia* was destroyed when the convent at Rimini, where it was preserved, was ransacked and shut down by French revolutionary forces in 1797. If it had survived we might have objective evidence supporting Ciacconius' or Wion's role as recorders rather than presumed forgers."[17]

Marauding French revolutionaries aside, we have news for John Hogue and anyone who is fascinated by the prophecy. We found the remaining copy of the "Lost Book" and negotiated it through Yale University. It reveals that Hogue confused the data. While *La Profezia* did not burn up at Rimini, it does claim there was an ancient manu-script at a monastery there. Specifically, it mentions "a manuscript which could be dated earlier than the sixteenth century in the possession of the Olivetan monks at Rimini."[18] The 1794 "lost" book has yielded other game-changing revelations as well, which we will discuss later.

Historically, the Prophecy of the Popes has enjoyed mixed accep-tance. Four hundred years ago, with so many more popes to go, it was a mere novelty. However, as time runs short, the forecast understand-ably becomes more urgent and the criticism more caustic. Beginning in the nineteenth century, the Jesuits, save one, have been outspokenly critical. As a result, the most recent edition of the Catholic Encyclopedia suggests that the prophecy is a late sixteenth century forgery, while the older 1911 edition allows, "it is not conclusive if we adopt Cucherat's theory that they were hidden in the Archives during those four hundred years."[19] This refers to the nineteenth-century author, Abbé Cucherat, who is one of the few who argued for the authenticity of the prophecy in his book, *Revue du monde catholique*, published in 1871. Even so, scholars have reason to believe that the prophecy was not actually hidden for four hundred years because similar manuscripts like the *Vaticinia de summis pontificibus*, dated as early as 1280, appear to be modeled on the Malachy prophecy. Still, most critical scholars point out that Malachy's biographer and dear friend, St. Bernard, makes no mention of the papal prophecy in *Life of St. Malachy of Armagh*.[20] This argument from silence is ubiquitous in the literature. Most academic sources are also not very charitable. *The Oxford Dictionary of the Christian Church* bluntly states, "The so-called Prophecies of Malachy, which are contained in a document apparently composed in 1590, have no connection with St. Malachy except their erroneous attribution to him."[21] The majority of Jesuit scholarship presents a united front. The first to call the Malachy prophecy a forgery was Claude François Menestrier (1631–1705), whose *Réfutation des Prophéties, faussement attribuée à Saint Malachie sur l'élection des papes* became the dominant Jesuit party line claiming a 1590 conspiracy by a certain Cardinal within the papal conclave. Following suit, M.J. O'Brien's *An Historical and Critical Account of the So-Called Prophecy of St. Malachy Regarding the Succession of Popes* is a thorough attempt at debunking. Herbert Thurston, another Jesuit, was a prolific late nineteenth-century critic. He argues that "not one scrap of evidence has ever been adduced to show that St. Malachy's prophecy about the Popes had been quoted, or even heard of, before it was published by Wion in 1595."[22] This is not actually the case as the esteemed Catholic scholar, John Lupia, claims that Vatican librarian, Onofrio Panvinio, "in 1556 began to correct and revise the Vatican Library catalog [and] rediscovered the 12th century manuscript written by St. Malachy and appears to be the first to publish on his prophecies in 1557."[23] In addition to several oblique references, we will discuss another possible reference to the prophecy published by Nicholas Sanders in 1571. Most scholars bifurcate the list of 112 Latin phrases at number seventy-six, due to the circumstances surrounding its publication. Even so, because we have discovered ample evidence dating the manuscript's circulation to at least 1570, we will divide the list there. In so doing, two layers of context are established in the prophecy. This approach is adapted from biblical scholarship.

Exegesis in biblical studies is always an attempt to derive the original author's intention for his original reader and that is the methodology undertaken here. For instance, when scholars study the New Testament Gospels, they take into account layers of context. There is the context in which Jesus is interacting in the original historical setting and then there is a layer of context in which the author of the Gospel is presenting his account to a later audience. Careful study reveals that each evangelist author, Matthew, Mark, Luke, and John, frames the events of Jesus' life in unique ways for their own theological and evangelistic purposes. The underlying context of Jesus can be assimilated by studying first-century Judaism in Israel. We study the Pharisees to understand Jesus' criticism of their traditions. In the same way, the upper level, the author's context, can be discerned by how he presents Jesus. Still, the order in which a certain account is presented in a Gospel is often unique. This requires the careful student to "think vertically" for potential significance.

You might ask, "Is the author making a statement by where he places this parable?" The context of the evangelist author speaks to why and how he selected, arranged, and adapted the historical material about Jesus. Additionally, the scholar must "think horizontally" meaning to read each pericope with awareness of the parallels in other Gospels.[24] While each of the four accounts preserves actual historical data, they are not always chronologically identical because of the secondary layer of context pertaining to the unique purpose of Mark, Matthew, Luke, and John. This methodology unveils new insights into the Prophecy of the Popes as well.

At first glance, there appear to be at least two levels of historical context, that of the original author and then that of the publisher. We will examine the possibility of even deeper contextual layers in the next chapter but for now we might accept the Malachy legend or perhaps a pseudepigrapher as the lower contextual level. To determine the upper level, the context of the publisher/commentator, we discover that is has been suggested that a papal emissary, Nicholas Sanders (1530–1581), may have made reference to an original Celtic version of the prophecy to Rome during the reign of Pope Pius V (1566–72).[25] While he may have obliquely referred to the prophecy in a book published in 1571, it has also been suggested that the first publication showing the influence of the Malachy prophecy was by Panvinio in his *Epitome Romanorum pontificum* (Venice, 1557). The second-earliest mention is said to be by Girolamo Muzio in his 1570 work, *Il Choro Pontificale.*[26] There is also record that a specific mention of the prophecy was in a handwritten account by Don Alphonsus Ciacconus, a Spanish Dominican scholar in Rome, in the year 1590.[27] At that time, Ciacconus was a recognized expert on ancient Greco-Roman paleography and ancient manuscripts, as well as the history of the papacy. Apparently the publisher, Dom Wion, had received the text from someone and turned to Ciacconus for his opinion. Ciacconus ostensibly authenticated the manuscript. We cannot know exactly when it was altered but the textual and circumstantial evidence points to the original manuscript being tampered with by 1570–1590 to promote a particular papabile (some argue). In the meantime (1570–1595), it circulated surreptitiously amongst the Cardinals creating quite a stir. Wion published it with the previous popes named and interpretations of the fulfillments added in 1595.

Thus, we have discerned two layers of context:

- **Lower level of historical context**: An original document possibly by St. Malachy or a pseudepigrapher circa 1139 –1571.
- **Upper level of historical context**: Alterations imposed and interpretations added circa 1571–1595.

In examining the scans of the original 1595 Latin text, even with no comprehension of Latin, one can note that explanations of the mottos with papal names cease at the time of publication. Wion claimed that Ciacconus was responsible for the interpretations but this has been called into serious question by O'Brien, who suggests it was someone else who simply copied from Onuphrius Panvinius' short history of the Popes, *Epitome Romanorum Pontijicum usque ad Paulum IV*, printed in Venice in 1557. He bases this on the case that the interpretations presented by Wion match Panvinius' work but disagree with Ciacconus' own book about the popes, *Viltae et res Gesltae Romanorum Ponlificum el Cardinalium*, printed in 1601. While Ciacconius' work resembles Panvinius', it disagrees in important areas that Ciacconius made explicit. O'Brien ponders this issue: "Now, if Ciacconius was the interpreter of the prophecies, as Wion asserts, Ciacconius must be pitching into himself, for we find reproduced in Wion's book the errors of which he complains. Who then is the interpreter? Is it Panvinius? Or may not the prophecy as well as the explanation have come from the same hand? May not Wion have been merely duped (which could have been easily done considering his character); and may he not in good faith have given the prophecy as that of the great St. Malachy?"[28] John N. Lupia, a well-credentialed contemporary scholar, believes it was *vice versa*, that Panvinius actually altered his book based on the prophecy. He writes, "In 1557 Panvinio published a history of the pontiffs from the origins to Paul IV (1555–1559). In it he makes corrections and additions based on the Prophecies of St. Malachy."[29] Whoever Wion's interpreter was, the last comment in *Lignum Vitae* referred to Urban VII who died in 1590 and the last papal name listed was Clement VIII who took office in 1592 just prior to the prophecy's 1595 publication. In reading the Latin text, underneath "*Crux Romulea…Clemens VIII,*" the last page simply lists the remaining mottos in three columns ending with the famous apocalyptic stanza centered on *Petrus Romanus* and the destruction of Mystery Babylon headquartered on Vatican Hill in the seven-hilled city.

Here is the original 1595 Latin text from *Lignum Vitae*:

S. MALACHIAS, Hibernus, monachus Bencorensis, & Archi-
epitcopus Ardinacensis, cum aliquot annis fedi illi præfuiffet, humi
literis caufa Archiepifcopatu abdicauit anno circiter Domini 1137.
& Dunenfi fede contentus in ea ad finem ufque uitæ permanfit.
Obiit anno 1148. die 2. Nouembris. *S. Bernardus in eius uita*.

Ad eum extant epiftolæ S. Bernardi tres, uidelicet, 315. 316. &
317. Scripfiffe fertur & ipfe nonnulla opufcula, de quibus nihil ha
Etenus uidi, præter quandam prophetiam de Summis Pontificibus,
quæ quia breuis eft, & nondum quod fciam excufa, & à multis de-
fiderata, hic à me appofita eft.

Prophetia S. Malachiæ Archiepifcopi, de Summis Pontificibus.

Ex caftro Tiberis.	Cœleftinus. ij.	Typhernas,
Inimicus expulfus.	Lucius. ij.	De familia Caccianemica.
Ex magnitudine môtis.	Eugenius. iij.	Patria Ethrufcus oppido
		Montis magni.
Abbas Suburranus.	Anaftafius. iiij.	De familia Suburra.
De rure albo.	Adrianus. iiij.	Vilis natus in oppido Sanc-
		Eti Albani.
Ex tetro carcere.	Victor. iiij.	Fuit Cardinalis S. Nicolai
		in carcere Tulliano.
Via Tranftiberina.	Callistus. iij.	Guido Cremenfis, Cardina-
		lis S. Mariæ Tranftiberim.
De Pannonia Thufciæ.	Pafchalis. iij.	Antipapa. Hungarus natio
		ne, Epifcopus Card. Tufculanus.
Ex anfere cuftode.	Alexander. iij.	De familia Paparona.
Lux in oftio.	Lucius. iij.	Locenfis Card. Oftienfis.
Sus in cribro.	Vrbanus. iij.	Mediolanenfis, familia cri-
		bella, quæ Suem pro armis gerit.
Enfis Laurentii.	Gregorius. viij.	Card. S. Laurentii in Luci-
		V 2 na, cu-

The second paragraph above reads: "Three Epistles of St. Bernard addressed to St. Malachy are still extant (viz., 313, 316, and 317). Malachy himself is reported to have been the author of some little tractates, none of which I have seen up to the present time, except a certain prophecy of his concerning the Sovereign Pontiffs. This, as it is short, and so far as we know, has never before been printed, is inserted here, seeing that many people have asked for it."

The bottom two lines by Wion read, "What has been added to the popes is not the work of Malachy, but of Father Alphonsus Giacon, of the Order of Preachers, the interpreter of this prophecy." This may seem confusing in light of the above discussion about Ciacconius. Gaicon is also Chacon or Ciacconius because he was from Spain, na, cuius infignia enfes falcati.

De Schola exiet.	Clemens. iij. Romanus, domo Scholari.
De rure bouenfi.	Cœleftinus. ij. Familia Bouenfi.
Comes Signatus.	Innocentius. iij. Familia Comitum Signie.
Canonicus de latere.	Honorius. iij. Familia Sabella , Canonicus S.Ioannis Lateranenfis.
Auis Oftienfis.	Gregorius. ix. Familia Comitum Signie Episcopus Card.Oftienfis.
Leo Sabinus.	Cœleftinus.iiij. Mediolanenfis, cuius infignia Leo, Epifcopus Card.Sabinus.
Comes Laurentius,	Innocentius iiij. domo flifca, Comes Laaniæ,Cardinalis S.Laurentii in Lucina.
Signum Oftienfe.	Alexander. iiij. De comitatus Signiæ,Epifcopus Card. Oftienfis.
Hierufalem Campanie.	Vrbanus. iiii. Gallus , Trecenfis in Campania, Patriarcha Hierufalem.
Draco depreffus.	Clemens. iiii. cuius infignia Aquila vnguibus Draconem renens.
Anguinus uir.	Gregorius. x. Mediolanenfis,Familia vicecomitum,quæ anguè pro infigni gerit.
Concionator Gallus.	Innocentius. v. Gallus, ordinis Prædicatorum.
Bonus Comes.	Adrianus. v. Ottobonus familia Flifca ex comitibus Lauaniæ.
Pifcator Thufcus.	Ioannes. xxi. antea Ioannes Petrus Epifcopus Card.Tufculanus.
Rofa compofita.	Nicolaus. iij. Familia Vrfina,quæ rofam in infigni gerit, dictus compofitus.
Ex teloneo liliacei Martini.Martinus.iiii. cuius infignia lilia,canonicus,& thefaurarius S.Martini Turonen.	
Ex rofa leonina.	Honorius. iiii. Familia Sabella infignia rofa à leonibus geftata.
Picus inter efcas.	Nicolaus. iiii. Picenus patria Efcolanus.
Ex eterno celfus.	Cœleftinus. v. Vocatus Petrus de morrone Eremita.
Ex undari bñdictione. Bonifacius. viii. Vocatus prius Benedictus, Caetanus,cuius infignia undæ.	
Concionator patereus.Benedictus xi. qui uocabatur Frater Niclaus,ordinis Prædicatorum.	

De

Lupa Cœleftina,	Eugenius. IIII. Venetus, canonicus antea regularis Cœleftinus, & Epifcopus Senéfis.
Amator Crucis.	Felix. V. qui uocabatur Amadæus Dux Sabaudiæ, infignia Crux.
De modicitate Lunæ.	Nicolaus V. Lunenfis de Sarzana,humilibus parentibus natus.
Bos pafcens.	Calliftus. III. Hifpanus , cuius infignia Bos pafcens.
De Capra & Albergo.	Pius. II. Senenfis , qui fuit à Secretis Cardinalibus Capranico & Albergato.
De Ceruo & Leone.	Paulus. II. Venetus, qui fuit Commendatarius ecclefiæ Ceruienfis, & Cardinalis tituli S.Marci.
Pifcator minorita.	Sixtus. IIII. Pifcatoris filius , Francifcanus.
Præcurfor Siciliæ.	Innocentius VIII.qui uocabatur Iofnes Baptifta, & uixit in curia Alfonfi regis Siciliæ.
Bos Albanus in portu . Alexander VI. Epifcopus Cardinalis Albanus & Portuenfis,cuius infignia Bos.	
De paruo homine.	Pius. III. Senenfis,familia piccolominea.
Fructus Iouis iuuabit.	Iulius. II. Ligur,eius infignia Quercus,Iouis arbor.
De craticula Politiana. Leo.X.filius Laurentii medici , & fcholaris Angeli Politiani.	
Leo Florentius.	Adrian. VI. Florétii filius, eius infignia Leo.
Flos pilei ægri.	Clemens. VII. Florentinus de domo medicea,eius infignia pila,& lilia.
Hiacinthus medicorũ.Paulus. III. Farnefius,qui lilia pro infignibus geftat,& Card.fuit SS.Cofme, & Damiani.	
De corona montana. Iulius. III. antea uocatus Ioannes Maria de monte .	
Frumentum flocidum. Marcellos. II.cuius infignia ceruus & frumétum, ideo floccidum,quod pauco tempore nixit in papatu.	
De fide Petri.	Paulus. IIII. antea uocatus Ioannes Petrus Caraffa.
Efculapii pharmacum. Pius. IIII. antea dictus Io.Angelus Medices.	
Angelus nemorofus.	Pius. V. Michael uocatus , natus in oppido Bofchi.
Medium corpus pilarũ.Gregorius XIII. cuius infignia medius Dra	

60.

---

co , Cardinalis creatus à Pio. IIII. qui pila in armis geftabat.

Axis in medietate figni.Sixtus. V. qui axem in medio Leonis in armis geftat.		
De rore cœli.	Vrbanus. VII. qui fuit Archiepifcopus Roffanenfis in Calabria,ubi mãna colligitur.	
Ex antiquitate Vrbis.	Gregorius. XIIII.	Notice last description is
Pia ciuitas in bello.	Innocentius. IX.	Clemens 1592
Crux Romulea.	Clemens. VIII.	
Vndofus uir.		Paftor & nauta.
Gens peruerfa.	Animal rurale.	Flos florum.
In tribulatione pacis.	Rofa Vmbriæ.	De medietate lunæ.
Lilium & rofa.	Vrfus uelox.	De labore folis.
Iucunditas crucis.	Peregrinⁱ apoftolic⁹.	Gloria oliuæ.
Montium cuftos.	Aquila rapax.	
Sydus olorum.	Canis & coluber.	
De flumine magno.	Vir religiofus.	
Bellua infatiabilis.	De balneis Ethruriæ.	
Pœnitentia gloriofa.	Crux de cruce.	
Raftrum in porta.	Lumen in cœlo.	
Flores circundati.	Ignis ardens.	
De bona religione.	Religio depopulata.	
Miles in bello.	Fides intrepida.	
Columna excelfa.	Paftor angelicus.	

In plecutione. extrema S.R.E.fedebit.
Petrus Romanus, qui
pafcet oues in multis tribulationibus:
quibus tranfactis ciuitas fepticollis diruetur, & Iudex tremédus iudicabit populum fuum. Finis.

In the extreme persecution of the Holy Roman Church, there will sit Peter the Roman, who will pasture his sheep in many tribulations: and when these things are finished, the city of seven hills will be destroyed, and the terrible judge will judge his people. The End.

Quæ ad Pontifices adiecta,non funt ipfius Malachiæ, fed R.A.P. Alphonfi Giaconis,Ord.Prædicatorũ,huius Prophetiæ interpretis.

images note 1

his original name, Alphonso Chacon, was Italianized to preserve the soft Spanish sound of "ch" in his name into Ciacconius or alternately as Wion has it "Giacon." But this last line reveals that the original prophecy was a mere string of obscure Latin phrases, and that Giacon, Ciacconius, added each pope's name and explained how the prophecy applied to him. Because he was an expert on paleochristian and medieval paleography and manuscripts, Wion's assertion of Ciacconius' authentication and involvement carries weight.

Because the comments end with Urban VII who died in 1590 and the last papal name listed is Clement VIII, the Jesuit, Claude François Menestrier (1631–1705), believed that the prophecy first appeared in 1590. Starting from that assumption, he observed the next prophecy after Urban was "*ex antiquitate Urbis*" which translates to "from the old city" with no interpretation offered. This is the critical point where scholars detect an attempt to influence the conclave when Gregory XIIII was opposed by one Girolamo Simoncelli. If one were unaware of the previous mentions of the prophecy, this theory would be convincing. As a representative example of scholarly detective work, Louis Moreri, a native of Provence born in 1643 and doctor of theology, is chosen. He was the author of the acclaimed *Dictionnaire Historique*. As his life's work, the dictionary contains such a wide variety of information it is considered to be an early forerunner of the modern encyclopedia. In the 1759 edition, we read:

> "They attribute to him [Malachy] a prophecy concerning the popes from Celestine II. To the end of the world, but the learned know that this prophecy was forged, during the conclave of 1590, by the partisans of Cardinal Simoncelli, who was designated by these words: 'De anlzguilale Urbis,' because he was of Orvieto; in Latin, '*Urbs vetus.*'"[30]

The argument is that the oracle "from the old city" would seem to predict Girolamo Simoncelli who was at that time the Cardinal of

Orvieto which also means "old city." This is the dominant opinion of critical Malachy scholars. The scholars could be right; it does seem a little too perfect. It seems that the conspirators hoped to rig the papal conclave by encouraging the voters to fall in step with the much venerated Saint Malachy. But even if it were so, it would not undermine the entire prophecy and there is ample cause to question the conspiracy theory. The anonymous author of the 1794 "lost book" claims to have dug into the Vatican archives and discredited the Simoncelli conspiracy theory:

> "We have consulted good historical accounts, even though many are dated from the controversial period of 1590 (there are included a large number of secret manuscript reports from during the time of the Conclaves), and there is not the slightest hint of the plot, nor of any artifact of the prophecy, that in such circumstances had a lot of interest to the 'others' curiosity. Indeed, on the contrary, it is undoubted that the conclave, which was in every respect one of the more boisterous between the rival parties, no one present was supporting Simoncelli."[31]

According to this text, not a single Cardinal was in support of Simoncelli. It seems that the 1590 conclave conspiracy theory which began with Menestrier has been debunked. John Lupia remarks, "Menestrier claimed the prophecies were a forgery dating from the 1590 conclave election of Gregory XIV, and even names the forger as one of Cardinal Simoncelli's party, who, apparently, wanted his candidate to secure the victory. However, there were two editions on the prophecies of St. Malachy prior to 1590 that renders Menestrier's claim both impossible and invalid."[32] This new evidence is a slap in the face to the Jesuit debunkers. Yet it was never the most compelling reason to think that the Malachy manuscript was tampered with.

To demonstrate why many discern that at least some of the pre-1590 mottos were written after the fact, we will use an analogy from counter-cult apologetics, specifically in regard to Mormonism. Joseph Smith claimed that he miraculously translated the book of Mormon directly from gold plates which were written by a divine hand. Thus, it was a one-generation translation from plates to Smith's manuscript. Accordingly, one would then expect the book of Mormon to be sacred scripture of the most direct and pure translation. The insurmountable obstacle for the veracity of the book of Mormon is demonstrated by the fact that when the book of Mormon references passages from the Hebrew Bible, it follows the translated text of the King James Bible a little too perfectly. For instance, where the King James *italicized* words, the Book of Mormon follows suit. Obviously, this proves that Smith copied his references from a King James Bible and not more ancient source material like the mythological golden plates. A similar case (which will be discussed in detail in a subsequent chapter) is the so-called *Donation of Constantine.* For centuries, the popes used this forged document to claim title to certain lands before a scholar demonstrated that it was written in a style of Latin that did not exist when it was purportedly composed. We have similar lines of evidence with the Prophecy of the Popes.

Because we are examining the upper level of context from the time of the publisher (specifically the interpretations offered prior to 1590), it seems that they were manipulated in line with what was available at the time. Books were hard to come by. The prophecy follows the descriptions and details found in a work on the history of the popes by Onuphrius Panvinius: *Epitome Romanorum Pontijicum usque ad Paulum IV*, printed in Venice in 1557. The prophecy transparently follows this reference work. O'Brien argued, "Any person who opens this work and compares the account of the popes in it from Celestine II to Paul IV, with the corresponding part of the 'Prophecy of St. Malachy' will come to the conclusion that the writer of the latter, if not Panvinius himself, must have been someone who followed Panvinius' account rather too closely."[33] This is more than just an assertion; his evidence is detailed and specific:

> In Panvinius's *Epitome*, the popes' armorial bearings are given, but not in every case. When the arms are given, we usually find that they figure in the prophecy, when not given, the prophecy is a play upon or a description of the pope's name, country, family, or title, when cardinal. Moreover, we find in Panvinius the very same antipopes as given in the prophecy. Even when the pope's family-name, armorial bearings or cardinalic title is wrongly given by Panvinius, we find the forger of the prophecy to perfectly chime in with him.[34]

In other words, it matches too perfectly because, even in the few places where Panvinius' papal history makes mistakes, the interpretations of the prophecy follow those errors. This only makes sense if someone was using Panvinius' book or if it were Panvinius himself. John Lupia argues that it was Panvinius who discovered the Malachy manuscript and that he changed his papal history to match the prophecy. This seems a little suspicious and we think it far more likely the reverse. More than likely, Panvinius discovered the ancient document and altered it in accordance to his papal history. After all, he would be following Rome's well-estab- lished penchant for altering an authentic, ancient document to meet new purposes. As we will see later, the prophecies after the publication date shift focus and clearly reveal that there are two layers of context. The original prophecy (the lower, an older level of historical context) seems to have been manipulated to match the interpretation (the upper, the late sixteenth-century level). O'Brien's parting shot is a zinger:

> According to Wion, Malachy's prophecy was a mere string of meaningless Latin phrases. How did the supposed interpreter know with what pope to commence? How was he persuaded to take up the antipopes?[35]

While O'Brien's incredulity is clear, the answer to the first question is trivial. As the legend goes, Malachy was summoned to Rome in 1139 by Pope Innocent II (r. 1130–43). Thus, the prophecy commenced with the Pope following Innocent II who was Celestine II (r. 1143–44). The second quandary concerning antipopes is much more problematic. For instance, in the Malachy prophecy, predictions 6: Octavius ("Victor IV") (1159–1164); 7: Pascal III (1165–1168); 8: Callistus III (1168–1177) are antipopes. Antipopes are alternative popes elected in opposition to a standing pope during various schisms and controversies. The problem is that those antipopes listed opposed Alexander III (1159–81) but in reality there was another antipope Innocent III (1178–1180) who is not included in prophecy.[36] What makes this revealing is this is exactly the same way Panvinius recorded it. Panvinius neglected antipope Innocent III as well. Whether Panvinius altered his text to fit the prophecy or altered the prophecy to fit his own book, the fact remains that the inclusion of certain antipopes to the exclusion of others is powerful evidence of tampering.

This state of affairs points to the fact that someone, likely Panvinius, redacted the pre-1590 prophecies to conform to Panvinius' book. If their goal was to influence a conclave, it makes perfect sense. Panvinius' work was the authoritative source at the time and likely the only one most people had access to. By manipulating all of the pre-1590 mottos to have obvious fulfillments that any semi-studious Cardinal could verify, they launched an ingenious conspiracy to promote Simoncelli as the candidate of divine destiny. The inclusion of antipopes makes it likely that something of this nature occurred. Because the lower level of historical context, the original text, was just a series of nebulous Latin phrases, how could someone like Panvinius, the alleged interpreter Ciacconus or the publisher, Wion (who discovered the list over four hundred years after their composition), know to include these and only these specific antipopes? It is just not plausible. If the antipopes are not included, the whole list gets thrown out of sync. Of course, the original text left no such instructions. Even so, *it is* in sync…but not with actual history; rather, with Panvinius' book!

In summary, there is ample evidence pointing to Panvinius or a sixteenth-century pseudepigrapher who referenced Panvinius' book for all of the prophecies up until Paul IV in 1559 (when Panvinius' book ends). The five popes between him and Urban VII (Pius IV, Pius V, Gregory XIII, and Sixtus V) would be in recent memory and easy for anyone to describe. It is our belief that whoever perpetrated the ruse used an actual prophetic document and modified all of the entries prior to coincide with the principle text on Pontifical history of that time. While this evidence supports the idea that the older prophecies were altered, it does not explain what has happened over the last four hundred years since Wion's publication.

Acrostics, Anagrams, and a Real-Life Conspiracy Code?

Of the two layers of historical context discussed prior, now the lower older level demands our attention. While we can see ample motivation for the redactor to modify the pre-1590 phrases, there is no logical reason that a sixteenth-century forger would craft a list so long into the future. Even more so, there is no good reason he would forecast the destruction of Rome when the papists have an obvious vested interest to the contrary. This is a powerful argument that the post-1595 prophecies are indeed an accurate representation of the original document. We will likely never know for sure who wrote the original but it very well could have been Malachy. The reason the post publication prophecies have a different character and a stranger, ironic, even sarcastic realization is that they are very likely the genuine article.

It was suggested prior that an Englishman, Nicholas Sanders, may have referenced the original document in Rome after he journeyed from the British Isles. Sanders (1530–1581) was an Oxford professor from a staunch Roman Catholic background and a link in a long chain of missionaries sent to Ireland to combat the spread of Protestantism. His writings are credited as the basis of most Roman

Catholic histories of the English Reformation. Not surprising, given the dubious nature of that work, the large quantity of inflammatory spurious statements within earned Sanders the nickname of "Dr. Slanders" in England.

The historical context of this period is during the confusion and crisis surrounding the English reformation when Elizabeth I, Henry VIII's daughter, came to the throne of England and Ireland in 1558 advocating Protestant theology. Catholics fearing retaliation for their harsh treatment of Protestants panicked. This caused papal loyal, Sanders, to vacate his Oxford chair in 1560 and hightail it to Rome, where he became a priest and doctor of theology. While it lasted, Rome was good for Sanders.

While in Rome, he hobnobbed with influential papists like Cardinal Hosius whom he served for a time. It was during this time that he published his books that we will subsequently examine. Later, he conspired with James Fitzmaurice Fitzgerald to launch a papal military invasion of Ireland. They wanted to secure Ireland for the Pope and vacate Protestants. Sanders and Fitzgerald landed a force of some six hundred Spanish and Italian troops under papal authority at Smerwick harbor in Ireland, instigating the Second Desmond Rebellion. While they enjoyed some superficial success, this campaign was ultimately unsuccessful and Sanders is believed to have died of cold and starvation hiding out in hinterland of Ireland in 1581.

It was during the heady days in Rome, around 1571, that Sanders' authored *De Visibili Monarchia Ecclesiae* ("From the Monarchy of the Visible Church") which provided the first account of the travails of the English Roman Catholics as a consequence of the reformation. While the book's purpose was to generate sympathy for English Catholics, it leads scholars to suspect he could have had access to the original Prophecy of the Popes document. The clue which suggests that he must have been aware of the Prophecy of the Popes is that, in his book, he argues, "...to measure time, nothing is more advisable than the series of the Roman pontiffs!"[37]

This discussion derives from an extremely rare book written in

French entitled, *La Mystérieuse Prophétie des Papes* ("The Mysterious Prophecy of the Popes"), published in 1951. The authors of this book were fortunate to find a copy of this sixty-plus-year-old manuscript and to have worked diligently to translate it to English. What we found is astonishing: nothing short of a real-life conspiracy code. Written by René Thibaut (1883–1952), a Belgian Jesuit, the book is a meticulous reading of the prophecy which comes to completely different conclusions than his skeptical predecessors. Adopting the methodology of a mystic as well as a scholar, he makes a compelling case that the Prophecy of the Popes is a real supernatural prophecy. Nevertheless, he argues the author of the prophecy is probably not Saint Malachy but someone who prophesied pseudonymously in his honor, in the same way a nameless second temple period Jew may have composed 1 Enoch, perhaps also redacting ancient source material.[38] What Thibaut took into account that his more severe Jesuit brothers neglected are the layers of historical context discussed prior. He appropriately recognizes an authentic, more aged layer of text which was massaged by a sixteenth-century interloper.

Thibaut somewhat agrees with the former analysis that the earlier prophecies were subjected to tampering, but he argues that the last forty-one suggest a much older document of Celtic origin. While he is reluctant to authenticate the legend, he refers to the author as Pseudo-Malachy, believing him to be Irish. He bases this on the stylistic use of numbers and word plays which form many acrostics and anagrams.[39] Commenting on the style, he observes, "Note that this way of dividing the words to sort various meanings is a method dear to the ancient Irish."[40] A simple example of an anagram is seen in the Latin text "*Peregrinus apostolicus*"[41] which was the prophecy for the ninety-sixth pope on the list, Pius VI. The anagram not only reveals the papal name, it does it twice: *PeregIinUS aPostolIcUS*. That's right! The name "Pius" is rather transparently embedded in the original Latin text twice! Can you imagine that perhaps we now have even a *third* level of context to examine?

This appearance of the name "Pius" is rather astounding considering we have a published copy dated almost two hundred years before Pius VI was elected. Furthermore, he argues the encrypted couplet within "Apostolic pilgrim" signifies both Pius VI and the very next pope Pius VII who were both forced into foreign exile (i.e., pilgrims). He also suggests that the repetition serves as a poetic refrain. In other words, "Pius! Pius!" is similar to the excited binary "Mayday, Mayday!" that sailors cry out in dire circumstances.[42] He demonstrates many similar patterns of words and numbers embedded in the list incorporating them into detailed charts and illustrations. His work is challenging and numinous. The most electrifying is his calculation of the forty popes prior to *Petrus Romanus*. Most startling for us, he demonstrates that many of these cryptograms point to *one particular year*. But first, he distinguishes the Malachian prophet from those who have set dates for the end of the world in the past:

> But even if he believed that, one has no right to compare it to the false prophets who, in troubled times like today announced the imminent coming of the Antichrist and the Last Judgment. For, unlike those birds of ill omen, our prophet has so little intent to frighten his contemporaries that he provides 40 popes before the supreme deadline! 40 popes, that is to say more than four centuries! Exactly, in the present case 440 years! The Prophet has an average 11-year pontificate. How do we know? We shall see later, when, in many ways, we will go up from the election of Gregory XIII (1572) **to 2012 and the Judgment of God.** (bold added)[43]

As we write, it is two days before Christmas, 2011. At the risk of sounding like a "bird of ill omen," 2012 is here folks! Over sixty years ago, Thibaut derived the ominous date of 2012 by calculating the average length of papal reign up until the time he wrote his book circa 1950 to be eleven years. We have verified his math and extrapolated it to our current time. Astonishingly, the average of eleven has held true to three decimal places, 1/1000th accuracy. For this simple derivation, allowing the average of eleven years per reign and a total of forty popes (11 x 40) he extrapolated 440 years from 1572 (1572 + 440) to arrive at the date for the arrival of Petrus Romanus in **2012**.[44] In other words, 2012 was seen as an end-times "event horizon" by at least one Jesuit priest before most readers were born.

Back when gas was nineteen cents a gallon, and certainly well before the apocalyptic frenzy surrounding the Mayan long count calendar's finale, Thibaut derived 2012 from the Prophecy of the Popes. Also note the quote above asserts, "in many ways" this means he derives 2012 from *several* distinct methods of cryptographic analysis. These will be examined after we survey some essential background, but as the final year he derived 2012 exclusively. Indeed, while he (and us) acknowledges the folly of setting a date for Christ's coming, he still centers on 2012 but for no other reason than he believes the prophecy demands it. Because this is a rare book and is written in French, few of you will be able to do as we have done to verify these claims. But, Google Books makes it available in snippet view where one can verify multiple instances of 2012.[45] As a means of illustration, when running a computer search on the original French text of the book, the search term "2012" returns a whopping twenty-four hits. He argues that so many factors point to 2012 as the culmination that the prophecy demands it. Even so, he represents it more as the conclusion of an age than the great tribulation.[46] This seems like special pleading. Apparently, he did not want to accept Rome's prophesied demise. Thibaut ends with the quip, "*L'année 2012 dira si, oui ou non, le prophète a vu clair*" ("The year 2012 will show whether or not the prophet saw clearly").[47] Indeed, it will.

Page 101

s'opposent tant qu'ils peuvent (¹). On sait bien aujourd'hui que la méthode est stérile et qu'il faut *apparemment* déraisonner pour trouver du neuf.

L'année 2012 dira si, oui ou non, le « prophète » a vu clair.

2 | Prophecy of the Popes and the Year 2012

t is the glory of God to conceal a thing: but the honor of kings is to search out a matter" (Proverbs 25:2). When we began researching the prophecy, we started with a healthy dose of skepticism. In light of the Counter Reformation and the Vatican's well-documented trail of forgeries, one might suspect the Prophecy of the Popes to be some sort of manipulation. As we initially delved into the scholarship on the subject, our worst suspicions seemed to be confirmed. Early on, the evidence that the pre-1590 prophecies were written after the fact was so convincing that we considered shelving the project. However, there were a few remarkable twentieth-century fulfillments like Benedict XV, assigned the motto *Religio depopulate,* that merited serious pause. There is well-documented history of the prophecy in the sixteenth century, so any fulfilled mottos after that time demand serious consideration.

Even more, as our research progressed, unresolved issues fell into place and yielded unexpected results. We have uncovered a wealth of source material seldom mentioned in the popular literature. At worst, we have a Jesuit hoax or some papal propaganda. If that is the case, then at the very least this work provides a platform to refute some errors in theology. We have no illusions of grandeur and we do not fancy ourselves as end-time prophets with special revelation. Even so, there is something remarkable about the fortune we have encountered in the research. We have asked if this prophecy is really genuine and have concluded at a minimum there is strong evidence that Rome has (and is) intentionally promoting the prophecy, even though some Jesuits have called it a forgery. Thus we would not put it past Rome to have arranged events in accordance with a Catholic prophecy and in some cases they clearly have. Even so, some of the fulfillments were beyond human control. While we believe demons can make educated guesses and manipulate events to give the illusion of prophecy, only God can inspire real prophecy (Isaiah 46:9–10). So why would the God of the Bible allow the Prophecy of the Popes? We offer three considerations.

First, let us offer a very simple rationale. God uses the most unlikely events to accomplish His sovereign purpose. He is uniquely capable of turning the tables in unexpected ways. Think of how God used Satan's diabolic designs against Jesus. Satan played right into to the Father's hands, ensured his own defeat and surrendered the atonement for sins of the world (1 John 2:2). The cosmic inquisition was ended when Satan, the cosmic grand inquisitor, defeated himself. It seems just that his earthly counterpart ("grand inquisitor") meet a similar fate. Through the cross of Calvary, God effectively, "spoiled principalities and powers [Satan and demons], he made a shew of them openly, triumphing over them in it" (Colossians 2:15). In the Prophecy of the Popes, Mystery Babylon and her *Pontifex Maximi* are similarly made a public horror as the City of Seven Hills is engulfed in flames. It is truly chilling to imagine.

Second, it seems from the Scriptures that God has a sense of irony that is second to none. Even a cursory reading of the Old Testament will yield God pouring out His emotions in the livid, sardonic tones of a jilted lover, "And they shall no more offer their sacrifices unto devils, after whom they have gone a whoring" (Le 17:7a); and "Go and cry unto the gods which ye have chosen; let them deliver you in the time of your tribulation" (Judges 10:14). Consider how the Prophet Elijah taunts the priests of Baal, "Cry aloud: for he is a god; either he is talking, or he is pursuing, or he is in a journey, or peradventure he sleepeth, and must be awaked" (1 Ki 18:27). Some versions render this Hebrew, "Cry aloud, for he is a god. Either he is musing, or he is relieving himself…" (1 Kings 18:27a, ESV). The point is that God appreciates irony and often employs sarcasm. He also appreciates a clever riddle (Proverbs 25:2).

Third, God often uses the most unlikely people. From a Catholic perspective, we offer the words of Pope Benedict XIV: "The recipients of prophecy may be angels, devils, men, women, children, heathens, or gentiles; nor is it necessary that a man should be gifted with any particular disposition in order to receive the light of prophecy provided his intellect and senses be adapted for making manifest the things which God reveals to him. Though moral goodness is most profitable to a prophet, yet it is not necessary in order to obtain the gift of prophecy."[48] While we are duly cautious to agree with a pope, it is helpful to recall Nebuchadnezzar's dream from Daniel 2. God chose to reveal a prophecy spanning from 605 BC through the second coming of Christ to an arrogant narcissistic pagan king. Of course, it required God's holy servant, Daniel, to interpret the dream. Similarly, God used Balaam, a sorcerer hired by Balak, a Moabite king, who was exceedingly fearful of the encroaching multitude of Israelites. Accordingly, the king sent for Balaam, a darkened wizard who now lives in prophetic infamy (2 Peter 2:15; Jude 11; Revelation 2:14). Despite Balaam's incorrigible status, God used him to prophesy, "I see Him, but not now; I behold Him, but not near; A Star shall come out of Jacob; A Scepter shall rise out of Israel, And batter the brow of Moab, And destroy all the sons of tumult" (Numbers 24:17).

Ronald Allen, professor of Hebrew Scripture at Western Baptist

Seminary writes, "In agreement with many in the early church and in early Judaism, we believe this text speaks unmistakably of the coming of the Messiah. That this prophecy should come from one who was unworthy makes it all the more dramatic and startling."[49] Thus, we see that God uses the most unlikely characters and situations to get His message across. This Pethorian prophecy was well over one thousand years before the birth of Christ and from a hostile source yet it is probably what led the Magi to Bethlehem. The nameless author of the allegedly lost *La profezia* used Balaam as an example as well, remarking that the gift of prophecy, "is essentially a free supernatural gift, in which God certifies the truth of His faith by communicating to different souls, sometimes even infidels like Balaam, in whom altered states have occurred inspiring them spontaneously to speak marvelously of the most sublime mystery of God."[50] If we conclude the Prophecy of the Popes is authentic prophecy, then it is so impossibly ironic and judiciously just that it could indeed be *inspired.* So, we must decide where to draw the line between the authentic and the forged.

John Hogue acknowledges that there is a line of demarcation after 1590: "roughly halfway through the succession, the mottoes of St. Malachy suffer a credibility crisis."[51] He concurs with the Jesuit's conspiracy hypothesis that the prophecy was a sixteenth-century propaganda ploy. Yet, its counterfeit status is of no ultimate concern as he argues, "Whether these Latin phrases were composed in 1140 or by someone in the 1590s under the pseudonym of a medieval saint, their author is a prophet."[52] Hogue rates the Malachy prophecies accuracy post 1590 at around 80 percent, but observes that the predictions have only seemed to gain precision through time. In other words, to Hogue, the more recent ones have exhibited even more remarkable accuracy. He agrees that the Jesuits went to work discrediting it because the prophesied demise of popery was intolerable no matter who the source. It follows that Rome would seek to discredit the prophecy because Catholic eschatology promotes the idea that the Roman Church conquers the world rather than the Malachian destruction of the City of Seven Hills during the reign of *Petrus Romanus*. Does Rome believe that it is destined for destruction?

That is why the favorable work of one Jesuit, Rene' Thibaut is more intriguing. His background has been particularly difficult to track down. We know he was Belgian-born in a tiny municipality named Ciney on December 13, 1883. He entered the Jesuit order in September of 1901. He was on the faculty of a University De Namur which was founded by the Jesuit order in 1831 in Namur, Belgium. His published books on theology and biblical studies are exclusively in French, but we have translated a few titles as examples: *The Meaning of Christ's Words* (1940), *The Meaning of the God Man* (1946), and of course our specimen *The Mysterious Prophecy of the Popes* (1951).[53] He died at age sixty-nine in Egenhoven, Belgium on November 23, 1952, shortly after his book on the Prophecy of the Popes was published.

Of course he is not alone as other Catholics like the Abbe Cucherat and the anonymous author of *La profezia dei sommi pontefici romani* have argued for the veracity of the prophecy. Contrary to Hogue's dramatic speculations about this allegedly lost volume burning up containing the evidence for the Cucherat's account of the Janiculum Hill vision (a book which we located, translated, and read) the unknown author admits the prophecy may or not be authored by Malachy. He wrote,

> So what if he is not Malachy? But even so, one might ask, "What are the benefits of such an argument?" Who has ever claimed that to prove indisputably it is the Saint? Nobody so far has attempted, and we are far from demanding it and agree with ease that the author is unknown.[54]

Even so, the anonymous author did mention an older manuscript at a monastery in Rimini and a later author Joseph Maitre says that it burned up.[55] The unnamed author goes on to say that we should judge the prophecy on its merits and not by who allegedly wrote it. In the modern era, perhaps one of the better-presented cases is in the Tan Books publication *The Prophecies of St. Malachy* with commentary by Catholic scholar Peter Bander van Duren who was a British expert on heraldry and orders of knighthood. Bander writes, "It is fair to say that the vast majority of Malachy's predictions about successive Popes are amazingly accurate—always remembering that he gives only a minimum of information."[56] Thibaut and Bander are not alone as there are other contemporary scholars who are impressed by the prophecy.

An Islamic scholar, Martin Lings, who was keeper of oriental manuscripts and printed books at the British Museum and a friend of C.S. Lewis, has also published in support of the Prophecy of the Popes in the peer-reviewed journal *Studies in Comparative Religion*.[57] Lings writes, "Its brief descriptions continue to be so apt that confirmed skeptics have been driven to wonder whether the Cardinals did not sometimes choose a Pope to fit the prophecy, or in other cases whether the Pope himself had not deliberately taken action to make the prophecy 'come true.'"[58] Quite frankly, when we first read that, we identified with it. That being the case, his article was one of the first from a respectable journal which argued it to be a genuine prophetic oracle. He adds, "The prophecy not seldom refers to unforeseeable things over which neither Pope nor Cardinals could have the slightest control."[59] He also points out that the prophecy does not always refer directly to the pope, himself, and sometimes even after the election it may continue to be a riddle, which is resolved prior to the demise of the particular pontiff. He provides some pertinent examples which we shall refer to as we examine the popes in order.

As mentioned in the first chapter, John Lupia, a Catholic scholar and editor of Roman Catholic News, has written authoritatively in favor of the prophecy. His opinion carries some force as he is an accomplished researcher with advanced degrees in biblical studies and archeology and a PhD in art history. In his two article series for *Roman Catholic News*, he posted the most complete bibliography we have come across on the Malachy prophecy. He is also a true believer. He comments, "After 35 years of research on this subject it is my opinion that they are authentic."[60] He explains that the Church has had over four hundred fifty years to officially reject the prophecies, yet it never has. Indeed, we see evidence that the Church has intentionally encouraged belief in the Malachy prophecy. They even produced a 1942 documentary entitled *Pastor Angelicus* (the prophecy for Pius XII) which incidentally features the pope saluting the fascist soldiers.[61] That aside, Lupia presents the most scholarly case for the prophecy's origin and authenticity we have seen.

As we explained in chapter one, he cites evidence that Vatican librarian Onofrio Panvinius discovered the manuscript in 1556. However, whereas Lupia argues that Panvinius altered his papal history to match the prophecy, we find this to be special pleading of the highest order. Why would the Vatican librarian use a string of nebulous Latin phrases instead of the historical records at his disposal to write a papal history? It just does not make sense. Because the prophecy as published by Wion reflects the same antipopes and errors in heraldry later identified in Panvinius' book, it seems far more likely that he altered the prophecy manuscript according to what he *believed* were the historical facts. To what end, we don't know, but most likely it entailed a Vatican-politico propaganda effort of some sort. Without the original manuscript it is impossible to make an authoritative assertion, but it seems the most prudent response is to accept the prophecies which occur sometime after the publication of his book. Because Lupia cites the second-oldest mention of the prophecy by Girolamo Muzio in his 1570 work, *Il Choro Pontificale* and Thibaut argues the same line of demarcation, we adopt that position.

Because most scholars dismiss the prophecies before the publication date as *vaticinia ex eventu*, the task of evaluation is greatly reduced. To critically evaluate the prophecy we only need examine the lower level of context. Hogue follows the conventional theory dividing the prophecy at Wion's 1595 publication: "He left us a list of 35 mottos, numbered 77 through 111 that, unlike the previous 76, are not 100 percent accurate; however, the average of success makes their author one of the most astounding prophets in history."[62] Yet, Rene Thibaut has a slightly different theory and a much more sophisticated methodology. Because the Simoncelli conspiracy theory seems to be a diversion and Thibaut believes the original manuscript begins circa 1571 which concurs with Lupia's data, we expand the range to include forty Latin mottos: 71 through 111. As we will endeavor to show, this range yields some surprising results that seem to authenticate Thibaut's work.

Thibaut believes Nicholas Sanders referenced the Malachy manuscript in his 1571 book, *From the Monarchy of the Visible Church*, when he argued that, "to measure time, nothing is more advisable than the series of the Roman pontiffs."[63] As a result, he was convinced that the last forty represent the original context. He went so far as to argue, "We also believe we have the right to ensure the complete integrity of the last 40 reports."[64] He also discounts the Simoncelli conspiracy but detects the work of the forger in the first seventy-one prophecies. He argues that the prophecies prior to seventy-two rather obviously point to heraldry (coats of arms) and acknowledges the all-too-perfect agreement with Panvinius' work. Thus, he begins the authentic portion of the manuscript at Gregory XIII in 1572 which adds a few more popes to the list than Hogue and the Jesuit critics allow.

So how do we evaluate something so mystical, so weird, and so utterly unique? While we must allow for supernaturalism *a priori*, our evaluation must acknowledge the standards of science. Good science is a search for what is true. First, we need to look at the mechanics of the prophecy and what constitutes a viable fulfillment. Second, we will discuss critical methodology. Critics argue that the phrases are vague and can be easily twisted into shape in an *ad hoc* (improvised) manner. This is largely because of the malleable nature of their referents. For instance, sometimes they refer to heraldry (Coat of Arms), other times the pope's name, perhaps his birthplace, or even events in his career. Thibaut believed that the authentic prophecies spoke more to events that occurred during the papal reign than specific items like heraldry. Frankly, the prophecies lack a precise target. If the prophecies had all referred to the same aspect like heraldry, then they would be much more convincing. We must acknowledge that this elasticity in the target is a major weakness. But even so, this is a puzzle, not an evangelistic tract. It is not supposed to be easy.

Science is defined by a process called the scientific method. Typically, this includes an observation about a phenomenon, a hypothesis formulated to explain it, and a test performed via a controlled experiment. The key to the testing process is falsifiability. A positive test result means a hypothesis is plausible, not proven, but a negative test result proves it false. Hence, the proper test of a hypothesis is to make a prediction and devise a test such that at least one outcome proves the theory false. Karl Popper is generally regarded as one of the greatest philosophers of science of the twentieth century. He is famous for establishing the criteria for modern scientific inquiry, two of which are suggested as:

1. It is easy to obtain confirmations, or verifications, for nearly every theory—if we look for confirmations.
2. Confirmations should count only if they are the result of *risky predictions*; that is to say, if, unenlightened by the theory in question, we should have expected an event which was incompatible with the theory—an event which would have refuted the theory.[65]

Now, we are not exactly trying to prove a scientific theory, but the idea is that we want to have this sort of methodology in mind as we evaluate the Prophecy of the Popes. We are confident that the Christian worldview explains the reality we observe much better than the naturalistic theories advocated by most scientists. Our

faith is grounded in evidence of a historical nature and we are confident and encouraged by the level of intellectual scrutiny that things
like the evidence for Jesus' resurrection can endure. Accordingly, we
have no agenda to meet with the Prophecy of the Popes. It either
authenticates itself on its merit or it becomes a conversation piece.
We mentioned above that one prophecy in particular grabbed
our attention in a way that prompted willingness to invest in the
research. Benedict XV was assigned the motto *Religio depopulate*:
"religion destroyed." That prophecy alone should give the skeptic
pause. While only a few of the prophecies show this level of overt
prescience, we now undertake an evaluation of the last ten as a representative sample of the first level of context: what we now believe
represents the original document.

Leo XIII
February 20, 1878 to July 20, 1903
Lumen in caelo "Light in the sky"

His coat of arms features a shooting star. Our first thought is that
this would be easy for the pope to intentionally fulfill. However,
heraldry is considered an art and science in Roman Catholicism,
and there are explicit rules. According to the rules, all bishops
adopt a coat of arms.[66] He necessarily adopted the coat of arms
with a light in the sky many years prior to his papal ambitions.
According to the Catholic Encyclopedia, he was made an archbishop in 1843: a full thirty-five years prior to becoming pope.[67] It
doesn't seem likely that he could have anticipated his own papacy
and intentionally fulfilled the prophecy. Nobody knows how long
the current pope is going to live. If one were to adopt the next
prophecy on Malachy's list as part of his coat of arms upon becoming a bishop, he would likely miss because someone else would
be elected prior to his ever-achieving papabile status. Notice the
shooting start in the top left corner:

images note 2

Because many of the previous prophecies do seem to speak to heraldry, this is a compelling fulfillment.

Pius X
August 4, 1903 to August 20, 1914
Ignis ardens "Burning fire"

During an audience with the general Chapter of the Franciscans in 1909, Pius X fell into a semi-trance with his head sunk on his chest, and after a few minutes he came to and opened his eyes with a look of horror on his face. He reputedly cried out: "What I have seen was terrible... Will it be myself? Will it be my successor? What is certain is that the Pope will quit Rome, and in fleeing from the Vatican he will have to walk over the dead bodies of his priests. Do not tell anyone while I am alive."[68]

Just prior to his death (August 20, 1914), Pope Pius X had another vision: "I saw one of my successors taking to flight over the bodies of his brethren. He will take refuge in disguise somewhere; and after a short retirement he will die a cruel death. The present wickedness of the world, is only the beginning of the sorrows which must take place before the end of the world."[69]

Is this a vision of the destruction of Rome forecasted in the ending of the Prophecy of the Popes? It certainly appears to be. Whereas other books about the Prophecy of the Popes point to a star on his coat of arms as a "burning fire," we wonder if perhaps this vision of

Rome burning isn't a better match? This one is debatable; we will leave it to the reader to decide.

Benedict XV
September 3, 1914 to January 22, 1922
Religio depopulata "Religion depopulated"

This is the kind of prediction we like because it was easily falsifiable. For instance, his reign could have been marked by a remarkable revival in the Church. It was a risky prediction and according to Popper, "Confirmations should count only if they are the result of risky predictions."[70] If Roman Catholicism had grown or even stayed the same this would have been necessarily falsified. Yet, in remarkable fulfillment, this was the time when Catholicism lost more adherents in one short period than at any other time in history.

World War I was devastating to the Roman Catholic Church, and then to add insult to injury, some 200 million left the Russian Orthodox fold to join the Bolshevik revolution or were killed or persecuted by the communists. A papal historian confirms, "Lenin declared war on religion and on assuming power was immediately to subject both the Orthodox and the Roman Catholic Churches in Russia to murderous persecution."[71] According to a leading expert on democide (death by government), "the Soviet Union appears the greatest megamurderer of all, apparently killing near 61,000,000 people. Stalin himself is responsible for almost 43,000,000 of these. Most of the deaths, perhaps around 39,000,000 are due to lethal forced labor in gulag and transit thereto."[72] Lenin and Stalin specifically targeted religious leaders as they viewed them as a threat. Religion was heavily depopulated during this period. Indeed, the prophecy demonstrates breathtaking accuracy here.

Pius XI

February 6, 1922 to February 10, 1939
Fides intrepida "Intrepid faith"

This pope reinstituted the Faustian bargain, which began with the Donation of Constantine fraud. Pius XI infamously struck a bargain with the fascist dictator Mussolini signing a concordat February 11, 1929. This deal made the Vatican a temporal power once again (Napoleon had taken it away). It was eerily similar to the unscrupulous events of AD 752–756. According to John Norwich's papal history:

> Under the Lateran Treaty the pope regained a vestige of his temporal power. Admittedly the land over which he was sovereign ruler amounted to a mere 109 acres—about a quarter the area of the Principality of Monaco—with a population of rather less than five hundred, but the Holy See was once again to rank among the nations of the world. Moreover, in return for his renunciation of his claim to the previous papal territories he was given a payment, in cash and Italian state securities, of 1.75 billion lire, which at that time amounted to some $100 million. Anticlerical laws passed by the Italian government since 1870, including the Law of Guarantees, were declared null and void. In return, the Vatican promised to remain neutral and not to involve itself in international politics or diplomacy.[73]

Dante likely rolled over in his grave. His "intrepid faith" led to a compromise with a ruthless dictator in order to put the Vatican back in business as a political state. Norwich adds, "The pope had even hailed Mussolini as 'a man sent by Providence,' and in the 1929 elections most Catholics were encouraged by their priests to vote Fascist."[74] He also signed a concordat with the Nazis in July 20, 1933. A Latin dictionary defines *intrepidus* as calm, brave, and undisturbed.[75] Perhaps "cold and calculating" fulfills this one?

Pius XII
March 2, 1939 to October 9, 1958
Pastor angelicus "Angelic shepherd"

There were rumors of visions and "angelic" phenomena associated with Pius XII during his papacy. We will discuss one of his visions below but if one understands "angelic" to mean well-behaved it seems falsified by the revelations from John Cornwell that he was Hitler's pope. Cornwell reveals:

> Even as news of the Final Solution was coming into the Vatican, he was collaborating with Luigi Gedda, president of Catholic Action in Italy, to make an hour long movie intended for world distribution entitled *Pastor Angelicus*, depicting the "daily life of the Pope and how he exemplifies the prophecy of the Irish monk Malachy that the 262nd successor to St. Peter was to be indicated by the name Angelic Shepherd."[76]

images note 3

The Concordat effectively legitimized Hitler and the Nazi government to the eyes of Roman Catholics. In light of this, perhaps "fallen angelic shepherd" would have been more fitting? Even though he intentionally claimed his prophetic motto, it amounts to an ironic sort of fulfillment.

images note 4

Not many popes have claimed their Malachy mottos so publicly. Also, if the papists truly believed it to be a complete sixteenth-century forgery (as most Jesuits would lead us to believe) why would a pope legitimize it? Pius XII also prophesied, "We believe that the present hour is the dread phase of the events foretold by Christ. It seems that darkness is about to fall over the world. Humanity is in the grip of a supreme crisis."[77]

John XXIII
October 28, 1958 to June 3, 1963
Pastor & nauta "Shepherd and sailor"

Being the patriarch of Venice, the city famous for its gondolas and a nautical street system, this one is another match. An interesting sideline is that the ambitious Cardinal Spellman of New York wanted the papacy bad enough to attempt to make this one happen. The word on the street is that after reading about the Malachy prophecies, he hired a boat, filled it with sheep and sailed up and down the Tiber River in full view of the conclave. If it is true, it reveals a tendency of the Romanists to force the prophecy.

This is the pope that called the Vatican II ecumenical council although he did not live to see its completion. In light of the false idea that Vatican II was a reversal of the hardline anathemas pronounced on all true Christians by the Council of Trent, it is essential to document that this pope affirmed and praised the Council of Trent during his opening address for Vatican II on April 29, 1963:

> In truth, at the present time, it is necessary that Christian doctrine in its entirety, and with nothing taken away from it, is accepted with renewed enthusiasm, and serene and tranquil adherence delivered to the exact words of conceiving and reducing to the form, which especially shines forth from the acts of the Council of Trent and the First Vatican Council. It is necessary that the very same doctrine be understood more widely and more profoundly as all those who sincerely adhere to the Christian, Catholic and Apostolic faith greatly desire, the same doctrine more fully known and higher instilled in the mind; it is necessary that this certain and unchangeable doctrine, to which is owed the obedience of faith, be explored and expounded in the manner required by our times.[78]

Thus, Vatican II cannot in any way, shape, or form be represented as a genuine step away from the extreme hubris displayed at the Council of Trent. Catholic apologists who represent it as such are engaging in sophistry. They have never truly taken back a single anathema. Even so, this pope is another feather in Pseudo-Malachy's cap.

Paul VI
June 21, 1963 to August 6, 1978
Flos florum "Flower of flowers"

He was another apparition devotee but of course he called the unidentified phantom by the name of Jesus' birth mother, "Mary." He spoke at Marian events, visited Marian shrines and issued three encyclicals relating to the femme phantom. He officially instituted "Mary, Mother of Christ, Mother of the Church" that is part of the Catechism.[79] This motto is another clear match to heraldry as his coat of arms includes 3 *fleurs-de-lis*, the flower symbol used by the French monarchy. This heraldic device is unique to him amongst the papists. *Fleur-de-lis* literally means "flower of lily," which matches "flower of a flower" quite well.[80]

images note 5

Paul VI was also the pope that Malachi Martin quoted as having said, "the smoke of Satan which has entered the Sanctuary"[81] in reference to the satanic enthronement ceremony of 1963. We also uncovered that Paul VI was active in campaigning for the New World Order. Carl Teichrib obtained a copy of a little-known speech by Paul VI to the United Nations on October 4, 1965. In his address, he calls for an expanded UN role in global affairs:

> Your Charter goes further than this, and Our message advances with it. You exist and operate to unite the Nations, to bind States together. Let Us use this second formula: to bring

the ones together with the others. You are an association. You are a bridge between peoples. You are a network of relations between States. We would almost say that your chief characteristic is a reflection, as it were, in the temporal field, of what our Catholic Church aspires to be in the spiritual field: unique and universal. In the ideological construction of mankind, there is on the natural level nothing superior to this. Your vocation is to make brothers not only of some, but of all peoples. A difficult undertaking, indeed; but this is it, your most noble undertaking. Is there anyone who does not see the necessity of coming thus progressively to the establishment of a world authority, able to act efficaciously on the juridical and political levels?[82]

This little-known speech supports the idea the UN and Vatican are working together toward a global government and New World Order. Will Peter the Roman make this long-sought ambition a reality?

John Paul I
August 26, 1978 to September 28, 1978
De medietate lunae "From the midst of the moon"

He is famous for the shortest papacy in history; he only lived thirty-three days as pope. It is widely believed that he was poisoned because his body was embalmed within one day of his death, in violation of Italian law (the Vatican is a sovereign state and so is not bound by Italian law). The sudden embalming raised suspicions that it had been done to prevent an autopsy. However, the Vatican insisted that a papal post-mortem was prohibited under Vatican law. This was later revealed to be untrue. It must not be against canon law because in 1830 an autopsy was carried out on the remains of Pope Pius VIII who was also suspected of being poisoned. The disingenuous 1978 claim forbidding an autopsy seemingly substantiates claims that John

Paul I was poisoned. If not, then why the obfuscation to prevent a proper investigation?

David Yallop's book, *In God's Name*, proposed a theory involving the Vatican bank's Paul Marcinkus and Roberto Calvi of the Banco Ambrosiano. Significant corruption did come to light and Calvi was revealed to be a member of an illegal Masonic lodge in Italy known as P2. Calvi was found hung by a rope under Blackfriar's Bridge in London with what appears to be Masonic symbolism.[83] Catholic theologian George de Nantesgo believes it was murder and has written about the banking conspiracy and the pope's alleged discovery of Freemason priests in the Vatican.[84] Could this be the same element Malachi Martin called the Roman Phalanx?

As far as his motto, John Paul I was born in the diocese of Belluno (*luno* is Latin for moon) and ascended to the papacy August 26, 1978 on the precise day of a half-moon in its waning phase, which corresponds quite neatly to the phrase "midst of the moon."[85] This is another compelling match.

John Paul II
October 16, 1978 to April 2, 2005
De labore solis "From the labor of the sun"

Pope John Paul II was extremely dedicated to the Mother-goddess worship under the guise of Mary. Many have called him "Mary's pope" because of his personal motto *Totus Tuus*, (Totally yours), signifying his complete devotion to Mary. A reasonable inference follows that if he was totally possessed by the goddess apparition then he could not be devoted to Jesus Christ. He spent a great deal of papacy making pilgrimages to apparition haunting sites and according to the National Catholic Reporter, "in the assassination attempt of May 13, 1981—the Feast of Our Lady of Fátima…John Paul believed Mary changed the flight path of the assassin's bullet to keep him alive."[86] In other words, he did not thank the Lord, he credited "Mary."

There are some that argue this motto refers to elements of sun worship still detectable in Romanism. But this prophecy seems to very accurately describe his origin. The motto is also said to possibly mean "eclipse of the sun," "pregnancy of the sun," or "travails of the sun." John Paul II was born May 18, 1920, during a partial solar eclipse over the Indian Ocean. He was buried on April 8, 2005, during a rare "hybrid" eclipse over South America and the Pacific.[87] We commend you to follow the footnoted links as we verified the eclipses at NASA. This is one fulfillment that is clearly beyond human control.

Pope Benedict XVI
April 19, 2005–?
Gloria olivae "Glory of the olive"

Grand Inquisitor Joseph Ratzinger picked the name Benedict XVI which makes it another self-fulfilling prophecy. He was born on the feast day of Saint Benedict formerly Joseph Labre thus sharing the name Joseph as well as Benedict.[88] Because the olive branch is a symbol of the Benedictine monks, most call this the fulfillment of the prophecy. Many commentators are eager to connect this to the Olivet discourse in Matthew 24 and the end times. Thibaut speculated on this motto and the two preceding ones back in 1951, "Signs of God's judgment are obviously figured. Is it civil (moon) and religious (sun) anarchy?"[89] His comment seems prescient considering the recent increase in earthquakes, Muslim uprisings, and global financial collapses. An allusion to the Olivet discourse may not be so fanciful because world is poised for something.

The Vatican issued a statement in October of 2011 calling for "some form of global monetary management."[90] Of course to the biblically literate this harkens, "And that no man might buy or sell, save he that had the mark, or the name of the beast, or the number of his name" (Re 13:17). Benedict XVI is the oldest pope to be elected since Clement XII in 1730. He will be eighty-five years old on April 16, 2012, shortly after this book is released. The reign of Benedict XVI will necessarily not last much longer. If the Prophecy of the

Popes holds true, Peter the Roman could be in office as early as 2012 but we really do not claim to know. We are simply pointing out what others have written. Tom Horn and Cris Putnam are not prophets or apocalyptic date-setters, just researchers and commentators.

The Next and Final Pope? Enter Peter the Roman and a Latin Cipher Predicting 2012

Even though there seem to be some remarkable fulfillments, what if we have been investigating the Prophecy of the Popes in the wrong way? What if the real prophecy lies hidden beneath the surface of the Latin phrases? Jesuit priest Rene Thibaut's book, *The Mysterious Prophecy of the Popes*, has unlocked an entirely different means of investigating fulfillment that no one else seems to have imagined possible. His work is deeply mystical and prohibitively complex to explain exhaustively. It is also out of print, exceedingly rare, and written in French which makes it exorbitantly inaccessible to all but the most dedicated. We can only claim to be scratching the surface of what he presents. Frankly, we are astounded that the 2012 meme of the last few years did not bring this forgotten volume to light. Please note that we do realize that date-setting has a well-documented 100 percent failure rate but, even so, we must acknowledge, there it is, 2012, brazened all over the pages of this 1951 tome. The simplest calculation which derives 2012 for the last pope is based on extrapolating the average papal reign of eleven years.

Forty popes times eleven years is four hundred forty years:

$40 \times 11 = 440$

Add that to the year 1572 (the year the genuine portion begins) and you land in 2012:

$440 + 1572 = 2012$

Although Thibaut wrote in 1951, we continued his thesis forward by adding the additional popes. The average eleven-year reign he predicted held true through John Paul II. It certainly did not have to. This was a risky prediction and it was confirmed. If John Paul I had lived a normal lifespan and held a much longer reign instead of dying mysteriously after thirty-three days, this trend might have ended. We even used papal reigns in days to get 1/365th accuracy and our results not only confirmed Thibaut's work but revealed a potential we did not expect. The following is a chart rendered from a software spread sheet we used to verify Thibaut's theory:

Pope (Reign)	Prophecy	Days	Reign in Years
Gregory XIII (May 13, 1572 to April 10, 1585)	72. *Medium corpus pilarum* "Half body of the balls"	4715	12.90924568
Sixtus V (April 24, 1585 to August 27, 1596)	73. *Axis in medietate signi* "Axle in the midst of a sign"	4143	11.34316115
Urban VII (September 15, 1590 to September 27, 1590)	74. *De rore caeli* "From the dew of the sky"	12	0.03285492
Gregory XIV (December 5, 1590 to October 15, 1591)	75. *Ex antiquitate Urbis* "Of the antiquity of the city"	314	0.859703742
Innocent IX (October 29, 1591 to December 30, 1591)	76. *Pia civitas in bello* "Pious city in war"	62	0.16975042
Clement VIII (January 30, 1592 to March 3, 1605)	77. *Crux Romulea* "Cross of Romulus"	4781	13.08994774
Leo XI (April 1, 1605 to Saturday, April 27, 1605)	78. *Undosus vir* "Wavy man"	26	0.07118566
Paul V (May 16, 1605 to Sunday, January 28, 1621)	79. *Gens perversa* "Corrupted nation"	5736	15.70465179
Gregory XV (February 9, 1621 to July 8, 1623)	80. *In tribulatione pads* "In the trouble of peace"	879	2.406622895
Urban VIII (August 6, 1623 to July 29, 1644)	81. *Lilium & rosa* "Lily and rose"	7663	20.98060437
Innocent X (September 15, 1644 to January 7, 1655)	82. *Iucunditas cruds* "Delight of the cross"	3766	10.31096908
Alexander VII (April 7, 1655 to May 22, 1667)	83. *Montium custos* "Guard of the mountains"	4428	12.1234655
Clement IX (June 20, 1667 to December 9, 1669)	84. *Sydus olorum* "Star of the swans"	903	2.472332735
Clement X (April 29, 1670 to July 22, 1676)	85. *De flumine magno* "From a great river"	2276	6.231483172
IInnocent XI (September 21, 1676 to August 12, 1689)	86. *Bellua insatiabilis* "Insatiable beast"	4708	12.89008031

Pope (Reign)	Prophecy	Days	Reign in Years
Alexander VIII (October 6, 1689 to February 1, 1691)	87. *Pœnitentia gloriosa* "Glorious penitence"	483	1.322410533
Innocent XII (July 12, 1691 to September 27, 1700)	88. *Rastrum in porta* "Rake in the door"	3365	9.213067168
Clement XI (November 23, 1700 to March 19, 1721)	89. *Flores drcundati* "Surrounded flowers"	7421	20.31803015
Innocent XIII (May 8, 1721 to May 29, 1724)	90. *De bona religione* "From good religion"	1117	3.058245476
Benedict XIII (May 29, 1724 - February 21, 1730)	91. *Miles in bello* "Soldier in War"	2094	5.733183551
Clement XII (July 12, 1730 - February 6, 1740)	92. *Columna excelsa* "Lofty column"	3496	9.571733379
Benedict XIV (August 17, 1740 to May 3, 1758)	93. *Animal rurale* "Country animal"	6457	17.67868491
Clement XIII (July 6, 1758 to February 2, 1769)	94. *Rosa Umbriae* "Rose of Umbria"	3864	10.57928426
Clement XIV (May 18, 1769 to September 22, 1774)	95. *Ursus velox* "Swift bear"	1953	5.347138241
Pius VI (February 15, 1775 to August 29, 1799)	96. *Peregrinus apostolicus* "Apostolic pilgrim"	8961	24.53441156
Pius VII (March 14, 1800 to August 20, 1823)	97. *Aquila rapax* "Rapacious eagle"	8559	23.43377174
Leo XII (September 28, 1823 to February 10, 1829)	98. *Cants & coluber* "Dog and adder"	1962	5.371779431
Pius VIII (March 31, 1829 to December 1, 1830)	99. *Vir religiosus* "Religious man"	610	1.670125103
Gregory XVI (February 2, 1831 to June 1, 1846)	100. *De balneis Ethruriae* "From the baths of Tuscany"	5598	15.32682021
Pius IX (June 16, 1846 to February 7, 1878)	101. *Crux de cruce* "Cross from cross"	11,559	31.64750175
Leo XIII (February 20, 1878 to July 20, 1903)	102. *Lumen in caelo* "Light in the sky"	9280	25.40780485
St. Pius X (August 4, 1903 to August 20, 1914)	103. *Ignis ardens* "Burning fire"	4034	11.04472896
Benedict XV (September 3, 1914 to January 22, 1922)	104. *Religio depopulata* "Religion depopulated"	2698	7.386881195
Pius XI (February 6, 1922 to February 10, 1939)	105. *Fides intrepida* "Intrepid faith"	6213	17.01063486

Pope (Reign)	Prophecy	Days	Reign in Years
Pius XII (March 2, 1939 to October 9, 1958)	106. *Pastor angelicus* "Angelic shepherd"	7154	19.58700818
John XXIII (October 28 , 1958 to June 3, 1963)	107. *Pastor & nauta* "Shepherd and sailor"	1679	4.596950899
Paul VI (June 21, 1963 to August 6, 1978)	108. *Flos florum* "Flower of flowers"	5525	15.12695278
John Paul I (August 26, 1978 to September 28, 1978)	109. *De medietate lunae* "From the midst of the moon"	33	0.09035103
John Paul II (October 16, 1978 to April 2, 2005)	110. *De labore solis* "From the labor of the sun"	9665	26.4619002
Benedict XVI (April 19, 2005 - April 29, 2012)	111. *Gloria olivae* "Glory of the olive"	2567	7.028214984
?	112. *Petrus Romanus* "Peter the Roman"		

Period	Average Reign
Average reign 1572 to 1951 (when Thibaut published)	11.05255156
Average reign 1572 to 2005 (through John Paul II)	11.1055246
Average reign if Benedict XVI is no longer pope by April 29, 2012 =	11.00359186
Days in a year =	365.2421
Thibaut's Formula =	40 popes x average 11-year reign = 440 years
Arrival of Petrus Romanus =	1572 + 440 = 2012

What makes this particularly interesting is that if Pope Benedict were to step down in April, it would yield a near-perfect eleven. Thibaut did not use decimal numbers, so anytime during 2012 would verify he got it right. He simply predicted it would be in the year 2012. Even so, you can imagine our shock as we were translating this from French when we saw this story:

images note 6

However, that is not the end of his 2012 derivations. Thibaut detects that dates are encoded into the Latin text in the form of Roman numerals revealing the time span from the election of Gregory XIII in 1572 to the last pope in the year 2012. He believes the first two prophecies on our list of forty reveal the year 2012.

71. *Medium corpus pilarum*
72. *Axis in medietate signi*

*Mediu**m** corpus pilaru**m** Axis in **m**edietate signi* = 4M
*Me**d**ium corpus pilarum Axis in me**d**ietate signi* = 2D
*Medium **C**orpus pilarum Axis in medietate signi* = 1C

And so on… To get the time span in years, we must first extract the Roman numerals from the text.

We find 4 M, 2 D, 1 C, 1 L, 1 X, 3 V, 7 I, and then adding up the Roman numerals like such:

M+M+M+M+ D+D+C+ L+ X+V+V+V+I+I+I+I+I+I+I = 5182

CONVERSION TABLE

Roman Numeral	Value
I	1
V (note that the Latin u counts as numeral v)	5
X	10
L	50
C	100
D	500
M	1,000

Thibaut then argues:

This total does not mean anything; it suggests at the most 1582. We know that in that year Pope Gregory XIII reformed the calendar. So 1582 would mark out the beginning of a new era. Thus, it is suggested: M D L V V V X IIIIIII = 1582.[91]

Honestly, at first this seems a little forced, but he is right that in 1582, Gregory XIII (the same pope from which the seventy-first motto *Medium corpus pilarum* was taken) corrected the Julian calendar with the papal bull *Inter gravissimas* issued on February 24, 1582. The adjustment took place officially when October 5, 1582 had ten days added to make it October 15, making up for the lack of precision in the old calendar. The reason for the reform was that the average length of the year in the Julian calendar was too long. It treated each year as 365 days, six hours in length, whereas improved astronomical calculations by the Jesuit Christopher Clavius had proved that actual length of a year was eleven minutes less. While eleven minutes doesn't seem like much, over a few centuries, it starts to make a significant difference in the seasons. Because of Gregory's involvement, the reformed Julian calendar came to be known as the Gregorian calendar which is still in use today. Thus, 1582 really was the beginning of a new way of measuring time and this seems to reinforce the idea that the genuine portion of the prophecy also begins with Gregory VIII who is number 72, *Medium corpus pilarum.*

Picking up Thibaut's argument, we now have: M D L V V V X IIIIIII = 1582. This leaves a remainder of 3M's, 1 D and 1 C which he arranges as MDC = 1000 + 500 +100 = 1600 and MM = 1000 + 1000 = 2,000. Thus, he derives 1600 and 2000. From these he argues the pattern reveals that the year 2000 will be reached after forty popes. He then says it must be exceeded by twelve years because between the last M in *Medium corpus pilarum* and the first M in *Axis in medietate signi* we have XII = 12.

*Medium corpus pilarum| **Axis in** |medietate signi*

Thus, MM (2000) + XII (12) = 2012

If you are like us, you are now scratching your head thinking that this whole calculation seems completely *ad hoc.* Frankly, it does, and if we weren't absolutely certain that this was published in 1951, we would accuse the author of going to extravagant lengths to derive 2012. However, we can think of no obvious reason the Jesuit mathematician would want to derive 2012 other than he believed it to be the case. The year 2012 was not even on the radar in 1951, and Thibaut died in 1952. It certainly did not make him famous and his book is now extremely obscure. But, bear with us, Thibaut does offer a rationale.

He argues that the first motto *"Medium corpus pilarum"* alone has a value of MMM D C L VVV II = 3667. From the 3667 he deducts the outer year boundary of 2000 and gets 1667. Now he seeks a means to reduce this to 1572 (the beginning of Gregory XIII's pontificate) in the same manner as he increased 2000 to 2012. He accomplishes this by extracting C and V from the text of *"Medium corpus pilarum"* and then subtracting the V from the C.

Thus, he derives 100 – 5 = 95.

And then 1667 – 95 = 1572.

Now he has derived the outward boundaries of the Prophecy of the Popes to be 1572 to 2012 from an encrypted Roman numeral scheme in the text of the first two mottos of the authentic text. Does it seem fanciful? You bet it does! Thibaut realized he was stretching credulity. He wrote, "Did the author think of this substitution? No, no doubt, but we do not think it is by chance alone! This data 1572–2012 we will find more than once, is it not likely that it is suggested from the beginning of the 40 reports?"[92] In other words, he seems to be saying that he doubts the prophet actually designed this, but rather it was the product of supernatural intelligence. He also believes the fact that this span of years 1572–2012 is supported by enough other means to make it more than likely that even this multifarious encryption scheme is valid.

His next calculation is a little more compelling to us. This is derived from the famous apocalyptic conclusion of the Prophecy of the Popes:

> *In persecutione extrema S. R. E. sedebit Petrus Romanus qui pascet oves in multis tribulationibus; quibus transactis, civitas septicollis diruetur et Iudex tremendus iudicabit populum suum.*

In case you are wondering, S.R.E. is liturgical short hand for *Sancta Romana Ecclesia* (The Holy Roman Church) and this is the famous apocalyptic passage:

> In extreme persecution, the seat of the Holy Roman Church will be occupied by Peter the Roman, who will feed the sheep through many tribulations; when they are over, the City of Seven Hills will be destroyed, and the terrible or fearsome Judge will judge his people.

But now we must deal with the Latin and endure the counting of letters. The Latin text contains 26 words with 158 letters[93] out which 64 serve as Roman numerals: 6 M, 5 D, 6 C, 5 L, 2 X 20 V, 20 I. Thibaut proposes bifurcating the set into a group with the M and C and a group with the D and L. (The number in parenthesis is the value of the Roman Numerals totaled.)

6M (6000) + 6C (600) = 6600 & 5D (2500) + 5L (250) = 2750

He then uses 15 of the 20 available "I" to add to the second number 2750 + 15 = 2765. (Only 5 "I" remain.)

Now he adds the remaining 2X (20) + 20V (100) + 5I (5) = 125.

Then: 6660 + 125 = 6725.

Now things get interesting. First, we need to think big, as in astronomical. Whereas most folks commonly use the Gregorian calendar, astronomers use the Julian Period, a chronological system based on the consecutive number of days from January 1, 4713 BC.[94] If we add 6725 years to 4713 BC we land squarely on 2012. For our other figure, we must acknowledge that we are dealing with Roman Catholic prophecy. Of course, we have argued that the historical evidence favors it being more Roman than Christian. The official year system of pagan Rome was known as the *Ab urbe condita* which is Latin for "since the foundation of Rome" and it is 753 BC.[95] If we add the 2765 figure to 753 BC, we also arrive squarely on 2012. Thibaut remarks, "Indeed is it not suitable to date the ruin of the city of seven hills from its construction?"[96]

Thibaut calculates this period in several more ways based on Jubilee cycles and extracting Roman numerals that frankly are just too difficult for us to present coherently. We have a rough English translation of the book and are still processing the extremely complex ciphers. As a representative example, consider this calculation:

mE(1572**)D(1573)ium C(1574)orpus pilA(1576*)rum
A(1595)xis in mE(1592*)D(1587)iE(1586) tA(1581)tE(1578) siG(1576**)ni

D(1598)E(1603) rorE( ) C(1604**)E(1608**)li
E(1620*)x A(1617)ntiquitA( )tE(1614) urB(1611)is

piA(1623) C(1627)ivitA(1628**) in B(1633)E(1636**)llo
C(1644*)rux romulE(1642)A(1640*)

unD(1648**)osus vir
G(1657)E(1653)ns pE( )rvE( )rsA(1651)

in triB(1661)ulA(1662)tionE(1664**) pA(1668*)C(1672*)is
lilium E(1676*)t rosA(1673).

images note 7

iuC(1677)un D(1682)itA(1684**)s C(1688**)ruC( )is
montium C(1694)ustos

siD(1699)us olorum
D(1716**)E(1716*) F(1715)luminE(1710) mA(1708*)G(1703)no

B(1718)E(1721)lluA(1724**) insA( )tiA( )B(1729)ilis
pE(1738)nitE( )ntiA(1736*) G(1731)loriosA(1730)

rA(1741)strum in portA ( )
F(1760*)lorE(1755)s C(1751)irC( )umD(1750)A(1747)ti.

D(1761)E(1766) B(1768**)onA(1769) rE(1772*)liG(1776*)ionE(1777)
milE(1788**)s in B(1785)E(1783)llo.

C(1790)olumnA(1792*) E(1794)xC(1796*)E(1800)lsA(1804*)
A(1809)nimA( )l rurA( )lE(1806)

rosA(1815) umB(1820*)riE(1823)
ursus vE(1828**)lox.

pE(1834)rE( )G(1838)rinus A(1843)postoliC(1847)us
A(1848**)quilA( ) rA( )pA( )x

C(1852**)A(1854)nis E(1856**)t C(1858)oluB(1859)E(1862)r
vir rE(1868*)liG(1866)iosus.

D(1874)E(1879) B(1881)A(1882)lnE(1884**)is E( )truriE( ) (¹)
C(1897)rux D(1896**) E(1896*) C(1892*)ruC( )E(1890)

lumE(1902)n in C(1904*)E(1908*) lo
iG(1917)nis A(1916**)rD(1914)E(1913)ns

rE(1919)liG(1923)io D(1925)E(1930)populA(1933)tA( )
F(1952*)iD(1948*)E(1947)s intrE( )piD(1942)A(1939)

pA(1956*)stor A( )nG(1956**)E(1958)liC(1960*)us
pA(1967)stor E(1964*)t nA(1961)utA( )

F(1968**)los F( )lorum
D(1981)E(1980**)mE( )D(1976*)iE(1975)tA(1972**)tE(1969) lunE( )

D(1987)E(1992*) lA(1995)B(2000*)orE(2003) solis
G(2012**) loriA(2012*) olivE(2008**).

Durant la période embrassée par les 40 derniers signalements
(1er mai 1572-30 avril 2012) on compte exactement 22957 di-

images note 8

Indeed, you can see in the parenthesis he arrives at April 2012 from this torturous calculation. We commend the reader to try and obtain a copy of the book and work this through. In the interest of getting our book published prior to the dates Thibaut derived we must stick to the basics. You might be thinking, "As if *any* of the above was easy to comprehend?" If some of the above seems overly complex, then we think this next cipher is clear enough to be impressive.

Ancient languages like Latin, Greek, and Hebrew have numbers associated with their letters which made practice of gematria popular. The mystic use of numbers was familiar to the Babylonian Jews, and passed from them to the Greeks in Asia. It occurs in the Cabbala, in the Sibylline Books (I. 324–331), in the Epistle of Barnabas, and was very common also among the Gnostic sects. The practice also passed into the New Testament with the number of beast: 666. We will get to that later, but let's take a look at one more Latin cipher which is based on the one-to-one correspondence cipher rather than Roman numerals. The last forty Malachy prophecies in Latin contain nineteen letters which correspond to numbers like this:

A	B	C	D	E	F	G	I	L	M	N	O	P	Q	R	S	T	U	X
1	2	3	4	5	6	7	8	9	10	11	12	13	14	15	16	17	18	19

Thibaut wanted to know if the prophecy verified his 440 years from May, 1572 to May, 2012 in an explicit manner. He discovered one method using lunar cycles that is pretty impressive. He explains, "The lunar cycle consists of 19 lunations. Each lunation or lunar month lasts 29 days, 12 h., 44 m. The lunar cycle of 19 years therefore has 235 lunations. Consequently, in 440 years there will 235 lunations 23 times and 37 more moons, in short: 5442."[97] Let us try to explain this more plainly.

There are approximately 29.53 days in a lunar month which is the time between two full moons. This is what he also calls one lunation. In astronomy, the Metonic cycle is a period of very close to nineteen years. The Greek astronomer, Meton, discovered that a period of nineteen years is almost exactly equal to 235 lunar months.

Thibaut divides the 440 years between May, 1572 and May, 2012 by the nineteen-year Metonic cycle (19 years x 23 = 437 years). This is as close as you can get with Metonic cycles of nineteen years. Hence, he has calculated the remaining three years; 29.53 days in a lunar month into 365.24 days a year times 3 years equals 37 lunar months:

19 years = 235 lunar months

19 years x 23 = 437 years (remainder of 3 years)

437 years x 23 lunar months = 5405

3 years = 3(365) / 29.5 = 37 lunar months

Lunar months in 440 years = 5405 + 37 = 5442

Actually, it is much easier just to take 440 years x 365.24 days in a year = 160705.6 and then divide that number by 29.53 days in a lunar year to get 5442.11. This basically just confirms his calculation. Now we get back to the Latin text! Stay with us, this is simpler than it might appear. He takes the entire Latin text of the prophecy from 1572 forward and out of the 557 letters he extracts thirteen letters that equal 5442 in Roman numerals: MMMMM CCCC XL II and then he evaluates the remaining 544 letters. What follows are scans from the book:

Intervention des 19 lettres.

Chaque lettre vaut la quantité de son numéro dans la série des 19. En faisant la somme de ces valeurs, n'obtiendrait-on pas le nombre des lunaisons de mai 1572 à mai 2012 ? Le cycle lunaire de 19 ans fait songer aux lunaisons. Chaque lunaison ou mois lunaire dure 29 j. 12 h. 44 m. Le cycle lunaire de 19 ans compte donc 235 lunaisons. En 440 ans révolus, il y aura par conséquent 23 fois 235 lunaisons, plus 37 lunaisons : en somme : 5442.

Des 557 lettres retenons de quoi effectuer 5442 en chiffres romains : MMMMM CCCC XL II. Le choix de XL pour XXXX est arbitraire, mais l'usage l'autorise et la suite prouvera qu'il est heureux. Évaluons les 544 lettres qui restent :

48 A	=	1 font	48
11 B	=	2	22
17 C	=	3	51
18 D	=	4	72
(N. B. : AE, OE = E) 60 E	=	5	300
5 F	=	6	30
11 G	=	7	77
64 I	=	8	512
40 L	=	9	360
15 M	=	10	150
32 N	=	11	352

LA MYSTÉRIEUSE PROPHÉTIE DES PAPES   **65**

37 O = 12	444
15 P = 13	195
2 Q = 14	28
44 R = 15	660
43 S = 16	688
29 T = 17	493
47 V = 18	846
6 X = 19	114
544	5442

Nous retrouvons exactement la somme 5442. Remarquez qu'il n'est pas nécessaire que le « prophète » ait effectué le calcul que nous venons de faire *ad cautelam*. Il pouvait légitimement prendre la valeur moyenne 10, celle de la lettre M qu'il répète trois fois dans le 1ᵉʳ signalement *MediuM corpus pilaruM*. Dès lors, il lui suffisait de compter 544 lettres pour obtenir probablement 5440. S'il a compté 557 lettres, c'est pour fournir autrement le nombre exact 5442 (grâce aux 13 surnuméraires MMMMM CCCC XL II).

Au demeurant, si hasard il y a, la merveille est-elle moindre ?

images note 9

Translation:

We find exactly the sum 5442. Note, it is not necessary that the "prophet" has made the calculation that we have. He could legitimately take the average value 10, the letter M that he repeats three times in the report *MediuM corpus pilaruM*. Therefore, it was enough to have 544 letters for probably 5440. If he counted 557 letters, otherwise it is to provide the exact number 5442 (with 13 supernumeraries MMMMM CCCC XL II). Moreover, if it is random, is the wonder of it less?

Thibaut found 5442 lunar cycles encrypted in the Latin text of the last forty prophecies. That is four hundred forty years with an average of eleven years per pope which lands squarely on 2012. What are we to make of all of this? We must observe that much of his work is circular. In other words, he presumes a time period and then goes looking for it in the text. Given the fanciful lengths he goes to it seems forced. But what did he have to gain by predicting 2012 back in 1951? We can only conclude that he believed what he wrote. Furthermore, the obscurity of the book does not support it being disinformation. The one fact that we cannot argue against is that the average eleven-year reign had held true since the publication of his book in 1951. Furthermore, he cites April 29, 2012 twice which makes for a nearly perfect eleven average.[98] If Pope Benedict XVI steps down in April it will be a staggering authentication of Thibaut's work but anytime in 2012 will still be incredible. We affirm his concluding watchword, "The year 2012 will show whether or not the prophet saw clearly"[99] but exchange the referent to Rene Thibaut rather than St. Malachy.

The Number of the Beast?

What also makes Thibaut's work interesting is that he is in line with a long history of scholars who attempted to decipher encrypted codes within various sacred texts. One of our earliest known examples of a Christian working like this comes from the second-century Church father, Irenaeus, who cautioned against the practice of superficially labeling various figures as the Antichrist based on deriving 666. As an example, he derived several names but he thought one possibility had the most merit, which has relevance to our discussion here. He wrote, "Then also *Lateinos* (LATEINOS) has the number six hundred and sixty-six; and it is a very probable [solution], this being the name of the last kingdom [of the four seen by Daniel]. For the Latins are they who at present bear rule."[100] In other words, he thought that the number of the beast is associated with Rome because it is the fourth kingdom in Daniel's prophecy. He derived 666 using gematria on the ancient Greek word Λατεινος or i n all caps ΛΑΤΕΙΝΟΣ which is transliterated *lateinos* in English.

$$
\begin{aligned}
\textbf{L} = 30 &= \quad \Lambda \text{ lambda} \\
\textbf{a} = 1 &= \quad \alpha \text{ alpha} \\
\textbf{t} = 300 &= \quad \tau \text{ tau} \\
\textbf{e} = 5 &= \quad \varepsilon \text{ epsilon} \\
\textbf{i} = 10 &= \quad \iota \text{ iota} \\
\textbf{n} = 50 &= \quad \nu \text{ nu} \\
\textbf{o} = 70 &= \quad \text{o omicron} \\
\textbf{s} = 200 &= \quad \varsigma \text{ sigma}
\end{aligned}
$$

666

During the Renaissance period, King James I of England was convinced that Irenaeus was on to something. He wrote: "Now as to the Mystery anent the *Number* of his name; whether it shall be understood by the number composed of the Letters in that Greek word ΛΑΤΕΙΝΟΣ; which word well suites with the *Romish* Church, *Romish* Faith, and *Latine* Service."[101] The Bishop of Derry and Chaplain to King James I, George Downame, wrote more extensively on the matter:

> Irenaeus, whose master, Polycarp, was a disciple of St. John, reports that those who had seen John face to face did teach that the number of the name of the beast according to the computation of the Greeks by the letters which be in it, shall contain 666. He, therefore, set down three names in Greek letters containing that number, the third of which is LATEINOS, whereof he writes, But the name Lateinos also contains the number 666, and it is very likely, because the most true kingdom has this name. For they are Latins which now reign.[102] In effect, it is as if he had said the name Latin is very likely because it has the number 666, and is the name

of the beast which figures as the most true kingdom, that is the Latin or Roman State. Therefore, the name of the beast is LATEINOS, that is to say, Latin.

In Hebrew the beast's name of Roman also comprehends that number. For the beast's name, being a noun or collective name may, according to the manner of the Hebrews, be uttered either in the Masculine or Feminine gender. The Feminine doth better fit the prophecy, not only because it renders the exact number 666, but because as the beast is the adulterous Roman State under Antichrist, is elsewhere in the Feminine called the Whore of Babylon, the mother of fornications. The most usual name of the beast in its own language, that is, the Latin tongue, is Romanus, which in Hebrew characters, as Master John Foxe theorizes, having reached this conclusion by earnest prayer, also contains the number 666. That the name Latin or Roman in the learned tongues is the name whereof the holy Ghost speaks must be true because everything here spoken of the name agrees perfectly and properly:

(1) It is the name of the beast.

(2) It contains the number 666.

(3) He is such a name, to whom all other notes of Antichrist do agree.

(4) Because the name Latinus [being Latin and Lateinos translated into the Latin language] or Romanus [being Roman translated into the Latin language] is also the name of a man. For Latinus was one of the ancient Kings of Italy, and Romanus was one of the Popes.[103] Wherefore I doubt not that the name of the beast is Roman or Latin in the learned tongues.[104]

Of course, Irenaeus was making a point that it is relatively trivial to derive 666 from a name so it is always mere speculation. Many scholars point to Nero as the most likely solution, as his gematria also yields the number of the beast. Here is another interesting figure of note, the current pope, *Benedictos*:

ΒΕΝΕΔΙΚΤΟΣ
B=2, E=5, N=50, E=5, Δ=4, I=10, K=20, T=300, O=70, Σ=200
666

3 | Antichrist and the False Prophet

No one likes waiting. Patience, persistence, and perseverance are not popular words. They convey capricious craving, laborious longing, and unrequited love. While Augustine advised, "Patience is the companion of wisdom,"[105] waiting is always proportionately difficult to the object of one's passion. How much more intense is the longing when waiting for one of infinite worth?

Christians live in the tension of what is called the "already, but not yet" paradigm. This refers to the idea that Christ inaugurated the kingdom at the first advent but it will not be fully realized until the second at the *eschaton.* Gordon Fee writes, "The theological framework of the entire New Testament is eschatological."[106] Thus, there is a tension inherent in the Christian worldview that eclipses all the yearnings of adolescence. It is the groaning of creation itself (Rom 8:22). Christians eagerly anticipate the *Parousia,* which is the transliteration of Greek word which means "presence" or "coming."

In New Testament theology, it is often used generally to include all of the events involving the second coming of Christ.[107] Yet we are told that before this restoration of all things there will be an apostasy and the rise of a man of lawlessness, the infamous Antichrist. Thus, it is really not so surprising that sincere Christians have been predicting and even identifying the antichrist throughout history.

The concept of antichrist traces back to Israelite history where Israel as the chosen people of God were threatened or opposed by a pernicious pagan kings. For example, concerning the Babylonian king, Isaiah writes, "For thou hast said in thine heart, I will ascend into heaven, I will exalt my throne above the stars of God: I will sit also upon the mount of the congregation, in the sides of the north" (Is 14:13). Ezekiel paints a similar portrait of the King of Tyre (28:2) and King Gog of Magog (38–39). While some believe these speak of Satan himself, these passages are also applied directly to a man as well. This suggests a satanic indwelling reminiscent of Judas in Luke 22:3. This self-proclaimed apotheosis is also found in the "little horn" of Daniel 7 and 8. Even more, it is seen in Daniel 11:36–37. Antiochus IV Epiphanes who desecrated the second temple typifies the eschatological figure, and the infamous "abomination of desolation" is seemingly spoken of as a still future event by Jesus (Mt 24:15). This deified tyrant figure appears in the New Testament in Paul's description of the "man of sin" who proclaims himself to be God (2 Thes 2:3–4). In John's Apocalypse, he is the beast from the abyss whose image is idolatrously worshiped (13:1–18). In Mark 13:22, Jesus warns near the time of His return that false Christs (*pseudochristoi*) and false prophets (*pseudoprophētai*) will deceive people by doing signs and wonders (cf. Matt 7:15; 24:11, 23–24). All of these texts form a composite picture from which scholars and expositors have formed a model of who this is and how he might manifest. Historically, the majority of interpreters including many Catholic scholars (whom we discuss later) have seen the earmarks of Rome in these prophetic Scriptures.

The Greek term *antichristos* can be taken two ways as "opponent of Christ" or as "false Christ." This is due to the twofold meaning of the prefix "*anti.*" It can mean "against" or "instead of."[108] It is only used explicitly in 1 John 2:18, 22; 4:3; 2 John 7, and in other apocryphal Christian literature. If we look to John's epistles, we see that "antichrist" is defined as "he who denies the Father and the Son" (1 John 2:22b). This meets the "against" sense of the prefix "anti." Yet, John also seems to distinguish between a single Antichrist "who shall come" and a plural "now are there many antichrists" (1 John 2:18). Leon Morris offers, "Perhaps we should bear in mind that John refers to 'the spirit of the antichrist' as well as 'the Antichrist' (thus using both neuter and masculine); indeed, he refers to 'many antichrists' in whom that spirit finds expression (1 John 4:3; 2:18)."[109] Thus, it seems judicious to be flexible in one's view. Even so, in 2 Thessalonians 2, Paul's use of: 1) "man of sin"; 2) "son of perdition"; 3) "opposeth and exalteth himself above all that is called God"; and 4) "whose coming is after the working of Satan" points to a single individual. Accordingly, special attention will be given to Paul's second letter to the Thessalonian church in this chapter. Due to Paul's description of a "man" and because Jesus is described as defeating an individual (cf. 2 Th 2:8; Re 19:20), it seems best to understand the general term "antichrist" culminating with an ultimate incarnation, "the Antichrist," just prior to the parousia. What we see in the Thessalonian letters is that Paul is shepherding a flock acutely experiencing eschatological tension. While the second (2 Thes 2:1–12) has the important data on the antichrist, it is also important to look back to Paul's first letter. Fortunately, a portion of Paul's eschatological teaching can be gleaned from the first letter. Fatefully, that letter also addressed a serious misunderstanding concerning the Lord's return.

It seems that Paul taught the fledgling Thessalonian congregation a good deal about eschatology. Nevertheless, because some believers had died since Paul had been there, some members of the fledgling church feared the deceased would miss out. Paul assured them that at the coming of Christ, the *parousia*, the dead would rise first and go to meet the Lord. Then the living believers would be caught up in clouds and both would remain with the Lord forever (1 Thes 4:13–18). This famous "rapture" passage is connected to the day of the Lord a few lines later in 1 Thessalonians 5:2. Paradoxically, 1 Thessalonians 5 anticipates the very error that 2 Thessalonians addresses. Paul had told them, "But ye, brethren, are not in darkness, that that day should overtake you as a thief" (1 Th 5:4). Even so, this is exactly what they thought had occurred a short while later albeit due to an intentional deception.

In the second letter, Paul is correcting a dangerous and cruel teaching that the realization of the kingdom was underway to the exclusion of the Church he founded and dearly loves. Paul's thanksgiving in 2 Thessalonians (1:3–12), similar to that in 1 Thessalonians, extols their characteristic loyalty in suffering and their example to others. The problem is that some believed that "the day of the Lord" had already occurred. Even worse, the lie was perpetrated under Paul's name (2 Thes 2:2). The main text discussed here (2:1–12) is the substantive doctrinal basis for Paul's correction.

Paul's solution to their fear is that "for *that day shall not come*, except there come a falling away first, and that man of sin be revealed, the son of perdition" (2 Thes 2:3). The "falling away" can also be rendered as "rebellion" from the Greek *apostasia* and most likely predicts a mass departure within the Church from solid theology and classical Christian doctrine. This is certainly the position we defend, as one cannot "fall away" or rebel against something as an outsider (rebellion necessarily occurs from within). While there are those who believe the term *apostasia* means a "departure" in the sense of the "rapture"— the church being gathered bodily and departing the earth before the start of Great Tribulation and the coming of the Antichrist—this idea has been discredited by many scholars who contend that the word *apostasia* almost certainly refers to a "religious apostasy."[110] G. K. Beale makes a solid case that *apostasia* "in the Greek Old and New

Testaments always refers to a "departure from faith."[111] For instance, in the book of Acts, the term is used to render: "thou teachest all the Jews which are among the Gentiles to <u>forsake</u> Moses" (Acts 21:21a; underline added). Because of Paul's extensive Pharisaic training, it is also important to note this word's similar use in the LXX,[112] which implies conclusion that "a religious apostasy" is how Paul and his first-century readers understood this phrasing.

The second sign is much more enigmatic and occurs when Paul mentions the man of sin who is revealed, "the son of perdition; Who opposeth and exalteth himself above all that is called God, or that is worshipped; so that he as God sitteth in the temple of God, shewing himself that he is God" (2 Th 2:3–4). This man of sin or alternately "man of lawlessness" is widely considered to be the Antichrist or the Beast from the abyss in the book of Revelation (Revelation 13, 17). There is debate on whether these two signs, the apostasy and coming of antichrist, are separate or contingent events. Some scholars read it as an apostasy and revealing of antichrist, while others see the apostasy led by the antichrist or vice versa. As with all exegesis, what is essential to interpreting the Thessalonian letter is what Paul had in mind. Clearly, Paul seems to reference the prophecy of Daniel. Specifically, the little horn (Dan 7:8; 8:9) and the willful king (11:36).

The parallels between Daniel's prophecy and Paul's teaching in vv.3–4 are obvious. Daniel wrote of a king who would "do according to his will; and he shall exalt himself, and magnify himself above every god, and shall speak marvellous things against the God of gods" (Dn 11:36). While Daniel's predictions find some fulfillment in Antiochus IV, many scholars see a pivot point at verse 36 where Daniel shifts to the end-time Antichrist. For instance, Stephen Miller contends, "Exegetical necessity requires that 11:36–45 be applied to someone other than Antiochus IV. The context indicates that the ruler now in view will live in the last days, immediately prior to the coming of the Lord."[113] Daniel also predicts, "And in the latter time of their kingdom, when the transgressors are come to the full, a king of fierce countenance, and understanding dark sentences, shall stand up" (Da 8:23) which places him at the eschaton.[114] This blasphemous event also seems to be in focus in Daniel 12:11. However, in the final analysis, Jesus makes the decisive call on this issue.

What essentially locks the futurist interpretation in for evangelicals is what Jesus predicted in Matthew 24, "When ye therefore shall see the abomination of desolation, spoken of by Daniel the prophet, stand in the holy place" (Mt 24:15; underline added). This was, of course, long after the demonically inspired deeds of Antiochus IV, and yet Jesus speaks of Daniel's prophecy as a future event. While it is demonstrable by textual comparison that Paul was informed of Jesus' warning in Matthew 24:15,[115] we can infer this had not occurred to the Thessalonians. How much of Jesus' eschatology Paul's Thessalonian readers would be aware of is a matter of speculation, but it is clear that Paul meant for them to understand there would be an appearance of an end-time individual with an apotheosis ambition preceding and forecasting Christ's return.

Another important exegetical issue is what Paul intended by "temple of God." Amillennial supercessionists, like Beale and historicists like Calvin, argue forcefully for a non-literal meaning where Paul is metaphorically referring to the church. Beale argues, "The same phrase, *God's temple*, is found nine other times in the New Testament outside of 2 Thessalonians, and it almost always refers either to Christ or the church."[116] From the same line of reasoning, Calvin views it exclusively as the pope.[117] We will explore these ideas thoroughly elsewhere and while many of the popes were seen by Catholic and evangelical fathers as prophetic types of the final antichrist and false prophet, John wrote in the first century that many antichrists had already come (1 John 2:18). It seems that in 2 Thessalonians, Paul is necessarily referring to a final manifestation directly signaling the day of the Lord sitting in the only "temple of God" known to his readers, the one in Jerusalem. Paul's readers obviously did not have the New Testament.

While Beale, Calvin, and other strict historicists can rightly argue from later Pauline theology that the Christian is a temple, this is the exegetical fallacy of presumptuously imposing developed New Testament theology onto a very early context. The New Testament did not exist and Paul is speaking instructively and pastorally. He is correcting an error, not speaking mystically. There is nothing in 1 or 2 Thessalonians which would lead Paul's readers to think what Beale and Calvin prefer. The temple was not a symbol in this early context. If anything, the background from Daniel and Antiochus IV would be in their minds and they would most certainly envision the temple in Jerusalem. If theological presuppositions are laid aside, it seems clear that Paul meant for his readers to understand the then-extant temple in Jerusalem and not the metaphorical Church. How does this fit into the Prophecy of the Popes? The Vatican has always had its eyes on Jerusalem (covered in our chapter titled "The Burdensome Stone"), which is literally playing out as we write this book.

Paul then discusses some particulars about this man of lawlessness: 1) he is currently restrained (2:6–7); 2) he will be killed by Christ (2:8); 3) he is empowered to perform signs by Satan (2:9); and 4) his followers face fearsome judgment (2:10–12). The identity of the restrainer is discussed in the chapter "From Peter to Constantine," but what demands immediate attention is the "mystery of inequity." He uses the word *mystery* in 2:7 because he understands the antichrist prophecy from Daniel as beginning to be fulfilled in a mysterious manner not clearly anticipated by Daniel. Although Daniel wrote that the ultimate antichrist appears in full force for all to see, now Paul sees that, while this devil has not yet come as he will at the eschaton, he is nonetheless *already at work* in the early Church through his diabolical deceivers, the false prophets. As far as antichrist, many interpreters conflate the two meanings of "anti" into a figure who poses as Christ while initially clandestinely opposing God in allegiance with Satan.

The man of lawlessness is "whom the Lord shall consume with the spirit of his mouth, and shall destroy with the brightness of his coming" (2 Th 2:8b). This is a quote from Isaiah, "with the breath of his lips shall he slay the wicked" (Is 11:4b). Daniel also predicts, "he shall be broken but by no [human] hand" (8:25b). Perhaps Paul also had the Armageddon scenarios from Zechariah 14:12 and Ezekiel 39:4 in mind with this statement. Of course, there is a direct parallel of this end-time face-off written by John a few decades after Paul's letter (Rev 19:15–20). In line with his pastoral intent, Paul's readers would be comforted to know that the man of sin's reign of terror would be short lived. However, as for them then, so with us today, confidence should not lead to complacency, the text speaks to the future revealing of this figure that will be empowered by Satan to perform deceptive miracles. Jesus was emphatic, "For there shall arise false Christs, and false prophets, and shall shew great signs and wonders; insomuch that, if it were possible, they shall deceive the very elect" (Mt 24:24; underline added). This is a call for Christians to be vigilant and discerning.

The *parousia* of the antichrist, "is after the working of Satan with all power and signs and lying wonders" (2 Thes 2:9). The word rendered "working" is from the Greek *energeian* and it is always used of supernatural activity in the New Testament (Acts 2:22, 43; 4:30; 5:12; 6:8; 7:36; 14:3; 15:12; Rom 15:19; 2 Cor 12:12; Heb 2:4).[118] This supernatural "working" has a parallel in Revelation 13:2 where the great red dragon empowers the beast. It also appears this beast is not alone but accompanied by a magic-working compatriot. Paul and his readers were not influenced by the naturalistic philosophy of our day. Accordingly, he did not likely mean the signs and wonders will be mere parlor tricks or illusions, but rather genuine, paranormal phenomena. The purpose of the supernatural acts is to deceive but the works themselves are very real. It seems God allows this manifestation of supernatural power as a means to execute judgment on the unbelieving world.

The "strong delusion," from the Greek *energeian planes*, is highly controversial because it arguably implies that God intentionally deceives. However, Paul wanted his readers to understand that it is ultimately self-imposed because they refuse the truth. God is not deceiving innocents and it is not without precedent. In the Hebrew Bible, God punished people with a "perverse spirit" (Is 19:14) and intoxication, "but not with wine; they stagger, but not with strong drink" (Is 29:9). The Jews believed this was because the other nations chose to turn away from Yahweh and only Israel accepted his law.[119] God also sent a deceiving spirit to apostate King Ahab that his plans might fail (1 Kgs 22:22). Here, a similar idea is expressed in that those "who believed not the truth, but had pleasure in unrighteousness" (v. 12b) are given a "strong delusion" from God so that they believe what is false. It is also implied by the parable of the sower (Mk 4:15 ff.) as wells as in Romans where Paul writes, "God gave them over..." (Ro 1:24, 26). From the flow of Paul's argument here, it seems likely that Paul had the Antichrist's claim to deity in mind with "what is false." The final Antichrist will be irresistible to the unbelieving world and this is their due judgment.

There are some important lessons for the contemporary church to be gleaned from 2 Thessalonians. Paul stated clearly that the mystery of iniquity was already at work (2:7). This seems to infer that since his time, the spirit of antichrist has been working to deceive not only the worldly culture but also the church. Accordingly, Christians should have anticipated the mass falling away from classical Christian doctrine and values now evident in contemporary society. Evangelicals and Roman Catholics alike have increasingly deviated from biblical Christianity to espouse heretical notions like Dominionism, the Prosperity Movement, and Dual Covenant Theology (wherein Jews do not need to accept Jesus as Messiah). Similarly equated with the coming of the False Prophet and Antichrist is Ecumenical Modernism, which has witnessed Anglicans and evangelicals reuniting with Rome and even the development among major mainline curiosities like the

ELCA[120] and PCUSA[121] to not only accept homosexual unions but to endorse homosexual clergy. John MacArthur has argued this represents God's judgment on our nation in line with Romans 1:18–32.[122] John Piper points out that these denominations are knowingly leading people to hell (1 Cor 6:9).[123] Then there is the attack of the "new" atheists like Dawkins, Harris, and Hitchens. Does all of this represent impetus of the great apostasy? It seems the church is on the very edge of destruction and yet Christianity is spreading like wildfire in China.[124] This too could represent the fulfillment of Jesus' prophecy, "And this gospel of the kingdom will be proclaimed throughout the whole world as a testimony to all nations, and then the end will come" (Matthew 24:14)?

This of course begs the question about Petrus Romanus (who pastures his sheep until these things are finished and the City of Seven Hills will be destroyed): "Is he the end time's false prophet or even perhaps the Antichrist?" It seems clear to Catholics and Evangelicals that the City of Seven Hills is Rome and to many of them that it is Mystery Babylon as well. But when we turn to the parallel passages in the Book of Revelation we find not one but two beasts described. Both are apocalyptic symbols for antichristian forces and/or persons empowered by Satan. The first beast, commonly referred to as the "Antichrist," is from the abyss, and the second beast, the one from the earth, is usually called the "false prophet" (Rev. 16:13; 19:20; 20:10).[125] In Daniel's prophecy, there is a cryptic reference to a ram with two horns, one larger than the other: "…a ram which had *two* horns: and the *two* horns *were* high; but one *was* higher than the other, and the higher came up last" (Daniel 8:3). In Revelation, we see something similar. The land beast or false prophet "had two horns like a lamb, but he spoke like a dragon" (Rev. 13:11), showing that although he appears as a Christian leader, his message is deceptive and satanic.

This prophetic tradition appears to be more ancient than many are aware. Some scholars think John is drawing on the Leviathan and

Behemoth monsters for the sea and land beast images from the intertestamental pseudepigrapha, 1 Enoch 60:9–10:

> And I besought the other angel that he should show me the might of those monsters, how they were parted on one day and cast, the one into the abysses of the sea, and the other unto the dry land of the wilderness. And he said to me: "Thou son of man, herein thou dost seek to know what is hidden."[126]

Scholars of apocalyptic literature also argue the second beast, the false prophet, represents false religion in general, but we contend here that it is counterfeit Christianity specifically. The false prophet's mission is to convince human beings to worship the Antichrist and he is empowered to do so through overt supernatural signs and wonders. It is here that John's Apocalypse supplies a sharper image than what we saw in Paul's letter to the Thessalonians, which was nearly forty years prior. In Revelation, we read that it is the second beast that "doeth great wonders, so that he maketh fire come down from heaven on the earth in the sight of men" (Rev 13:13). With this in mind, we consider Paul's teaching that his "coming is after the working of Satan with all power and signs and lying wonders" (2 Th 2:9). When viewed together, it seems that it is likely the false prophet figure that instigates the Antichrist's arrival. According to the respected academic source, *Dictionary of Biblical Prophecy and End Times*, "If the dragon, the beast, and the false prophet comprise the satanic trinity, the false prophet serves as the demonic counterpart to the Holy Spirit."[127] Perhaps this was the satanic enthronement ritual (discussed in the next chapter) performed in the Vatican as described by Malachi Martin in *Windswept House*? Maybe Petrus Romanus is the satisfaction of that diabolic incantation.

Peter Goodgame has argued convincingly that the Roman prince seen in Daniel 9:27 who sets up the Abomination of Desolation is the false prophet rather than the Antichrist.[128] He cites Revelation 13:14 in which the false prophet "deceiveth them that dwell on the earth by the means of those miracles which he had power to do in the sight of the beast; saying to them that dwell on the earth, that they should make an image to the beast, which had the wound by a sword, and did live," and Daniel 11:31 which prophecies, "And <u>arms shall stand on his part</u>, and they shall pollute the sanctuary of strength, and shall take away the daily sacrifice, and they shall place the abomination that maketh desolate" (underline added). These passages clearly show it is the confederates of the Antichrist who set up the desolating image. Goodgame also argues that because Daniel refers to the Antichrist as a king (Hebrew *melek*) in 7:24, 8:23 and 11:21–35, it seems unlikely that he would call him a prince (Hebrew *nagiyd*) in 9:26–27. We can safely assume he is Roman by the phrase, "And <u>the people of the prince</u> who is to come, shall destroy the city and the sanctuary" (v. 26; underline added) which necessarily refers to the Roman sacking of Jerusalem in AD 70. Goodgame's exegesis and reasoning are sound and compelling.

The implications to the prophecy of Petrus Romanus are self-evident too. In line with Daniel 9:27's prediction of a covenant for one week, Goodgame argues this infers that a pope will broker an agreement over Jerusalem. This final seven year period will begin when the future Roman prince "confirms a covenant" that will involve the nation of Israel and the city of Jerusalem. This researcher has been led to the belief that this future Roman prince will be the False Prophet of Bible prophecy, and that he may indeed be a leader of the apostate Roman Catholic Church. It is clear from Scripture that the False Prophet will be a powerful and well-respected global spiritual leader, and there is none more powerful or more respected in religious matters than the Roman Catholic Pope.[129]

To some, this may seem like a scenario lifted right out of the *Left Behind* novels, but it coheres nicely with Malachi Martin's finishing assertions. As far as Jerusalem, we have gathered considerable evidence that this process is underway in earnest. Formally classified US State department memos have been obtained which suggest that "religious figures, non-governmental people" should be put in charge of the Holy City.[130] This is handled in detail in our chapter "The Burdensome Stone."

4 | Rosemary's Baby (Petrus) and the Priests Who Were *Dying* to See Him

In the 1968 horror film *Rosemary's Baby* by director Roman Polanski, Mia Farrow plays Rosemary Woodhouse, a naïve young housewife who agrees to become pregnant but through a series of spooky events comes to believe her husband has made a pact with eccentric neighbors Minnie and Roman Castevet (Ruth Gordon and Sidney Blackmer) to use the unborn child in some sort of occult ritual.

On the night they have planned to try to conceive, Mrs. Castevet brings separate dishes of chocolate mousse to Rosemary and her husband Guy. Rosemary takes a few bites, but disliking the chalky under-taste, quietly throws it away. A few minutes later, she becomes dizzy and passes out. She then has what she thinks is a nightmare in which the Castevets and other neighbors are in her bedroom watching as she is raped by a demonic presence. The dream is so vivid she suddenly screams out, "This is no dream—this is really happening!" When she wakes, there are scratches all over her body, and her husband tells her that in order not to miss the opportunity for conception, he had engaged her body for sex while she slept.

(Note that Polanski had wanted his wife Sharon Tate to play the role of Rosemary, and Tate reportedly provided the idea for the key scene in which Rosemary is raped and impregnated. In tragic, real-life irony, on August 9, 1969, Tate was eight and a half months pregnant when she and her unborn child were brutally murdered by followers of Charles Manson—Susan Atkins and Tex Watson. When screenwriter Wojciech Frykowski, who was at Sharon Tate's home the night of the murders [and also murdered] asked Tex who he was and what he was doing there, Watson replied, "I'm the devil, and I'm here to do the devil's business.")

Following the horrific "nightmare" scene experienced by the movie character Rosemary, she learns she is pregnant and that the baby is due June 28, 1966 (666). The Castevets recommend an obstetrician named Dr. Abraham Sapirstein (Ralph Bellamy) who prescribes a daily "vitamin drink" for her, which he assures is good for her and the unborn child. Minnie Castevet gives her an odd-smelling "good luck charm" to wear, which also smells of the main ingredient in the vitamin drink—*tannis root* (a phonetic play on the term *Satanas*, *Satan*).

When before long Rosemary's dear friend Hutch (Maurice Evans) notices her appearance becoming gaunt and hears her complaining of severe abdominal pains, loss of weight, and unusual cravings for raw meat and chicken liver (an ancient witches fertility prescription), he decides to research the "tannis root" concoction. Mysteriously, before he can share what he finds, he falls into a coma and dies, but not before waking up long enough to ask a friend to deliver a book on witchcraft—in which he has marked photographs and passages—to Rosemary, along with a cryptic message: "the name is an anagram." From this, she deciphers that her neighbor Roman Castevet's name is the anagram and that he is actually Steven Marcato, son of Adrian Marcato, a former resident and devoted Satanist.

Her suspicions grow as she becomes convinced that her husband and neighbors really are practicing witchcraft, and that somehow this involves her unborn child. Dr. Sapirstein and Rosemary's husband Guy learn of her mistrusts, and tell her that neither she nor the baby will be harmed so long as she cooperates. Right after, she goes into labor and is sedated, and when she awakens, her baby is gone. She is told the infant died, but she hears a baby crying in another room at the apartment. Finding a secret door connecting her residence to the neighbors, she discovers a congregation gathered around her infant son. The baby boy's eyes are frighteningly deformed, and she is told that her husband is not the father, that the child is the spawn of Satan.

Although Rosemary's Baby is based on a novel, ritualized sexual magic is real and the plan to use it to incarnate the devil's seed has had a long and curious history among Satanists, secret societies, freemasons, and even, according to some Catholic priests, the Vatican.

Highly guarded instruction manuals used by secretive Satanist organizations such as The Order of Nine Angels, the Church of Satan founded by Anton LaVey, and even further back by members of Ordo Templi Orientis including works by infamous 33rd-degree freemason, Aleister Crowley, have described how it is through sex that a being is brought into the world and housed in a body of flesh. Thus it is a mystical exercise that, when combined with magick rituals such as chanting of specific syllables to project proper vibrations (which open the inner mind and mesmerize the conscious mind), invite the nebulous spirit to fill the embryonic host. As the participating priestess lies upon the ground or upon the altar and is aroused by activity of the priest, copulation proceeds while the priestess visualizes the opening of a celestial gateway and Dark Chaos flowing out of it downward upon her, providing the mystical seed. Like the ancient Pythian of Apollo, the priestess is also at this moment a portal to the abode of dark gods.

Rocket scientist and cofounder of the Jet Propulsion Laboratory,

Jack Parsons, and his pal L. Ron Hubbard (Church of Scientology founder) were disciples of Aleister Crowley and recorded one such event called the "Babalon Working," which they performed in hopes of incarnating the whore of Babylon—a demon child or *gibbori*—through a portal during ritual sex. Parsons later wrote that the ceremony was successful and that "Babalon is incarnate upon the earth today awaiting the proper hour of her manifestation."[131]

According to *Magick, Liber ABA, Book 4* (widely considered the magnum opus of occultist Aleister Crowley), ritual magic sex can include (what sounds like) cannibalism and human sacrifice. Crowley says, "It would be unwise to condemn as irrational the practice of devouring the heart and liver of an adversary while yet warm. For the highest spiritual working one must choose that victim which contains the greatest and purest force; a male child of perfect innocence and high intelligence is the most satisfactory."[132]

As far back as 200 AD, the Christian apologetic work *Octavius* by Marcus Minucius Felix described apostate Christians participating in orgiastic rituals in a dark room while worshiping the head of a donkey and sacrificing a baby for the Host during Black Mass. Most experts believe similar activity has secretly continued throughout the ages, and that true "Hosts"—that is, the bread and grape wine used after consecration, which is, according to dogma, changed into the literal substance of the Body and the Blood of Jesus Christ via transubstantiation—are given by Catholic priests, who have made diabolical pacts with Satanists, to the attendants of the Black Sabbath. Among highly placed Church experts who assert such activity is real and even occurs inside the leonine walls of the Holy See would be: Monsignor Luigi Marinelli (whose 1999 book *Gone with the Wind in the Vatican* sold one hundred thousand copies in just the first three weeks); exorcist and Archbishop Emmanuel Milingo, who in a speech at the Our Lady of Fátima 2000 International Conference on World Peace, charged high-ranking members of the Church hierarchy of being in league with "Satan"; and the late exorcist and maverick professor of the Pontifical Biblical Institute, eminent Catholic theologian and former

Jesuit, Malachi Martin. When the Manhatten magazine *The Fátima Crusader* asked Martin about the public alarm raised over Archbishop Milingo's claim that high-ranking Vatican officials were "followers of Satan," Martin replied, "Anybody who is acquainted with the state of affairs in the Vatican in the last 35 years is well aware that the prince of darkness has had and continues to have his surrogates in the court of St. Peter in Rome."[133] While a few have tried to discredit Martin by claiming that he was everything from a double agent for Jewish lobbying groups during Vatican II (to effect the final draft of Nostra Aetate, which would, among other things, absolve the Jews of the death of Jesus) to maligning him as an outright "pathological liar" (which the dead cannot defend themselves against), Malachi was in fact a close personal friend of Pope Paul VI and worked within the Holy See doing research on the Dead Sea Scrolls, publishing articles in journals on Semitic paleography, and teaching Aramaic, Hebrew, and Sacred Scripture.

In 1965, Paul VI granted Martin a dispensation from his Jesuit and priestly duties, and Martin moved to New York, where he dedicated himself to writing about—and sometimes speaking out on—a variety of issues stemming from the Second Vatican Council, to detailed insider accounts of papal history, Catholic dogma, and geopolitics. As a member of the Vatican Advisory Council and a formidable polyglot who could speak seventeen languages (not to mention being personal secretary to renowned Jesuit Cardinal Augustin Bea), Martin had privileged information pertaining to secretive church and world issues, including the Third Secret of Fátima, which Martin hinted spelled out parts of the plan to formerly install the dreaded False Prophet during a "Final Conclave."

On this, Martin's claim that an Illuminati-Masonic group made up of Western plutocrats called "The Assembly" or the "Superforce" had infiltrated the highest levels of Vatican administration and were working to bring about a New World Order, may have led to involvement by operatives of the same group concerning his untimely (some say "suspicious") death in 1999.

This raises questions as well about John Paul I, who was elected pope in 1978 but who died only thirty-three days later (33 is an occult masonic marker). Shortly after becoming pope, John Paul I learned of cardinals, bishops, and high-ranking prelates that were Freemasons. He may have been murdered to keep him from exposing these men's plans and/or to deter an investigation he had launched into the Vatican bank connected with Roberto Calvi, a Grand Orient Freemason and the Chairman of the Ambrosiano Bank, which the Vatican Bank was primary shareholder of. When in 1978 it was discovered that monies had been illegally laundered for the Mafia through that bank, Calvi fled Italy and three days later, the Bank's shares crashed. One day after that, Calvi's secretary conveniently committed suicide, and on June 18, Calvi himself was found hanging beneath the Blackfriar (connected to Freemasons) Bridge in London with a Masonic Cabletow around his neck and chunks of masonry (left as a symbol?) in his pockets. John Daniel says of this in *Scarlet and the Beast*: "At Masonic ritual murders, Masonic symbols are left at the scene for several reasons: (1) to show Masons that this was a Masonic murder; (2) to warn Masons to follow the Masonic code, or suffer like fate; and (3) to prove to Masonic paymasters that the 'hit' was accomplished."[134]

But was John Paul I, like Calvi may have been (and like Malachi Martin infers in *Windswept House*), murdered by a Masonic "Superforce" too large and too powerful for him to contain; one that Martin would later claim was behind the scenes, secretly working to use the Vatican to bring about a global Antichrist system? "Suddenly it became unarguable that now… the Roman Catholic organization carried a permanent presence of clerics who worshipped Satan and liked it," wrote Martin. "The facts that brought the Pope to a new level of suffering were mainly two: The systematic organizational links—the network, in other words that had been established between certain clerical homosexual groups and Satanist covens. And the inordinate power and influence of that network."[135]

Ten years before something "pulled his feet" out from under him while he was preparing for an exorcism and Malachi Martin fell and later died (at the time he was working on what he promised would be his most explosive book yet under the telling title: *Primacy: How the Institutional Roman Catholic Church became a Creature of The New World Order*), he had become increasingly outspoken about pedophilic Satanism at the heart of the Vatican throughout the College of Cardinals and all the way down to local parishes, which he said were in league with a secret Masonic diabolicus that began following the "enthronement of the fallen Archangel Lucifer" in the Roman Catholic Citadel on June 29, 1963. This horrid *rituale*, as Martin had called it, had two primary objectives: 1) to enthrone Lucifer as the Prince over Rome; and 2) to assure the sorcerous inception and embodiment in flesh of that immaterial spirit that would fill Petrus Romanus.

In *The Keys of This Blood: The Struggle of World Dominion*, Martin had written:

> Most frighteningly for John Paul, he had come up against the irremovable presence of a malign strength in his own Vatican and in certain bishops' chanceries. It was what knowledgeable Churchmen called the "superforce." Rumors, always difficult to verify, tied its installation to the beginning of Pope Paul VI's reign in 1963. Indeed Paul had alluded somberly to "the smoke of Satan which has entered the Sanctuary"…an oblique reference to an enthronement ceremony by Satanists in the Vatican.[136]

Martin concealed even greater detail of this luciferic "enthronement ceremony by Satanists in the Vatican" in his book, *Windswept House*:

> The Enthronement of the Fallen Archangel Lucifer was effected within the Roman Catholic Citadel on June 29,

1963; a fitting date for the historic promise about to be fulfilled. As the principal agents of this Ceremonial well knew, Satanist tradition had long predicted that the Time of the Prince would be ushered in at the moment when a Pope would take the name of the Apostle Paul [Pope Paul VI]. That requirement—the signal that the Availing Time had begun—had been accomplished just eight days before with the election of the latest Peter-in-the-Line.[137]

The specific date given by Martin—June 29, 1963—and the combination of the specific names Peter (whom the Pope is successor of in Catholicism) and Paul, is important. June 29 is the Feast or Solemnity of both apostles, Peter and Paul. This is a liturgical feast in honor of the martyrdom of both Saints and according to Wikipedia a holy day of obligation in the universal Church in which the faithful are "obliged" to participate in mass. Among other things, this means on this specific date a perfectly timed sacrilegious parody of the Catholic mass was completed during the Enthronement of the Fallen Archangel Lucifer (which occultists know would hold high satanic energy) as well as simultaneously an offense made against the martyrdom of Peter and Paul during the Church's Feast in their names.

Martin stated publicly on more than one occasion that this enthronement of Lucifer in Rome was based on fact, and that to facilitate the black magic, a parallel ceremony was conducted simultaneously in the United States in Charleston, South Carolina. The reason this location was selected has remained obscure to many, but given what Malachi said about the Masonic connection, it makes sense that South Carolina was chosen: It is the site of the first Supreme Council of the Scottish Rite Freemasonry in the United States, called "the Mother Lodge of the World," where in 1859, champion of luciferian dogma for the Masonic-Illuminatus, Albert Pike became Grand Commander of the Supreme Council, where he served the Order of the Quest until his death in Washington DC on

April 2, 1892. Pike was known as a Satanist in his adopted state of Arkansas and loved to sit naked in the woods astride a phallic throne while participating for days in drunkenness and debauchery. Today, his body is proudly entombed at the House of the Temple, headquarters of the Southern Jurisdiction of the Scottish Rite Freemasonry in Washington DC.

According to the logic of former Sirhan Sirhan attorney, Day Williams, this makes Charleston, at the thirty-third parallel, even more perfect for the sacrifice and parallel ceremony described by Martin because, "If a life is taken close to the…33rd Parallel, this fits with the Masons' demonic mythology in which they demonstrate their worldly power by spilling human blood at a predetermined locale."[138] Martin added additional reasons for the South Carolina location:

> Such unobtrusive elements as the Pentagram and the black candles and the appropriate draperies could be part of the Ceremonial in Rome. But other Ruberics—the Bowl of Bones and the Ritual Din, for example, the sacrificial animals and the victim—would be too much. There would have to be a Parallel Enthronement. A Concelebration could be accomplished with the same effect by the Brethren in an Authorized Targeting Chapel. Provided all the participants in both locations "targeted" every element of the Event on the Roman Chapel, then the Event in its fullness would be accomplished specifically in the target area. It would all be a matter of unanimity of hearts, identity of intention and perfect synchronization of words and actions between the Targeting Chapel and the Target Chapel. The living wills and the thinking minds of the Participants concentrated on the specific Aim of the Prince would transcend all distance.[139]

Martin's chilling description in *Windswept House* of the methodical profanation of everything virtuous and innocent during the

"Parallel Enthronement" between the Targeting Chapel and the Target Chapel included indescribably foul Invocations, sadistic animal sacrifices, and repeated violations of a young "Ritual Victim" on an altar. For the uninitiated, the very idea this happened strains credulity. Yet when John F. McManus, for The New American, June 9, 1997, asked Father Martin if the Black Mass in South Carolina had actually occurred, it led to an enlightening Q and A:

> McManus: Your book begins with a vivid description of a sacrilegious "Black Mass" held in 1963 in Charleston, South Carolina. Did this really happen?
>
> Martin: Yes it did. And the participation by telephone of some high officials of the church in the Vatican is also a fact. The young female who was forced to be a part of this satanic ritual is very much alive and, happily, has been able to marry and lead a normal life. She supplied details about the event....
>
> McManus: In addition…you depict numerous other cardinals and bishops in a very bad light. Are these characterizations based on fact?
>
> Martin: Yes, among the cardinals and the hierarchy there are satanists, homosexuals, anti-papists, and cooperators in the drive for world rule.[140]

Even more explosive, near the end of *Windswept House* there is an often overlooked section providing explicit details of the enthronement ceremony and its true purpose to create a satanic pope. Martin provides details of the "Roman Phalanx," another name for the Vatican satanic cult, as well as describing their ultimate goal:

As a body, they had sworn "the Sacred Oath of Commitment" administered by the Delegate. Then each man had approached the Altar to give "Evidence" of his personal dedication. With blood drawn by the prick of a golden pin, each had pressed his fingerprint beside his name on the Bill of Authorization. Henceforth, the life and work of every member of the Phalanx in the Roman Citadel was to be focused on the transformation of the papacy itself. No longer was the Petrine Office to be an instrument of the "Nameless Weakling" [Jesus]. It was to be fashioned into a willing instrument of the Prince, and a living model for "the New Age of Man."[141]

Thus it appears frighteningly evident that, like in the movie *Rosemary's Baby* and in the visions and fears of so many Catholic seers, a ceremony for invoking the incarnation of Satan's seed—or installing it ritualistically inside a young person or chosen priest—was indeed performed, and a blood oath of dedication enacted for its goals by highly placed Satanists inside the Roman Catholic Citadel a little less than fifty years ago.

Whether Martin was killed and his death covered up for revealing this satanic scheme to use the Catholic Church as a launching pad for a luciferic *novus ordo seclorum* may never be known. One year before he died, however, Martin's very good friend, Father Alfred Kunz, was brutally murdered at his St. Michael Catholic Church in Dane, Wisconsin. Kunz had been investigating the same Satanism among "priests" that Martin had warned about, and had told Martin in the weeks before his murder that he feared for his life.

When Kunz was found dead with his throat slit, Martin claimed in various media that he had "inside information" that the Vatican "luciferians" had murdered him because he was getting ready to blow the lid off their conspiracy. The satanic animal sacrifice described by Martin in *Windswept House* as part of the "enthronement of the Fallen Archangel Lucifer in the Vatican" seems eerily comparable to what was indeed discovered in Dane County during the first hours of the murder investigation, including a calf which had been found sacrificed on a farm near St. Michael's Church exactly twenty-four hours before Kunz was last seen alive. According to police reports, the calf's throat was slit, as was Father Kunz, and its genitals cut off. There are details we will not discuss in this book due to their horrific nature, but deep within occultism there are reasons for removing the genitals of a sacrifice having to do with blasphemy of the Old Testament description of animals being accounted unworthy as offerings to the Lord if their testicles are bruised, crushed, torn, or cut (Lev. 22:24). According to survivors of ritual Satanic abuse (including Egyptian-Masonic Satanism), human sacrificial victims are sometimes laid on a table and their genitals likewise removed in order to make them "unworthy" or unfit for salvation (though versions of such abuse in South Africa are called "muti" murders, and some people pay large sums of money for genitalia from these human sacrifices in the belief it will bring them fertility, health, and good fortune). Then there is the ancient occult idea that decapitated persons cannot partake in the resurrection, thus dark rituals can include mutilation of the head, throat, and genitals where damnation of the victim is meant as a magical curse. In the case of the Dane County murder, was a black ritual performed between the hours of 10 p.m. March 2 and 4 a.m. March 3, 1998, to "target" Father Kunz and to "mark" him unfit for redemption?

During our investigative research for this book, we made formal requests of the Dane County Sheriff's Office for pertinent case files (DCSO Case # 98011295) pertaining to the ongoing investigation of the Father Kunz homicide. After first being told the files we requested would be given us, on December 15, 2011 we received a letter from the office of Lieutenant Mark Twombly signed by Sheriff Mahoney that the District Attorney would need to approve the release of the files (in other words it would take a court order) and therefore the request had been denied. Since this is an active, ongoing case, the sensitive records are not to be made public at this time and this is understandable. In filing a second request for less delicate documents, we were able to obtain a packet of files, but none of these provided solid clues to the larger question of conspiracy related to the murder of Father Kunz—specifically, was evidence discovered at the crime scene that his murder was somehow connected to his conservative position on Vatican II, and, more importantly, that he had information on certain pedophile priests and Satanists (that had earned him fierce enemies within the Church) reaching all the way to the Catholic hierarchy in Rome involved in ceremonies or behavior related to the enthronement of Lucifer and a ritual conducted for the purpose of transmigrating a particular spirit into Petrus Romanus?

"In the absence of an arrest, the Kunz case has developed into a sinister religious Rorschach for many—certainly among those close to the case who consider themselves traditionalists within the troubled Roman Catholic Church,"[142] wrote Chuck Nowlen in the 2001 cover story for Las Vegas Weekly, *The Devil and Father Kunz*. At that time, Nowlen had interviewed Peter Kelly, a Monroe, Wis., attorney and master's divinity student who had produced Kunz's weekly radio show. Given that Kelly was a good friend of Kunz and had spent substantial time with him in private conversations, his response to Nowlen's questions reveal a lot about what Kelly personally believed lay at the root of the murder: "This is a time of major crisis within the church, and the breakdown tends to be along traditional and conservative versus liberal lines. I think it's getting almost to the point of complete collapse. And, yeah, I know: Some people delve into a so-called satanic influence in the church, and everybody sort of rolls their eyes and laughs. But, I tell you, the nexus is really there."[143]

Still, Nowlen wondered, could someone within the Church really have killed Kunz—or ordered him killed?

"Absolutely," the lawyer confirmed, "as unbelievable as that might sound to some people."[144]

SHERIFF DAVID J. MAHONEY
DANE COUNTY SHERIFF'S OFFICE
JEFF HOOK, Chief Deputy
(608) 284-6167

JANICE L. TETZLAFF	TIMOTHY F. RITTER	JEFFREY A. TEUSCHER	RICHELLE J. ANHALT
Captain, Executive Services	Captain, Support Services	Captain, Security Services	Captain, Field Services
(608) 284-6175	(608) 284-6186	(608) 284-6165	(608) 394-6870

December 15th, 2011

Defender Publishing
PO Box

Dear ████████

This is in response to your request for records that we received on December 12th, 2011. You requested a copy of reports under DCSO Case # 98011295.

Your request for portions of these records is denied pursuant to §19.35(1)(am)1., Wis. Stats., in that any record containing personally identifiable information that is collected or maintained in connection with a complaint, investigation or other circumstances that may lead to an enforcement action or proceeding, or any such record that is collected or maintained in connection with such an action or proceeding is exempt. The records you have requested are being maintained by the Dane County Sheriff's Office in connection with an active law enforcement action.

As this is an active case, you will need to obtain a release from the DA's Office before we can release any video, photographs, or reports.

Pursuant to §19.35(4)(b), Wis. Stats., this decision is subject to review by mandamus under §19.37(1), Wis. Stats., or upon application to the Attorney General or a district attorney.

Sincerely,

DAVID MAHONEY
SHERIFF OF DANE COUNTY

Lieutenant Mark Twombly
Dane County Sheriffs Office

Public Safety Building, 115 W. Doty Street, Madison, Wisconsin 53703 (608)284-6800

ADMINISTRATION FAX (608)284-6163   SUPPORT SERVICES FAX (608)284-6156   SECURITY SERVICES FAX (608)284-6050   FIELD SERVICES FAX (608)284-6858
www.danesheriff.com

Letter received by Defender Publishing from Dane County Sheriff's Office denying request for records

5 | Mysticism and the Guardians of the Hidden Knowledge

With what Malachi Martin swore to in the previous chapter concerning a Masonic diabolicalus inside the Vatican, a few years ago, during research for the book *Apollyon Rising 2012*, our team made a trip to Washington, DC where we met with two members of the Scottish Rite Freemasonry. We joined one of them at The House of the Temple, the headquarters building of the Scottish Rite of Freemasonry, Southern Jurisdiction, where the Rite's Supreme Council, 33rd-Degree, have their meetings, and the other at the George Washington Masonic Memorial in Alexandria, Virginia. While both men were very helpful and informative, they became evasive when we started asking specific questions about a DC connection to the Vatican and secret rituals that are performed in the Temple Room on the third floor at the House of the Temple invoking the "birth" of a promised seed. We discuss that in particular in the next chapter, but for now, stay with us, as this is going to take a few pages to unveil.

What most in the public do not understand is that, in spite of denial by some Masons, theirs is a religious institution with rituals and even prophetic beliefs concerning a human-transforming final world order, founded on and maintained by dozens of doctrines defined by Manly P. Hall, in *The Lost Keys of Freemasonry*[145] as "the principles of mysticism and the occult rites." The reason lower-degree Masons would deny this is because the Masters of the Craft intentionally mislead them. Speaking of the first three degrees of Freemasonry, Albert Pike admitted in *Morals & Dogma*:

> The Blue Degrees are but the outer court or portico of the Temple. Part of the symbols are displayed there to the initiate, but he is intentionally misled by false interpretations. It is not intended that he shall understand them; but it is intended that he shall imagine he understands them. Their true explication is reserved for the Adepts, the Princes of Masonry.... It is well enough for the mass of those called Masons to imagine that all is contained in the Blue Degrees; and whoso attempts to undeceive them will labor in vain, and without any true reward violate his obligations as an Adept.[146]

At these lower degrees, most members of Freemasonry belong to what is maintained as a fraternal organization that simply requires belief in a "Supreme Being" while avoiding discussion of politics and religion in the lodge, using metaphors of stonemasons building Solomon's temple to convey what they publically describe as "a system of morality veiled in allegory and illustrated by symbols." We've known several of these types of Masons, all of whom were sincere members of society who worked together in a brotherhood for common benefit and to pool resources for charitable goals. None of these lower-degree Masons with whom we have been acquainted would ever, insofar as we know, participate in a conspiracy toward a global world order in which people will be politically and spiritually enslaved. But as one former Freemason told us, "This is the veneer of the lower degrees that exists on the Order's public face. What is happening with at least some of the members at the 33rd level, or among the York Rite Knights Templar and the Shriners, is another matter altogether. When I was part of the brotherhood, I watched as specific members with the correct disposition and ideology were identified, separated, groomed, and initiated into the higher degrees for reasons you *would* find corresponding with the goals of a New World Order."[147]

Famous Freemason Foster Bailey once described how the Masons not included among this elite are unaware of an "Illuminati" presence among Master Masons, who in turn are the guardians of a secret "Plan":

> Little as it may be realised by the unthinking Mason who is interested only in the outer aspects of the Craft work, the whole fabric of Masonry may be regarded as an externalisation of that inner spiritual group whose members, down the ages, have been the Custodians of the Plan.... These Master Masons, to whom TGAOTU [The Great Architect of the Universe] has given the design and Who are familiar with the tracing board of the G.M. [Grand Master] on high, are...sometimes known as the Illuminati and can direct the searchlight of truth wherever its beams are needed to guide the pilgrim on his way. They are the Rishis of the oriental philosophy, the Builders of the occult tradition.[148]

Part of the carefully guarded Illuminati "Plan" Bailey referred to involves the need for each Mason to navigate the meaning behind the various rituals in order to discover the secret doctrine of Masonry involving the true identity of deity and what this means now and for the future. Manly Hall, who rightly called the Great Seal of the United States "the signature" of that exalted body of Masons who designed America for a "peculiar and particular purpose," described these two kinds of Masons as members of a "fraternity within a fraternity," the elect of which are dedicated to a mysterious *arcanum arcandrum* (a "sacred secret") unknown to the rest of the Order:

> Freemasonry is a fraternity within a fraternity—an outer organization concealing an inner brotherhood of the elect.
>
> ...it is necessary to establish the existence of these two separate yet independent orders, the one visible and the other invisible.
>
> The visible society is a splendid camaraderie of "free and accepted" men enjoined to devote themselves to ethical, educational, fraternal, patriotic, and humanitarian concerns.
>
> The invisible society is a secret and most august fraternity whose members are dedicated to the service of a mysterious arcanum arcandrum.
>
> Those brethren who have essayed to write the history of their craft have not included in their disquisitions the story of that truly secret inner society which is to the body Freemasonic what the heart is to the body human.
>
> In each generation only a few are accepted into the inner sanctuary of the work...the great initiate-philosophers of Freemasonry are...masters of that secret doctrine which forms the invisible foundation of every great theological and rational institution.[149]

Among dedicatories to those who support this "invisible" secret doctrine, there is a memorial alcove in the heart of the House of the Temple called the "Pillars of Charity." Here, between two vaults on either side—one containing the exhumed remains of former

Sovereign Grand Commander Albert Pike and the other containing Sovereign Grand Commander John Henry Cowles, marked by busts of each man on marble pedestals—a stained-glass window depicts the all-seeing eye above the words *Fiat Lux* emitting thirty-three beams of light downward onto the phrase *ordo ab chao* from ancient craft Masonic doctrine, "order out of chaos."

In between meetings with the anonymous Masons who met with us during research for *Apollyon Rising 2012*, we stepped into this shrine and read the names of those who are hallowed there on reflective golden inscriptions for contributing at least 1 million dollars to advance the cause of Scottish Rite Freemasonry, including the George Bush family, whose work to initiate the New World Order is universally understood.

At the House of the Temple, like elsewhere, "The Brotherhood of Darkness" (as our friend Dr. Stanley Monteith calls it) intentionally hides in plain sight the occult aspirations of the secret plan, which ultimately will be realized in a one-world order and one-world religion under Petrus Romanus and the son of Lucifer—Apollo/Osiris/Nimrod—or, as Manly Hall put it:

> The outcome of the "secret destiny" is a World Order ruled by a King with supernatural powers. This King was descended of a divine race; that is, he belonged to the Order of the Illumined for those who come to a state of wisdom then belong to a family of heroes-perfected human beings.[150]

When Hall offered this astonishingly perceptive commentary about the future Masonic "King" who is "descended of a divine race" of "Illumined" (luciferic) "heroes-perfected" (half-man, half-god) human beings, he nailed exactly what the Cumaean Sibyl's prophecy on the Great Seal of the United States says will occur concerning the coming of Apollo/Osiris/Nimrod. But it may surprise some readers to learn that even US Presidents and Vice Presidents believed in this hidden message on the Great Seal…and were dedicated to seeing the prophecy fulfilled.

Roosevelt, Wallace, and the Mystic from Russia

Of all the Masonic symbols associated with the founding of America, Manly Hall viewed the design of the Great Seal of the United States as the highest signature of occult planning by those men who were dedicated to fulfilling Bacon's Rosicrucian dream of the New Atlantis. Other scholars agreed with this assessment and recognized the symbolism of the Seal as pointing to the "secret destiny of America." This included Rhodes Scholar James H. Billington and Harvard professor Charles Eliot Norton, who described the Great Seal as hardly other than an "emblem of a Masonic Fraternity." In 1846, 33rd-Degree Freemason and noted author James D. Carter inadvertently confirmed this as well when he admitted the Masonic symbolism is clearly known whenever "an informed Mason examines the Great Seal."

Yet for all the volumes written in the early years about the arcane meaning behind the symbols and mottoes of the Great Seal, it was not until the 1940s that, perhaps by providence, the significance of the seal started finding its defining moment.

It happened when during the summer of 1940, two-term President Franklin D. Roosevelt decided to run for an unprecedented third term and chose as his running mate for the Vice-Presidency, secretary of agriculture and 32nd-Degree Mason, Henry Wallace. Among other things, Roosevelt needed an unyielding supporter for the fading New Deal and saw in Wallace a farm-bred intellectual whose scrubbed Midwestern looks would appeal to a cross section of Americans— from ranchers to big-city unionists. Democratic National Committee Chairman Jim Farley couldn't have disagreed more, and made his opinion known not only to Roosevelt but to his wife, Eleanor, a strong and respected civil rights activist who, after discussing the liberalism and mysticism of Wallace, phoned her husband and told him, "I've been talking with Jim Farley and I agree with him. Henry Wallace won't do." But FDR was determined to have his Masonic brother as his second in command and drafted a speech in which he would refuse the party's nomination unless Wallace was designated for VP. The first lady followed by giving a speech of her own—a first time in which a woman addressed the Democratic National Convention—asking the delegates to respect her husband's reasoning. Wallace went on to become thirty-third vice president of the United States under the thirty-second president, Franklin D. Roosevelt—himself a 32nd-Degree Mason and Knight of Pythias (Shriner) with an equal thirst for mysticism. Of course, at the time, the delegates could hardly have imagined such weird instruments as a 1938 White House interoffice memo from Wallace to Roosevelt that illustrated how deeply mysticism was already a part of the two men's relationship. It read in part:

> I feel for a short time yet that we must deal with the "strong ones," the "turbulent ones," the "fervent ones," and perhaps even with a temporary resurgence, with the "flameless ones," who with the last dying gasp will strive to reanimate their dying giant "Capitalism." Mr. President, you can be the "flaming one," the one with an ever-upsurging spirit to lead into the time when the children of men can sing again.[151]

If at first this strange language befuddles the reader, it becomes much clearer when the history of Wallace, who openly referred to himself as a "practical mystic," is brought to light, including his veneration of Agni Yoga Society founder and theosophist Nicholas Roerich. Known in his native land as Nicolai Rerikh, Roerich and his wife had migrated from the Soviet Union to the United States in the 1920s where they made a name for themselves on the New York scene as teachers of Madam Blavatsky's theosophical *Secret Doctrine*. Roerich's particular devotion to mysticism was, however, increasingly focused on apocalyptic themes surrounding the coming of a new earthly order, which struck a chord with Wallace. This came to light later when Wallace began the VP race and was threatened with embarrassment by the Republicans, who had come into possession of a series of letters written by Wallace in the 1930s. Some of the communications were addressed to Roerich as "Dear Guru," and described the anticipation Wallace felt for "the breaking of the New Day," a time when a mythical kingdom would arrive on earth accompanied by a special breed of people. Earlier letters by Wallace simply addressed the mystic as "Dear Prof. R," and reflected the yearning Wallace felt to become Roerich's disciple and to make contact with those supernatural masters who populated Blavatsky's spiritual universe. In early 1934, Wallace wrote Roerich:

> …Long have I been aware of the occasional fragrance from that other world which is the real world. But now I must live in the outer world and at the same time make over my mind and body to serve as fit instruments for the Lord of Justice. The changes in awareness must come as a result of steady, earnest recollectedness. I shall strive to grow as rapidly as possible…. Yes, the Chalice is filling.[152]

The phrase by Wallace "I must…make over my mind and body to serve as fit instruments for the Lord of Justice" is a direct reference to Helena Blavatsky's *Secret Doctrine* to which Wallace and Roerich were dedicated. On page 332 of her related work, Blavatsky explains that "Osiris" is this Lord of Justice who rules over the "Seven Luminous Ones" or seven stars that Wallace would later speak of and under which the United States would serve following the inauguration of the New World Order and the resurrection of Osiris/Apollo.[153] The other phrase, "Yes, the Chalice is filling" corresponds to Holy Grail teachings by Roerich concerning a mystical cup, called the "Chalice of Buddha" or sometimes "the Blessed One" which was (at least metaphorically) a vessel of knowledge to those who honored the messianic figure and which would be filled by the appearance of the King of the New World Order—Osiris/Apollo to Masons. Though in the 1930s and 40s such coded letters gave Wallace an air of mystery as well as space for criticism in his political life; Roosevelt, too, was more than a casual acquaintance of Roerich. John C. Culver and John Hyde in their biography *American Dreamer: The Life and Times of Henry A. Wallace* note how:

> Roosevelt, perhaps influenced by his mother's enthusiasm for Eastern art and mysticism, took a personal interest in the Roerichs' causes. Roosevelt met Roerich at least once, met with Roerich's associates on several occasions, and between 1934 and 1936 personally corresponded with Helena Roerich several times. "Mr. President," she wrote in a typical letter, "Your message was transmitted to me. I am happy that your great heart has so beautifully accepted the Message and Your lightbearing mind was free from prejudice."
>
> Indeed, it was Roosevelt who suggested to Wallace that he read an allegory by Arthur Hopkins called *The Glory Road*, which served as the basis for the coded language in the guru letters.[154]

Behind the Guru Letters: Belief in the Great Seal Prophecy

Although Roosevelt would be the one to set in motion the push to place the Great Seal of the United States on the US one-dollar bill, Wallace claimed it was he who first brought the seal's oracular significance to Roosevelt, believing the symbolism of the emblems carried inference to Roosevelt's "New Deal," and, more important, a Masonic prophecy toward a New World Order. Wallace describes the meeting he had with Roosevelt:

> Roosevelt as he looked at the colored reproduction of the Seal was first struck with the representation of the All-Seeing Eye—a Masonic representation of the Great Architect of

the Universe. Next, he was impressed with the idea that the foundation for the new order of the ages had been laid in 1776 but that it would be completed only under the eye of the Great Architect. Roosevelt, like myself, was a 32nd-degree Mason. He suggested that the Seal be put on the dollar bill…and took the matter up with the Secretary of the Treasury [also a Freemason].… He brought it up in a Cabinet meeting and asked James Farley [Postmaster General and a Roman Catholic] if he thought the Catholics would have any objection to the "all-seeing Eye," which he as a Mason looked on as a Masonic symbol of Deity. Farley said, "No, there would be no objection."[155]

Regardless of who between Roosevelt and Wallace first perceived the seal's Masonic prophetic significance, surviving records clearly show it was Roosevelt (and in his own handwriting no less) who instructed that the obverse side of the seal be placed on the right back of the dollar and the reverse side of the seal with the pyramid and all-seeing eye be put on the left so that it would be the first thing a person saw when reading the back of the dollar from left to right. Thus, most Americans "were left with the impression that the mysterious pyramid and its heralding of a 'new order' were the foremost symbols of the American republic," notes Mitch Horowitz in *Occult America*.[156] It is natural to thus assume Wallace and Roosevelt also pondered the eagle on the Great Seal with its thirty-two feathers on the right wing and thirty-three on the left, representing the 32nd and 33rd degrees of Freemasonry, because in addition to being 32nd-Degree Masons, Roosevelt was the thirty-second president and Wallace the thirty-third vice president, an especially remarkable numerological "coincidence" given that Roosevelt was succeeded by Harry Truman, the thirty-third president of the United States and a 33rd-Degree Freemason! Additionally, in a 1991 hardcover book on American Presidents by the Smithsonian Institution (the world's largest research complex, founded by Freemason James Smithson) titled *The Smithsonian Treasury: Presidents*, it says on page 72 that when Franklin Roosevelt died during the closing days of World War II, the responsibility "<u>to formulate policies for a new world order</u>" fell to Freemason Harry Truman.[157] A painting on the same page depicts Truman standing over four other Masons—Joint Chiefs of Staff Admiral William D. Leahy; Army Air Force General Henry H. Arnold; Army Chief of Staff George C. Marshall; and Navy Commander in Chief Ernest J. King—a fitting diagram given that all this is depicted on page 72 of a Smithsonian work, an intriguing choice for a statement on the vision for a new world order given what the number seventy-two means within Masonic Gnosticism regarding the seventy-two fallen angels or "kosmokrators" that currently administer the affairs of earth and who are magically bound within the US Capitol Dome to bring about a New World Order (discussed elsewhere).

As a mystic and Mason, Wallace (like we do) undoubtedly believed these numerologies were not coincidence. Furthermore, what is now known is that Wallace viewed the unfinished pyramid with the all-seeing eye hovering above it on the Great Seal as a prophecy about the dawn of a new world with America at its head. Whenever the United States assumed its position as the new capital of the world, Wallace wrote, the Grand Architect would return and metaphorically the all-seeing eye would be fitted atop the Great Seal pyramid as the finished "apex stone." For that to happen, Wallace penned in 1934, "It will take a more definite recognition of the Grand Architect of the Universe before the apex stone [capstone of the pyramid] is finally fitted into place and this nation in the full strength of its power is in position to assume leadership among the nations in inaugurating 'the New Order of the Ages.'"[158]

Finding or making "a more definite recognition" of this messianic figure appears to have secretly obsessed Wallace (as well as Roosevelt) while also playing a key role in the decision to include the Great Seal on the US dollar. Both men were fascinated with the concept of a new breed of people—new Atlantians for the New Atlantis similar to Hitler's contemporaneous exploration for the Aryan supermen—led by an earthly messiah. Incredibly, if this supernatural leader were to be a magical reincarnation or resurrection of deity, the body or DNA of this savior may have been kept in or represented by a coffin (echoing the coffin symbolism on Masonic aprons), cryptically mentioned in correspondence between Wallace and Nicholas Roerich. On March 12, 1933, Wallace wrote Roerich:

> Dear Guru,
>
> I have been thinking of you holding the casket—the sacred most precious casket. And I have thought of the New Country going forward to meet the seven stars [Blavatsky's "Seven Luminous Ones" that serve under "Osiris," the Lord of Justice, and under which the U.S. would serve at the fulfillment of the Sibyl's *novus ordo seclorum* prophecy on the Great Seal] under the sign of the three stars [possibly the three belt stars of Orion, related in myth to Osiris]. And I have thought of the admonition "Await the Stone."
>
> We await the Stone and we welcome you again to this glorious land of destiny, clouded though it may be with strange fumbling fears. Who shall hold up the compelling vision to those who wander in darkness? In answer to this question we again welcome you. To drive out depression. To drive out fear.... And so I await your convenience prepared to do what I am to do.[159]

Investigative mythologist William Henry says this letter from Wallace made it clear that Roosevelt, Nicholas Roerich, and Henry Wallace "were in search of this Divine Child...and his secret... Stone...[and that] they awaited...in the 'New Country' [America as the New Atlantis]."[160] Central to the fulfillment of this scheme was the "sacred casket" that Wallace mentioned in his letter to Roerich, considered in esoteric circles to be the same as the casket or "coffin" of Osiris, and the Chintamani "Stone" or magical meteorite and holy relic believed to have been left by "missionaries" to Earth from the region of the star Sirius in the constellation Canis Major (The Great Dog). The "Stone" supposedly held properties that could give eternal life and was believed by devotees to be the true Cup of Christ. This mythology is also connected with Shambhala (which Roerich was looking for), a legendary kingdom in Tibet where supposedly enlightened immortals secretly live and who currently are guiding human evolution toward a one-world order. In fact, a portion of the Chintamani Stone was reportedly carried by Roerich as an emissary in 1935 to the founders of the now defunct League of Nations, whose goal also was to create a one-world order.

Whatever the case for Wallace, like Manly Hall had, he and Roosevelt viewed the all-seeing eye above the unfinished pyramid as pointing to the return (or reincarnation) of this coming savior, whose arrival would cap the pyramid and launch the New World Order. The all-seeing eye on the Great Seal is fashioned after the Eye of Horus, the offspring of Osiris (or Osiris resurrected), as both men surely understood. Aliester Crowley, 33rd-Degree Freemason (the "wickedest man on earth") and a Roerich occult contemporary, often spoke of this as the "New Age of Horus" and the breaking dawn of the rebirth of Osiris. That such mystics and Freemasons simultaneously used such identical language is telling, given that the Great Seal's mottoes and symbolism relate to both Osiris and Apollo specifically, yet as one. Osiris is the dominant theme of the Egyptian symbols, his resurrection and return, while the *mottoes* of the seal point directly to Apollo, and the eagle, a pagan emblem of Jupiter, to Apollo's father. For instance, the motto *annuit coeptis* is from Virgil's *Aeneid*, in which Ascanius, the son of Aeneas from conquered Troy, prays to Apollo's father, Jupiter [Zeus]. Charles Thompson, designer of the Great Seal's final version, condensed line 625 of book IX of Virgil's *Aeneid*, which reads, *Juppiter omnipotes, audacibus annue coeptis* ("All-powerful Jupiter favors [the] daring undertakings"), to *Annuit coeptis* ("He approves [our] undertakings"), while the phrase *novus ordo seclorum* ("a new order of the ages") was adapted in 1782 from inspiration Thompson found in a prophetic line in Virgil's Eclogue IV: *Magnus ab integro seclorum nascitur ordo* (Virgil's *Eclogue IV*, line 5), the interpretation of the original Latin being, "And the majestic roll of circling centuries begins anew." This phrase is from the Cumaean Sibyl (a pagan prophetess of Apollo, identified in the Bible as a demonic deceiver) and involves the future birth of a divine son, spawned of "a new breed of men sent down from heaven" (what Roosevelt, Wallace, and Roerich were looking for) when he receives "the life of gods, and sees Heroes with gods commingling." According to the prophecy, this is Apollo, son of Jupiter (Zeus), who returns to Earth through mystical "life" given to him from the gods when the deity Saturn (Saturn is the Roman version of the biblical *Satan*) returns to reign over the Earth in a new Pagan Golden Age.

From the beginning of the prophecy we read:

Now the last age by Cumae's Sibyl sung Has come and gone, and the majestic roll Of circling centuries begins anew: Justice returns, returns old Saturn's reign, With a new breed of men sent down from heaven. Only do thou, at the boy's birth in whom The iron shall cease, the golden race arise, Befriend him, chaste Lucina; 'tis thine own Apollo reigns.

He shall receive the life of gods, and see Heroes with gods commingling, and himself Be seen of them, and with his father's worth Reign o'er a world....

Assume thy greatness, for the time draws nigh, Dear child of gods, great progeny of Jove [Jupiter/Zeus]! See how it totters—the world's orbed might, Earth, and wide ocean, and the vault profound, All, see, enraptured of the coming time![161]

According to Virgil and the Cumaean Sibyl, whose prophecy formed the *novus ordo seclorum* of the Great Seal of the United States, the New World Order begins during a time of chaos when the earth and oceans are tottering—a time like today. This is when the "son" of promise arrives on earth—Apollo incarnate—a pagan savior born of "a new breed of men sent down from heaven" when "heroes" and "gods" are blended together. This sounds eerily similar to what the Watchers did during the creation of the nephilim and to what scientists are doing this century through genetic engineering of human-animal chimeras. But to understand why such a fanciful prophecy about Apollo, son of Jupiter, returning to Earth should be important to you: In ancient literature, Jupiter was the Roman replacement of Yahweh as the greatest of the gods—a "counter-Yahweh." His son Apollo is a replacement of Jesus, a "counter-Jesus." This Apollo comes to rule the final New World Order, when "Justice returns, returns old Saturn's [Satan's] reign." The ancient goddess Justice, who returns Satan's reign (*Saturnia regna*, the pagan golden age), was known to the Egyptians as Ma'at and to the Greeks as Themis, while to the Romans she was Lustitia. Statues and reliefs of her adorn thousands of government buildings and courts around the world, especially in Washington DC, as familiar Lady Justice, blindfolded and holding scales and a sword. She represents the enforcement of secular law and is, according to the Sibyl's conjure, the authority that will require global compliance to the zenith of Satan's dominion concurrent with the coming of Apollo. What's more, the Bible's accuracy concerning this subject is alarming, including the idea that "pagan justice" will require surrender to a satanic system in a final world order under the rule of Jupiter's son.

In the New Testament, the identity of the god Apollo, repeat-coded in the Great Seal of the United States as the Masonic "messiah" who returns to rule the earth, is the same spirit—verified by the *same name*—that will inhabit the political leader of the end-times New World Order. According to key Bible prophecies, the Antichrist will be the progeny or incarnation of the ancient spirit, *Apollo*. Second Thessalonians 2:3 warns: "Let no man deceive you by any means: for that day shall not come, except there come a falling away first, and that man of sin be revealed, the son of *perdition* [*Apoleia*; Apollyon, Apollo]" (emphasis added). Numerous scholarly and classical works identify "Apollyon" as the god "Apollo"—the Greek deity "of death and pestilence," and Webster's Dictionary points out that "Apollyon" was a common variant of "Apollo" throughout history. An example of this is found in the classical play by the ancient Greek playwright Aeschylus, *The Agamemnon of Aeschylus*, in which Cassandra repeats more than once, "Apollo, thou destroyer, O Apollo, Lord of fair streets, Apollyon to me."[162] Accordingly, the name Apollo turns up in ancient literature with the verb *apollymi* or *apollyo* (destroy), and scholars including W. R. F. Browning believe apostle Paul may have identified the god Apollo as the "spirit of Antichrist" operating behind the persecuting Roman emperor, Domitian, who wanted to be recognized as "Apollo incarnate" in his day. Such identifying of Apollo with despots and "the spirit of Antichrist" is consistent even in modern history. For instance, note how Napoleon's name literally translates to "the true Apollo."

Revelation 17:8 likewise ties the coming of Antichrist with Apollo, revealing that the Beast shall ascend from the bottomless pit and enter him:

> The Beast that thou sawest was, and is not; and shall ascend out of the Bottomless Pit, and go into *perdition* [*Apolia*, Apollo]: and they that dwell on the Earth shall wonder, whose names were not written in the Book of Life from the foundation of the world, when they behold the Beast that was, and is not, and yet is. (emphasis added)

Among other things, this means the Great Seal of the United States is a prophecy, hidden in plain sight by the Founding Fathers and devotees of Bacon's New Atlantis for more than two hundred years, foretelling the return of a terrifying demonic god who seizes control of Earth in the new order of the ages. This supernatural entity was known and feared in ancient times by different names: Apollo, Osiris, and even farther back as Nimrod, whom Masons consider to be the father of their institution.

We are willing to bet, however, few people know how Washington D.C.'s mirror city, the Vatican, also believes in the Cumaean Sibyl's *novus ordo seclorum* prophecy, so much so in fact that they even had Michelangelo gloriously encode it on the ceiling of the Sistine Chapel.

Pythians, Romanists, and the Sign of the 6th Knuckle

According to the Greeks, the greatest outcome of the love affair between Zeus and Leto was the birth of the most beloved—and soon to reappear oracle gods—Apollo. More than any other deity in ancient history, Apollo represented the passion for prophetic inquiry among the nations. Though mostly associated with classical Greece, scholars agree that Apollo existed before the Olympian pantheon and some even claim that he was at first the god of the Hyperboreans—an ancient and legendary people to the north. Herodotus came to this conclusion and recorded how the Hyperboreans continued in worship of Apollo even after his induction into the Greek pantheon, making an annual pilgrimage to the land of Delos, where they participated in the famous Greek festivals of Apollo. Lycia—a small country in southwest Turkey—also had an early connection with Apollo, where he was known as *Lykeios*, which some have joined to the Greek *Lykos* or "wolf," thus making one of his ancient titles, "the wolf slayer."

Apollo, with his twin sister Artemis, was said by the Greeks to have been born in the land of Delos—the children of Zeus (Jupiter) and of the Titaness Leto. While an important oracle existed there and played a role in the festivals of the god, it was the famous oracle at Delphi that became the celebrated mouthpiece of the Olympian. Located on the mainland of Greece, the *omphalos* of Delphi (the stone the Greeks believed marked the center of the earth) can still be found among the ruins of Apollo's Delphic temple. So important was Apollo's oracle at Delphi that wherever Hellenism existed, its citizens and kings, including some from as far away as Spain, ordered their lives, colonies, and wars by its sacred communications. It was here that the Olympian gods spoke to mortal men through the use of a priesthood, which interpreted the trance-induced utterances of the Pythoness or Pythia. She was a middle-aged woman who sat on a copper-and-gold tripod, or, much earlier, on the "rock of the sibyl" (medium), and crouched over a fire while inhaling the smoke of burning laurel leaves, barley, marijuana, and oil, until a sufficient intoxication for her prophecies had been produced. While the use of the laurel leaves may have referred to the nymph Daphne (Greek for "laurel"), who escaped from Apollo's sexual intentions by transforming herself into a laurel tree, the leaves also served the practical purpose of supplying the necessary amounts of hydrocyanic acid and complex alkaloids which, when combined with hemp, created powerful hallucinogenic visions. Another drug possibly used by the Pythia is known as DMT [dimethyltryptamine]. This chemical—naturally produced in the pineal gland and present in some wild plants—has been used for thousands of years by shamans to contact the spirit world. Others suggest that the Pythia may have employed a version of the psychoactive drug "absinthe" to induce a spirit-traversing mental gateway—a practice also employed throughout Greek paganism as well as by shamans of other cultures but condemned in the Scriptures (Galatians 5:20; Revelation 9:21 and 18:23) as *pharmakeia*—the administering of drugs for sorcery or magical arts in connection with demonic contact. The book, *Forbidden Gates: How Genetics, Robotics, Artificial Intelligence, Synthetic Biology, Nanotechnology, and Human Enhancement Herald the Dawn of TechoDimensional Spiritual Warfare*, discusses this phenomenon in more recent times, saying of absinthe in particular:

> This unique, distinctive distilled liquid of pale green color was
> known in the late nineteenth and early twentieth centuries as

the "green fairy." Although its consumption almost became an obsession across Europe and more mystical cosmopolitan centers in America like New Orleans, it was most closely associated with the bohemian artistic culture thriving at the time. It was a favorite of eclectic artists such as the painter Salvador Dali and writer Oscar Wilde, due to its reliable propensity to facilitate their contact directly with their inspirational spirit "muses." Occult magician Aleister Crowley was so devoted to absinthe for its spiritual invocation capabilities that he wrote his famous lengthy poem, "The Green Goddess," in its honor. It was the only alcoholic beverage banned across Europe (as well as North America) because the diagnosed "absinthism" addiction and effects were deemed much worse than regular alcohol. *The curious matter about absinthe is that it is distilled from the wormwood plant, which has the official name of Artemis absinthium. Artemis was a Greek and Roman goddess who was (a) considered a "huntress"; (b) associated with fire and keys; and (c) the sister of Apollo. She was associated with the goddess Hecate, who was known as a "luminal" god who controlled the access to portals in the spirit world.*[163] (emphasis added)

Whatever the case may have been for the ancient Pythian or Sibyl, it was under the influence of such "forces" that she prophesied in an unfamiliar voice thought to be that of Apollo, himself. During the Pythian trance, the medium's personality often changed, becoming melancholic, defiant, or even animal-like, exhibiting a "possession" psychosis that may have been the source of the werewolf myth, or *lycanthropy*, as the Pythia reacted to an encounter with Apollo/Lykeios—the wolf god. Delphic "women of python" prophesied in this way for nearly a thousand years and were considered to be a vital part of the pagan order and local economy of every Hellenistic community.

Whether by trickery or occult power, the prophecies of the Sibyls were sometimes amazingly accurate. The Greek historian Herodotus (considered the father of history) recorded an interesting example of this. Croesus, the king of Lydia, had expressed doubt regarding the accuracy of Apollo's oracle at Delphi. To test the oracle, Croesus sent messengers to inquire of the Pythian prophetess as to what he, the king, was doing on a certain day. The priestess surprised the king's messengers by visualizing the question and by formulating the answer before they arrived. A portion of the historian's account says:

> The moment that the Lydians (the messengers of Croesus) entered the sanctuary, and before they put their questions, the Pythoness thus answered them in hexameter verse: "Lo! on my sense there striketh the smell of a shell-covered tortoise, Boiling now on a fire, with the flesh of a lamb, in a cauldron. Brass is the vessel below, and brass the cover above it." These words the Lydians wrote down at the mouth of the Pythoness as she prophesied, and then set off on their return to Sardis.... [When] Croesus undid the rolls...[he] instantly made an act of adoration...declaring that the Delphic was the only really oracular shrine.... For on the departure of his messengers he had set himself to think what was most impossible for any one to conceive of his doing, and then, waiting till the day agreed on came, he acted as he had determined. He took a tortoise and a lamb, and cutting them in pieces with his own hands, boiled them together in a brazen cauldron, covered over with a lid which was also of brass.[164] (*Herodotus, Book 1, 47*)

Another interesting example of supernatural insight by an Apollonian Sibyl is found in the New Testament book of Acts. Here, the demonic resource that energized her visions is revealed.

And it came to pass, as we went to prayer, a certain damsel possessed with a spirit of divination [*of python*, a seeress of Delphi] met us, which brought her masters much gain by soothsaying: The same followed Paul and us, and cried, saying, These men are the servants of the most high God, which shew unto us the way of salvation. And this did she many days. But Paul, being grieved, turned and said to the spirit, I command thee in the name of Jesus Christ to come out of her. And he came out the same hour. And when her masters saw that the hope of their gains was gone, they caught Paul and Silas.... And brought them to the magistrates, saying, These men, being Jews, do exceedingly trouble our city. (Acts 16:16–20)

The story in Acts is interesting because it illustrates the level of culture and economy that had been built around the oracle worship of Apollo. It cost the average Athenian more than two days' wages for an oracular inquiry, and the average cost to a lawmaker or military official seeking important state information was charged at ten times that rate. This is why, in some ways, the action of the woman in the book of Acts is difficult to understand. She undoubtedly grasped the damage Paul's preaching could do to her industry. Furthermore, the Pythia of Delphi had a historically unfriendly relationship with the Jews and was considered a pawn of demonic power. Quoting from *Spiritual Warfare: The Invisible Invasion*, we read:

Delphi with its surrounding area, in which the famous oracle ordained and approved the worship of Asclepius, was earlier known by the name Pytho, a chief city of Phocis. In Greek mythology, Python—the namesake of the city of Pytho—was the great serpent who dwelt in the mountains of Parnassus.... In Acts 16:16, the demonic woman who troubled Paul was possessed with a spirit of divination. In Greek this means a spirit of python (a seeress of Delphi, a pythoness)...[and]

reflects...the accepted Jewish belief...that the worship of Asclepius [Apollo's son] and other such idolatries were, as Paul would later articulate in 1 Corinthians 10:20, the worship of demons.[165]

The Cumaean Sibyl (also known as Amalthaea), whose prophecy about the return of the god Apollo is encoded in the Great Seal of the United States, was the oldest of these Sibyls and the seer of the underworld who, in the *Aeneid*, gave Aeneas a tour of the infernal region. This adds to a mystery of adoption of the Pythians and Sibyls by the Vatican as "vessels of truth." These seers, whose lives were dedicated to channeling from frenzied lips the messages of gods and goddesses, turn up in Catholic art, from altars to illustrated books and even upon the ceiling of the Sistine Chapel, where five Sibyls including the Delphic (like Paul cast a demon out of) join the Old Testament prophets in places of sacred honor. Yet it is the Cumaean who not only sits so prominently inside Catholicism's most celebrated chapel, but who's painting, on close examination, unveils a secret—a magnificent clue—which her Italian Renaissance artist left concerning her, and her returning Lord's, origin and identity. For upon consideration, the portrait reveals "the sign of the 6th knuckle." The Cumaean's left thumb is inside a book and the fingers of her left hand wrapped outside in standard book-holding fashion. A clearly visible extra knuckle is portrayed, secreted perhaps by Michelangelo to depict a sixth digit bent under the palm, or to illustrate that a sixth finger had been lost or cut off at the knuckle. Either meaning is deeply occultic, and as students of history and the Bible clearly know, this ties both the Sibyl and her prophesied savior Apollo to the offspring of the fallen Watchers, the Nephilim (see 2 Samuel 21:20), of which Apollo/Osiris/Nimrod was chief.

This is the tip of the iceberg. What it has to do with Petrus Romanus and his Apollonian master continues in the following chapter.

The Sign of the Sixth Knuckle in the Sistine Chapel

images note 10

6 | Domes, Obelisks, Grimoires, and Magic Squares

The Dark Secret behind Washington, DC and the Vatican City

U ndoubtedly the vast majority of people, when looking at Washington, DC and at the Vatican, never comprehend how these cities constitute one of the greatest open conspiracies of all time. There, reproduced in all their glory and right before the world's eyes, is an ancient talismanic diagram based on the history and cult of Isis, Osiris, and Horus, including the magical utilities meant to generate the deity's return.

The primeval concept—especially that of sacred Domes facing Obelisks—was designed in antiquity for the express purpose of regeneration, resurrection, and apotheosis, for deity incarnation from the underworld to earth's surface through union of the respective figures—the Dome (ancient structural representation of the womb of Isis) and the Obelisk (ancient representation of the erect male phallus of Osiris).

This layout, as modeled in antiquity, exists today on the grandest scale at the heart of the capital of the most powerful government on earth—the United States—as well as in the heart of the most politically influential Church on earth—the Vatican. Given this fact and the pattern provided by the apostle Paul and the Apocalypse of John (the book of Revelation) that the end times would culminate in a marriage between political (Antichrist) and religious (False Prophet) authorities at the return of Osiris/Apollo, it behooves open-minded researchers to carefully consider this prophecy in stone, as it defines the spiritual energy that is knowingly or unknowingly being invoked at both locations with potential ramifications for Petrus Romanus, the year 2012, and beyond.

The US capital has been called the "Mirror Vatican" due to the strikingly similar layout and design of its primary buildings and streets. This is no accident. In fact, America's forefathers first named the capital city "Rome." But the parallelism between Washington and the Vatican is most clearly illustrated by the Capitol building and Dome facing the Obelisk known as the Washington Monument, and at St. Peter's Basilica in the Vatican by a similar Dome facing a familiar Obelisk—both of which were, according to their own official records, fashioned after the Roman Pantheon, the circular Domed Rotunda "dedicated to all pagan gods." This layout—a Domed temple facing an Obelisk—is an ancient, alchemical blueprint that holds significant esoteric meaning.

For those who may not know, the US Capitol building in Washington, DC is historically based on a pagan Masonic temple theme, Thomas Jefferson, who shepherded the antichristian "Roman Pantheon" design, wrote to the Capitol's architect, Benjamin LaTrobe, defining it as "the first temple dedicated to…embellishing with Athenian taste the course of a nation looking far beyond the range of Athenian destinies"[166] (the "Athenian" empire was first known as "Osiria," the kingdom of Osiris). In 1833, Massachusetts Representative Rufus Choate agreed, writing, "We have built no national temples but the Capitol."[167] Why is the Capitol building referred to as a "temple?" Apollyon Rising 2012 explains:

In 1793, when the cornerstone of the U.S. Capitol building was laid by George Washington in full Masonic garb and ritual, Maryland Grand Master Joseph Clark (who can be seen standing behind Washington in the mural[168] depicting the event at the George Washington Masonic National Memorial), the Annapolis architect and builder who designed and built the Maryland State House Dome,[169] was there that day as the Grand Master Pro Tempore. He proclaimed: "I have…every hope that the grand work we have done today will be handed down…to as late posterity as the like work of that ever memorable temple to our order erected by our Grand Master Solomon. The work we have done today, laying the cornerstone of this designed magnificent temple, the Capitol of our…States…by the virtuous achievements…of our most illustrious Brother George Washington" (emphasis added). In other words, Master Freemasons including George Washington, Ben Franklin, and Pierre L'Enfant designed and dedicated the Capitol building to be a temple of pagan spiritual energy modeled after their mystical version of Solomon's temple (they note that Solomon married himself to paganism through his wives) built by Hiram Abiff (Osiris). Freemason David Ovason adds that when the cornerstone ceremony was performed, it was intentionally set to coincide with a specific astrological time when, among other things, the head of the Dragon (Caput Draconis) would be in Virgo/Isis. This was, Ovason says, to procure approval of those pagan gods that Jefferson and Washington solicited. To futher illustrate that this was no coincidence, Ovasion points out how the cornerstones for the Washington Monument and the White House were likewise dedicated via Masonic ritual under the same astrological conditions related to Isis and Osiris, though laid in different years.[170]

William Henry and Mark Gray in their book, *Freedom's Gate: Lost Symbols in the U.S. Capitol*, add that, "The U.S. Capitol has numerous architectural and other features that unquestionably identify it with ancient temples."[171] After listing various features to make their case that the US Capitol building is a "religious temple"—including housing the image of a deified being, heavenly beings, gods, symbols, inscriptions, sacred geometry, columns, prayers, and orientation to the sun—they conclude:

The designers of the city of Washington DC oriented it to the Sun—especially the rising Sun on June 21 and December 21 [the same day and month as the end of the Mayan calendar in 2012]. The measurements for this orientation were made from the location of the center of the Dome of the U.S. Capitol, rendering it a "solar temple." Its alignment and encoded numerology point to the Sun as well as the stars. A golden circle on the Rotunda story and a white star in the Crypt marks this spot.... It is clear that the builders viewed the Capitol as America's sole temple: a solemn...Solar Temple to be exact.[172]

To understand what these statements may soon mean for the future of the world, one needs to comprehend how these aparati— the Dome and the Obelisk facing it—facilitate important archaic and modern protocols for invigorating *prophetic* supernatural alchemy. In ancient times, the Obelisk represented the god Osiris' "missing" male organ, which Isis was not able to find after her husband/brother was slain and chopped into fourteen pieces by his evil brother Seth (or Set). The story involves a detailed account of the envious brother and seventy-two conspirators tricking Osiris into climbing inside a box, which Seth quickly locked and threw into the Nile. Osiris drowned, and his body floated down the Nile River, where it snagged on the limbs of a tamarisk tree. In Byblos, Isis recovered his body from the river bank and took it into her care. In her absence, Seth stole the body again and chopped it into fourteen pieces, which he threw into the Nile. Isis searched the river bank until she recovered every piece, except for the genitals, which had been swallowed by a fish (Plutarch says a crocodile). Isis recombined the thirteen pieces of Osiris' corpse and replaced the missing organ with a magic facsimile (Obelisk), which she used to impregnate herself, thus giving rise to Osiris again in the person of his son, Horus. This legendary ritual for reincarnating Osiris formed the core of Egyptian cosmology (as well as the Rosicrucian/Masonic dying-and-rising myths) and was fantastically venerated on the most imposing scale throughout all of Egypt by towering Obelisks (representing the phallus of Osiris) and Domes (representing the pregnant belly of Isis) including at Karnak where the upright Obelisks were "vitalized" or "stimulated" from the energy of the masturbatory Sun god Ra shining down upon them.

There is historical evidence that this elaborate myth and its rituals may have been based originally on real characters and events. Regarding this, it is noteworthy that in 1998, former secretary general of Egypt's Supreme Council of Antiquities, Zahi Hawass, claimed to have found the burial tomb of the god Osiris (Apollo/Nimrod) at the Giza Plateau. In the article, "Sandpit of Royalty," from the newspaper *Extra Bladet* (Copenhagen), January 31, 1999, Hawass was quoted saying:

I have found a shaft, going twenty-nine meters vertically down into the ground, exactly halfway between the Chefren Pyramid and the Sphinx. At the bottom, which was filled with water, we have found a burial chamber with four pillars. In the middle is a large granite sarcophagus, which I expect to be the grave of Osiris, the god.... I have been digging in Egypt's sand for more than thirty years, and up to date this is the most exciting discovery I have made.... We found the shaft in November and began pumping up the water recently. So several years will pass before we have finished investigating the find.[173]

As far as we know, this discovery did not ultimately provide the physical remains of the deified person. But what it did illustrate is that at least some very powerful Egyptologists believe Osiris was a historical figure, and that his body was stored somewhere at or near the Great Pyramid. Manly P. Hall, who knew that the Masonic legend of Hiram Abiff was a thinly veiled prophecy of the resurrection of Osiris, may have understood what Zahi Hawass (not to mention Roerich, Roosevelt, and Wallace with their sacred Osiris Casket [see previous chapter]) was looking for, and why. Consider that he wrote in *The Secret Teachings of All Ages*: "The Dying God [Osiris] shall rise again! The secret room in the House of the Hidden Places shall be rediscovered. The Pyramid again shall stand as the ideal emblem of…resurrection, and regeneration."[174]

In Egypt, where rituals were performed to actually "raise" the spirit of Osiris into the reigning Pharaoh, political authority in the form of divine kingship or theocratic statesmanship was established (later reflected in the political and religious doctrine of royal and political legitimacy or "the divine right of kings," who supposedly derived their right to rule from the will of God, with the exception in some countries that the king is subject to the Church and the pope). This meant, among other things, the Egyptian Pharaoh enjoyed extraordinary authority as the "son of the sun god" (Ra) and the incarnation of the falcon god Horus during his lifetime. At death, Pharaoh became the Osiris, the divine judge of the netherworld, and on earth, his son and predecessor took his place as the newly anointed manifestation of Horus. Thus each generation of pharaohs provided the gods with a spokesman for the present world and for the afterlife while also offering the nation divinely appointed leadership.

Yet the observant reader may wonder, "Was there something more to the Pharaoh's deification than faith in ritual magic?" The cult center of Amun-Ra at Thebes may hold the answer, as it was the site of the largest religious structure ever built—the temple of Amun-Ra at Karnak—and the location of many extraordinary mysterious rites. The great temple with its one hundred miles of walls and gardens (the primary object of fascination and worship by the nemesis of Moses—the Pharaoh of the Exodus, Ramses II) was the place where each pharaoh reconciled his divinity in the company of Amun-Ra during the festival of Opet. The festival was held at the temple of Luxor and included a procession of gods carried on barges up the Nile River from Karnak to the temple. The royal family accompanied the gods on boats while the Egyptian laity walked along the shore, calling aloud and making requests of the gods. Once at Luxor, the Pharaoh and his entourage entered the holy of holies, where the ceremony to raise the spirit of Osiris into the king was performed and Pharaoh was transmogrified into a living deity. Outside, large groups of dancers and musicians waited anxiously. When the king emerged as the "born again" Osiris, the crowd erupted in gaiety. From that day forward, the Pharaoh was considered to be—just as the god ciphered in the Great Seal of the United States will be—the son and spiritual incarnation of the Supreme Deity. The all-seeing eye of Horus/Apollo/Osiris above the unfinished pyramid on the Great Seal represents this event.

Modern people, especially in America, may view the symbols used in this magic—the Dome representing the habitually pregnant belly of Isis, and the Obelisk, representing the erect phallus of Osiris—as profane or pornographic. But they were in fact ritualized fertility objects, which the ancients believed could produce tangible reactions, properties, or "manifestations" within the material world. The Obelisk and Dome as imitations of the deities' male and female reproductive organs could, through government representation, invoke into existence the being or beings symbolized by them. This is why inside the temple or Dome, temple prostitutes representing the human manifestation of the goddess were also available for ritual sex as a form of imitative magic. These prostitutes usually began their services to the goddess as children, and were deflowered at a very young age by a priest or, as Isis was, by a modeled Obelisk of Osiris' phallus. Sometimes these prostitutes were chosen, on the basis of their beauty, as the sexual mates of sacred temple bulls who were considered the incarnation of Osiris. In other places, such as at Mendes, temple prostitutes were offered in coitus to divine goats. Through such imitative sex, the Dome and Obelisk became "energy receivers," capable of assimilating Ra's essence from the rays of the sun, which in turn drew forth the "seed" of the underworld Osiris. The seed of the dead deity would, according to the supernaturalism, transmit upward from out of the underworld through the base (testes) of the Obelisk and magically emit from the tower's head into the womb (Dome) of Isis where incarnation into the sitting pharaoh/king/president would occur (during what Freemasons also call *the raising [of Osiris] ceremony*). In this way, Osiris could be habitually "born again" or reincarnated as Horus and constantly direct the spiritual destiny of the nation.

This metaphysical phenomenon, which originated with Nimrod/Semiramis and was central to numerous other ancient cultures, was especially developed in Egypt, where Nimrod/Semiramis were known as Osiris/Isis (and in Ezekiel chapter 8 the children of Israel set up the Obelisk ["image of jealousy," verse 5] facing the entry of their temple—just as the Dome faces the Obelisk in Washington, DC and in the Vatican City—and were condemned by God for worshipping the Sun [Ra] while weeping for Osiris [Tammuz]). The familiar Masonic figure of the point within a circle is the symbol of this union between Ra, Osiris, and Isis. The "point" represents Osiris' phallus in the center of the circle or womb of Isis, which in turn is enlivened by the sun rays from Ra, just as is represented today at the Vatican, where the Egyptian Obelisk of Osiris sits within a circle, and in Washington, DC, where the Obelisk does similarly, situated so as to be the first thing the sun (Ra) strikes as it rises over the capital city and which, when viewed from overhead, forms the magical point within a circle known as a *circumpunct*. The sorcery is further amplified, according to ancient occultic beliefs, by the presence of the Reflecting Pool in DC, which serves as a mirror to heaven and "transferring point" for those spirits and energies.

And just what is it the spirits see when they look downward on the Reflecting Pool in Washington? They find a city dedicated to and built in honor of the legendary deities Isis and Osiris complete with the thirteen gathered pieces of Osiris (America's original thirteen colonies); the required Obelisk known as the Washington Monument; the Capitol Dome (of Isis) for impregnation and incarnation of deity into each Pharaoh (President); and last but not least, the official government buildings erected to face their respective counterparts and whose cornerstones—including the US Capitol Dome—were dedicated during astrological alignments related to the zodiacal constellation Virgo (Isis) as required for the magic to occur.

Where the Vitality of Osiris/Apollo (the Beast that Was, and Is Not, and Yet Is) Pulsates in Anticipation of His Final "Raising"

The three-hundred-thirty ton Obelisk in St. Peter's Square in the Vatican City is not just any Obelisk. It was cut from a single block of red granite during the Fifth dynasty of Egypt to stand as Osiris' erect phallus at the Temple of the Sun in ancient Heliopolis (λιούπολις, meaning city of the sun or principal seat of Atum-Ra sun-worship), the city of "On" in the Bible, dedicated to Ra, Osiris, and Isis. The Obelisk was moved from Heliopolis to the Julian Forum of Alexandria by Emperor Augustus and later from thence (approximately 37 AD) by Caligula to Rome to stand at the spine of the Circus. There, under Nero, its excited presence maintained a counter-vigil over countless brutal Christian executions, including the martyrdom of the apostle Peter (according to some historians). Over fifteen hundred years following that, Pope Sixtus V ordered hundreds of workmen under celebrated engineer-architects Giovanni and Domenico Fontana (who also erected three other ancient obelisks in the old Roman city including one dedicated to Osiris by Rameses III—at the Piazza del Popolo, Piazza di S. Maria Maggiore, and Piazza di S. Giovanni in Laterano) to move the phallic pillar to the center of St. Peter's Square in Rome. This proved a daunting task, which took over four months, nine hundred laborers, one hundred forty horses, and seventy winches. Though worshipped at its present location ever since by countless admirers, the proximity of the Obelisk to the old Basilica was formerly "resented as something of a provocation, almost as a slight to the Christian religion. It had stood there like a false idol, as it were vaingloriously, on what was believed to be the center of the accursed circus where the early Christians and St. Peter had been put to death. Its sides, then as now, were graven with dedications to [the worst of ruthless pagans] Augustus and Tiberius."[175]

The fact that many traditional Catholics as well as Protestants perceived such idols of stone to be not only objects of heathen adoration but the worship of demons (see Acts 7:41–42; Psalms 96:5; and 1 Corinthians 10:20) makes what motivated Pope Sixtus to erect the phallus of Osiris in the heart of St. Peter's Square, located in Vatican City and bordering St. Peter's Basilica, very curious. To ancient Christians, the image of a cross and symbol of Jesus sitting atop (or emitting from) the head of a demonic god's erect manhood would have been at a minimum a very serious blasphemy. Yet Sixtus was not content with simply restoring and using such ancient pagan relics (which were believed in those days to actually house the pagan spirit they represented) but even destroyed Christian artifacts in the process. Michael W. Cole, Associate Professor in the Department of the History of Art at the University of Pennsylvania, and Professor Rebecca E. Zorach, Associate Professor of Art History at the University of Chicago, raise critical questions about this in their scholarly book *The Idol in the Age of Art* when they state:

Whereas Gregory, to follow the chroniclers, had ritually dismembered the city's *imagines daemonem* [demonic images], Sixtus fixed what was in disrepair, added missing parts, and made the "idols" into prominent urban features. Two of the four obelisks had to be reconstructed from found or excavated pieces... The pope was even content to destroy *Christian* antiquities in the process: as Jennifer Montagu has pointed out, the bronze for the statues of Peter and Paul came from the medieval doors of S. Agnese, from the Scala Santa at the Lateran, and from a ciborium at St. Peter's.

[Sixtus] must have realized that, especially in their work on the two [broken obelisks], they were not merely repairing injured objects, but also restoring a *type*... In his classic book *The Gothic Idol*, Michael Camille showed literally dozens of medieval images in which the freestanding figure atop a column betokened the pagan idol. The sheer quantity of Camille's examples makes it clear that the device, and what it stood for, would have been immediately recognizable to medieval viewers, and there is no reason to assume that, by Sixtus's time, this had ceased to be true.[176]

The important point made by Professors Cole and Zorach is that at the time Sixtus was busy reintroducing to the Roman public square restored images and statues on columns, the belief remained strong that these idols housed their patron deity, and further that, if these were not treated properly and even placed into service during proper constellations related to their myth, it could beckon evil omens. Leonardo da Vinci had even written in his Codex Urbinas how those who would adore and pray to the image were likely to believe the god represented by it was alive in the stone and watching their behavior. There is strong indication that Sixtus believed this too, and that he "worried about the powers that might inhabit his new urban markers."[177] This was clearly evident when the cross was placed on top of the Obelisk in the midst of St. Peter's Square and the pope marked the occasion by conducting the ancient rite of exorcism against the phallic symbol. First scheduled to occur on September 14th to coincide with the liturgical Feast of the Exaltation of the Cross and not coincidently under the zodiacal sign of Virgo (Isis), the event was delayed until later in the month and fell under the sign of Libra, representing a zenith event for the year. On that morning, a pontifical High Mass was held just before the cross was raised from a portable altar to the apex of Baal's Shaft (as such phallic towers were also known). While clergy prayed and a choir sang Psalms, Pope Sixtus stood facing the Obelisk and, extending his hand toward it, announced: "Exorcizote, creatura lapidis, in nomine Dei" ("I exorcize you, creature of stone, in the name of God"). Sixtus then cast sanctified water upon the pillar's middle, then its right side, then left, then above, and finally below to form a cross, followed by, "In nomine Patris, et Filij, et Spiritus sancti. Amen" ("In the Name of the Father and of the Son and of the Holy Ghost. Amen"). He then crossed himself three times and watched as the symbol of Christ was placed atop Osiris' erect phallus.

Washington Dome Facing Obelisk

Vatican Dome Facing Obelisk

Yet if what Sixtus established in the heart of Vatican City gives some readers pause (numerous other signature events by Sixtus aligned the Sistine city with constellations sacred to Osiris and Isis, which we are not taking time to discuss here but that caused Profs. Zorach and Cole to conclude that, in the end, Sixtus wanted to remain *in the good graces of the pagan gods*), in Washington, DC near the west end of the National Mall, the Obelisk built by Freemasons and dedicated to America's first president brings the fullest meaning to the nephilim-originated and modern porn-industry impression that "size matters." This is no crude declaration, as adepts of ritual sex-magic know, and dates back to ancient women who wanted to give birth to the offspring of the gods and who judged the size of the male generative organ as indicative of the "giant" genetics or divine seed needed for such offspring. While such phallic symbols have been and still are found in cultures around the world, in ancient Egypt, devotion to this type "obscene divinity" began with Amun-Min and reached its crescendo in the Obelisks of Osiris.

Throughout Greece and Rome the god Priapus (son of Aphrodite) was invoked as a symbol of such divine fertility and later became directly linked to the cult of pornography reflected in the more modern sentiments about "size." This is important because, in addition to the Washington Monument being intentionally constructed to be the tallest Obelisk of its kind in the world at 6,666 (some say 6,660) inches high and 666 inches wide along each side at the base, one of the original concepts for the Washington Monument included Apollo (the Greek version of Osiris) triumphantly returning in his heavenly chariot, and another illustrating a tower "like that of Babel" for its head. Any of these designs would have been equally appropriate to the thirty-three-hundred-pound pyramidal capstone it now displays, as all three concepts carried the meaning necessary to accomplish what late researcher David Flynn described as "the same secret knowledge preserved by the mystery schools since the time of the Pelasgians [that] display modern Isis Osiris worship."[178] This is to say, the "seed" discharged from a Tower-of-Babel-shaped head would magically issue forth the same as would proceed from the existing Egyptian capstone—the offspring of Apollo/Osiris/Nimrod.

The greatest minds in Freemasonry, whose beliefs set the tone for the design of the capital city, its Great Seal, its Dome, and its Obelisk, understood and wrote about this intent. Albert Pike described it as Isis and Osiris' "Active and Passive Principles of the Universe…commonly symbolized by the generative parts of man and woman,"[179] and Freemason writer Albert Mackey described not only the Obelisk, but added the importance of the circle around its base, saying, "The Phallus was an imitation of the male generative organ. It was represented…by a column [Obelisk] that was surrounded by a circle at the base."[180]

In Egypt, where the parodies and rituals for raising Osiris to life through these magical constructs was perfected, Pharaoh served as the "fit extension" for the reborn god to take residence in as the "sex act" was ritualized at the temple of Amun-Ra. The all-seeing eye of Horus/Osiris/Apollo above the unfinished pyramid on the Great Seal forecasts the culmination of this event—that is, the actual return of Osiris—for the United States during or closely following the year 2012, and the Dome and Obelisk stand ready for the metaphysical ritual to be performed in secret by the elite. We use the phrase "performed in secret" because what the vast majority of people throughout America do not know is that the "raising" ceremony is still conducted inside the headquarters of the Scottish Rite Freemasonry in the House of the Temple by the Supreme Council 33rd Degree over Washington, DC for at least two reasons. First, whenever a Mason reaches the Master level, the ritual includes a parody representing the death, burial, and future resurrection of Hiram Abiff (Osiris). The world at large finally caught a glimpse of this custom when Dan Brown, in his book *The Lost Symbol,* opened with a scene depicting the start of the tradition:

> The secret is how to die.
>
> Since the beginning of time, the secret had always been how to die.
>
> The thirty-four-year-old initiate gazed down at the human skull cradled in his palms. The skull was hollow, like a bowl, filled with bloodred wine.
>
> Drink it, he told himself. You have nothing to fear.
>
> As was tradition, he had begun his journey adorned in the ritualistic garb of a medieval heretic being led to the gallows, his loose-fitting shirt gaping open to reveal his pale chest, his left pant leg rolled up to the knee, and his right sleeve rolled up to the elbow. Around his neck hung a heavy rope noose—a "cable-tow" as the brethren called it. Tonight, however, like the brethren bearing witness, he was dressed as a master.
>
> The assembly of brothers encircling him all were adorned in their full regalia of lambskin aprons, sashes, and white gloves. Around their necks hung ceremonial jewels that glistened like ghostly eyes in the muted light. Many of these men held powerful stations in life, and yet the initiate knew their worldly ranks meant nothing within these walls. Here all men were equals, sworn brothers sharing a mystical bond.

As he surveyed the daunting assembly, the initiate wondered who on the outside would ever believe that this collection of men would assemble in one place…much less this place. The room looked like a holy sanctuary from the ancient world.

The truth, however, was stranger still.

I am just blocks away from the White House.

This colossal edifice, located at 1733 Sixteenth Street NW in Washington, D.C., was a replica of a pre-Christian temple—the temple of King Mausolus, the original mausoleum…a place to be taken after death. Outside the main entrance, two seventeen-ton sphinxes guarded the bronze doors. The interior was an ornate labyrinth of ritualistic chambers, halls, sealed vaults, libraries, and even a hallow wall that held the remains of two human bodies. The initiate had been told every room in the building held a secret, and yet he knew no room held deeper secrets than the gigantic chamber in which he was currently kneeling with a skull cradled in his palms.

The Temple Room.[181]

While such drama makes for excellent fiction, *The Lost Symbol* turns out to be at best a love fest and at worst a cover up between Dan Brown and the Freemasons. However, one thing Brown said is true—the Temple Room in the Heredom does hold an important *secret*. We've been there, stood inside and prayed for protection under our breath, because according to our sources (who provided facts that have not been denied when we were interviewed by a US Congressman, US Senator, and even a 33rd-Degree Freemason on his radio show), in addition to when a Mason reaches the Master level, the ancient raising ceremony is conducted following the election of an American President—just as their Egyptian forefathers did at the temple of Amun-Ra in Karnak—in keeping with the tradition of installing within him the representative spirit of Osiris until such time as the god himself shall fulfill the Great Seal prophecy and return in flesh.

In the prologue of 33rd-Degree Freemason Manly P. Hall's book, *The Lost Keys of Freemasonry*, detailed recounting of the underlying and familiar story of Hiram Abiff (Osiris) is told, who sets out to construct the temple of the Great Architect of the Universe, but is killed by three spectres. This story, impersonated every time an initiate reaches the level of Master Mason, is by admission of Freemasons a retelling of the death-epic of the god Osiris. In *Lost Keys*, Hall narrates how the Great Architect gives Hiram (Osiris) the trestleboard for the construction of the great temple, and when he is killed by three ruffians, the Great Architect bathes him in "a glory celestial," as in the glory surrounding the all-seeing eye of Osiris above the pyramid on the Great Seal. The Great Architect follows this by charging those who would finish the building with the task of finding the body of Hiram (Osiris) and raising him from the dead. When *this* has been accomplished, the great work will conclude and the god will inhabit the (third) temple:

> Seek ye where the broken twig lies and the dead stick molds away, where the clouds float together and the stones rest by the hillside, for all these mark the grave of Hiram [Osiris] who has carried my Will with him to the tomb. This eternal quest is yours until ye have found your Builder, until the cup giveth up its secret, until the grave giveth up its ghosts. No more shall I speak until ye have found and raised my beloved Son [Osiris], and have listened to the words of my Messenger and with Him as your guide have finished the temple which I shall then inhabit. Amen.[182]

Thus the appearance of the uncapped pyramid of Giza on the Great Seal of the United States echoes the ancient pagan as well as Masonic beliefs concerning the old mysteries and the prophecy of the return of Osiris/Apollo/Nimrod. In *Rosicrucian and Masonic Origins*, Hall, who had said in *The Secret Teachings of All Ages* that the Great Pyramid was "the tomb of Osiris,"[183] explains that Preston, Gould, Mackey,

Oliver, Pike, and nearly every other great historian of Freemasonry were aware of this connection between Freemasonry and the ancient mysteries and primitive ceremonials based on Osiris. "These eminent Masonic scholars have all recognized in the legend of Hiram Abiff an adaptation of the Osiris myth; nor do they deny that the major part of the symbolism of the craft is derived from the pagan institutions of antiquity when the gods were venerated in secret places with strange figures and appropriate rituals."[184] In *Morals and Dogma*, Albert Pike even enumerated the esoteric significance of the Osiris epic at length, adding that lower-level Masons (Blue Masonry) are ignorant of its true meaning, which is only known to those who are "initiated into the Mysteries."[185] Pike also spoke of the star Sirius—connected to Isis and at length to Lucifer/Satan—as "still glittering" in the Masonic lodges as "the Blazing Star." Elsewhere in *Morals and Dogma*, Pike reiterated that the "All-Seeing Eye…was the emblem of Osiris"[186] and that the "Sun was termed by the Greeks the Eye of Jupiter, and the Eye of the World; and his is the All-Seeing Eye in our Lodges."[187]

Magic Squares, 666, and Human Sacrifice?

While finding the body of Osiris and resurrecting it—either figuratively or literally—is central to the prophetic beliefs of Freemasonry, until Apollo/Osiris return, formal procedures will continue in secret for installing within America's national leader the divine right of Kingship through the raising of Osiris ceremony. It is very important to note how, when this ritual is carried out in the Temple Room of the Heredom, it unfolds below a vast thirty-six-paneled skylight that forms a stylized Magic 666 Square. Around the four sides of the skylight can be seen the Winged Sun-Disc. This positioning above the altar is in keeping with historical occultism. Egyptian magicians employed the same symbolism above the altar for invoking the sun deity. In the St. Martin's Press book *Practical Egyptian Magic* it is noted: "Emblematic of the element of air, this consists of a circle or solar-type disk enclosed by a pair of wings. In ritual magic it is suspended over the altar in an easterly direction and used when invoking the protection and co-operation of the sylphs."[188] The Renaissance occultist Paracelsus describes these sylphs as invisible beings of the air, entities that the New Testament book of Ephesians (2:2) describes as working beneath "the prince [Lucifer/Satan] of the power of the air, the spirit that now worketh in the children of disobedience." In applied magic, the "magic square of the sun" itself was associated in antiquity with binding or loosing the sun god Apollo/Osiris and was the most famous of all magical utilities because the sum of any row, column, or diagonal is equal to the number 111, while the total of all the numbers in the square from 1 to 36 equals 666. In the magical Hebrew Kabbalah, each planet is associated with a number, intelligence, and spirit. The intelligence of the Sun is Nakiel, which equals 111, while the spirit of the Sun is Sorath and equals 666. It makes sense therefore that Freemasons built the Washington Monument Obelisk to form a magic square at its base and to stand 555 feet above earth, so that when a line is drawn 111 feet directly below it toward the underworld of Osiris, it equals the total of 666 (555+111=666)—the exact values of the binding square of the Sun God Apollo/Osiris installed in the ceiling above where the Osiris raising ceremony is conducted in the House of the Temple.

6	32	3	34	35	1
7	11	27	28	8	30
19	14	16	15	23	24
18	20	22	21	17	13
25	29	10	9	26	12
36	5	33	4	2	31

Magic 666 Square

36-paneled magic-square skylight above the altar in the House of the Temple

Freemason and occultist Aleister Crowley practiced such Kabbalah and likewise connected the number 111 with the number 6, which he described as the greatest number of the Sun or sun god. He employed the magic square in rituals to make contact with a spirit described in *The Book of the Sacred Magic of Abramelin the Mage*, a work from the 1600s or 1700s that involves evocation of demons. In Book Four of the magic text, a set of magical word-square talismans provides for the magician's Holy Guardian Angel who appears and reveals occult secrets for calling forth and gaining control over the twelve under-world authorities including Lucifer, Satan, Leviathan, and Belial. In addition to Crowley, the most influential founding father and Freemason, Benjamin Franklin, not only used such magic squares, but according to his own biography and numerous other authorita-tive sources even created magic squares and circles for use by himself and his brethren. Yet the gentle appearance and keen astuteness of America's most famous bespeckled Freemason might have hidden an even darker history than the story told by those magic squares, which his strong, deft hands once held. Award-winning filmmaker Christian J. Pinto explains:

> One of the most influential founding fathers, and the only one of them to have signed all of the original founding documents (the Declaration of Independence, the Treaty of Paris, and the U.S. Constitution) was Benjamin Franklin. Franklin was…without question, deeply involved in Freemasonry and in other secret societies. He belonged to secret groups in the three countries involved in the War of Independence: America, France, and England. He was master of the Masonic Lodge of Philadelphia; while over in France, he was master of the Nine Sisters Lodge, from which sprang the French Revolution. In England, he joined a rakish political group founded by Sir Francis Dashwood (member of Parliament, advisor to King George III) called the "Monks of Medmenham Abbey," otherwise known as the "Hellfire Club." This eighteenth-century group is described as follows:

>> The Hellfire Club was an exclusive, English club that met sporadically during the mid-eighteenth century. Its purpose, at best, was to mock traditional religion and conduct orgies. At worst, it involved the indulgence of satanic rites and sacrifices. The club to which Franklin belonged was established by Francis Dashwood, a member of Parliament and friend of Franklin. The club, which consisted of "The Superior Order" of twelve members, allegedly took part in basic forms of satanic worship. In addition to taking part in the occult, orgies and parties with prostitutes were also said to be the norm.

Pinto continues this connection between Benjamin Franklin and dark occultism:

> On February 11, 1998, the Sunday Times reported that ten bodies were dug up from beneath Benjamin Franklin's home at 36 Craven Street in London. The bodies were of four adults and six children. They were discovered during a costly renovation of Franklin's former home. The Times reported: "Initial estimates are that the bones are about two hundred years old and were buried at the time Franklin was living in the house, which was his home from 1757 to 1762 and from 1764 to 1775. Most of the bones show signs of having been dissected, sawn or cut. One skull has been drilled with several holes."
>
> The original Times article reported that the bones were "deeply buried, probably to hide them because grave robbing was illegal." They said, "There could be more buried, and there probably are." But the story doesn't end there. Later reports from the Benjamin Franklin House reveal that not only were human remains found, but animal remains were discovered as well. This is where things get very interesting. From the published photographs, some of the bones appear to be blackened or charred, as if by fire… It is well documented that Satanists perform ritual killings of both humans and animals alike.[189]

While many students of history are aware of the magic 666 square and its use by occultists down through time to control the spirit of Apollo/Osiris, what some will not know is how this magical binding and loosing of supernatural entities also extends to the testes of Washington's 6,666 inch-high phallic Obelisk, dedicated by Freemasons seventy-two years following 1776 (note the magic number 72), where a Bible (that Dan Brown identified as the "Lost Symbol" in his latest book) is encased within the cornerstone of its 666-inch-square base. One wonders what type of Bible this is. If a Masonic version, it is covered with occult symbols of the Brotherhood and

Rosicrucianism and the purpose for having it so encased might be to energize the Mason's interpretation of Scripture in bringing forth the seed of Osiris/Apollo from the testes/cornerstone. If it is a non-Masonic Bible, the purpose may be to "bind" its influence inside the 666 square and thus allow the seed of Osiris/Apollo to prevail. The dedication of the cornerstone during the astrological alignment with Virgo/Isis as the sun was passing over Sirius indicates a high degree of magic was indeed intended by those in charge.

The First American Osiris

Through Masonic alchemistry, presidential *apotheosis*—that is, the leader of the United States (America's Pharaoh) being transformed into a god within the Capitol Dome/womb of Isis in sight of the Obelisk of Osiris (the Washington Monument to those whom Masons call "profane," the uninitiated)—actually began with America's first and most revered president, Master Freemason George Washington. In fact, Masons in attendance at Washington's funeral in 1799 cast sprigs of acacia "to symbolize both Osiris' resurrection and Washington's imminent resurrection in the realm where Osiris presides."[190] According to this Masonic enchantment, Osiris (Horus) was rising within a new president in DC as Washington took his role as Osiris of the underworld. This is further simulated and symbolized by the three-story design of the Capitol building. Freemasons point out how the Great Pyramid of Giza was made up of three main chambers to facilitate Pharaoh's transference to Osiris, just as the temple of Solomon was a three-sectioned tabernacle made up of the ground floor, middle chamber, and Holy of Holies. The US Capitol building was thus designed with three stories—Washington's Tomb, the Crypt, and the Rotunda—capped by a Dome. Each floor has significant esoteric meaning regarding apotheosis, and the tomb of Washington is empty. The official narrative is that a legal issue kept the government from placing Washington's body there. However, just as the tomb of Jesus Christ was emptied before His ascension, Washington is not in his tomb because he has travelled to the home of Osiris, as depicted high overhead in the womb/Dome of Isis.

When visitors to Washington DC tour the Capitol, one of the unquestionable highlights is to visit the womb of Isis—the Capitol Dome—where, when peering upward from inside Isis' continuously pregnant belly, tourists can see hidden in plain sight Brumidi's 4,664-square-foot fresco, *The Apotheosis of George Washington.* The word "apotheosis" means to "deify" or to "become a god," and explains part of the reason US presidents, military commanders, and members of Congress lay in state in the Capitol Dome. The womb of Isis is where they go at death to magically reach apotheosis and transform into gods.

Those who believe the United States was founded on Christianity and visit the Capitol for the first time will be surprised by the stark contrast to historic Christian artwork of the ascension of Jesus Christ compared to the "heaven" George Washington rises into from within the energized Capitol Dome/womb of Isis. It is not occupied by angels, but with devils and pagan deities important to Masonic belief. These include Hermes, Neptune, Venus (Isis), Ceres, Minerva, and Vulcan (Satan), of course, the son of Jupiter and Juno to which human sacrifices are made and about whom Manly Hall said brings "the seething energies of Lucifer" into the Mason's hands.[191]

Beside those pagan gods which accompany Washington inside the Capitol Dome, the scene is rich with symbols analogous with ancient and modern magic, including the powerful trident—considered of the utmost importance for sorcery and indispensable to the efficacy of infernal rites—and the caduceus, tied to Apollo and Freemasonic Gnosticism in which Jesus was a myth based on Apollo's son, Asclepius, the god of medicine and healing whose snake-entwined staff remains a symbol of medicine today. Occult numerology associated with the legend of Isis and Osiris is also encoded throughout the painting, such as the thirteen maidens, the six scenes of pagan gods around the perimeter forming a hexagram, and the entire scene bounded by the powerful Pythagorian/Freemasonic "binding" utility—seventy-two five-pointed stars within circles.

The Apotheosis of George Washington Above 72 Pentagrams

Much has been written by historians within and without Masonry as to the relevance of the number seventy-two (72) and the alchemy related to it. In the Kabbalah, Freemasonry, and Jewish apocalyptic writings, the number equals the total of wings Enoch received when transformed into Metatron (3 Enoch 9:2). This plays an important role for the Brotherhood, as Metatron or "the angel in the whirlwind" was enabled as the guiding spirit over America during George W. Bush's administration for the purpose of directing the *future* and *fate* of the United States (as also prayed by Congressman Major R. Owens of New York before the House of Representatives on Wednesday, February 28, 2001).

But in the context of the Capitol Dome and the seventy-two stars that circle Washington's apotheosis in the womb of Isis, the significance of this symbolism is far more important. In sacred literature, including the Bible, stars are symbolic of angels, and within Masonic Gnosticism, seventy-two is the number of fallen angels or "kosmokrators" (reflected in the seventy-two conspirators that controlled Osiris' life in Egyptian myth) that currently administer the affairs of earth. Experts in the study of the Divine Council believe that, beginning at the Tower of Babel, the world and its inhabitants were disinherited by the sovereign God of Israel and placed under the authority of seventy-two angels (the earliest records had the number of angels at seventy, but this was later changed to seventy-two) which became corrupt and disloyal to God in their administration of those nations (Psalm 82). These beings quickly became worshipped on earth as gods following Babel, led by Nimrod/Gilgamesh/Osiris/Apollo. Consistent with this tradition, the designers of the Capitol Dome, the Great Seal of the United States, and the Obelisk Washington Monument circled the *Apotheosis of Washington* with seventy-two pentagram stars, dedicated the Obelisk seventy-two years after the signing of the Declaration of Independence, and placed seventy-two stones on the Great Seal's uncapped pyramid, above which the eye of Horus/Osiris/Apollo stares. These three sets of seventy-two (72), combined with the imagery and occult numerology of the Osiris/Obelisk, the Isis/Dome, and the oracular Great Seal, are richly symbolic of the influence of Satan and his angels over the world (see Luke 4:5–6, 2 Corinthians 4:4, and Ephesians 6:12) with a prophecy toward Satan's final earthly empire—the coming *novus ordo seclorum,* or new golden pagan age.

In order for the "inevitable" worship of Osiris to be "reestablished" on earth, the seventy-two demons that govern the nations must be controlled, thus they are set in magical constraints on the Great Seal, the Washington Obelisk, and the pentagram circles around the *Apotheosis of Washington* to bind and force the desired effect.

In *The Secret Destiny of America,* Hall noted as well that the seventy-two stones of the pyramid on the Great Seal correspond to the seventy-two arrangements of the Tetragrammaton, or the four-lettered name of God in Hebrew. "These four letters can be combined in seventy-two combinations, resulting in what is called the Shemhamforesh, which represents, in turn, the laws, powers, and energies of Nature."[192] The idea that the mystical name of God could be invoked to bind or loose those supernatural agents (powers and energies of nature, as Hall called them) is meaningful creed within many occult tenets, including Kabbalah and Freemasonry. This is why the seventy-two stars are pentagram-shaped around the deified Freemason, George Washington. Medieval books of magic, or grimoires such as the Key of Solomon and the Lesser Key of Solomon not only identify the star systems Orion (Osiris) and Pleiades (Apollo) as the "home" of these powers, but applies great importance to the pentagram shape of the stars for binding and loosing their influence. Adept Rosicrucians and Freemasons have long used these magical texts—the Key of Solomon and the Lesser Key of Solomon—to do just that. Peter Goodgame makes an important observation about this in "The Giza Discovery":

One of the co-founders of the occult society known as the Golden Dawn193 was a Rosicrucian Freemason named S. L.

MacGregor Mathers, who was the first to print and publish the Key of Solomon (in 1889) making it readily available to the public. Mathers describes it as a primary occult text: "The fountainhead and storehouse of Qabalistic Magic, and the origin of much of the Ceremonial Magic of mediaeval times, the 'Key' has been ever valued by occult writers as a work of the highest authority." Of the 519 esoteric titles included in the catalogue of the Golden Dawn library, the Key was listed as number one. As far as contents are concerned, the Key included instructions on how to prepare for the summoning of spirits including…demons…. One of the most well-known members of the Golden Dawn was the magician [and 33rd-degree freemason] Aleister Crowley. In 1904 Crowley published the first part of the five-part Lesser Key of Solomon known as the Ars Goetia,194 which is Latin for "art of sorcery." The Goetia is a grimoire for summoning seventy-two different demons that were allegedly summoned, restrained, and put to work by King Solomon [according to Masonic mysticism] during the construction of the Temple of YHWH.[195]

Unlike other grimoires including the sixteenth-century *Pseudomonarchia Daemonum* and the seventeenth-century *Lemegeton*, the Key of Solomon does not contain the "Diabolical Signature" of the devil or demons, which the Ars Goetia describes as numbering seventy-two and who were, according to legend, constrained to assist King Solomon after he bound them in a bronze vessel sealed by magic symbols. Such books routinely contain invocations and curses for summoning, binding, and loosing these demons in order to force them to do the conjurers will. Even members of the Church of Satan sign letters using the Shemhamforash, from the Hebrew name of God or Tetragrammaton, producing a blasphemous reinterpretation of the seventy-two entities. And then there is Michelangelo, who painted what we have called the "Sign of the Sixth Knuckle" inside the Sistine Chapel (mentioned elsewhere in this book) that tied the prophecy on the Great Seal of the United States from the Cumaean Sibyl to the return of the Nephilim Apollo. But incredibly, Michelangelo also produced the Shemhamforash on the Vatican's famous ceiling, as his fresco has "an architectural design of 24 columns. On each of these columns are two cherubs, which are mirror imaged on the adjoining column totaling 48 cherubs figures. Then on the 12 triangular spandrels flanking the ceiling borders are an additional 24 nude figures (two bronze nude figures per triangular spandrel) also mirror imaging each other. This totals to 72 cherub figures or the 72 angels of God or names of God [or conversely, the 72 angels that fell and are now the demons or kosmokrators over the nations of the earth]."[196]

Once one understands the importance that these mystical keys hold in Kabbalah, Rosicrucianism, Freemasonic mysticism, and other mystery traditions, there can be (and is) but one reasonable interpretation for the connection in the Vatican and the seventy-two pentagrams at the base of the Apotheosis of Washington. These are there to bind and control the demons over the nations to honor the dedication made by early American Freemasons and certain Roman devotees for a New Atlantis and New World Order under the coming antichrist deity Osiris/Apollo.

From Seventy-Two Demons to Feathered Serpents: What You Do— and Do Not—Learn in School about American History

In public school, children are taught how a world map was created in 1507 by German cartographer Martin Waldseemüller. On this map, the lands of the Western Hemisphere are first called "America," named so after an Italian explorer and navigator named Amerigo Vespucci. According to the official account, the United States of America received the latter part of its name when Waldseemüller used the feminized Latin version of *Amerigo* to call this land *America*.

Or, at least that's what we are told.

What kiddies in public education are not taught, however (and which mainstream academia has yet been willing to accept), is a rival explanation for the origin of "America" related to Mesoamerican serpent-worship, biblical giants, Freemasonry, and even the year 2012.

The story begins long before the Spaniards arrived on this continent and was chronicled in the hieroglyphic characters (and repeated in oral history) of the sacred, indigenous Maya narrative called the Popol Vuh. Sometime between 1701 and 1703, a Dominican priest named Father Francisco Ximénez transcribed and translated the Mayan work into Spanish. Later his text was taken from Guatemala to Europe by Abbott Brasseur de Bourbough where it was translated into French. Today the Popol Vuh rests in Chicago's Newberry Library, but what makes the script interesting is its creation narrative, history, and cosmology, especially as it relates to the worship of the great "feathered serpent" creator deity known as *Q'uq'umatz*, a god considered by scholars to be roughly equivalent to the Aztec god *Quetzalcoatl* and the Yucatec Mayan *Kukulkan*. According to Freemasons like Manly P. Hall, no other ancient work sets forth so completely the initiatory rituals of the great school of philosophic mystery, which was so central to America's Baconian dream of the New Atlantis, than the Popol Vuh. What's more, Hall says, it is in this region where we find the true origin of America's name and destiny.

In *The Secret Teachings of All Ages*, Hall writes:

This volume [Popol Vuh] alone is sufficient to establish incontestably the philosophical excellence of the red race.

"The Red 'Children of the Sun,'" writes James Morgan Pryse, "do not worship the One God. For them that One God is absolutely impersonal, and all the Forces emanated from that One God are personal. This is the exact reverse of the popular western conception of a personal God and impersonal working forces in nature. Decide for yourself which of these beliefs is the more philosophical [Hall says sarcastically]. These Children of the Sun adore the Plumèd Serpent, who is the messenger of the Sun. *He was the God Quetzalcoatl in Mexico, Gucumatz in Quiché; and in Peru he was called Amaru. From the latter name comes our word America. Amaruca is, literally translated, 'Land of the Plumèd Serpent.'* The priests of this [flying dragon], from their chief centre in the Cordilleras, once ruled both Americas. All the Red men who have remained true to the ancient religion are still under their sway. One of their strong centres was in Guatemala, and of their Order was the author of the book called Popol Vuh. In the Quiché tongue Gucumatz is the exact equivalent of Quetzalcoatl in the Nahuatl language; quetzal, the bird of Paradise; coatl, serpent—'the Serpent veiled in plumes of the paradise-bird'!"

The Popol Vuh was discovered by Father Ximinez in the seventeenth century. It was translated into French by Brasseur de Bourbourg and published in 1861. The only complete English translation is that by Kenneth Sylvan Guthrie, which ran through the early files of The Word magazine and which is used as the basis of this article. A portion of the Popol Vuh was translated into English, with *extremely valuable commentaries,* by James Morgan Pryse, but unfortunately his translation was never completed. The second book of the Popol Vuh is largely devoted to the initiatory rituals of the Quiché nation. *These ceremonials are of first importance to students of Masonic symbolism and mystical philosophy, since they establish beyond doubt the existence of ancient and divinely instituted Mystery schools on the American Continent.* (emphasis added)[197]

Thus from Hall we learn that Freemasons like him believe "ancient and divinely instituted" mystery religion important to students of Masonry came to Amaruca/America—*the Land of the*

Plumèd Serpent—from knowledge that the Red Man received from the dragon himself. What Hall conceals is that when he refers to those "extremely valuable commentaries" made by James Pryes, he is referencing an article from Helena Blavatsky's *Lucifer* magazine, which was published by the Theosophical Society and that illuminated the inner doctrine of Rosicrucianism, Freemasonry, and all the secret orders—that Lucifer is the "angel of light" who, in the form of a serpent, bids mankind to partake of the "Tree of Knowledge of Good and Evil" so that their eyes would be open and they could become as gods. Even to this day, in the secret societies, Lucifer is considered this benevolent serpent-god who has nothing more than the best intentions for man, while Jehovah is an evil entity who tries to keep mankind in the dark and punishes him if he seeks the truest wisdom. Since these ancient serpent legends include the Mesoamerican feathered serpent gods and can be looked upon as a historical testament of that Angel thrown down by God, "then perhaps The Land of the Plumèd Serpent may also be known as *the Land of Lucifer*," concludes Ken Hudnall in *The Occult Connection II: The Hidden Race.*[198]

This raises serious questions about what type of "divinely instituted" wisdom Hall had in mind for Amaruca/America, as part of the legitimate concern revolving around this disclosure stems from the fact that the Inca, Aztec, and Maya were either unquestionably gifted mathematicians and astronomers, or they really did receive advanced knowledge from *someone or something*. They measured the length of the solar year far more accurately than did the Europeans in their Gregorian calendar, and precisely oriented their sacred buildings and cities with stars and star clusters, particularly Pleiades and the Orion Nebula associated throughout the ancient Middle East with Osiris/Apollo/Nimrod. The pre-Columbian book, *Codex Dresdensis* (a.k.a. the *Dresden Codex*) by the Yucatecan Maya is famous for its first-known related illustrations of advanced calculations and astronomical phenomena. But how were the pre-telescopic Mesoamericans uniquely aware of such important knowledge? They themselves—like other archaic cultures did—credited ancient "gods" with bringing the heavenly information to Earth.

In 2008, fellow researcher David Flynn may have uncovered important information related to this legend, the size and scope of which simply surpass comprehension. It involves mammoth traces of intelligence carved in stone and covering hundreds of square miles: possibly the strongest evidence ever detected of prehistoric engineering by those who were known and feared throughout the ancient world as gods—the giant offspring of the Watchers.

In the same way modern archeologists only recently found the ruins of hidden Mayan temples in the Guatemalan jungle by using satellites, Flynn employed above-Earth orbiting satellites to image a vast network of patterns that surround Lake Titicaca in Bolivia, South America, which extend for more than one hundred miles south into the Bolivian desert. The patterns display geometric repetition and intelligent designs, including interlocking rectangular cells and mounds, perfectly straight lines, and repeated sharp-angle turns that do not occur naturally. These cover every topographical feature of the high plateau surrounding the lake, over flood plains, hills, cliffs, and mountains. The full report of this remarkable research plus numerous satellite images is available at RaidersNewsUpdate.com/Giants.htm.

Twelve miles south of Lake Titicaca, located within the center of the array of geoglyphs, lies the megalithic ruins of Tiahuanaco. Known as the "American Stonehenge" or the "Baalbek of the New World," its architecture exhibits technological skill that exceeds modern feats of building. At Tiahuanaco, immense stone works were joined with modular fittings and complex breach-locking levels that have never been seen in any other ancient culture. According to engineers, one of the largest single stones ever to be moved and put into a building anywhere on earth (about four hundred tons) was transported to Tiahuanaco from a quarry over two hundred miles away. This feat is even more incomprehensible when one realizes the route of transport was through a mountain range up to fifteen thousand feet.

Conventional historians try to assign the age of the structures at Tiahuanaco to around 600 BC, postulating that a pre-Inca civilization, without benefit of the wheel, modern tools, or even a written language constructed these architectural marvels. But historian Arthur Posnansky studied the area for more than fifty years and observed that sediment had been deposited over the site to the depth of six feet. Within this overburden, produced by a massive flood of water sometime around the Pleistocene age (thirteen thousand years ago), fossilized human skulls were unearthed together with seashells and remnants of tropical plants. The skulls have nearly three times the cranial capacity of modern man and are displayed in the La Paz museum in Bolivia.

In addition, when the first Spanish chroniclers arrived with the conquistador Pizaro, the Inca explained that Tiahuanaco had been constructed by a race of giants called "Huaris" before *Chamak-pacha*, the "period of darkness," and was already in ruins before their civilization began. They said these giants had been created by Viracocha ("Kukulkan" to the Maya and "Quetzalcoatl" to the Aztecs), *the god who came from the heavens* (a.k.a. the Watchers).

> He (Viracocha) created animals and a race of giants. These beings enraged the Lord, and he turned them into stone. Then he flooded the earth till all was under water, and all life extinguished. This flood was called uñu pachacuti, by the Inca which means "water that overturns the land." They say that it rained sixty days and nights, that it drowned all created things, and that there alone remained some vestiges of those who were turned into stones. Viracocha rose from the bosom of Lake Titicaca, and presided over the erection of those wondrous cities whose ruins still dot its islands and western shores, and whose history is totally lost in the night of time.[199]

Near Lake Titicaca in the Hayu Marca Mountain region of Southern Peru at fourteen thousand feet exists a huge, mysterious, door-like structure carved into a solid rock face in an area long revered by Peruvian Indians as the "City of the Gods." Shamans still come to perform rituals at this site, which they call *Puerta de Hayu Marca* or the Gate of the Gods. It measures exactly twenty-three feet in height and width, with a recess in the center slightly smaller than six-feet high. Native Indians say the site is "a gateway to the lands of the Gods" through which, in their ancient past, great heroes arrived and then departed with a "key" that could open the mysterious doorway. Another legend tells of the first Incan priest—the Amaru Meru (note again the Amaru-ca/America connection)—who used a golden disk to open the portal, which turned the solid rock into a stargate. According to local legend, this priest was the first of other "kings" who came to Earth from heavenly locations specifically associated with the Pleiades (Apollo) and Orion (Osiris). This disc-key section of the Gate of the Gods may be depicted by a small, circular depression on the right side of the recess of *Puerta de Hayu Marca*, which in turn could be related to another "portal" not far away—the Gate of the Sun at Tiahuanaco, identified by some historians and archaeologists as the gate of the god Viracocha who created the race of giants.

Mythology involving such giants, followed by world deluge, is universally recorded in the legends of the Inca, Maya, Olmec, and Aztec cultures of Mexico. These stories are consistent with Sumerian and Hebrew accounts of the Great Flood and of the subsequent destruction of giant nephilim whose history of human sacrifices parallel Mayan rituals (victims of Maya had their arms and legs held down while a priest cut their chests open and ripped out their hearts). The Greeks likewise recorded how prehistoric giants were responsible for the creation of megalithic structures discovered around the world, and Islamic folklore ascribes this prehistoric "building" activity to a race of super beings called "jinn" (genies):

The Jinn were before Adam: They built huge cities whose ruins still stand in forgotten places.[200]

In Egypt, the Edfu temple texts, believed to predate the Egyptians themselves, explain something of additional significance, reminiscent of nephilim activity before and after the Flood:

The most ancient of earth's temples and monuments were built to bring about the resurrection of the destroyed world of the gods.[201]

Within the Inca religious paradigm, the oldest record of the Andean region available, the Tiahuanaco geoglyphs are therefore viewed as the vestiges of a lost civilization that knew its destiny…to be destroyed by world cataclysm. In this regard, the geoglyphs serve not only as a memorial of an ancient existence, but also as a warning for future humanity and the return of a destructive epoch, or as David Flynn concluded:

The geoglyphs seem to be physical evidence that supports the Middle and South American myths of world deluge and giants. Their discovery in modern times fits Inca and Mayan prophecies of an "awakening" to knowledge of the ancient past, of the "builder gods" and of their return. It is perhaps testament to the accuracy of these prophecies that the date, December 21, 2012, is known so widely in modern times… the end of the Mayan calendar.[202]

Secrets of Amaru-Ca in the US Capital Dome

That the Maya prehistory echoes the advent of the mysterious Watchers, their giant offspring, the end date 2012, and a connection between these histories and early American freemasonry could be beyond coincidence. In fact, what appears to be fabulous evidence that early Freemasons and those working with them were not only aware of the Mesoamerican belief system and the calendar ending date 2012, but actually incorporated it directly into the design of the Capital Dome in Washington, DC, is vividly illustrated in the commissioned artwork of Constantino Brumidi, the artist who also painted the Apotheosis of George Washington. The book *Apollyon Rising 2012* explains:

> Born July 26, 1805, in Rome, Brumidi was an Italian/Greek painter who made his name restoring sixteenth-century Vatican frescos, as well as artwork in several Roman palaces. Following the French occupation of Rome in 1849, Brumidi immigrated to the United States, where he became a citizen and began work for the Jesuits in New York (viewed at that time as the "hidden power and authority" of the Roman Catholic Church). This work included frescos in the Church of St. Ignatius in Baltimore, Maryland; the Church of St. Aloysius in Washington DC; and St. Stephen's Church in Philadelphia, namely, the Crucifixion, the Martydom of St. Stephen, and the Assumption of Mary.
>
> Abruptly in 1854, the Jesuits financed a trip for Brumidi to Mexico, where he... engaged in the curious task of making copious notes of the ancient Aztec Calendar Stone (also known as the "Stone of the Sun"), which ends in the year 2012.
>
> Immediately upon his return from Mexico, Brumidi took his collection of notes and drawings to Washington DC, where he met with Quartermaster General Montgomery C. Meigs, supervisor of construction over the wings and Dome of the United States Capitol. Brumidi was quickly commissioned to be the "government painter," and began adorning the hallways and Rotunda of the Capitol with pagan frescos sacred to Freemasonry, including the *Apotheosis of George Washington* and the famous *Frieze of American History*. Brumidi died in 1880 and three other artists completed the frieze, but not

before Brumidi attached to his historic work—sometime between 1878–1880—a scene called *Cortez and Montezuma at Mexican Temple*, featuring the Aztec Calendar Stone and other important symbolism.

The Stone of the Sun depicted in Brumidi's frieze (the circular object behind the figures on the right) is based on the actual twelve-foot tall, four-foot thick, twenty-four-ton, monolithic Aztec Calendar Stone. During the pinnacle of Aztec civilization when the Aztec dominated all other tribes of Mexico, this Stone rested atop the Tenochtitlan Temple in the midst of the most powerful and largest city in Mesoamerica. Today, Mexico City's Cathedral, where Brumidi worked, occupies this site. The Spaniards buried the Stone there, and it remained hidden beneath the Cathedral until it was rediscovered in 1790. Then it was raised and embedded into the wall of the Cathedral, where it remained until 1885. Today, the Stone of the Sun is on display in the National Museum of Anthropology in Mexico City's Chapultepec Park.

The inclusion of this symbolism and its accompanying idols in the U.S. Capitol Dome is important. The sun god Tonatiuh, whose face and protruding tongue are seen at the center of the Sun Stone, is the god of the present (fifth) time, which began in 3114 BC and ends in 2012. The Aztec solar calendar is second only in accuracy to the Mayan calendar, which also ends on December 21, 2012. Tonatiuh—who delivered important prophecies and demanded human sacrifices (more than twenty thousand victims per year were offered to him, according to Aztec and Spanish records, and in the single year of 1487, Aztec priests sacrificed eighty thousand people to him at the dedication of the reconstructed temple of the sun god)—was also known as the lord of the thirteen days (from 1 Death to 13 Flint), a number sacred to Aztec, Maya, *and Freemasons* for prophetic and mystical reasons.

Cortez and Montezuma at Mexican Temple, by Brumidi

Like the Maya, Aztecs believed the first age, or "First Sun," was a time when giants had lived on earth who were destroyed by a great flood or deluge long before the Mayan or Toltec civilizations came along. The final age, or "Fifth Sun," would end in 2012. While the Aztecs assimilated such knowledge from the Maya, they built their culture primarily on Toltec ideas. Their great city of Tenochtitlan, on an island in Lake Texcoco with its causeways, canals, marketplaces, and vast towers and temples rising majestically into the air, was so spectacular that when the conquistador Bernal Díaz del Castillo, who wrote an eyewitness account of the conquest of Mexico by the Spaniards, saw it, he exclaimed:

> When we saw so many cities and villages built in the water and other great towns on dry land we were amazed and said that it was like the enchantments... on account of the great towers and cues and buildings rising from the water, and all built of masonry. And some of our soldiers even asked whether the things

that we saw were not a dream.... I do not know how to describe it, seeing things as we did that had never been heard of or seen before, not even dreamed about.[203]

Not only was the Aztec culture so advanced in engineering, astronomy, and mathematics, but the warriors of Montezuma outnumbered the expedition of Cortez by a thousand to one. How then did the Spaniards conquer the Aztecs so easily? Toltec prophecy had told of Quetzalcoatl, who would come from the east as a light-skinned priest to rule their civilization. Nezhaulcoyotl, a great astrologer who supported Montezuma, believed this vision, and when Cortez arrived exactly when the prophecy said the god would return, Montezuma received him as the coming of Quetzalcoatl, and surrendered. This event is symbolized in the *Cortez and Montezuma* frieze by Brumidi.

Another connection between Brumidi's prophetic Stone of the Sun depiction and Freemasonry can be seen in the serpent coiled around the sacred fire, toward which Montezuma's left hand intentionally gestures. The sacred fire was connected to the seven-star Pleiades (Tianquiztli, the "gathering place") by the Aztecs, and represented the final year in a fifty-two-year cycle called "calendar round," which ended when the Pleiades crossed the fifth cardinal point at midnight that year. At this time, the Aztecs would let the fires go out and conduct the "dance of the new fire" to start the cycle again. When the priests lit the new "sacred fire" as well as the hearth fires, it ensured the movement of the sun (the serpent coiled around the sacred fire in Brumidi's painting) along the precession anew. In the year 2012, not only will the Pleiades be in this zenith over Mesoamerica, but the alignment will come into full conjunction with the sun... This sacred knowledge is why the Pyramid of the Sun at Teotihuacan near Mexico City also corresponds with the Pleiades. Its west side and surrounding streets are aligned directly with the setting point of the Pleiades, a configuration held in high esteem by the Maya as well. They built the Kukulcan pyramid at Chichen Itza so that during the spring and autumn equinox, at the rising and setting of the sun, a slithering, snake-like shadow representing Kukulcan (Quetzalcoatl, the plumed serpent) would cast along the north stairway to the serpent's head at the bottom. Sixty days later, when the sun rises over the Pyramid at midday, it aligns with the Pleiades again.

By portraying the Stone of the Sun that ends in 2012, the sacred fire that ends in 2012, and the astrological alignment with the Pleiades in the *Frieze of American History*, Brumidi is telling us quite clearly that the designers of the Capitol were aware of the implications of 2012. This adds clarity to the reasons the designers of the Great Seal of the United States similarly incorporated the Mayan 13 katun system—which started in 1776 and ends in 2012—on the nation's primary cipher.[204]

Yet a deeper and related message is also openly hidden in the Capitol Dome. A third piece of imagery from Brumidi's *Cortez and Montezuma* scene that not only connects Mesoamerican belief to the Freemasons and prophecy, but to the Vatican, can be found in the drum behind the kneeling Aztec. The drum bears the shape of the Maltese cross, a symbol connected in history with the empire of Osiris as starting on the island of Malta. The Maltese cross was adopted by the Knights of Malta (connected with Freemasonry) and the Vatican (where Brumidi first worked and found favor). We believe this is not by chance. Captain Montgomery C. Meigs, the engineer who placed Brumidi over the paintings for the new Dome, wanted artwork reminiscent of that at the Vatican. With Brumidi's ties to the Vatican and the Jesuits, it was a match "made in heaven." By including this well-known Mayan, Illuminati, and Freemasonic symbol, Brumidi cleverly connected the deisgn of the Capitol Dome in Washington, DC with the Vatican, Masonic mysticism, and the year 2012 in more ways than one. Yet to understand the significance of where we are today facing the arrival of Petrus Romanus, it is essential in the next section of this book to examine the history of the Roman Catholic Church and the basis for the papacy itself.

SECTION TWO

ESSENTIAL HISTORY OF THE PAPACY

7 | The Petrine Myth of Apostolic Succession

A prophecy predicting the imminent end of the papacy is particularly enthralling, because the papacy is the oldest continuously functioning institution in the world. Consider that when the American War of Independence was being fought, there had already been some 250 popes in office. Before the United States elected its first President in 1789, they had already elected the two-hundred-fifty-first pope. Today, Benedict XVI stands as the two-hundred-sixty-fifth official pontiff. As leader of the Roman Catholic Church, the pope is considered the successor of the apostle Peter and the Vicar of Christ. That means he is Christ's exclusive representative on earth. The word "pope" is derived from the term *papa*, which originated in ancient Greek as a child-like term for "father." A critical figure was Pope Stephen I (r. 254–257), who was the first, as far as we know, to assert forcefully the *Petrine doctrine* of Roman authority. He insisted that he held the "chair of Peter" (*cathedra Petri*) in direct succession from the apostle Peter. This assertion inaugurates the idea that each pope is Peter's successor, albeit it began nearly two hundred years after Peter's martyrdom. The papacy, as it is today, simply did not exist in the first few centuries of Christianity.

Things changed drastically with Constantine. He ordered the building of St. Peter's and St. Paul's basilicas, and he bequeathed the Lateran Palace to Pope Sylvester. In the West, the title "pope" was largely reserved to the city of Rome when Leo the Great (440–461) infamously assumed the historic pagan title of *Pontifex Maximus* favored by Emperor Constantine. In the eighth century, the papacy broke with the Eastern emperor and allied itself with a Western royal and claimed land in central Italy for political autonomy, a pivotal event which will be discussed in detail herein. Throughout the early Middle Ages (600–1050), the Eastern and Western Church honored the bishop of Rome as the "vicar of St. Peter," but the East ignored him for all intents and purposes and the Western Emperors only paid attention when it was expedient.

During the Middle Ages, the titles "Vicar of St. Peter," "Vicar of the Prince of the Apostles," and "Vicar of the Apostolic See" were all employed interchangeably. It was only in the eleventh century that Gregory VII made "Pope" or "Pontiff" the official title. Accordingly, the term "papacy" originated in the later eleventh century to differentiate the Roman bishop from the bishops of all other diocese. During this time political maneuvers allowed the Church to assert more and more worldly power. In the thirteenth century, largely due to Pope Innocent III, the Pontifex Maximus asserted the priority of the spiritual over the material world and adopted a supercilious new title, "Vicar of Christ." This renders into English literally as "instead of Christ." Of course, to one with a coherent biblical worldview, this seems outrageously blasphemous.

The authority for the papacy comes from what is called the *Petrine doctrine*. This idea takes its name from Peter the apostle of

Jesus who is alleged to be the first pope. In ecclesiology, the theory of church government, this has been termed the *Petrine Office.* Today that office is audaciously alleged to have infallible authority. For this discussion we jump forward to the nineteenth century when Pius IX (1846–1878) called the Council, Vatican I, which declared that all Christians must affirm:

> And so, supported by the clear witness of Holy Scripture, and adhering to the manifest and explicit decrees both of our predecessors the Roman Pontiffs and of general councils, we promulgate anew the definition of the ecumenical Council of Florence [49], which must be believed by all faithful Christians, namely that the Apostolic See and the Roman Pontiff hold a world-wide primacy, and that the Roman Pontiff <u>is the successor of blessed Peter, the prince of the apostles, true vicar of Christ</u>, head of the whole Church and father and teacher of all Christian people.
>
> To him, <u>in blessed Peter</u>, full power has been given by our lord Jesus Christ to tend, rule and govern the universal Church.[205] (underline added)

Moreover, the Council went on to affirm "the Infallible 'Magisterium' of the Roman Pontiff," proclaiming:

> ...that the Roman Pontiff, when he speaks *ex cathedra*, that is, when in discharge of the office of Pastor and Teacher of all Christians, by virtue of his supreme Apostolic authority, he defines a doctrine regarding faith or morals to be held by the universal Church, is, by the divine assistance promised to him in Blessed Peter, <u>possessed of that infallibility</u> with which the divine Redeemer willed that His Church should be endowed in defining doctrine regarding faith or morals; and that, therefore, such definitions of the Roman Pontiff

are of themselves, and not from the consent of the Church, irreformable.[206]

In other words, when the Pontifex Maximus speaks in his alleged apostolic authority, his words are inerrant scripture and cannot be changed. Thus, Catholic dogma has set its own terms and cannot correct itself without being internally contradictory. Even worse, if one chooses to question this alleged papal perfection, then they are cursed by the church, "But if anyone—which may God avert!—presume to contradict this our definition, let him be anathema."[207] Thus, according to official Roman doctrine, one is doomed to hell for denying papal authority and even infallibility. This unfortunate state of affairs stands today despite that many, called Old Catholics, left the Roman Church because papal fallibility is demonstrable by their actions and doctrines. Even more, we shall demonstrate that the *Petrine doctrine* upon which it rests is tenuous indeed.

Undermining the Basis

From the statements above, the claim to authority rests on the handing down, over the last two thousand years, of Peter's apostolic authority. If their claims about Peter are demonstrated false, then whole magisterium of the Roman Church crumbles. The papists claim rests upon two bases, one historical and the other theological. First addressing the theological, they argue that the papacy was divinely instituted by Christ in his declarations to Peter (Matthew 16:18–19; John 21:15–17) and due to its divine institution, the pontiff demands devotion and submission even as to Christ.

Matthew 16:18–19

"And I say also unto thee, That thou art Peter, and upon this rock I will build my church; and the gates of hell shall not prevail against it. And I will give unto thee the keys of the kingdom of heaven: and whatsoever thou shalt bind on earth shall be bound in heaven: and whatsoever thou shalt loose on earth shall be loosed in heaven" (Mt 16:18–19).

Traditionally, Romanists base their case primarily on this passage, claiming that Peter is the "rock" upon which the Church is founded, thus giving his successors the full power of binding and loosing. There is certainly a word-play evident in the Greek. The name Peter is *Petros* and rock is *petras*. Even so, it is not clear in the original language that Christ was referring to Peter being the foundation of the Church when He spoke of "this rock." "Peter" is in the second person but "this rock" is in the third person. Furthermore, "Peter" is a masculine, singular term but "rock" is a feminine, singular term. Thus, it seems unlikely that they have the same referent. Jesus could have easily said, "and upon *you* the rock," had He intended Rome's meaning. Instead, He switches from direct address to the demonstrative "this."

Arguing this in non-technical language is somewhat strained but when going from second person, "you, Peter," to third person, "this rock," then "this rock" is referring to something *other than* the person who was being addressed in the preceding phrase, something that we find in the immediate context.

Sound exegesis of sacred Scripture entails thinking in paragraphs or textual units rather than proof texting with short decontextualized passages. What is the most important idea in this Gospel narrative? If you recall from your formative years in Sunday school, when in doubt, the correct Sunday school answer was nearly always, "Jesus." Indeed, Jesus is the answer here as well. The misappropriated response to Peter is praise from Jesus for Peter's inspired confession: "Thou art the Christ, the Son of the living God" (Matthew 16:16). In this author's (Putnam) view, it is on this confession of Christ that the Church is built. In Peter's own words, Christ is the cornerstone that the builders rejected which has become the capstone (1 Peter 2:7). Even early Catholic theologian Augustine agreed, "On this rock, therefore, He said, which thou hast confessed. I will build my Church. For the Rock *(Petra)* is Christ; and on this foundation was Peter himself built."[208] The head of the universal Church is Christ alone.

For the sake of argument, even if we were to grant that Peter is the rock in Matthew 16:18, it still would not make him a Pontifex Maximus. The same authority Jesus gave to Peter (Matthew 16:18) is also given to all the apostles (Matthew 18:18). Paul also affirms the Church is, "built upon the foundation of the apostles and prophets, Jesus Christ himself being the chief corner stone" (Eph 2:20). Furthermore, Paul received his revelation independently of the other apostles (Gal. 1:12; 2:2) and even used his revelation to scold Peter (Galatians 2:11–14). It is also telling that Catholic apologists seldom mention that only a few verses later Jesus rebukes Peter as Satan: "Get thee behind me, Satan: thou art an offence unto me: for thou savourest not the things that be of God, but those that be of men"(Matthew 16:23). No one gives Peter superiority in apostasy because of this condemnation, thus it seems wise we not give him supremacy in the ecclesia for a commendation.

According to Revelation 3:7, the Lord Jesus holds the key of David. What He opens no one can shut, and what He shuts no one can open. Peter is given the "keys" through preaching the Gospel, an authority subsequently granted to all who are called to proclaim the Gospel. In Acts, Peter is the apostle who first preaches the message of the kingdom to the Jews at Pentecost (Acts 2), to the Samaritans (Acts 8), and to the Gentiles (Acts 10). Peter was an important apostle but no more preeminent than Paul. Peter helped establish the Jerusalem church, but James the brother of Jesus assumed the leadership of the Jerusalem church (Acts 15).[209] It was Paul who defined Christian doctrine having written thirteen of the twenty-seven New Testament books. Paul became "the apostle to the Gentiles" (Acts 14; 16–28). Peter became the "apostle to the Jews," preaching throughout Palestine (Gal. 2:7–8).

John 21:15–17

"He saith unto him the third time, Simon, son of Jonas, lovest thou me? Peter was grieved because he said unto him the third time, Lovest thou me? And he said unto him, Lord, thou knowest all things; thou knowest that I love thee. Jesus saith unto him, Feed my sheep" (John 21:17).

"Feed my sheep" implied nothing more than pastoral care and Peter was assigned to be the apostle to the Jews. Again one needs to think exegetically in context. Contrary to the papists claim, the passage speaks more to Peter's weakness than to his preeminence. The reason Peter is asked three times by Jesus, "Do you love me more than these [other disciples]?" was that Peter denied the Lord three times and he needed to be restored (Luke 22:31–32 c.f. 22:54–62). At the tomb of Jesus' resurrection, the Angel instructed the women to get the disciples and rather oddly he added, "*and* Peter" (Mark 16:8), seemingly implying that Peter had lost his apostolic status. Thus, Jesus was not exalting Peter above the other apostles in John 21, rather restoring him to their level!

Historical Basis

The New Testament, the only contemporary account of Peter's life, reveals him as having a wife living in Capernaum (Matthew 8:14) and makes no reference to his having been in Rome, nor to his martyrdom. Capernaum was located on the northwest shore of the Sea of Galilee about two and a half miles west from the entrance of the Jordan River, and was the economic center of Galilee.[210] The house of Simon Peter at Capernaum is mentioned many times in the Gospels (Matthew 8:14; 17:25; Mark 1:29; 2:1; 3:20; 9:33). This house, including evidence of an internal house church, was located in 1968 during the archeological excavations led by V. Corbo and S. Loffreda.[211]

In the Book of Acts, which chronicles the Apostles' deeds after Jesus died, Peter is seen as preaching in Jerusalem as late as AD 45 (Acts 12), and last appears at the Jerusalem council which is dated around AD 48–49 (this date is crucial because as we will see later it undermines his direct founding of the Church in Rome). Peter cannot have been where Catholic tradition places him as the Bishop of Rome and where the book of Acts reports him to be at the same time. It is quite literally a decision between the Bible and third-century tradition.

Catholicism has taught for centuries that Peter was martyred and buried in Rome and that all popes succeed from him. It is true that early tradition supports the idea that Peter died at the hand of Nero by crucifixion near the time of the Great Fire of Rome in AD 64. Even so, the story of Peter in Rome is flimsy at best and reeks of special pleading and vested interest. Although some Early Church fathers wrote in the late second century that Peter and Paul founded the Roman church, it is likely that neither apostle had a role in its original establishment.[212] According to the director of the Medieval Institute and Professor of history at the University of Notre Dame, Thomas F. X. Noble, the Roman Catholic dates of Peter as bishop of Rome from 42 to 67 are wrong. Noble is certainly a preeminent authority on the papacy and his lecture notes state unequivocally, "Peter did not found the Roman community, and there is no good evidence that that community had a bishop—an 'overseer'—in the 1st century."[213] The New Testament evidence simply does not support the official Catholic history.

The spurious and unbiblical nature of the Catholic claim is seen clearly in Paul's epistle to the Romans. Paul's letter was written in AD 56–57 during the time the Catholics claim Peter was there. However, the omission of a salutation to Peter in the epistle to the Romans suggests that Peter was not in Rome at the time. In fact, nothing in Paul's inspired letter to the Early Roman Church remotely suggests that Peter was there or had even a minor part in its foundation. Even more, if Peter had truly founded the church, it seems disingenuous that Paul, who claimed a policy of never building on the foundation of another, gave them such defining doctrinal instruction (Romans

15:20). Evangelical scholars believe that converts from the day of Pentecost (Acts 2) probably carried Christianity to Rome. J. C. Waters makes this case: "It is most probable that Christianity made its way to Rome spontaneously as the personal baggage of Jews, proselytes, and sympathizers, who brought faith in Jesus as Messiah with them from the East [see Acts 2:10]. They came to Rome for commercial reasons, as immigrants, or against their will as slaves."[214] In the interest of being charitable, perhaps Peter is given credit as a founder of the Church in Rome simply from his inspired sermon at Pentecost?

Suetonius was a prominent Roman historian who recorded the lives of the Roman Caesars and the historical events surrounding their reigns. He served as a court official under Hadrian and as an annalist for the Imperial House. Suetonius records the expulsion of the Christian Jews from Rome (mentioned in Acts 18:2) in AD 49–50. "As the Jews were making constant disturbances at the instigation of Chrestus (Christ), [Claudius] expelled them from Rome."[215] Chrestus is simply a variant spelling of "Christ" and is virtually the same as Tacitus' Latin spelling.[216] It appears the Christian's preaching had elicited a protest amongst the Jews as it had in Jerusalem. Furthermore, the expulsion of the Jews from Rome under the emperor Claudius infers that a Christian Church *had already been established* by that time because Paul's later tent-making partners, Priscilla and Aquila, were among those who had been exiled. F. F. Bruce contends, "In none of Paul's references to them is there any hint that they were converts of his: all the indications are that they were Christians before they met him, and that accordingly they were Christians while they lived in Rome—which may throw light on Suetonius's statement that the Jews were expelled by Claudius because of their constant rioting 'at the instigation of Chrestus.'"[217] Thus, the New Testament evidence clearly supports the likelihood of the Roman Church existing during the time that Peter is reported to still be in Jerusalem in the Book of Acts. But there is more biblical data opposing Rome's claim.

Perhaps more decisive is the fact Paul also omits Peter from his extensive list of greetings to Rome's prominent Christians in the salu-

tation of his epistle (Romans 16:3–16). Paul greeted these residents of
the city of Rome at exactly the time the Vatican would place him there.
He greeted entire families and mentioned twenty-nine folks by name.
But he did not mention Peter. That is surely an unimaginable oversight if Peter was residing there as the Bishop of Rome. Furthermore,
a few years after he wrote the book of Romans, Paul was taken to
Rome stand trial before Caesar. When the Christian community in
Rome heard of Paul's arrival, they all went to meet him (Acts 28:15).
This is only a few years before Peter's martyrdom. Again, there is not
a single mention of Peter among them. Luke certainly would have
mentioned him had he been there. The New Testament stands in
sharp relief to the papists claim. What about archeology? Doesn't the
Church claim Peter is buried underneath St. Peter's square?

In ancient Roman paganism, an aedicula is a small shrine. The
term "aedicule" derives from the Latin "aedes," a temple building or
house. Many aediculae were household shrines that held small altars
or statues of the Lares and Penates. The Lares were Roman deities
protecting the house. The Penates were patron gods or household
gods. It was proximate to a pagan shrine like this that the bones of
Peter were allegedly discovered. But it is not at all clear that the bones
originated from there. The tale is quite suspicious. Catholic arche-
ologist, Padre Antonio Ferrua, excavated a vast Roman cemetery
that underlies St. Peter's Square and basilica. According to his 1951
report, the excavations that had begun there in 1939 had unearthed a
necropolis and some twenty pagan mausoleums but no trace of Peter.
According to investigative journalist Tom Mueller, "Ferrua and his
colleagues had in fact worked with remarkable objectivity: despite
intense pressure from the Vatican community, they reported no trace
of Peter—not one inscription that named him, not even amid all the
graffiti on his supposed tomb. Strangest of all, they discovered that
the earth directly beneath the *aedicula* was empty."[218]

Frustrated, Pope Pius XII demanded further research by Vatican
loyal epigraphist, Margherita Guarducci. She inverted the previous
findings, discovering drawings and inscriptions that Ferrua's team had

bizarrely overlooked after over a decade of investigation, including an inscription near the *aedicula* that she rendered as "Peter is within." It is dubious that the original investigation reported nothing of the sort and innuendo and accusation still continue.

The grave that is now claimed by the Church to be that of St. Peter lies at the foot of the aedicula beneath the floor. In 1953, long after the initial twelve-year archeological effort had come up empty, another set of bones were found that were said to have been removed without the archeologists' knowledge from a niche in the north side of a wall on the right of the aedicula. Subsequent testing indicated that these were the bones of a sixty- to seventy-year-old man. Meuller reported:

> In the snarl of graffiti on Peter's tomb she discerned a "mystic cryptography," with countless coded messages about the Apostle. At length she even produced Peter's remains. A *sampietrino* had shown her a wooden box of bones, she explained, which were inside the masonry surrounding the *aedicula* when the archaeologists first discovered it. Somehow they had overlooked the precious relics, and Monsignor Kaas later tucked them away for safekeeping. Scientific tests arranged by Guarducci indicated that the bones had been wrapped in a cloth of royal purple stitched with gold, and were those of a man of sixty to seventy years and a robust physique—the bones, she argued, of the Apostle.[219]

In other words, these bones were not even discovered at the actual site; rather, they were found in a storeroom and alleged to have been spirited away from the site. In addition to the human remains, the suspicious box contained sheep, ox, pig, and mouse bones. Most discrediting, there are no witnesses to place its origin at the site. This level of contamination makes the dubious discovery invalid by scientific standards. Who can say these bones were not simply planted by the demonstrably frustrated Vatican? This appears to be the case. Dr. Robert Beckford, a theology lecturer at Oxford Brookes University remarked, "We found that there is no scientific evidence to support the idea that Peter was buried in Rome, but yet the rival theory has not got out because it challenges the Church. If you undermine its basis for power you undermine the Church. It's tragic that the faith gets reduced to manipulating the facts and to one Church trying to make itself superior to others."[220]

Pope Pius XII stated in December 1950 that it could not be confirmed to be Saint Peter's grave with absolute certainty. However, following the discovery of further bones and an inscription, much later in 1968, Pope Paul VI announced that the relics of St. Peter had been identified.

While there is no good reason to believe the Vatican's evidence, scientifically rigorous archeological evidence suggests that Peter was not buried in the pagan capital. Over a century ago, a French Christian archaeologist, Charles Claremont-Gannueau, wrote a little-known report, dated November 13, 1873, from Jerusalem to the Palestine Exploration Fund. In this report he told of his monumental discovery. In a cave near Bethany in the Mount of Olives, a group of Jewish ossuaries (stone coffins) from the first century of the Christian era were found. To his great surprise, Claremont-Gannueau found that these ancient Jewish stone coffins contained the names of numerous individuals mentioned in the New Testament as members of the Jerusalem Church. Even more interesting were the signs of the cross etched on several of the ossuaries.

In John's Gospel, we read, "Now a certain man was sick, named Lazarus, of Bethany, the town of Mary and her sister Martha" (John 11:1). The Mount of Olives was within walking distance of the ancient town of Bethany and the tomb discovered by Clermont-Ganneau contained names which correspond to the names in the New Testament. He discovered inscriptions including the names of "Eleazar" ("Lazarus"), "Martha," and "Mary" on three different coffins. He also found inscriptions of the name "Yeshua" ("Jesus") inscribed commemoratively on several the ossuaries. One coffin, also bearing cross marks on it, was inscribed with the name "Shlom-

zion" followed by the designation "daughter of Simon the Priest."
Clermont-Ganneau wrote in his report:

> This catacomb on the Mount of Olives belonged apparently
> to one of the earliest families which joined the new religion
> of Christianity. In this group of sarcophagi [coffins], some
> of which have the Christian symbol [cross marks] and
> some have not, we are, so to speak, [witnessing the] actual
> unfolding of Christianity. Personally, I think that many of
> the Hebrew-speaking people whose remains are contained in
> these ossuaries were among the first followers of Christ... The
> appearance of Christianity at the very gates of Jerusalem is,
> in my opinion, extraordinary and unprecedented. Somehow
> the new [Christian] doctrine must have made its way into
> the Jewish system... The association of the sign of the cross
> with written in Hebrew alone constitutes a valuable fact.[221]

The French archaeologist realized that there was a high degree of
probability that these tombs belonged to the family of Mary, Martha,
and Lazarus, the close friends of Jesus. Claremont-Gannueau wrote
further, "By a singular coincidence, which from the first struck me
forcibly, these inscriptions, found close to the Bethany road, and very
near the site of the village, contain nearly all the names of the per-
sonages in the Gospel scenes which belonged to the place: Eleazar
(Lazarus), Simon, Martha...a host of other coincidences occur at the
sight of all these most evangelical names."[222] Despite its monumental
historical importance, this report was mysteriously never mentioned in
the newspapers of the day. As a result, it was virtually lost to history.

Several years later very close by on the Mount of Olives, another
by archaeologist, P. Bagatti, found and excavated another catacomb
holding one hundred ossuaries. Based on inscribed crosses, the Chi
Rho symbol, and the name "Yeshua," Baggati concluded that these
were also Jewish followers of Jesus Christ. Coins minted by Roman
Governor Varius Gratus (AD 16) proved that these tombs were used

for burial of Christians before the fall of Jerusalem in AD 70. The ossuaries contained the following names inscribed on their sides, together with Christian symbols or the name of Jesus: Jonathan, Joseph, Jarius, Judah, Matthias, Menahem, Salome, Simon, and Zechariah. While many of these names appear in the New Testament records of the Early Church at Jerusalem, the most fascinating ossuary was the one inscribed with crosses and the name "Sapphira." This is a very unique name which has not been found in Jewish literature of the period outside the New Testament passage Acts 5: 1. Luke recorded the death of this woman and her husband when they lied to God and the Church (Acts 5:1, 5–10). "But a certain man named Ananias, with Sapphira his wife, sold a possession…" This very unique name eliminates reasonable doubt that this was indeed the tomb of early Christians.

Fot. 81.

Aramaic Inscription	‮רויראוצצ‬

Hebrew from Strong's Concordance	שִׁמְעוֹן בַּר יוֹנָה
	H3124 H1247 H8095
	Jonah Bar Simon
	(Hebrew reads right to left)

images note 11

Of course, the most controversial find of all was a coffin bearing the unusual inscription "Shimon bar Yonah" which is the full name Jesus used in the Matthew 16:17, ironically the favorite proof text of the papists. It seems improbable that a three-term name could refer to any other than the apostle Peter. Compounding a fully intact name with the fact it was found in a Christian burial ground amongst probable New Testament contemporaries from the very time in which Peter lived, the evidence is very convincing. The archeology was also conducted with scientific rigor sorely lacking in the Vatican's Rome effort. One marvels at the Vatican's feigned indifference at what is likely one of most important archeological finds in Christian history. This blatant neglect of evidence can only be explained by their vested interest in maintaining the mythology of the papacy.

Unfortunately, the Vatican seems all too willing to deceive its faithful. According to F. Paul Peterson, a Franciscan monk who knew the archaeologist Bagatti:

> "Father Bagatti told me personally that three years ago he went to the Pope (Pius XII) in Rome and showed him the evidence and the Pope said to him, 'Well, we will have to make some changes, but for the time being, keep this thing quiet'." In awe I asked also in a subdued voice, "So the Pope really believes that those are the bones of St. Peter?"
>
> "Yes," was his answer. "The documentary evidence is there, he could not help but believe."[223]

It truly seems that the Vatican has sought to suppress this important archaeological find simply to preserve their legend that Peter was the first pope. Yet right before our eyes lays the greatest proof that Peter was never a pope in Rome. If he had been, it would have certainly been written in the New Testament. The traditions of Peter in Rome can only be traced back to the second century, yet the archeological evidence at the Mount of Olives traces right back to the time of apostles.

The earliest tradition for Peter's martyrdom in Rome is Clement of Rome's letter to the Corinthians (AD 96) but it gives little detail: "Peter, through unrighteous envy, endured not one or two, but numerous labors and when he had at length suffered martyrdom, departed to the place of glory due to him."[224] It only supports martyrdom, that's all there is. It is in *The Acts of Peter* (second century AD), that we find the story of Peter engaging in a spectacular supernatural showdown with his arch nemesis Simon Magus. In the story, through demonic power, Simon has stolen away the faith of Roman church, but Peter challenges him in the name of Christ. At the peak of the contest, Peter raises three men from the dead and exposes Simon's inferiority and identity as an angel of Satan. In an attempt to regain his status, Simon takes flight above the city of Rome, but he is brought down by Peter's prayer.

> And behold when he [Simon Magus] was lifted up on high, and all beheld him raised up above all Rome and the temples thereof and the mountains, the faithful looked toward Peter. And Peter seeing the strangeness of the sight cried unto the Lord Jesus Christ: If thou suffer this man to accomplish that which he hath set about, now will all they that have believed on thee be offended, and the signs and wonders which thou hast given them through me will not be believed: hasten thy grace, O Lord, and let him fall from the height and be disabled; and let him not die but be brought to nought, and break his leg in three places. And he fell from the height and brake his leg in three places. Then every man cast stones at him and went away home, and thenceforth believed Peter.[225]

Simon is whisked away by two associates but later dies from the fall. Peter is convicted on trumped-up charges and sentenced for crucifixion. Interestingly, Justin Martyr reports Simon's visit to Rome, but places it during the reign of Claudius (41–54), and makes no mention of an encounter with Peter.[226] The tradition of Peter's burial is not found in the earliest manuscripts of the tradition; these were added after as it was theologically expedient. The *Anchor Bible Dictionary* article explains,

"The failure of the *Martyrdom of Peter* to locate the place of Peter's execution or burial was corrected in later developments of the tradition, such as the *Passion of Peter* and the *Passion of Peter and* Paul."[227]

It is from this account, soaring Simon Magus in tow, which Rome's tradition of Peter being crucified upside-down derives. Ostensibly this was at Peter's request, because he was unworthy to die in the same manner as the Lord. It seems that Origen adopted elements of this account mid-third century in his commentary on Genesis, which were recorded by Eusebius.[228] Of course, the historicity of this account is not accepted by scholars. Nevertheless, the papacy is still symbolized by an inverted cross. It is quite ironic that Satanists have adopted the same inverted cross symbol as the papacy. Satanists consider it to represent the opposite of Christianity by inverting its principal symbol. As a result, this symbol has become very popular within anti-religious groups and black metal groups. It appears frequently in cinematic representations of Satan worship. Might this connection with the papacy suggest something beyond mere coincidence? Has the papacy been duped into adopting a satanic symbol? Still, in line with Protestant tradition, the papacy represents a similar inversion by promoting a purveyor of false doctrine, a *pseudoprophētai*, as the Vicar of "in place of" Christ.

images note 12

The preponderance of theological and historical evidence shows that by the standard of apostolic succession the Romanists fall far short. Eusebius of Caesarea, acknowledged as the father of Church History, writing about 300 AD, reported that Origen had written: "Peter is reported to have preached to the Jews throughout Pontius, Galatia, Bithynia, Cappadocia and, <u>about the end of his days</u>, tarrying at Rome, was crucified" (underline added).[229] Even the earliest traditions report Peter was in Rome for only a short time near the end of his life. One could even allow that Peter was crucified in Rome but reconcile the archeological evidence with the possibility that, in accordance with Jewish tradition, his friends and family carried his body home to the Mount of Olives for a proper Jewish burial via ossuary (e.g. Joseph in Joshua 24:32).

In conclusion, this argument has been an academic exercise because the concept of apostolic succession is in and of itself incoherent. Apostles by definition only lived in the first century. The criterion for being an apostle was that one was an eyewitness of the resurrected Christ (cf. Acts 1:22; 1 Cor. 9:1; 15:5–8). These unique individuals were given certain distinctive supernatural "signs of an apostle" (2 Cor. 12:12). It follows that there could be no apostolic succession in the pope nor anyone else. The authority of apostles has been replaced by the authority of the writings of the apostles. Only the teaching of the apostles remains in the Church today, neither the office nor its authority can be claimed legitimately by anyone. Furthermore, even if it were possible to transfer spiritual authority, a cursory examination of the decadent lifestyles of the pontiffs from the middle ages demonstrates a broken chain. In summary, popes are merely posers, not apostles. It is with that in mind, that we turn to Constantine who was supposedly the first Christian Roman emperor.

8 | From Peter to Constantine

The Roman Church has made it an article of faith that popes are successors of St. Peter as the first bishop of Rome. But Peter demonstrably never had that title, and he was only so endowed centuries after his death. While Peter was a leader in Jerusalem, James, the Lord's brother, had the title of bishop. James wrote a pertinent word to the present discussion in his ancient epistle of wisdom, "…know ye not that the friendship of the world is enmity with God? Whosoever therefore will be a friend of the world is the enemy of God" (James 4:4). We believe that when the Church of Rome realized her ambition to become a worldly dominion, she lost her way. With this in mind, this chapter will show that the bishop of Rome sold out to the prince of this world many centuries ago. While somewhat speculative, a plausible scenario based on historical research and biblical theology will be suggested as to how and why this began. We believe this error has inevitably led Romanism into the system of the Antichrist.

The former chapter demonstrated the incompatibility of the papists claim to apostolic succession with the Bible. Further inconsistencies with the *Petrine myth* are seen in the earliest known lists of bishops of Rome. When scrutinizing these records, we quickly see that Peter's name is conspicuously absent. Irenaeus, the disciple of Polycarp (a disciple of John the Apostle), listed all the Roman bishops up to the twelfth, Eleutherius. According to Irenaeus, the first bishop of Rome was not Peter but Linus.[230] The Apostolic Constitution in the year 270 also named Linus as first bishop of Rome, allegedly appointed by the Apostle Paul. In case you are still wondering why I am making a federal case out of this issue, it is because the Roman Catholic Church bases all of its authority on this myth that Peter was the first pope. I mean myth in the most charitable sense of an expedient lie. Furthermore, it still affects our world today. Case in point, John Paul II spoke these deluded words at the inauguration of his Pontificate on Sunday October 22, 1978 in St Peter's Square: "Yes, Brothers and sons and daughters, Rome is the See of Peter. Down the centuries new Bishops continually succeeded him in this See. Today a new, Bishop comes to the Chair of Peter in Rome, a Bishop full of trepidation, conscious of his unworthiness. And how could one not tremble before the greatness of this call and before the universal mission of this See of Rome!"[231]

The "See of Peter" and "See of Rome" simply refers to a "seat" as in the seat of power. That power so claimed from it being Peter's chair or "seat" which it clearly never was. Indeed the pomp and circumstance of the papacy has been a charade since the third century. You will also encounter the term "Holy See" in reference to the Vatican. Yet, there is nothing holy about it, rather rapacious perversion. The Vatican has a history of forgery and expedient deceit which is second to none.

"For the mystery of iniquity doth already work: only he who now letteth will let, until he be taken out of the way" (2 Thessalonians 2:7; Apostle Paul, circa AD 51).

From this passage we see that the "mystery of iniquity" was necessarily active when Paul wrote the Thessalonians in AD 51. Thus, it infected the early Church and is still festering today. Ultimately this malignant mystery manifests as the ultimate "man of sin" when the restraining influence is removed. The eminent theologian, Charles Hodge, explained that the Roman Catholic Church uniquely meets the necessary requirements of the mystery of iniquity in this way:

> The two elements of which the papacy is the development are the desire of preeminence or lust of power, and the idea of a priesthood, that is, that Christian ministers are mediators whose intervention is necessary to secure access to God, and that they are authorized to make atonement for sin; to which was added the claim to grant absolution. Both these elements were at work in the apostolic age. The papacy is the product of the transfer of Jewish and Pagan ideas to the Christian system. The Jews had a high priest, and all the ministers of the sanctuary were sacrificing priests. The Romans had a "Pontifex Maximus" and the ministers of religion among them were priests. Nothing was more natural and nothing is plainer as a historical fact than that the assumption of a priestly character and functions by the Christian ministry, was one of the earliest corruptions of the Church.[232]

The papacy is the oldest institution on earth representing the most ancient succession of false prophets. The ambitions of false prophets were a problem evident in the New Testament. What other influence has held sway since Paul wrote the Thessalonians in AD 51 and is still corrupting the Church? Paul also indicated that this malevolent entity was restrained until such time when the restraint would be removed resulting in a great apostasy from biblical truth which would consummate in the final end-time Antichrist. The identity of the restraining influence is controversial.

What makes identifying this with precision difficult, is that we are missing a lot of information. Paul's Thessalonian readers knew what he was talking about from previous teachings (2 Thessalonians 2:5–6). He says, "And now ye know what withholdeth…" (2:6a; underline added). This infers that, whatever it is, it was active in the first century and is still today as per "until he be taken out of the way" (v. 7b; underline added). Accordingly, the identity of the "what withholdeth" or the restraining influence is a much-debated topic by New Testament scholars, and it is far too nebulous to take a dogmatic position. Suggestions include the Roman Empire, the Jewish state, Satan and the fallen angels, the angel Michael and holy angels, and the preaching of the Gospel and the Holy Spirit.[233] Even so, the wide variety of opinion should suggest something to the reader. While the Holy Spirit is a popular choice in contemporary evangelical circles, the most widely advocated view historically was the Roman Empire. By this it is meant that the Roman government held back the spirit of iniquity from invading the Church. Given the first few centuries of state-mandated paganism and emperor worship, this may seem odd, but the Church thrived under Roman persecution. In fact it seems that the Church was more biblical when it was underground. Noted Biblical scholar F.F. Bruce argues: "But no more convincing account of the restrainer has been suggested than that put forward by Tertullian (*De resurr. carn.* 24): 'What is this but the Roman state, whose removal when it has been divided among ten kings will bring on Antichrist?' (the reference to the ten kings is an importation from Rev 17:12–14)."[234]

The idea is that the secular government kept a check on the temptation of the Church to become entangled in political power with all of its corruptions. Even so, it still seems difficult for most to credit the Roman Empire as the restraining influence of 2 Thessalonians 2:6. Yet, it is possible to generalize it to secular government in a general way as in the case of separation of church and state.

What one can detect by exegesis of the Greek text was that Paul speaks of it as a force (v.6, *to katechon*, "*what* withholdeth": neuter participle) and as a personal figure (v.7, *ho katechōn*, "*he* who letteth":

masculine participle). The ongoing withholding seemingly rules out the Roman Empire and Jewish state as they died out and Christ did not return. Still, it is possible to think of this as "the rule of law" or government generally as F.F. Bruce advocates.[235] If so, the personal participle seems odd. Because of this, it seems that a personal, supernatural power is required. The Bible speaks of angels or spirits that exercise significant influence and control over people groups, empires, countries, and cities (Ephesians 6:12). Although there is not exhaustive biblical revelation about these powers and principalities, there is enough discussion to affirm their reality and provide some insight. Michael Heiser calls this the "Deuteronomy 32 Worldview": a theological construct based on the oldest manuscripts. Whereas older English translations like the King James read, "according to the number of the children of Israel," they did not have the luxury of the more ancient Hebrew manuscripts discovered in Qumran known as the Dead Sea Scrolls. In those versions of Deuteronomy, as well as in the Greek Septuagint (which was the standard Bible quoted by Jesus and the apostles), God is said to have divided humanity "according to the number of the sons of God," which is a clear reference to angels (Deut. 32:8, ESV; underline added).[236] The passage seems to be teaching that the number of the nations is proportional to the number of angels. In Judaism, the passage was broadly understood to mean that certain angels are associated with specific countries and people groups. The big idea is that there is an underlying spiritual analog to temporal governments.

Of course, in reality, these powers and principalities masquerading as gods are fallen angels and demonic spirits. The same chapter of Deuteronomy that reveals the allocation of the nations to angelic supervision speaks of Israel aggravating God's jealousy by worshipping foreign gods (32:16). It says Israel actually "sacrificed unto devils, not to God; to gods whom they knew not, to new gods that came newly up, whom your fathers feared not" (32:17). These principalities pulled off an effective ruse by deceiving people into thinking that they were the omnipotent potentates of heaven and earth. It is important to make note of their *modus operandi* as I am arguing this is precisely what happened with Roman Catholicism. The Septuagint version of Psalm 96:5 also tears the mask off the pretenders: "For all the gods of the nations <u>are demons</u>, but the Lord made the heavens" (underline added). In other words, all of the prayers, rituals, and sacrifices offered to false gods are, in reality, to fallen angelic imposters appropriating the rightful place of the one true God. Unfortunately, the Roman Catholic Church's many idolatrous and occult practices, like praying to statues of deceased human beings, have placed it under this indictment. This is likely due to the influence of *Roma Dea*, a fallen angel who empowered the Roman Empire.

In the Book of Daniel, the angel Gabriel reports to Daniel that he was delayed twenty-one days due to a battle with the "Prince of the Kingdom of Persia," and was only able to escape when Israel's champion, the arch angel Michael, came to assist (Daniel 10:13–14). Even more, he reports that once he is done battling the Persian spirit he will then face the "Prince of Greece." What immediately comes to mind is that at the time of Daniel's writing, the Persian Empire was in control of most of the world, but it was soon to be conquered by Alexander the Great of Greece. What we have in Daniel is a peek behind the curtain of an extradimensional battle, which finds its analog in our material political sphere. Apparently, some of these angelic powers rebelled against God and have sought worship for themselves by falsely presenting themselves to the people as "gods" (Ps. 82:1–8). The prophet Isaiah foretells the future judgment of these so called gods: "On that day the LORD will punish the host of heaven, in heaven, and the kings of the earth, on the earth" (Isaiah 24:21). It seems likely that the mystery of lawlessness that was already at work was a fallen angelic influence which is still behind Roman popery today. The restraining influence could be Holy angels or the Holy Spirit. The demonic influence was likely behind many of the early heretics and false teachers that Paul and the early Church faced but came in full force as the Church compromised its values by entanglement in worldly affairs.

While it was there from the outset, it began in earnest with the emperor Constantine. Widely heralded as the first Christian Emperor, I (Putnam) am skeptical that he was ever truly converted. After his alleged conversion in AD 312, he retained the title of *Pontifex Maximus* (a title Roman emperors bore as head priests of the pagan priesthood), until his death. This infers his faith was syncretistic, much like the ancient Samaritans, a smorgasbord of occult, pagan, and biblical beliefs. The first references to Constantine's alleged conversion come from the writings of the early Christian writers, Lactantius and Eusebius, both of whom lived during the time of Constantine. While both agree his conversion story is centered on a decisive battle of the Milvian Bridge, they disagree dramatically on the details. Lactantius' account says he converted due to an encounter with the God of the Bible in his dreams, "Constantine was directed in a dream to cause the heavenly sign to be delineated on the shields of his soldiers, and so to proceed to battle. He did as he had been commanded, and he marked on their shields the letter X, with a perpendicular line drawn through it and turned round thus at the top, being the cipher of CHRIST."[237] In Eusebius' account, the *Pontifex Maximus* fears the powerful sorcery of his enemies and turns to the God of his father, Constantius, who was allegedly a Christian (yet his ongoing paganism is well supported):

> [28.1] Accordingly be besought his father's god in prayer, beseeching and imploring him to tell him who he was and to stretch out his right hand to help him in his present difficulties. And while he was thus praying with fervent entreaty, a most incredible sign appeared to him from heaven, the account of which it might have been hard to believe had it been related by any other person. But since the victorious emperor himself long afterwards declared it to the writer of this history, when he was honoured with his acquaintance and society, and confirmed his statement by an oath, who could hesitate to accredit the relation, especially since the

testimony of aftertime has established its truth? He said that about noon, when the day was already beginning to decline, he saw with his own eyes the trophy of a cross of light in the heavens, above the sun, and an inscription, Conquer by This attached to it. At this sight he himself was struck with amazement, and his whole army also, which followed him on an expedition, and witnessed the miracle. [29.1]He said, moreover, that he doubted within himself what the import of this portent could be. And while he continued to ponder and reason on its meaning, night overtook him; then in his sleep the Christ of God appeared to him with the sign which he had seen in the heavens, and commanded him to make a likeness of that sign which he had seen in the heavens, and to use it as a safeguard in all engagements with his enemies.[238]

There are obvious problems reconciling the two accounts. In Eusebius, the paranormal experience took place right before the battle of the Milvian Bridge; but in Lactantius, the dream occurred the night before in his bed and there is no mention of the fantastic heavenly cross-shaped apparition. It is also important to observe that his response does not seem to be the Spirit-led conviction of an undone repentant sinner. His response does not acknowledge his moral need nor the salvation only found in Christ; rather, Constantine makes a pragmatic decision based on his ambition to be victorious in battle. This has none of the earmarks of a true conversion, but rather an expedient stratagem.

Historians are in wide agreement that a year after the battle of the Milvian Bridge, Constantine was instrumental in ending all persecution against the Christians by issuing the Edict of Milan (also known as the Edict of Toleration), which made Christianity a *Religio licita*, or a "legal religion." Nevertheless, it is also clear that Constantine did not patronize Christ exclusively. If he had, it is rather odd that he commemorated the battle he supposedly won through Christ by erecting a triumphal arch of pagan pageantry: the Arch of Constantine. The arch is decorated with images of Victoria the Roman goddess of victory, equivalent of the Greek goddess Nike and all sorts of demonic despotism. It portrays sacrifices to gods like Apollo, Diana, and Hercules, but contains absolutely no Christian symbolism. This is perplexing considering this is supposed to celebrate his alleged vision and victory given by the Christian God. Perhaps he simply had a taste for pagan architecture like America's founding fathers? (Christian J. Pinto's *Riddles in Stone* DVD documentary might lead one to new understanding of America's origins as well.) The historical record and archeological evidence supports the idea that Constantine did continue to worship pagan deities long after his "conversion."

In 321, a full nine years after his alleged conversion, Constantine instructed that Christians and non-Christians should be united in observing the pagan "day of the sun," referencing the esoteric eastern sun-worship which Aurelian had helped introduce, and his coins still were minted with symbols of the sun cult until 324. For example, a bronze coin dated to AD 315 has the image of the Ancient Roman Sun God, Sol Invictus, proudly depicted on the inverse side, with the text: *SOLI INVICTO COMITI* (or, *"To the invincible Sun god, companion of the Emperor"*).[239]

images note 13

Thus, the evidence is very clear that for at least a decade *after* Constantine's alleged conversion, he still worshipped the pagan sun god. Specifically, Sol Invictus (Latin for "Invincible Sun") was around as early as the second century. The previous *Pontifex Maximus* Aurelian made him the official sun god and a state-certified cult alongside the traditional pagan cults in 274. This practice continued for centuries even infiltrating Gnosticism prompting Augustine to address it, "As there is an unconscious worship of idols and devils in the fanciful legends of the Manichaeans, so they knowingly serve the creature in their worship of the sun and moon."[240] Clearly, he did not view it charitably, but there are elements of sun-worship still seen in the Roman religion today.[241]

If we turn to the apostle Paul for our theology, it is abundantly clear that Constantine was still in fellowship with demons. Paul argued to the Church in Corinth, "Rather, that the things which the Gentiles sacrifice they sacrifice to demons and not to God, and I do not want you to have fellowship with demons" (1 Co 10:20). Constantine played both sides. At no time did he make Christianity the official religion. Some might point out the many good works done by the Emperor like his building projects including the Church of the Holy Sepulcher and Old Saint Peter's Basilica. Theologically, Constantine intervened in two doctrinal disputes, one involving Donatism and the other, Arianism.

Donatism, named for Bishop Donatus, entailed the intolerance of the *lapsi*. Because the Church had previously faced intense persecution for not worshipping the official deities, facing death, many relapsed to the required pagan practices. Accordingly, they were called the *lapsi*. When Constantine granted legal status to Christianity, most Christians wanted to welcome back those who apostatized, but the Donatists stridently objected to this forgiveness. Constantine ruled against them. Arianism was the great Trinitarian heresy of antiquity. Arius was a priest from Egypt who taught that Jesus Christ was a created being subordinate to God the Father. Arians were declared heretics. While these were good decisions, Constantine set a dangerous precedent by involving the Roman state in the affairs of the Church. Of course, in the interest of being charitable, Protestants do understand good works to be *evidence* of conversion rather than the impetus of it. So does his post "conversion" behavior support his relationship with Christ?

After his purported conversion experience, Constantine had his wife, Fausta, killed in an over-heated bath[242] and had his eldest son Crispus put to death as well.[243] While the reasons are debated, the rumor was an incestuous affair. Even so, he can be credited with establishing the long lived tradition of Roman Catholic revisionist history, as their names were wiped from the face of many inscriptions, and references to their lives in the literary record were virtually erased by church historians loyal to Constantine.

For instance, some versions of Eusebius' history contain lavish praise for Crispus, but later editions have no mention of him or Fausta. He also ordered the execution of his brother-in-law, Licinius, after a solemn promise of mercy.[244] Is this evidence of saving faith and a contrite heart? One must seriously question the character of anyone who murders his own wife and son and does not keep his solemn vow. While his behavior stands in stark opposition to everything Christ taught, it is remarkably consistent with the record of the Roman Catholic Church with all of its murderous inquisitions. It seems that the Christian faith would have been better served had it remained persecuted and underground. The true Church thrives in persecution. After all, Jesus promised it to His real followers (Mark 13:13; Matthew 10:22).

Finally, I allow a glimmer of hope for Constantine's salvation. It seems clear that he struggled with his faith. The record does indicate his pagan sympathies waned as he matured. His behavior was depraved and deplorable, but short of the sanctification of the spirit, this should be expected of an Emperor with absolute power. It seems that he resisted and doubted the Gospel for most of his career as a

Pontifex Maximus, but God still used him. In this way, he reminds me of King Nebuchadnezzar whom God ultimately humbled and arguably saved as well (cf. Daniel 4). Perhaps Constantine did have a miraculous, divine encounter on the bridge of Milvia. Even so, the evidence does not lead one to conclude this represented his actual conversion. It has been suggested that it could have been a manifestation of the "prince of the power of the air" who had designs on infiltrating the Church with Roman paganism (Ephesians 2:2). Arguably, those designs succeeded as there are elements of sun-worship and necromancy still present in Roman Catholicism.

In fact, the 1908 edition of the Catholic Encyclopedia states that the Sol Invictus festival "has a strong claim on the responsibility for our December date" of Christmas.[245] Whether his vision on the bridge was divine or demonic, the net effect was the same. Pagan rituals and idolatry endure in Roman Catholicism, but even so, Constantine did make life easier for the average Christian believer. It appears that at the very end of his life, much like the thief on the cross, perhaps the Emperor accepted the Gospel on his death bed.

Contrary to the party line on his earlier conversion, Constantine was only baptized after the Feast of Easter in 337 when he fell seriously ill. Ever bargaining with God by promising to live a more Christian life if he survived, the bishops "performed the sacred ceremonies according to custom."[246] Constantine died soon after, on the last day of Pentecost, following the Easter of May 22, 337.[247] The mystery of lawlessness was busy at work establishing the *Pontifex Maximus* as head of the Christian Church. It was when the Church became respectable after Emperor Constantine that venomous rivalries ensued. The Church was granted lands and special privileges. Accordingly, the wrong sort of candidates came forward for the priesthood. Ambition came into conflict with God in the Church. Ultimately, it was a forgery perpetrated in Constantine's name that seems to have decisively carried the Roman church into the kingdom of the Antichrist.

9 | Donation of Constantine and the Road to Hell

When Satan confronted Jesus in the desert, he offered Him the world. Indeed, Satan is often acknowledged as the "god of this world" as in the biblical sense of the term *kosmos* comprising the sensual, the nonspiritual, and the temporal. This is why Faust sells his soul to Mephistopheles for twenty-five years of youth and wealth in the famous legend. Satan is quite happy to trade the things of this world for the one "thing" over which he has no authority…your soul—that is unless you invite him to. Even so, Satan does not really take souls, nor does he really gain anything tangible. He simply hates mankind and takes pride in encouraging rebellion and idolatry. It's the tact he took with Jesus and it is only logical that this was also his strategy with the early Church as well.

The Christian Church began as a small, maltreated minority, worshipping Christ despite the potential horrors of being used as sport

for ravenous lions and suffering the supreme agony of Roman crucifixion. The tales of the early martyrs like Perpetua and Felicity are
awe-inspiring. During the first few hundred years, there were many
great and godly men who led the Church. It was in the crucible of
persecution that the early apologists, Justin Martyr and Tertullian,
were shaped. In the early days after Constantine, the Church, now
highly regarded, was able to take advantage of the infrastructure from
the *Pax Romana* or "Roman peace" which had established a common language and suitable roads in which to evangelize the Empire.
Where the state had once imposed its will on the Church, now the
tables began to slowly turn as the Church began to assert itself over
the kings. Soon, the Church became one with the state and as we
demonstrated prior, the cost to the Gospel was horrific. This did not
happen overnight but there was a pivotal moment when the Church
made a Faustian bargain.

One would hope that after centuries of hiding in the catacombs,
a spirit of religious tolerance would prevail. Unfortunately, the common man had little sway and Christianity, as the new Roman state
religion, was no more tolerant that it's predacious pagan predecessor:

> The code of Justinian confirmed the laws of Theodosius and
> his successors, which declared certain heresies, Manicheism
> and Donatism, crimes against the State, as affecting the
> common welfare. The crime was punishable by confiscation
> of all property, and incompetency to inherit or to bequeath.
> Death did not secure the hidden heretic from prosecution; as
> in high treason, he might be convicted in his grave.[248]

These were brutal times when your religious convictions were legal
matters. Embroiled by the fiery heat from the great schisms between
Rome as the spiritual power and Constantinople as the temporal, the
Emperor Justinian had asserted that the Roman See was the highest
ecclesiastical authority.[249] Be that as it may, Pope Vigilius (r. 537–555)

had a serious bout with the Emperor. It seems that the emperor's wife, Theodora, was an avowed monophysite, the eastern heterodoxy that Jesus had only one nature rather than two. Of course, the biblical view, asserted in the Chalcedonian decree, is that Jesus was both fully God and fully man. Nevertheless, in 553, Justinian called the Fifth General Council to mitigate the findings of the Chaldonian council in order to appease his enraged wife. When Pope Vigilius cowardly pled illness, his absence was not important enough to postpone the proceedings. So much for the primacy of Rome, in this case, doctrine was dictated by the Emperor.

Among other things, the Council expediently decided that the pontiff was a heretic and he was promptly excommunicated. Later, upon exile to an inhospitable island, his doctrinal convictions mysteriously conformed. A prominent Catholic historian writes, "On 8 December 553, he sent a letter to the new Patriarch of Constantinople in which he claimed that till now he had been deluded by 'the wiles of the devil'. Satan had divided him from his fellow bishops but, through the penalty of excommunication, he had seen the light."[250] This frames the papist's claim of Justinian's *Novellae* in support of Rome's primacy in a perverse irony. It was later in 606 that Pope Boniface III sought and gained a reaffirmation from Emperor Phocas for the primacy of Rome. While some regard his arrogant assertion of himself as "Universal Bishop" to be Rome's initial embrace of the Antichrist, it was more like the precursor to a more substantial Faustian bond.

The document, popularly called the "Donation of Constantine," is a counterfeit imperial decree by which the emperor Constantine I supposedly transferred authority over the Western empire and city of Rome along with Judea, Greece, Asia, Thrace, and Africa to pope Sylvester while retaining his imperial authority in the Eastern Roman Empire from his new capital of Constantinople. The forged text claims that the land was Constantine's gift to Pope Sylvester (r. 314–335) for baptizing him, discipling him in the Christian faith, and miraculously healing his leprosy. The forgery clearly telegraphs the papist's lust for worldly power:

> I together with all our satraps and the whole senate and the nobles and all the Roman people, who are subject to the glory of our rule—considered it advisable that, as on earth he (Peter) is seen to have been constituted vicar of the Son of God, so the pontiffs, who are the representatives of that same chief of the apostles, should obtain from us and our empire the power of a supremacy greater than the earthly clemency of our imperial serenity is seen to have had conceded to it— we choosing that same prince of the apostles, or his vicars, to be our constant intercessors with God. And, to the extent of our earthly imperial power, we decree that his holy Roman church shall be honored with veneration; and that, more than our empire and earthly throne, the most sacred seat of St. Peter shall be gloriously exalted; we giving to it the imperial power, and dignity of glory, and vigor and honor. (Donation of Constantine)[251]

It is believed to have been forged near the middle of the eighth century in order to assist Pope Stephen II in his negotiations with the Frankish Mayor of the Palace, Pepin the Short. Pope Stephen had a big problem. He was being boxed in by the invading Lombard armies and desperately needed military aid. Esteemed historian, Edward Gibbon, recorded that Pope Stephen even wrote a letter signed with the Apostle Peter's name as if he were still alive:

> The apostle [Peter] assures his adopted sons, the king, the clergy, and the nobles of France, that, dead in the flesh, he is still alive in the spirit; that they now hear, and must obey, the voice of the founder and guardian of the Roman church; that the Virgin, the angels, the saints, and the martyrs, and

all the host of heaven, unanimously urge the request, and will confess the obligation; that riches, victory, and paradise, will crown their pious enterprise, and that eternal damnation will be the penalty of their neglect, if they suffer his tomb, his temple, and his people, to fall into the hands of the perfidious Lombards.[252]

Stephen had already helped Pepin ascend the throne as part of a political maneuver in which the pope anointed Pepin as king in 751, enabling the Carolingian family to supplant the old Merovingian royal line, which had become decadent and lackadaisical. In return, Pepin promised to give the pope the lands in Italy which the Lombards had taken.

Eventually, Pepin led a military campaign which defeated the Lombards seizing a sizable territory. The fiction of Constantine's gift made it possible for observers to interpret Pepin's land grant, not as a benefaction, but as a restoration. In other words, the king could claim that he was returning (not *giving*) the papal lands to the Church. In this way, the myth of Constantine's donation added legitimacy to the conspiracy between the Roman Church and the Frankish state. Pepin's pay off, known as "the donation of Pepin," was fulfilled in 756. It is a pivotal date because these lands became the basis of the papacy's temporal power which continues to this day as Vatican City. In fact, the Roman religion is the only faith in existence assigned its own US ambassador.

The Roman ecclesia's formal entry into the realm of the *kosmos*, the evil world system in New Testament theology,[253] should not be mitigated to a simple act of political expediency. It marks a proverbial journey down to the crossroads to sell one's soul to the devil. Satan's subsequent occupation of the "See of Rome" is demonstrably evident in the historical record. While this chapter can only scratch the surface of the available evidence, it was during that same mid-eighth-century period, during the reign of Stephen III that particular patterns of brutality (including the torture and blinding of Constantine II who had occupied the papal throne for eighteen months) beckoned the wickedness to come. Not only did the Roman Church continually perpetrate large-scale fraud, they became everything that Jesus passionately argued that His kingdom was not.

Jesus taught clearly that in this present age the devil is the prince of this world (John 12:31; 14:30). It is not surprising that the Gospel was abandoned as the popes sought Satan's role. The Church's business is to worship, nurture the flock, declare the good news and make disciples until *Jesus returns to deal with the temporal.* The role of the Church certainly is not the impertinent pursuit of world domination through political power and dishonest manipulation in His name. But that is exactly what Rome has always done. It should be instructive that it was the devil's device in the temptation of Christ (Matthew 4:9). Over and over again, Christ rejected such an aim, saying that His kingdom is not of this world (John 18:36) and He taught His disciples not to behave like the rulers of the world (Matthew 20:25). Recognizing this, Martin Luther argued:

> He [Christ] says even more clearly in Luke 17[:20–21], "The kingdom of God is not coming with signs to be observed; nor will anyone say, 'Lo, here it is!' 'There!' for behold, the kingdom of God is within you." I am surprised that these Romanists regard such a clear and strong saying of Christ as nothing but a carnival mask. Everyone can clearly understand from it that the kingdom of God (for this is what he calls his Christendom) is not in Rome, is not bound to Rome, and is neither here nor there. Rather, it is where there is inward faith, whether the man be in Rome, or wherever he may be. Therefore, it is a stinking lie and opposes Christ as though he were a liar to say that Christendom is in Rome, or is bound to Rome, much less that its head and power are there because of divine order.[254]

Of course, living a few centuries later, Luther had the advantage of scholarship which turned the Romanist's quest for power by deception on its ear. In the Renaissance, better training made it possible for scholars to compare such documents with the genuine articles from antiquity.

While Nicholas of Cusa was one of the first to notice that the *Donation* did not agree with other ancient documents, the brilliant scholar Lorenzo Valla proved conclusively that the document was a fraud. Catholic historian, Peter De Rosa, writes, "Valla showed that the pope at the alleged time of the Donation was not Sylvester but Miltiades. The text refers to 'Constantinople' whereas Constantine's city in the East still retained its original name of Byzantium. The Donation was written not in classical Latin but in a later bastardized form. Also, explanations are given, say, of Constantine's regalia, which would not have been needed in the fourth century but were necessary in the eighth. In a hundred irrefutable ways, Valla shot the document to pieces."[255] To any scholar, it is full of sophomoric errors, as the Latin in the document could not have been written in the fourth century and the purported date is internally inconsistent.[256] Valla revealed this around 1450 in the service of King Alfonso of Aragon, Sicily and Naples, who was attempting to make property claims to various parts of Italy. Even so, his work was not published until 1517. Although, it was obvious to the intellectually honest, Rome did not concede and continued to use the document for centuries. We now turn back to the end of the first millennium as Rome asserted her debase determination to dominate.

As the Roman church became a worldly power, the popes increasingly relegated their spiritual duties secondary to their function as the heads of an Italian state. They used the Donation of Constantine extensively to oppose the territorial ambitions of their neighbors while justifying their own. Apathy toward spiritual matters grew as they built an empire on a lie. During this phase of Western history, there was a marked decline in the moral character of those who came into positions of power in both the secular and ecclesiastical realms. Within the Roman religious system, the last vestiges of spiritual fruit putrefied. Many of the priesthood were biblically illiterate and had little theological training. Beginning about the middle of the eighth century and continuing into the eleventh, one uncovers nearly three centuries of continuous apostasy, sorcery, lasciviousness, war, and wanton destruction. The integrity of the ecclesiastical system collapsed of its own internal rot.

These resulting years of darkness (757–1046) are ignominiously titled the "Pornocracy" or "Dark Age" by historians because of their unparalleled licentiousness. Demonic weirdness defines the era. In one extremely odd legend, even Rome's scholars have allowed for the possibility that a woman surreptitiously served as pope during this time. Bartolomeo Platina (1421–1481), the prefect of the Vatican Library, recorded an accounting of the Pope Joan legend. Platina dealt with the possibility of its veracity in the person of Pope John VIII (r. 872–82) writing, "John, of English extraction but born at Mentz, is said to have arrived at the Popedom by evil arts; for disguising herself like a man, whereas she was a woman, she went."[257] While we cannot know for sure whether John VIII was a John or a Joan, the papal practice of evil arts is much more defined than the Pope Joan legends. The ex-Jesuit, De Rosa, writes of the medieval popes, "They were less disciples of Christ than of Belial, the Prince of Darkness. Very many were libertines, murderers, adulterers, warmongers, tyrants, simoniacs who were prepared to sell everything holy. They were nearly all more wrapped up in money and intrigue than in religion."[258] A macabre model of this papal wickedness is vividly demonstrated by the "Cadaver Synod."

Pope Formosus (r. 891–896) was a pro-Carolingian Pontiff who had political opponents in Spoleto and northern Italy. When Formosus died, his opponents secured the election of Stephen VII (r. 896–897), who hated Formosus with a passion. Pope Stephen VII dug up his departed predecessor nine months post-interment and held a bizarre tribunal. He adorned the rotten corpse in full papal regalia, placed him on the throne, and proceeded to interrogate him while an altar boy sheepishly served as the deceased defendant's voice. Pope Stephen charged Formosus with taking office under false pretenses and declared all of his papal acts and ordinations invalid. After he was condemned as an antipope, his fingers used for blessing were cut off and his malodorous corpse was unceremoniously pitched into the Tiber River. Within a year, the fickle tide of political favor went back out and Pope Stephen VII was snatched up by a mob, arrested, and strangled.[259] While it hardly seems possible, things actually go downhill from here.

As the first millennium approached, debauchery ruled the day. For two generations, the corrupted houses of Theophylact, Alberic, and Marozia dominated Rome and the papacy. Marozia, a Roman noblewoman, was the mother of one pope, John XI, and the concubine of another, Pope Sergius III. While most people are familiar with the papal practice of changing names upon election, few are aware of its inauspicious beginnings. It has been the common practice since 955, like when Cardinal Joseph Aloisius Ratzinger became known simply as Benedict XVI. Unbeknownst to most, the practice began institutionally at the height of the pornocracy, when the teenaged Octavianus, a descendent of King Charlemagne, called himself Pope John XII in 955.[260] He was the pinnacle of a pornocrat. Even the Catholic encyclopedia concedes that, "The temporal and spiritual authority in Rome were thus again united in one person—a coarse, immoral man, whose life was such that the Lateran was spoken of as a brothel, and the moral corruption in Rome became the subject of general odium."[261] It is also a matter of record that during Pope John XII's reign, overt papal Satanism infected Rome's infrastructure. In the *Patrologia Latina*, an enormous collection of ancient manuscripts, it was recorded that, "All clerics as well as laymen, declared that he had toasted to the devil with wine. They said when playing at dice, he invoked Jupiter, Venus and other demons."[262] The pope toasted to the devil. One would think that constitutes a break in the chain of apostolic succession. While Rome's apologists play this off as an aberration, the fruit of the medieval papacy reveal it was closer to the rule.

Pope Sylvester II (r. 999–1003), born Gerbert d'Aurillac, was reputed to have studied occult lore while a young man in Seville, then under the control of the Muslims. He was the first French Pope and undoubtedly a very gifted man in science and math, having studied under the Moors in Spain. As the legend goes he had lived there with a practitioner of the black arts who possessed a grimoire which could subdue the devil to its masters will. As the account goes, he stole the book and made a pact with the devil, trading his soul to become pope. The bargain entailed that he was to enjoy the opulence of the papacy as long as he refrained from conducting high mass in Jerusalem. Cambridge scholar E. M. Butler reveals, "Gerbert was believed to have carnal intercourse with the devil and to be accompanied by a familiar spirit in the form of a shaggy black dog. He was supposed to be able to blind his adversaries and to divine hidden treasure by the much-execrated practice of necromancy."[263] He was also one of the first medieval magicians to purportedly create a "brazen head" (a robotic human head that could answer yes or no questions). Based on his pact, Pope Sylvester thought he was secure as long as he avoided the Holy Land; but he was tricked when he conducted mass in the Jerusalem church at Rome (*Santa Croce in Jersalemme*).[264] After he realized he had been hoodwinked, he was already surrounded by demons. Knowing his number was up, he allegedly made a full confession denouncing his relations with the demonic and instructed that his body be dismembered and interred at the spot dictated by two free roaming horses. The horses delivered his hacked remains to the Lateran church. To this day, it is believed that his tomb at the Lateran church moans and his bones audibly rattle just prior to the death of the sitting pope. If the Prophecy of the Popes holds true, the time to listen draws near. While this is the stuff of legends, our next example is firmly rooted in historical fact.

Pope Silvester II and the Devil
images note 14

According to Clunian monk Raoul Glaber, Pope Benedict IX (1012–1056) was elected at an unprecedented eleven years of age. Born in Rome as Theophylactus of Tusculum, he holds the great privilege of being the only pope to hold office on more than one occasion and the only pontiff to ever have sold the papacy. The German scholar, Ferdinand Gregorovius, wrote in his acclaimed history of the city of Rome that Pope Benedict was, "a demon from hell in the disguise of a priest, [who] occupied the chair of Peter and profaned the sacred mysteries of religion by his insolent courses."[265] The Catholic encyclopedia demurs only reporting, "He was a disgrace to the Chair of Peter."[266] That appears to be a colossal understatement as he was reported to have indulged in sorcery and demonolatry as well as being a practicing homosexual who indulged in an occasional fling of bestiality.[267] Various murderous intrigues resulted in his leaving and reclaiming the pontificate three times. Eventually, he tired of papal orgies and decided to marry. He summarily auctioned off the papacy for a couple thousand pounds of gold. Now how about that for the doctrine of apostolic succession?

Because of the rampant sexual immorality, many scholars of the medieval period would promote Pope Gregory VII (r. 1073–85) as a fresh breeze of morality because he is credited with establishing the rule of priestly celibacy. In truth, the rule of celibacy has been an albatross to the priesthood by forcing them to pursue proscribed means of satisfaction. He also ostensibly fought against corruption, and attempted to reconcile the Eastern and Western Churches. Although the Catholic encyclopedia hails him as a great reformer, he attempted to vastly expand the papal empire by corrupt means. Using forged documents, the Donation of Constantine and pseudo-Isidorian Decretals, he laid claim to Corsica, Sardinia, Spain, and Hungary as papal property.[268] Johann Joseph Ignaz von Döllinger, a renowned Roman Catholic historian, who taught Church history for nearly half a century in Rome's service, remarks:

In the middle of the ninth century, about 845, there arose the huge fabrication of the Isidorian decretals. About a hundred pretended decrees of the earliest Popes, together with certain spurious writings of other Church dignitaries and acts of Synods, were then fabricated in the west of Gaul, and eagerly seized upon Pope Nicholas I at Rome, to be used as genuine documents in support of the new claims put forward by himself and his successors. That the pseudo–Isidorian principles eventually revolutionized the whole constitution of the Church, and introduced a new system in place of the old, on that point there can be no controversy among candid historians. The most potent instrument of the new

Papal system was Gratian's *Decretum*, which issued about the middle of the twelfth century from the first school of Law in Europe, the juristic teacher of the whole of Western Christendom, Bologna. In this work the Isidorian forgeries were combined with those of the other Gregorian (Gregory VII) writers...and with Gratia's own additions. His work displaced all the older collections of canon law, and became the manual and repertory, not for canonists only, but for the scholastic theologians, who, for the most part, derived all their knowledge of Fathers and Councils from it. No book has ever come near it in its influence in the Church, although there is scarcely another so chokeful of gross errors, both intentional and unintentional.[269]

As we saw in chapter 2, the pseudo-Isidorian Decretals have important implications for the Malachian Prophecy of the Popes because they are an early example of the practice of altering original ancient documents in such a way as to promote a political agenda. Rome is a master at changing history to affect the future. It is undisputed by historians that the majority of the Gregory VII's claims were based on lies and forgeries. Even so, he excommunicated King Henry IV twice over various political power struggles between Church and Empire. His megalomania is also well-documented.

What follows is a small sample taken from the twenty-seven propositions of the *Dictatus Papae*, otherwise known as the *Dictates of Hildebrand* (under the name of Pope Gregory VII):

- 2. That the Roman pontiff alone is justly styled universal.
- 6. That no person...may live under the same roof with one excommunicated by the Pope.
- 9. That all princes should kiss his [the pope's] feet only.

- 12. That it may be permitted to him to depose emperors.
- 19. That he [the pope] can be judged by no one.
- 22. That the Roman Church never erred, nor will it, according to the scripture, ever err.[270]

The unmitigated arrogance is breathtaking. Since the Roman Church ostensibly never erred, he necessarily endorsed the most debauched deeds of the pornocracy as a form of piety. Of course, he identified himself with Peter, as the rock on which the Church was built and the keeper of the keys of the kingdom but he forgot that in temporal affairs, Peter was a humble subject under a persecuting government, and still urged the Christians to honor the king at a time when an antichristian despot, Nero, reigned supreme (1 Peter 2:17). But Gregory VII was likely more than a simple megalomaniac.

While he is still held in high esteem by modern Romanists, Gregory VII was widely believed to be a practicing occultist. There are many such legends, but as a representative example, we offer a fascinating incident preserved in the writings of John Foxe:

Upon a certain time this Gregory, coming from Albanus to Rome, had forgot behind him his familiar book of necromancy, which he was wont commonly to carry always with him. Whereupon remembering himself, on entering the port of Lateran, he calleth two of his most trusty familiars to fetch the book, charging them on no account to look within it. But they being so restrained, were the more desirous to open it, and to peruse it, and so did. After they had read a little the secrets of the satanical book, suddenly there came about them the messengers of Satan, the multitude and terror of whom made them almost out of their wits. At length, they coming to themselves, the spirits were instant upon them to know wherefore they were called up, wherefore they were vexed; "quickly," said they, "tell us what ye would us to do, or else we will fall upon you, if ye retain us longer." Then spake one of the young men to them, bidding them go and pluck down yonder walls, pointing unto certain high walls there nigh to Rome, which they did in a moment. The young men crossing them for fear of the spirits, and scarcely recovering themselves, at length came to their master.[271]

Rome's apologists may attempt to diminish it all as legends and trumped up charges, but the historical record is clear. Henry the IV called him "The False Monk" due to all of his high-handed deceptions. In the end, Henry IV won the day and Pope Gregory VII was unseated on the grounds of sorcery and magic and replaced by anti-pope Clement III.[272] Accordingly, he died in infamy while exiled to the southwestern city of Salerno.

There have been many other popes who were suspected of sorcery; for example, John XXI (1276–77) and Benedict XII (1334–42). Pope Gregory XII (1406–15) was formally questioned about magical practices in 1409 at the Council of Pisa. The Dominican Bishop and Catholic Saint Albertus Magnus was believed to be an occultist who conjured a talking brazen head similar to that of Silvester II, albeit it was smashed for annoying his disciple Thomas Aquinas. Poor Aquinas, an erudite apologist, has nevertheless earned his infamy for basing much of his argumentation on Rome's forgeries of the Church fathers in the *Thesaurus of Greek Fathers*. Aquinas used many of the spurious passages in his work, *Against the Errors of the Greeks*, probably thinking they were genuine.[273] Whether he knew it or not, he was under the tutelage of a known occultist, alchemist, and magician in Albertus Magnus. Rome's sorcery will be dealt with in a more direct fashion in another chapter; the point here is that there is a well-documented basis for the assertion that with the Donation of Pepin in 756, the Roman Church sold their ecclesiastic soul and, as a result, their lampstand was removed.

There is abundant historical evidence to sustain the conclusion of correlation between the beginning of the pornocracy and the formation of the Papal States. In 756, the Faustian bargain was transacted bringing all of its inherent potential for despotism. It seems inevitable that unsavory individuals would actively seek the power of the office and use it for Satan's purposes. During this time, the Bible was banned and the Gospel was suppressed. A leading evangelist of the first great awakening, Jonathan Edwards, wrote:

> During this time also superstition and ignorance more and more prevailed. The Holy Scriptures by degrees were taken out of the hands of the laity, the better to promote the unscriptural and wicked designs of the pope and the clergy; and instead of promoting knowledge among the people, they industriously promoted ignorance. It was a received maxim among them, That ignorance is the mother of devotion: and so great was the darkness of those times, that learning was almost extinct in the world. The very priests themselves, most of them, were barbarously ignorant as to any commendable learning, or any other knowledge, than their hellish craft in oppressing and tyrannizing over the souls of the people. —The superstition and wickedness of the church of Rome, kept growing worse and worse till the very time of the Reformation, and the whole christian [*sic*] world were led away into this great defection, excepting the remains of the christian [*sic*] church in the Eastern empire that had not been utterly overthrown by the Turks. The Greek church, and some others, were also sunk into great darkness and gross superstition, excepting also those few that were the people of God, who are represented by the woman in the wilderness, and God's two witnesses, of which more hereafter. —This is one of those two great kingdoms which the devil in this period erected in opposition to the kingdom of Christ, and was the greatest and chief.[274]

In the fusing together of tremendous political, temporal, and military strength along with ecclesiastical authority, there was produced, albeit unintentionally, almost unlimited potential for tyrannical power. In view of the great emphasis which has traditionally been placed upon the Petrine Doctrine and the concept of apostolic succession, it follows that all modern popes are necessarily the successors of these devils.

This brief examination of papal darkness should be mistaken as the condemnation of all Catholics. There were always true followers of Jesus in the Church despite its rampant corruption. The problem is that when men of conscience spoke up, they were often excommunicated and killed. Even so, some spoke out boldly. One was John Peter of Oliva (died 1297), whose works were anathematized as "blasphemous and heretical." One of the more revealing in reference to Mystery Babylon of Revelation 17 reads:

> The woman here stands for the people and empire of Rome, both as she existed formerly in a state of Paganism, and as she has since existed, holding the faith of Christ, though by many crimes committing harlotry with this world. And, therefore, she is called a great harlot; for, departing from the faithful worship, the true love and delights of her Bridegroom, even Christ her God, she cleaves to this world, its riches and delights; yea, for their sake she cleaves to the devil, also to kings, nobles, and prelates, and to all other lovers of this world. She saith in her heart, that is, in her pride, I sit a queen: —I am at rest; I rule over my kingdom with great dominion and glory. And I am no widow: —I am not destitute of glorious bishops and kings.[275]

It seems that many within the Church increasingly saw the painful truth and this was the impetus for the Protestant Reformation.

10 | Mystery Babylon Meets Dante's Inferno

T|he *Divine Comedy* by Dante Alighieri, written between 1308 and 1321, is widely considered to be one of the greatest works of world literature. The epic poem's ingenious allegorical vision of the afterlife is the zenith of the medieval worldview as developed by the Roman Church. Some dubious theology aside, it is divided into three parts: the Inferno (Hell), Purgatorio (Purgatory), and Paradiso (Heaven). The poem spins a theatrical yarn, weaving Dante's travels through hell, purgatory, and heaven with subtle yet subversive social commentary on the papacy and other controversial topics. Dante's revolutionary skill is often lost on modern readers unfamiliar with the issues of his day.

The poem begins the night before Good Friday in the year 1300. Dante is lost in a dark wood where he is assailed by wild beasts: a lion, leopard, and a wolf. After realizing he cannot find his way (salvation) he knows that he is falling into a deep, dark place where the sun never shines (damnation). At last, he is rescued by Virgil, the heroic Roman poet of the Augustan era, and the two of them begin a journey into the darkest depths of the underworld. Allegorically, the three beasts he encountered represent three types of sin: the self-indulgent, the violent, and the malicious. These categories also correspond to levels of punishment in the inferno. The popes invariably merit the worst of the worst.

There are nine circles of hell in Dante's Inferno. While the upper levels are reserved for self-indulgent sins like lust and gluttony, it is quite telling that the sins of the Roman Church are reserved for the lower levels of eight and nine. These are sins of malice like fraud and treachery. Interestingly, in the sub circles, one through six of circle eight, we find headings of fraud, pimping, seducing, flattery, simony, and sorcery. Within these are allusions to Pope Nicholas III, Pope Boniface VIII, Pope Clement V, and the infamous *Donation of Constantine.*

> Your avarice O'ercasts the world with mourning, under foot
> Treading the good, and raising bad men up.
> Of shepherds like to you, the Evangelist
> Was ware, when her, who sits upon the waves,
> With kings in filthy whoredom he beheld;
> She who with seven heads tower'd at her birth,
> And from ten horns her proof of glory drew,
> Long as her spouse in virtue took delight.
> Of gold and silver ye have made your god,
> Differing wherein from the idolater,
> But that he worships one, a hundred ye?
> Ah, Constantine! to how much ill gave birth,
> Not thy conversion, but that plenteous dower,
> Which the first wealthy Father gain'd from thee.[276]

With the line "Ah, Constantine! to how much ill gave birth," Dante alludes to the bogus temporal gifting by Constantine to Pope

Sylvester. In this way, Dante understood the New Testament concept of a composite society much better than the supposed scriptural authorities of his day. Accordingly, Dante was an early advocate for the proper separation of church and state. Although he was unaware it was a complete fraud, he blamed the *Donation of Constantine* as the cause of the worldly ambitions of the papacy (*Infero* 19.115–7). This seems to support our overarching thesis that AD 756 marked a Faustian bargain. Dante alluded to the donation of Constantine again. This time in the *Paradisio* section of the Divine Comedy (20.55):

> The other following, with the laws and me,
> To yield the Shepherd room, pass'd o'er to Greece;
> From good intent, producing evil fruit:
> Now knoweth he, how all the ill, derived
> From his well doing, doth not harm him aught;
> Though it have brought destruction on the world.[277]

In this brief passage, Dante expresses that the destruction of the world had been wrought by the marriage of church and state. It harkens Malachy's apocalypse under Petrus Romanus. The line to "yield the shepherd room" refers to the pope as a shepherd and "pass'd o'er to Greece" is reflective of Constantine's ostensibly gifting the entire Roman state to the pope while moving to Constantinople. *The Divine Comedy* was not alone in its disdain for the papist's worldly ambitions. Dante's *De Monarchâ* book 3 explicitly challenges the theocratic conception of the power elaborated by the papal bull *Unam Sanctam* of 1302. Pope Boniface VIII is regarded by many as one of the most evil persons who ever lived. He was incessantly battling King Phillip IV over power and wealth. Dante was not alone; it is widely known that Boniface purchased the papal office and was corrupt to his core. They even tried him for simony *after* he died. Even worse, at his posthumous trial he was also charged with sodomy.[278] The notorious papal bull which follows, *Unam Sanctum*, was also a major impetus for the

Protestant reformation. It is so foundational to a proper understanding of Rome's disease we have reproduced it in its entirety for your own evaluation.

UNAM SANCTAM

Urged by faith, we are obliged to believe and to maintain that the Church is one, holy, catholic, and also apostolic. We believe in her firmly and we confess with simplicity that outside of her there is neither salvation nor the remission of sins, as the Spouse in the Canticles [Sgs 6:8] proclaims: "One is my dove, my perfect one. She is the only one, the chosen of her who bore her," and she represents one sole mystical body whose Head is Christ and the head of Christ is God [1 Cor 11:3]. In her then is one Lord, one faith, one baptism [Eph 4:5]. There had been at the time of the deluge only one ark of Noah, prefiguring the one Church, which ark, having been finished to a single cubit, had only one pilot and guide, i.e., Noah, and we read that, outside of this ark, all that subsisted on the earth was destroyed.

We venerate this Church as one, the Lord having said by the mouth of the prophet: "Deliver, O God, my soul from the sword and my only one from the hand of the dog [Ps 21:20]." He has prayed for his soul, that is for himself, heart and body; and this body, that is to say, the Church, He has called one because of the unity of the Spouse, of the faith, of the sacraments, and of the charity of the Church. This is the tunic of the Lord, the seamless tunic, which was not rent but which was cast by lot [Jn 19:23–24]. Therefore, of the one and only Church there is one body and one head, not two heads like a monster; that is, Christ and the Vicar of Christ, Peter and the successor of Peter, since the Lord speaking to Peter Himself said: "Feed my sheep [Jn 21:17]," meaning, my sheep in general, not these, nor those in particular, whence we understand that He entrusted all to him [Peter]. Therefore, if the Greeks or others should say that they are not confided to Peter and to his successors, they must confess not being the sheep of Christ, since Our Lord says in John "there is one sheepfold and one shepherd." We are informed by the texts of the gospels that in this Church and <u>in its power are two swords</u>; namely, the spiritual <u>and the temporal</u>. For when the Apostles say: "Behold, here are two swords" [Lk 22:38] that is to say, in the Church, since the Apostles were speaking, the Lord did not reply that there were too many, but sufficient. Certainly the one who denies that the temporal sword is in the power of Peter has not listened well to the word of the Lord commanding: "Put up thy sword into thy scabbard [Mt 26:52]." Both, therefore, are in the power of the Church, that is to say, the spiritual and the material sword, but the former is to be administered _for_ the Church but the latter by the Church; the former in the hands of the priest; the latter by the hands of kings and soldiers, but at the will and sufferance of the priest.

However, one sword ought to be subordinated to the other and <u>temporal authority, subjected to spiritual power</u>. For since the Apostle said: "There is no power except from God and the things that are, are ordained of God [Rom 13:1–2]," but they would not be ordained if one sword were not subordinated to the other and if the inferior one, as it were, were not led upwards by the other.

For, according to the Blessed Dionysius, it is a law of the divinity that the lowest things reach the highest place by intermediaries. Then, according to the order of the universe, all things are not led back to order equally and immediately, but the lowest by the intermediary, and the inferior by the superior. Hence we must recognize the more clearly that spiritual power surpasses in dignity and in nobility any temporal power whatever, as spiritual things surpass the temporal. This we see very clearly also by the payment, benediction, and consecration of the tithes, but the acceptance of power itself and by the government even of things. For with truth as our witness, it belongs to spiritual power to establish the terrestrial power and to pass judgment if it has not been good. Thus is accomplished the prophecy of Jeremias concerning the Church and the ecclesiastical power: "Behold to-day I have placed you over nations, and over kingdoms' and the rest. Therefore, if the terrestrial power err, it will be judged by the spiritual power; but if a minor spiritual power err, it will be judged by a superior spiritual power; but if the highest power of all err, it can be judged only by God, and not by man, according to the testimony of the Apostle: "The spiritual man judgeth of all things and he himself is judged by no man [1 Cor 2:15]." This authority, however, (though it has been given to man and is exercised by man), is not human but rather divine, granted to Peter by a divine word and reaffirmed to him (Peter) and his successors by the One Whom Peter confessed, the Lord saying to Peter himself, "Whatsoever you shall bind on earth, shall be bound also in Heaven" etc., [Mt 16:19]. Therefore whoever resists this power thus ordained by God, resists the ordinance of God [Rom 13:2], unless he invent like Manicheus two beginnings, which is false and judged by us heretical, since according to the testimony of Moses, it is not in the beginnings but in the beginning that God created heaven and earth [Gen 1:1]. Furthermore, we declare, we proclaim, we define that it is absolutely necessary for salvation that every human creature be subject to the Roman Pontiff.[279] (underline added)

Perhaps you can now imagine why in the *Inferno*, Dante placed Boniface VIII in the eighth circle of Hell, but not only that, he was upside down inside a furnace! Although previous popes had made similar claims, the theocratic treatise *Unam Sanctum* claimed virtual omnipotence for the pope. He truly believed he was God on earth. Of course, this meant the pope could legitimately intervene in matters usually controlled by secular authority. Ahead of his time in many ways, Dante expressed a philosophy that man essentially pursues two aspects: the earthly life and eternal life. Dante argued that the pope was assigned the spiritual (the eternal), but the emperor had charge over the earthly (the temporal). Accordingly, the emperor exercises autonomy over the material sphere, while the immaterial sphere is under the pope. In other words, he saw the *Donation of Constantine* and megalomaniacal tirades like *Unam Sanctum* as an assault on proper church/state separation. Although the fact that the *Donation* was a sophomoric forgery had yet to be proved, Dante shows remarkable prescience in his skepticism. This is an excerpt from *De Monarchâ:*

> Their proof is no proof, for Constantine had not the power to alienate the imperial dignity, nor had the Church power to receive it. Their insistent objection to what I say can be met thus. No one is free to do through an office assigned him anything contrary to the office, for thereby the same thing, in virtue of being the same, would be contrary to itself, which is impossible. But to divide the Empire would be contrary to the office assigned the Emperor, for as is easily seen from the first book of the treatise, his office is to hold the human race subject to one will in all things. Therefore, division of his Empire is not allowed an Emperor. If, as they claim, certain dignities were alienated by Constantine from the Empire and ceded to the power of the Church, the "seamless coat" would have been rent, which even they had not dared to mutilate who with their spears pierced Christ, the very God. Moreover, as the Church has its own foundation, so has the

Empire its own. The foundation of the Church is Christ, as the Apostle writes to the Corinthians: "Other foundation can no man lay than that is laid, which is Jesus Christ." He is the rock on which the Church is founded, but the foundation of the Empire is human right.[280]

Dante believed that the Emperor and the pope were both fallible humans and that both derived their power and authority only from God. He contended that, as a fallen creature, man occupies an intermediate position between sinfulness and holiness. Because man is composed of body and soul, he is corruptible. Ultimately, because of death it is only in terms of the soul that he is incorruptible. Man, then, has the function of reconciling corruptibility with incorruptibility. Because both the emperor and pope are human, only a higher power could judge the two "equal swords," as each was given power by God to rule over their respected domains. Dante's argument had force then and it still rings true in a broad sense today. It is the same line of reasoning that is behind the separation clause in the United States Constitution: a document which has also been viciously attacked by the Vatican.

Lest the reader be bewitched by Rome's current sophistry that such papal megalomania was all relegated to ancient history, we leap forward in time to reproduce a small sampling of the 1864 *Syllabus of Errors* by Pope Pius IX. When reading these, keep in mind these items are *condemned.*

15. That each person is free to adopt and follow that religion which seems best to the light of reason…
18. That Protestantism is simply a different form of the same Christian religion, and that it is possible to please God in it as well as in the true Catholic church…
21. That the church does not have the power to declare as a dogma that its religion is the only true religion…

24. That the church has no authority to make use of force, nor does it have temporal power...
30. That the immunity of the church and of ecclesiastics is based on civil law...
37. That it is lawful to institute national churches, separate and completely independent of the Roman pontiff...
47. That the good order of civil society requires that public schools, open to children of all classes, and in general all public institutions devoted to the teaching of literature and science, and to the education of youth, be free of all authority on the part of the church, of all its moderating influence, and be subject only to the civil and political authority, so that they may behave according to the opinions of civil magistrates and to the common opinion of the time...
55. That the church ought to be separate from the state, and the state from the church...
77. That in our time it is no longer convenient that the Catholic religion be the only religion of the state, or that every other religion be excluded.
78. That it is therefore praiseworthy that in some Catholic countries the law allows immigrants to practice publicly their own forms of worship.
79. That it is false that, if all religions are granted civil freedom, and all are allowed to express publicly their opinions and ideas, no matter what they may be, this will facilitate moral and mental corruption, and will spread the plague of indifferentism.
80. That the Roman pontiff can and should be reconciled with, and agree to, progress, liberalism, and modern civilization.[281]

It is beyond the scope of this book to provide an adequate accounting of events leading up to, including, and following the Protestant

Reformation and Roman Counter Reformation. The crusades and the inquisitions not only entailed brutalizing Muslims and Jews but also included the unmitigated slaughter of Bible-believing Christians like the Waldenses and Huguenots in the name of the Roman Catholic Church. We can hardly give them justice by our brief survey. If this history is all new to you and you would like to get up-to-speed quickly, we commend to the reader the documentary film, *A Lamp in the Dark: The Untold History of the Bible*, by our brother-in-Christ, Christian J. Pinto. It covers a lot of the ground about men like John Wycliffe, Martin Luther, William Tyndale, and Myles Coverdale who paid a high price to get the word of God into the hands of the common man. If anything, the Dark Ages were so black because of widespread biblical illiteracy which was institutionally promoted by the Romanists who feared what honest men would conclude if they compared the papists to the prophetic word. As the Bible increasingly made it into more men's hands, they quickly identified the papacy as the spirit of Antichrist and the Roman Magisterium as Mystery Babylon the Great. First, we shall examine Rome in light of Revelation chapter 17 and then we will examine the spirit of Antichrist.

Mystery Babylon the Great

Rome has never relinquished her dominionist dream of world domination under papal power. For instance, the Catholic interpretation of Nebuchadnezzar's famous dream in Daniel chapter 2 posits the Roman Catholic Church as the conquering champion in place of Christ. The Anglican-turned-Romanist, Cardinal John Henry Newman, presented it like this:

> Not even Daniel's prophecies are more exact to the letter, than those which invest the Church with powers which Protestants consider Babylonish. Nay, holy Daniel himself is in no small measure employed on this very subject. He it is who announces a fifth kingdom, like "a stone cut out

without hands," which "broke in pieces and consumed" all former kingdoms, but was itself to "stand forever." and to become "a great mountain," and "to fill the whole earth." He it is also who prophesies that "the Saints of the most High shall take the kingdom and possess the kingdom forever."[282]

In other words, he believes the Roman Catholic Church is "the stone cut out of the mountain without hands" (Daniel 2:45). It is Rome who is the "kingdom, which shall never be destroyed: and the kingdom shall not be left to other people, but it shall break in pieces and consume all these kingdoms, and it shall stand for ever" (Daniel 2:44). Charles Hodge presented this example in his seminal *Systematic Theology* and concluded, "If this be not to put itself in the place of God, it is hard to see how the prophecies concerning Antichrist can ever be fulfilled. No more conclusive argument to prove that the papacy is Antichrist, could be constructed, than that furnished by Dr. Newman, himself a Romanist. According to him the prophecies respecting the glory, the exaltation, the power, and the universal dominion of Christ, have their fulfilment in the popes."[283] Whereas Hodge sees the papacy as the Antichrist, we would qualify that to be more in the spirit of antichrist. Yet, Malachy's vision diverges significantly from Newman's Romanist megalomania. And, it is not denied by any Roman Catholic scholar that Malachy's prophecy very explicitly speaks of the destruction of Rome:

In extreme persecution, the seat of the Holy Roman Church will be occupied by Peter the Roman, who will feed the sheep through many tribulations; when they are over, <u>the city of seven hills will be destroyed</u>, and the terrible or fearsome Judge will judge his people.[284] (underline added)

But it is for this reason that the papists would most certainly have a vested interest in discrediting the Malachian vision. We took into account only two, O'Brien and Thurston, from amongst a large constituency of Jesuit scholars who have argued it was simply a forgery. It is for this reason that John Hogue argued, "Any document that predicted an end to the Roman Catholic Church and the final destruction of Rome would certainly warrant the launching of an anti-information campaign. Enter the Jesuits, the harshest critics of these prophecies."[285] This makes the favorable scholarship of the Belgian Jesuit, Rene Thibaut, even more exceptional. We will examine his interpretation of the apocalyptic codex in a later chapter, but we turn now to the pressing prophetic implications.

While Malachy's prediction seems devastating to their visions of worldwide Romanism, the ten-thousand-pound elephant in the room for the Roman Catholic Church is that the predicted destruction of the seven-hilled city also identifies the Roman Catholic Church as "MYSTERY, BABYLON THE GREAT, THE MOTHER OF HARLOTS AND ABOMINATIONS OF THE EARTH" (Revelation 17:5). The identification by association is inescapable. The woman that rides the scarlet-colored beast is very clearly described as a city that sits on seven mountains that rules over the kings of the earth (cf. Revelation 17:9; 17:8). The coherence is remarkable and it seems to us to be conclusive. If one accepts the veracity of Malachy's vision, then the Roman Catholic Church is necessarily the woman who rides the beast. Even so, biblical scholars have long associated the mysterious harlot with the city of Rome.

The literary genre of the book of Revelation is called apocalyptic. Because this is a visionary genre, it is notoriously difficult to interpret. According to the top scholars in conservative biblical studies today, "Apocalyptic describes prophecies in which God 'reveals' his hidden future plans, usually through dreams or visions with elaborate and at times strange symbolism or numbers. The form of apocalyptic (i.e., dreams, visions, symbols) makes its communication less direct than the spoken 'word' of prophecy proper. This explains in part why it poses such an interpretive challenge."[286] The symbolic nature of apocalyptic also explains the range of interpretative schools one encounters (preterist, historicist, futurist) from sincere Christian believers. Accordingly, we have endeavored to remain open to various schools of thought and encourage the reader to do the same. Even so, as the result of exegesis, it seems clear to us the title of "Babylon" is meant symbolically for Rome.

Exegesis is the systematic effort to determine what the original author intended. God chose specific individuals, like Paul or John, and inspired them to communicate His word for us. For instance, the book of Revelation was originally written to the seven churches. While it is also *for* us, it was written *to* them. The objective meaning of a passage is always the meaning the original, inspired author intended. While this may prove elusive, the goal of exegesis is to make an objective assessment of what the author was communicating to the original recipients. It follows necessarily that his meaning could be understood in the original context and was not based on our perspective of advanced historical developments. When the members of the seven churches received the book of Revelation as a letter from the apostle John, they necessarily understood the line, "And the woman which thou sawest is that great city, which reigneth over the kings of the earth" (Revelation 17:18) as a reference to Rome. To a first-century Christian, it was a "no-brainer"; there was no other viable option. Although prophecies of the future demand important qualifications to this rule, it follows that it would hold for symbols and types. This is why the vast majority of biblical scholars view the great harlot as Rome. When one looks deeply into the historical context, the identification is very compelling.

There are many connections between Revelation 17 and the ancient city of Rome. Of course the most obvious is how 17:9 portrays the great harlot and beast as sitting on seven hills. While there is no known association with ancient Babylon, the ancient city of Rome was famous for these seven hills. According to evangelical scholar, Craig Keener, "It was common knowledge that the original city of Rome sat on seven hills; this datum appears throughout Roman literature and on Roman coins and was celebrated in the name of the annual Roman festival called Septimontium. Here the hills have become mountains in characteristic apocalyptic hyperbole."[287] The Septimontium was the festival of the seven hills of Rome which was celebrated in September in which they sacrificed seven animals at seven times in seven different places.

But what makes this association inescapable for Roman Catholics is that their own chief defenders admit it as well. This is bittersweet in that they concede it when it suits their purposes only to deny it when it convicts. One of Rome's chief apologists, Karl Keating, issued a resounding refutation of many previously misguided efforts to rightfully expose the idolatry of Romanism. For instance, he makes sport of Ralph Woodrow's *Babylon Mystery Religion* which was based on the shoddy scholarship presented in Alexander Hislop's *The Two Babylons*, published in 1862.

The history of this debate is noteworthy because in an admirable display of intellectual honesty, Woodrow responded with deep study then issued his own refutation of Hislop, entitled *The Babylon Connection?*.[288] In the course of this research, we availed ourselves of Woodrow's new volume in an effort to treat the Catholic side honestly. While Keating had a field day burning straw men, his strained attempt to place Peter as the bishop of Rome found him arguing forcefully that, "Babylon is a code word for Rome. It is used that way six times in the last book of the Bible and in extra biblical books such as Sibylline Oracles (5; 159Q), the Apocalypse of Baruch (2:1) and Esdras (3:1)."[289] Of course Keating is arguing in reference to 1 Peter 5:13 to place Peter in Rome in support of the *Petrine mythology* repudiated back in chapter 7. However, in so doing, he has acknowledged that Rome appears six times in the book of Revelation: a concession which ought to bring conviction but is inexplicably brushed over.

Other Catholic apologists concede the same. Albert Nevins wrote, "Babylon is a Christian code word for Rome and the Roman Empire. Examine Revelation 17:5 where the author uses Babylon—mother of harlots and the earth's abomination, drunk on the blood of Christian martyrs—in this sense. At the time Peter was writing, Babylon was no longer a great city but a deserted relic of mud huts."[290] Actually there was a substantial Jewish population in Babylon at the time which is well evidenced in the Babylonian Talmud. Another item that Keating studiously referenced was that apocryphal books also reference the seven-hilled city at the eschaton. The Sibylline Oracles are Jewish pseudapigraphal prophecies modeled after pagan oracles of the same name which were attributed to the ancient prophetess Sibyl. It gives an overview of history in four kingdoms and ten generations: Assyria, Media, Persia, and Macedonia/Rome. The older Jewish oracles support the Rome's identity as Babylon and prophesy its destruction in the same manner as the Prophecy of the Popes:

> But when after the fourth year a great star shines, which by itself shall destroy the whole land, because of the honor which they first paid to Poseidon god of the sea, then shall come a great star from heaven into the divine sea, and shall burn up the deep sea and Babylon itself, and the land of Italy on whose account many faithful saints of the Hebrews have perished, and the true people. (S.O. 5:155–161; underline added)[291]

The Sibylline Oracles composition spans a wide range of time, and the later books from the Christian era also speak to Rome:

> Among most men, and robbery of temples.
> And then shall, after these, appear of men
> The tenth race, when the earth-shaking Lightener
> Shall break the zeal for idols and shall shake
> The people of seven-hilled Rome, and riches great.
> Shall perish, burned by Vulcan's fiery flame.
> And then shall bloody signs from heaven descend—
> But yet the whole world of unnumbered men
> Enraged shall kill each other, and in tumult

Shall God send famines, plagues, and thunderbolts
On men who, without justice, judge of rights.
And lack of men shall be in all the world,
So that if anyone beheld a trace
Of man on earth, he would be wonderstruck.
And then shall the great God who dwells in heaven
Saviour of pious men in all things prove.
And then shall there be peace and wisdom deep,
And the fruit-bearing land shall yield again
Abundant fruits, divided not in parts
Nor yet enslaved. And every harbor then,
And every haven, shall be free to men
As formerly, and shamelessness shall perish.
(S.O. 2:15–36; underline added)[292]

Scholars date these prophecies between the second to sixth centuries but it is quite telling that they seem to describe the idolatrous practices of the Roman Catholic Church and cohere with the destruction of Mystery Babylon in Revelation as well as with the apocalyptic finale of Malachy's Prophecy of the Popes. While the reference to the City on Seven Hills is compelling, it is by no means the extent of the historical evidence.

In chapter 14 of this book, "The Occult Queen of Heaven," we mention a likely candidate for the phantom apparition who dictates apostasy as the pagan goddess of Rome, *Dea Roma*. It seems to be beyond coincidence that one compelling piece of evidence for the identity of the Great Harlot is the *Dea Roma* coin. It was minted around AD 71 in Asia Minor which was the home of the seven churches to whom John originally sent the book of Revelation. One side of the coin features the emperor Vespasian who was the emperor about ten years prior to when scholars believe John composed Revelation, so the coin would have been in wide circulation and John and his readers were certainly familiar with it. It is the flip-side of the coin that supports our present case. This is a photograph of the back side:

Dea Roma Coin
images note 15

Right away we notice that the goddess Roma is sitting on the seven hills wearing a military dress and holding a Roman sword on her knee. She is bordered on both sides by the letters S and C which denote *senatus consultum* which is Latin meaning a "senate resolution." To the far right, the river deity Tiber lounges and on the left we see the twins Romulus and Remus, the mythological founders of Rome, suckling on the she-wolf who raised them. The parallels to the great harlot in Revelation 17 are ubiquitous. The most obvious are that both women sit on seven hills and the great whore sits on many waters while *Roma* sits on the waters of the Tiber River; but the correspondence goes much deeper into the Roman lore of which John and his readers were certainly aware.

In the legend of the foundation of Rome, Romulus and Remus are twin brothers abandoned by their parents and put into a basket that was set afloat on the River Tiber. The basket ran aground and the twins are discovered by a female wolf, *Lupa*. The she-wolf nurses the babies for a short time before they are found by a shepherd. The shepherd Faustulus and his wife Acca Larentia raise them as their own children.

What is particularly interesting is that one of the many Roman slang words for prostitute was *lupa* and that in some traditions their mother Acca Larentia is a sacred prostitute. For instance, the ancient historian Livy wrote, "Some there are who think that this Larentia, from her having been a prostitute, was, by the shepherds, called *Lupa*; and to this circumstance they ascribe the origin of this fabulous tale."[293]

According to Robert Utley, "Seneca's *Controversies* 1:2 and Juvenal's *Satires* 6:122–123 record that Roman whores wore a head band with either their own name or the name of their owner on their foreheads."[294] All of this has a striking semblance to "Babylon the Great the Mother of Harlots" whose name is similarly displayed, "upon her forehead" (Revelation 17:5). While Rome has certainly indulged in literal whoredom, most interpreters allow that the whore represents the apostate church or end-time spirituality in some form.

In the book of Revelation, the true Church is called the bride of Christ who attends the marriage supper of the Lamb as opposed to the great whore under examination here. In the Old Testament, God also used the theme of marriage in his tumultuous relationship with Israel. God had the prophets do some astonishing things as a form of symbolic prophecy. Typically, such narratives include: a command to perform an action, a report of the performance, and its interpretation through a follow-up prophetic word or vision. A prime example is God's commissioning of Hosea:

> The beginning of the word of the LORD by Hosea. And the LORD said to Hosea, Go, take unto thee a wife of whoredoms and children of whoredoms: for the land hath committed great whoredom, *departing* from the LORD. (Hosea 1:2)

God often compares His unfaithful people to a harlot. This is very much the same sort of image we see in Revelation 17. God would never accuse the secular or pagan world of being unfaithful as they were never His to begin with. But it seems most likely that He would accuse ostensibly Christian folks who indulge in sorcery, idolatry, and necromancy of spiritual fornication. It really follows necessarily from the first-century imagery and the biblical typology that the great whore represents God's people who have turned astray to idols and demonic spirits, the apostate church of Rome.

There is simply no competitor in the same class as Rome when one considers the prophetic parameters like, "With whom the kings of the earth have committed fornication, and the inhabitants of the earth have been made drunk with the wine of her fornication" (Revelation 17:2). With this in mind, relatively recent history records the Vatican literally putting the fascist dictator Mussolini into office, and Catholic scholar's John Cromwell's 1999 bestseller *Hitler's Pope* shocked the reading world with its compelling case that pope Pius XII legitimized Adolf Hitler's Nazi regime in Germany. While the Jesuits have undoubtedly been hard at the dubious deed of discrediting Cromwell's research, Hitler's association with Pius XII is well-known. While this present endeavor covers some of the same ground, we are only hitting the highlights for the uninitiated. We commend to the reader a much more exhaustive treatment of this subject in Dave Hunt's seminal work, *A Woman Rides the Beast*, which contends:

> The Vatican's backing of Hitler and Mussolini and the Nazi puppet regime in France during the Second World War was consistent with its desire to resurrect the Holy Roman Empire with secular leaders doing Rome's bidding. Such has long been the Vatican dream and still is. France (which Pius XI called "the first-born of the great Catholic Family"), together with Italy and Germany, were Europe's principal Catholic countries where the Church held great power. Their governments were willing to work with the Church and even to establish formal relations through concordats.[295]

The Vatican made a choice to sign the concordants and all the special pleading in the world will not explain it away. What is even more telling is the fact that they have never thought twice about pronouncing anathemas on every single Protestant alive, burning at the stake thousands and excommunicating great men of God. For instance, Martin Luther was quickly excommunicated by the papal bull *Exurge Domine* of June 15, 1520 for simply trying to keep the Church honest, but there is no such document for Mussolini or Hitler. Neither murderous Roman Catholic dictator has been excommunicated to this day. Rome's record of spiritual fornication is simply unparalleled.

Another fascinating but lesser-known connection to Mystery Babylon is that in some traditions the city of Rome was thought to be a deity with a mysterious or cryptic name. The word on the street in the first century was that it was the goddess of sexuality, *Amor*, which is really just *Roma* backwards. Accordingly, when John portrays a woman sitting on seven hills as "the mother of harlots," it really seems that he is making an allusion to this secret name as well. Hence, we have a "mystery" city connection to Rome which would also be familiar to John's readers. Even so, the prophetic word seems to address the Roman Catholic Church in a more literal and contemporary manner when it states that "the inhabitants of the earth have been made drunk with the wine of her fornication" (Revelation 17:2). While the references to whoredom and fornication speak symbolically to spiritual apostasy, is there any church in the world more known for sexual crimes against humanity than Rome?

Pope Benedict's role in the pedophile priest cover up is so well-documented that it hardly warrants extensive argumentation. There has been a systematic and intentional effort to cover up and protect the pedophile priests who have victimized countless innocent children. The evidence is clear. In 2001, while he was still Cardinal Ratzinger, Pope Benedict issued a once-secret Vatican edict, *Crimen Sollicitationis*, to Catholic bishops, instructing them to put the Church's interests ahead of children.[296] The BBC aired a documentary in which a former Vatican lawyer Father Tom Doyle argued persuasively:

> There's no policy to help the victims, there's absolutely no policy to help those who are trying to help the victims, and there's an

unwritten policy to lie about the existence of the problem. Then, as far as the perpetrators, the priests, when they're discovered, the systemic response has been not to investigate and prosecute, but to move them. To move them from one place to another in a secret way, and not reveal why they're being moved. So there's total disregard for the victims, total disregard for the fact that you're gonna have a whole new crop of victims in the next place. Now this is just…this is not in the United States where this is happening. This is all over the world. You see the same pattern and practice no matter what country you go to.[297]

New cases are still pouring as a recent 2011 report released in the Netherlands says over eight hundred Catholic clergy and church employees are responsible for tens of thousands of sexual abuses cases in the Dutch churches alone.[298] As we have documented in earlier chapters, this behavior is not new. We further suggest William H. Kennedy's book, *Lucifer's Lodge*, which provides a well-documented case that these are not simply sex crimes, rather they are also reflective of cults of ritualistic Satanism within the Church driving the pedophilia. This was also confirmed by Malachi Martin and is discussed in the chapter, "Rosemary's Baby (Petrus) and the Priests Who Were *Dying* to See Him." When framed in light of historical and recent events, it seems that there is no serious challenger for a Church "having a golden cup in her hand full of abominations and filthiness of her fornication" (Revelation 17:4). Rome wins, hands down.

Turning back to the imagery on the *Dea Roma* coin and Revelation 17, the pagan goddess is holding the Roman sword. While pagan Rome persecuted the Early Church, they cannot hold a candle to the Romanists. The woman who rides the beast is also said to be "drunken with the blood of the saints, and with the blood of the martyrs of Jesus" (Revelation 17:6). Dave Hunt provides a thorough case in the aforementioned book, and we can only scratch the surface, but Chuck Missler phrases it in a particularly persuasive manner in his briefing, "The Kingdom of Blood":

Innocent III murdered far more Christians in one afternoon than any Roman emperor did during his entire reign. In Spain alone over 3 million are recorded in Canon Llorente's *History of the Inquisition.* These horrors remain as memorials to the dogmas which remain in force today. Millions over the centuries who simply refused to align themselves with the Roman Catholic heresies, dogmas, and practices were martyred for their faith.[299]

Furthermore, in France on St. Bartholomew's Day, Sunday, August 24, 1572, and for days afterward, up to seventy thousand Bible-believing Christians were brutally murdered after being tricked into a ruse of toleration.[300] Pope Gregory XIII (the same pope whom Rene Thibaut argues inaugurates the genuine prophecy), ordered a celebratory *Te Deum*, a hymn of praise, to be sung and even had a commemorative medal molded with the motto *Ugonottorum strages* 1572, showing an angel bearing a cross and sword next to the bodies of slaughtered Protestants. Not only have they perpetrated mass genocide on Christians, they even threw a party and casted a medallion to celebrate it! Can there be any reasonable doubt that papal Rome is the only feasible candidate for an unfaithful spiritual spouse who has the blood of the martyrs on her hands?

Gregory XIII Slaughter of Huguenots, 1572
images note 16

From verse 7 on, the angel explains the symbolism of the vision to John and the reader. For instance, "The waters which thou sawest, where the whore sitteth, are peoples, and multitudes, and nations, and tongues" (Revelation 17:15). Is there any possible competition for a city which rules spiritually over people from all over the world? When one ponders the Angels explanation of the vision to John, Rome is the frontrunner beyond a doubt. The Catholic Encyclopedia agrees:

> The significance of Rome lies primarily in the fact that it is the city of the pope. The Bishop of Rome, as the successor of St. Peter, is the Vicar of Christ on earth and the visible head of the Catholic Church. Rome is consequently the centre of unity in belief, the source of ecclesiastical jurisdiction and the seat of the supreme authority which can bind by its enactments the faithful throughout the world.[301]

The chapter closes with "And the woman which thou sawest is that great city, which reigneth over the kings of the earth" (Re 17:18). Considering what the popes have written and said it seems even more certain. We ask the reader to think back to the previous chapter, "Donation of Constantine and the Road to Hell," where we cited the *Dictates of Hildebrand* also known as *Dictatus Papae* which demanded, "That it may be permitted to him to depose emperors" and more audacious things like, "That all princes should kiss his [the pope's] feet only."[302]

Seriously folks! Is this the humble servant leadership modeled by Jesus? Of course not, it's the polar opposite. We could quote popes for hundreds of pages making similar arrogant boasts, but we will leave that to the studious reader to research. In considering that closing verse of chapter 17, think about the doctrinal article *Papa* by Franciscan canonist Lucius Ferraris, "As to papal authority, the Pope is as it were God on earth, Sole sovereign of all the faithful of Christ, chief king of kings, having a plentitude of unbroken power, entrusted

by the omnipotent God to govern the earthly and heavenly kingdoms."[303] According to the pope, loyalty to him is as necessary as
the Gospel to one's eternal redemption, "We, moreover, proclaim,
declare and pronounce that it is altogether *necessary to salvation* for
every human being to be subject to the Roman Pontiff."[304]

Pope Pius XII and could it be?

images note 17

The Spirit of Antichrist, In Their Own Words

In light of the clear correspondence with Mystery Babylon the Great,
one ponders Jesus' warnings concerning Antichrist. If one understands the Greek prefix *anti* as "in place of" then it appears Jesus
was pointing right at the papacy. He warns, "For many will come in
my name, saying, 'I am the Christ,' and they will lead many astray"
(Mk 13:6; Mt 24:5; Lk 21:8). It seems fair to argue that He speaks
of the individual popes who have made a personal claim, "I am he."
Because, as we have shown, it is relatively trivial to cite incendiary
quotes and document papal debauchery from the Middle Ages; this
brief sampling will only examine more contemporary material. In
looking at the evidence, statements by more recent popes still support Antichrist status. For instance, this infamous blasphemy veiled
with fawned humility by Pius IX, "I alone despite my unworthiness,
am the successor of the Apostles, the Vicar of Jesus Christ: I alone
have the mission to guide and direct the barque of Peter; I am the

way, the truth and the life" (underline added).[305] Of course, Pius IX was the Pope who made papal infallibility an official dogma, so this is in line with his egotistical eccentricity. Even so, his predecessor carried on the tradition. During his inaugural sermon as Cardinal, the man who later became Pope Pius X boasted, "The Pope is not simply the representative of Jesus Christ: On the contrary, he is Jesus Christ Himself, under the veil of the flesh, and who by means of a being common to humanity continues His ministry amongst men" (underline added).[306] In case one might think this an anomalous pretension, the next pope, Pius XI argued, "Thus the priest, as is said with good reason, is indeed 'another Christ'; for, in some way, he is himself a continuation of Christ."[307]

One might be tempted to think the modernized attitude post Vatican II has changed things, yet even John Paul II affirmed, "The Pope is considered the man on earth who represents the Son of God, who 'takes the place' of the Second Person of the omnipotent God of the Trinity."[308] This is unbelievably blasphemous to one familiar with the Scripture, "I am the LORD: that is my name: and my glory will I not give to another, neither my praise to graven images" (Isaiah 42:8).

When Cardinal Joseph Ratzinger was elected as the new pope, it first seemed to contradict the *Glory of the Olive* motto in the Malachy prophecy. Then he declared his name as Benedict XVI, which established a firm connection to Benedictines. Benedict of Nursia was an innovator of sixth-century monasticism from which the name of the Benedictine order is derived. Accordingly, he is known as the "Patriarch of Western Monasticism."[309] The Olive branch is their symbol. The Olivetans are a branch within the Benedictines formed in 1319 Giovanni Tolomei (St. Bernard Ptolomei) who became a monk in response to an entity he assumed to be Mary restoring his eyesight.[310] Some see a connection in that Benedict XVI's papacy as the "Glory of the Olive" marks the escalation of the birth pains listed in the Olivet discourse (Matt 24:7). According to Hogue, "The Benedictines in general—and the Olivetan Benedictines in particular—prophesied a Benedictine pope arriving near the end of days before the apocalypse and God's judgment on the world. They expected him to live and tend his Christian flock at the onset of strange dire days fulfilling what Jesus Christ had imparted in Jerusalem to his disciples nearly 2,000 years ago."[311] This has some force as many in prophecy studies have observed the "birth pains" Jesus spoke of have increased in frequency and severity.

Before this, Cardinal Ratzinger headed up the Congregation for the Doctrine of the Faith, formerly known as the Office of the Inquisition. As noted above, recent reports reveal that he did more than just cover up information during the pedophile scandal. It seems he protected the perpetrators.[312] Whether this connects to Malachi Martin's allegations of Vatican Satanism is unknown, but considering Martin's allegations and subsequent suspicious death, it seems possible. The word on the street is that Martin had begun work on a book about the coming New World Order, tentatively titled *Primacy: How the Institutional Roman Catholic Church became a Creature of The New World Order*,[313] when he was killed by a dubious plummet down the stairs in his Manhattan apartment in 1999.[314] Some of his secrets died with him, but not all of them. We will have more on that later. In the next chapter, we will survey a wealth of historical scholarship concerning the papacy as Antichrist.

11 | The Pope as Antichrist

The idea that the Pope or office of the papacy is the biblical Antichrist offends modern sensibility. Contemporary culture elevates political correctness as a cardinal virtue albeit many of its staunchest proponents are intolerant of those who advocate objective truth. It seems pluralism rules the day in religious discourse. Even in evangelical circles, ecumenism disavows such an idea. However, protestant tradition is not politically correct. During the fourteenth century, the Waldenses, a truly evangelical group known for their remarkable holiness and simple lifestyle, published a treatise designed to prove that the papal system was Antichrist. This was a remarkable change in position from their earlier position in *The Noble Lesson* that taught that the Antichrist was an individual. Boldly defying the papists, they insisted on using translations of Scripture that the common man could understand. In obedience to the word of God, they rejected masses, purgatory, and prayers for the dead.[315] The Waldenses were severely persecuted for centuries. In 1545, some three to four thousand of them were massacred at what is now known as Massacre of Mérindol by Roman Catholic President of the parliament of Provence, France and the military commander Antoine Escalin des Aimars.[316] As early as 1631, scholars began to regard the Waldenses as early forerunners of the Protestant Reformation.

Following the Waldenses it was not long before other Christians were viciously persecuted by Rome: The Hussites, the Wycliffites, and the Lollards also proclaimed that the pope was the Antichrist, the Man of Sin, and that the papacy was the Beast system. These were persecuted Bible-believing Christians who simply wanted to worship and read their Bibles free from Roman popery. These early expressions of the papal antichrist could seemingly be easily dismissed for the all-too-common tactic of demonizing one's enemy. But as the reformation progressed, and the evidence mounted, it quickly became the dominant position. Contrary to the early rebels and polemicists, Martin Luther did not intend to break away from the Roman Catholic Church, but rather reform it. He did not start out with a bad opinion of the pope. He sincerely believed that the pope, being a man of God, would respond favorably when he nailed up his Ninety-five Theses on October 31, 1517. Yet, just a few years later, after burning the papal bull from the Diet of Worms, Luther had also come to the firm conclusion that the papacy was incorrigibly the Antichrist. He promoted the idea in many of his later writings, most forcefully in the Smalcald Articles:

> This business shows overwhelmingly that he is the true end-times Antichrist, who has raised himself over and set himself against Christ, because the Pope will not let Christians be saved without his authority (which amounts to nothing, since it is not ordered or commanded by God). This is precisely what St. Paul calls "setting oneself over God and against God." [317]

Here Luther argues unambiguously that the pope shows himself to be the "true end-times Antichrist." This polemic is concerning the papal bull, *Unam Sanctam*, which was issued to counter Philip the Fair's effort to separate the civil and spiritual domains. In that bull, promulgated November 18, 1302, the Latin text reads, "*Porro subesse Romano Pontifici omni humanae creaturae declaramus dicimus, definimus et pronunciamus omnino esse de necessitate salutis*" (underline added).[318] This substantiates Luther's argument, in that this bull unmistakably asserts that "every human creature" must submit to the pope for salvation. Of course, this bears no resemblance to the Gospel found in the New Testament and one is hard pressed to find a weakness in Luther's rationale. However, the idea that the "end times Antichrist" was present in 1302 is only coherent in light of it being the *office* of the papacy rather than an individual. Since the office of the papacy has endured to this day, Luther's argument still has some force.

Philipp Melanchthon was a German reformer and collaborator of Luther's. He is heralded as the first systematic theologian of the Protestant Reformation and an intellectual leader of the Lutheran Reformation.[319] In "Treatise on the Power and Primacy of the Pope," the seventh Lutheran creedal document of the *Book of Concord*, Melanchthon also forcefully argues that the pope is the Antichrist. He skillfully reveals how the Gospel was subverted by tradition. Truly, the papacy as antichrist is as characteristic of traditional Lutheranism as the hymn, "A Mighty Fortress is our God." While more will be said on modern Lutheran interpretations below, this presentation now turns to Geneva and Calvin.

Calvin shared and affirmed Luther's conclusions concerning the papacy. In his *Institutes*, he based his primary argument on the 2 Thessalonians passage and the "little horn" prophecies in Daniel, arguing that the papacy personifies arrogant displacement of the Gospel. He argues that this is so self-evident, that denying it is to dispute the Apostle Paul's credibility:

To some we seem slanderous and petulant, when we call the Roman Pontiff Antichrist. But those who think so perceive not that they are bringing a charge of intemperance against Paul, after whom we speak, nay, in whose very words we speak. But lest anyone object that Paul's words have a different meaning, and are wrested by us against the Roman Pontiff, I will briefly show that they can only be understood of the Papacy.[320]

He contends that the worldly pope sits in opposition to the spiritual kingdom of Christ. Based on the "mystery of inequity already at work" he denies that it could be, "introduced by one man, nor to terminate in one man." [321] Searching the *Institutes* for the terms "Antichrist" and "Papacy" occurring together with Libronix software returns a total of thirty-five occurrences in seven articles. Thus, it is safe to say that the view goes hand-in-hand with historic Calvinism. A later Swiss Calvinist Theologian, Francis Turretin, is famous for his polemic style in which he "sought to present the most complete set of logical deductions possible in order to reject unorthodox interpretations and to present a biblical and complete theology."[322] His book, *Seventh Disputation: Whether it Can Be Proven the Pope of Rome is the Antichrist*, published in 1661, is such a foundational treatment on the subject that it will be examined more thoroughly.

Turretin followed in Calvin's footsteps in Geneva where he was born and later buried. Even so, he was cut from broad cloth, educated in a variety of theological centers: Geneva, Leiden, Utrecht, Paris, Saumer, Montauban, and Nimes. He was ordained as a pastor to the Italian parishioners in Geneva in 1647; later in 1653 he became professor of theology.[323] Among his writings, his *Institutio Theologiae Elencticae*, a systematic theology written in argumentative form, became the standard text at Princeton Theological Seminary only until it was replaced by Charles Hodge's *Systematic Theology* in the late nineteenth century. His style of elenctic theology is still studied by reformed apologists and theologians today. The work considered in this presentation, *Seventh Disputation: Whether it Can Be Proven the Pope of Rome is the Antichrist*, is part of a larger work, *Concerning Our Necessary Secession from the Church of Rome and the Impossibility of Cooperation with Her*, published circa 1661. The point of this seventh argument in the larger work is that the seventh major reason Protestants can never be reconciled with the Roman Catholic Church is that the pope is certainly the Antichrist. This work is known as the classic apology for the papal antichrist and the Church of Rome as Mystery Babylon.

Turretin builds his case systematically from the ground up. He addresses the many ways in which the term "antichrist" may be used as was done at the beginning of this book. He establishes a semantic case that the Latin "vicar" carries a similar meaning to the Greek "anti" as "one who comes in the place of another."[324] He makes a powerful case from 2 Thessalonians that, "The Pope takes for himself not only the name of the Church, but with its name its privileges and all authority, as if he alone (with his faithful) were the temple of God, which is the Church (the Christians outside his belief system being viewed as heretics and schismatics)."[325] He then establishes that the location, Rome, matches the prophecy in Revelation 17 incorrigibly. He argues that Babylon was a known codeword for Rome used by early Christians (cf. 1 Pe 5:13) and "the seven heads are seven mountains" (Re 17:9) infers Rome which was famously called "the City on Seven Hills." He argues that, "the great seven-hilled city, which in John's day held power over the kings of the earth, and which, by her cup of fornications, was destined to inebriate all people, intoxicating them with the blood of the saints" cannot represent Pagan Rome because only Christian Rome could slide into apostasy.[326]

While some of exegesis is suspect, his reasoning is, for the most part, impeccable as he systematically builds the case. For instance, he argues Paul mentioning that the "mystery of lawlessness is already at work" (2 Th 2:7) can only describe an entity which had its roots at the onset of the Church. The Thessalonians had to know about it for Paul's letter to be coherent. Accordingly, he reasons the restraining influence was the Roman Empire. History bears this out as the papacy assumed greater temporal power as the Empire fell. He cites examples from history of various popes asserting their power over the earth as vicars of Christ. He argues that birth and revelation of the Antichrist came to fruition in AD 606 with Boniface III who claimed the title of "Universal Bishop."[327] Furthermore, their regalia match the descriptions in Revelation 17:3, 4 with uncanny accuracy. The Church of Rome martyred many Christian believers in accordance with Revelation 17:6, he goes on to claim. Less convincing, he even postulates that the mark of the beast is Catholic sign of the cross. At the end of his treatment, he addresses counter arguments and refutes them.

One particularly compelling counterargument is titled, "Antichrist's Attack and Denial of Christ is Hidden and Implicit; Not Open and Explicit." He makes the case that those who object to the papal antichrist often do so because the pope ostensibly believes in and promotes Jesus. (This sounds like many modern evangelicals today.) It seems valid because it ostensibly disagrees with John's definition, "he who denies the Father and the Son" (1 Jn 2:22b). This is still a popular objection today, so his work is quite relevant. On opposing Christ, he says the following:

> Is it to be understood as open and explicit as far as external profession, or implicit and hidden as far as the actual truth of the matter? We Reformed hold firmly that the Antichrist must deny Christ, not in the first, but in the second manner; that he must be a disguised enemy of Christ, who, under the pretence of the name of Christ would rule over the Church of Christ, attacking the person of Christ, his offices and his good works. It must not, therefore, be expected that the Antichrist would openly profess himself the enemy of Christ,

(although in reality he shows himself to be such), nor would he boast himself to actually be the Christ, which the pseudo-christs did.[328]

This argument has merit and is a fine example of his elenctic style. The explanation carries weight because only in this way can the Antichrist simultaneously meet both meanings of the prefix "anti." If he were to openly oppose Christ, no one would accept him instead of Christ. This explanatory scope is persuasive. Even so, not all of his arguments are as compelling.

He attacks the futurist theory of a Jewish Antichrist arguing that he must be a professing Christian. In this argument, he states the "temple of God" mentioned by Paul in 2 Thessalonians cannot possibly be a restored Jewish temple. This is weak because most modern exegetes would argue that Paul had the Jewish temple in mind or that it at least is a viable option. D. A. Carson comments:

> It may mean he will sit in the Jewish temple (destroyed in AD 70) or in a future rebuilt temple. Alternatively the temple may be a metaphor for the church. More probably, however, the imagery, which is drawn from Ezk. 28:2 and reflects the stories of Antiochus and Pompey who both entered the Jewish temple, is to be taken metaphorically of the totalitarian claims of the rebel.[329]

In biblical exegesis, one always defers to the author's intent. There is nothing in Paul's letters to the Thessalonians that infers he was speaking of the metaphorical church. That interpretation imposes a developed New Testament theology on to a primitive context. Paul's readers would have certainly understood him to mean the Jerusalem temple which was still standing at the time. Furthermore, the typology of the "abomination of desolation" mentioned by Jesus strongly implies a rebuilt Jewish temple (Mt 24:15). Even more, Turretin's arguments against a future end-time Antichrist, are rendered incoherent by Paul and John's teaching that Jesus will destroy an individual at his return (2 Th 2:8; Re 19:20). In the final analysis, he makes a powerful case for the papacy as a manifestation of antichrist but his polemic against a futurist view fails. Yet, the view was not limited to the Swiss reformers.

In the British Isles, Thomas Cranmer was the Archbishop of Canterbury during the reigns of Henry VIII, Edward VI, and for a very short time for Mary I. He was successful under the former two, famously composing the *Book of Common Prayer* which is still in use today. Of course, his Protestant stance was what led the staunchly Catholic Queen, "bloody Mary," to execute him. However, he was first tortured by watching his close friends being brutally executed. Under such duress, he signed a statement denying Protestantism and was scheduled to make a public profession just prior to his own execution. Instead, he recanted the coerced statement saying, "As for the Pope, I refuse him as Christ's enemy and Antichrist, with all his false doctrines" and thus he died honorably as a reformation martyr.[330]

The Scottish reformer, John Knox, held similar views to Calvin and other reformers. He had been captured from his native land by the French and forced into slave labor until he was released to England where he served the Anglican King Edward VI. When bloody Mary ascended to the throne, he moved to Geneva where he met Calvin. Accordingly, he learned reformed theology and on his subsequent return home led the Protestant Reformation in Scotland. His writings on the papacy as antichrist are extensive. A word search of *The Works of John Knox* using the search terms "antichrist" and "Roman" returns an astonishing 102 occurrences in thirty-six articles. He stated, "Yea, we doubt not to prove the kingdome of the Pope to be the kingdome and power of Antichrist."[331] Indeed, the reformers had little doubt. But is this just a Lutheran and Calvinist construct?

Lest one begin to think that this belief was particular to Calvinism, it is essential to examine the opinions of John Wesley. Of course,

Wesley was Arminian in his theology and the founder of Methodism. He wrote a book entitled, *Antichrist and His Ten Kingdoms*, where he said of the pope, "He is in an emphatical sense, the Man of Sin…"[332] In his commentary on Revelation, he wrote, "The beast with seven heads is the Papacy of many ages: the seventh head is the man of sin, antichrist. He is a body of men from Re 13:1–17:7; he is a body of men and an individual, Re 17:8–17:11; he is an individual, Re 17:12–19:20."[333] Wesley makes an apt observation that the biblical material points to an institution and an individual. This infers the historic/futurist hybrid interpretation mentioned earlier. It is also seen in the writings of Charles Spurgeon.

Spurgeon, the prince of preachers, wrote eloquently about the apostasy of the Church into the system of Antichrist. He also had little doubt and argued the point forcefully. For instance, in one sermon, he expounds on the clever strategy of Satan's evil world system:

> Then the world changed its tactics; it became nominally Christian, and Antichrist came forth in all its blasphemous glory. The Pope of Rome put on the triple crown, and called himself the Vicar of Christ; then came in the abomination of the worship of saints, angels, images, and pictures; then came the mass, and I know not what, of detestable error.[334]

Far from a fanciful eschatological theory relegated to the hinterland of his thought, it was demonstrably a cornerstone in his theological discourse. He was fond of elaborating on the metanarrative of salvation history as it progressed from the apostolic era. In a later sermon, he offered concerning the digression of Roman Catholic Church, "She became like the heathen around her, and began to set up the images of her saints and martyrs, till at last, after years of gradual declension, the Church of Rome ceased to be the church of Christ, and that which was once nominally the church of Christ actually became the Antichrist."[335] Yet, it is important to note that Spurgeon also saw a future time when the Jews would return to their own land and then, "that the power of antichrist shall be utterly and eternally destroyed, and that Babylon, that is to say, the Papal system, with all its abominations, shall be cast like a millstone into the flood, to rise no more forever."[336]

Another Englishman, John Henry Newman, was notorious for converting from Anglicanism back to Catholicism. His apostasy from Protestantism sprung from the Oxford movement which emphasized Catholic ideas like apostolic succession, the authority of tradition and high church communion. He was rewarded by being made a Cardinal by Pope Leo XIII. What is most fascinating about Newman's views is that they confirm the worst suspicions of the reformers, albeit unwittingly. The charge is summed up eloquently by Charles Hodge in his seminal systematic theology, "They [popes] assume the honour which belongs to God not merely by claiming to be the vicars of Christ on earth, and by allowing themselves to be addressed as Lord and God, but by exacting the submission of the reason, the conscience, and the life, to their authority."[337] Hodge goes on to quote Newman ascribing the glory of Christ in prophecy as applying to the papacy and Roman Catholic Church. After Newman explicitly ascribes the prophecies of Christ's Parousia and kingdom to the Pope, he justifies in this way, "Now Christ Himself was to depart from the earth. He could not then in his own person be intended in these great prophecies; if He acted it must be by delegacy."[338] Newman even claimed that the Roman Catholic Church is the stone in Nebuchadnezzar's dream which fills the whole earth (Da 2:45).

In America, Roger Williams, the first Baptist Pastor in America, spoke of the pope as "the pretended Vicar of Christ on earth, who sits as God over the Temple of God, exalting himself not only above all that is called God, but over the souls and consciences of all his vassals,"[339] George Whitefield concurred offering in one sermon, "A great many show much zeal in talking against the man of sin, and loudly (and indeed very justly) exclaim against the Pope for sitting in the temple, I mean the church of Christ, and 'exalting himself above all that is called God.'"[340] Jonathan Edwards was convinced as well. He held a somewhat unusual postmillennial view based on the 1260 days the woman is in the wilderness in Revelation 12:6. He interpreted those days as the years that the true Church was to be oppressed by the antichrist papists. Clarence Goen writes, "Edwards considered that the most likely time for the end of the reign of Antichrist was 1260 years after either AD 606 (the recognition of the universal authority of the bishop of Rome), or AD 756 (the acceding of temporal power to the Pope)."[341] That would place the former in 1866 and the latter in <u>2016</u>. Is this only a remarkable coincidence or can it be possible that the long-held historicist interpretation of prophecy was correct? This question will be addressed soon in the pages of this book, but it seems judicious to observe that 2016 falls in range of 3.5 years from June of 2012. Even so, Edwards, being an optimist, still hoped that the first great awakening was a harbinger of an early fall for Romanism. His remarkable success as an evangelist of the first great awakening supported his post-millennial view. But no matter what particular eschatological persuasion one subscribed to, the view of an antichrist pope dominated the late nineteenth and early twentieth century. Even Catholics came to similar conclusions.

George Tyrrell, a Jesuit priest and controversial modernist theologian, was excommunicated in 1908 after he also came to the conclusion that papacy was antichrist. He stated, "I believe in the Roman Church so far as it is Christian and Catholic; I disbelieve in it so far as it is papal. I see two spirits in it, as in myself, struggling for supremacy—Light and Darkness, Christ and Anti-Christ; God and the Devil."[342] Another figure in turn of the century theology, Charles Hodge, who served at Princeton theological seminary from 1812 to 1929, also argues convincingly that the papacy is antichrist. His treatment of the antichrist in his *Systematic Theology* is so influential that it will also be examined more thoroughly.

One can readily see why Turretin's theology text's remarkable shelf life at Princeton was ended by Hodge. It is a pleasure to read and study Hodge's work as he has a more winsome style and is more exegetically coherent. If the reader has any lingering doubt about the notion that the papacy is a manifestation of antichrist, studying Hodge will likely persuade. Hodge makes most of the same points as Turretin and the other reformers but he allows more flexibility. That tractability and his rigorous intellectual honesty are his strong points. Keeping in mind this work was published at the dawn of the twentieth century, Hodge addresses the "temple of God" reference in 2 Thessalonians: "Some, however, suppose that the reference is to the literal temple in Jerusalem; but this supposes, (*a.*) That the Jews are to be restored to their own land. (*b.*) That they are to be restored as Jews, or unconverted, and that the temple is to be there rebuilt."[343]

While Hodge was incredulous it would ever occur, it is more than a little exciting that since this writing the Jews have been restored to their land and that they are planning to rebuild the temple, already having placed a cornerstone, and still in an unconverted state.[344] As discussed elsewhere in this book, even more persuasive is the possibility that Rome is driving the process. Hodge also adds force to the argument that the Roman Empire was the restraining influence on the "mystery of lawlessness." Hodge cites, "And <u>you know</u> what is restraining him now so that he may be revealed in his time" (2 Th 2:6; underline added) and then asks, "How could the Thessalonians know to what he referred?"[345] This makes for an improved exegetical case that it was indeed the Roman Empire. Hodge also addresses counter arguments and Catholic apologists.

He demolishes Anglican turncoat John Henry Newman's argument that this line of reasoning necessarily condemns all Catholic believers. He argues it is a non-sequitur because the Church of Rome can be understood in different aspects, the arrogant hierarchy of the papacy and the body of professing believers. He breaks new ground in reformed polemics by generously offering, "That many Roman Catholics, past and present, are true Christians, is a palpable fact."[346] This is refreshing because it does not necessarily follow that the papacy being part of the antichrist system damns all Catholics. Additionally, he does not rigidly rule out other manifestations like Turretin. He states, "Admitting that the Apostle's predictions refer to the Roman pontiffs, it does not follow that the papacy is the only antichrist."[347] This accounts for John's teaching that the Antichrist (singular) is coming as many antichrists had come (1 Jn 2:18). Hodge carries this line of thinking further offering, "the same power, retaining all its essential characteristics, may change its form."[348] His intellectual honesty in accounting for more than one potential manifestation is inspirational. As noted above, Wesley and Spurgeon were also sympathetic to the possibility of an ultimate future Antichrist just prior to Jesus' return. Is it possible that papacy still might fulfill this ultimate sense as well? Could there be a satanic presence in the Vatican which is leading toward that final confrontation? There is fascinating evidence which suggests it.

Finally, despite political correctness and its nearly forgotten status in modern evangelicalism, almost all of the original protestant confessions affirm that the papacy is antichrist. For example, *The Second Scotch Confession* of AD 1580 states:

> And theirfoir we abhorre and detest all contrare Religion and Doctrine; but chiefly all kynde of *Papistrie* in generall and particular headis, even as they ar now damned and confuted by the word of God and kirk of *Scotland.* But in special, we detest and refuse the usurped authoritie of that *Romane* Antichrist upon the scriptures of God, upon the Kirk, the civill Magistrate, and consciences of men.[349]

Similarly, *The Westminster Confession of Faith* does not mince words concerning the papacy:

> There is no other head of the Church but the Lord Jesus Christ. Nor can the Pope of Rome, in any sense, be head thereof: but is that Antichrist, that man of sin, and son of perdition, that exalteth himself, in the Church, against Christ and all that is called God.[350]

This statement was repeated virtually verbatim in the Baptist Confession of 1688, otherwise known as the Philadelphia Confession. It was the most generally accepted confession of the Regular or Calvinistic Baptists in England and in the American south. The Westminster confession is still widely used today.

With all of this scholarship and tradition, it is appropriate to examine how this is handled in our contemporary situation. Many modern evangelicals are oblivious. Others have embraced ecumenism, often unaware of their own confessions. Unfortunately, recent agreements like "Evangelicals and Catholics Together: The Christian Mission in the Third Millennium" have advocated the practice of evangelicals not evangelizing Catholics. It ostensibly gives their unbiblical teachings a pass. This was signed by well-known leaders like Pat Robertson, Charles Colson, Bill Bright, J. I. Packer and others.[351] In the footnoted article, a Christian apologist, James White, does an excellent job of exposing its many flaws. It is truly sad that the blood of the reformation martyrs and centuries of scholarship are so frivolously brushed under the rug and forgotten.

Contemporary advocates of the papal antichrist include Dave Hunt of Berean Call Ministries (who wrote a popular book-turned-documentary-film, *A Woman Rides the Beast*) and nearly all Seventh Day Adventist prophecy teachers, notably Steve Wohlberg, Doug Batchelor and Walter Veith. Of course, this treatment would not be complete without mentioning Pastor Ian Paisley, a North Ireland politician and Presbyterian minister, famous for shouting "I denounce you as the Antichrist!" and holding up a sign to that effect when John Paul II was addressing European Parliament in 1988.[352] The South Atlantic Presbytery of the Bible Presbyterian Church affirmed a very strong statement in 2005, stating, "The Roman Catholic Church, Mystery, Babylon the Great, Mother of Harlots and abominations of the earth (Rev 17:5) constitutes the greatest threat to fundamental Christianity in the 21st century!"[353] In 2008, the South Atlantic Presbytery disassociated from the Bible Presbyterian Synod. The Presbytery is now called Faith Presbytery, Bible Presbyterian Church. It is comprised of churches in New Jersey, Pennsylvania, Maryland, Virginia, North Carolina, Missouri, and California. I obtained a copy of this document from Mr. Brad Gsell who stated unequivocally, "the Presbytery certainly considers the Pope to be an antichrist, but not necessarily The Antichrist."[354]

456

THE THREAT OF THE ROMAN CATHOLIC CHURCH IN THE 21ST CENTURY

WHEREAS: The mass media has captivated the world with the activities and pronouncements of Pope John Paul II during his visit to the Holy Land in March, 2000; and

WHEREAS: The Vatican and the Lutheran World Federation have signed, in October, 1999, a joint declaration of accord on the doctrine of justification (Only the synods of Wisconsin and Missouri dissented); and

WHEREAS: In the middle of February, 2000, PLO chairman Yasser Arafat met with Pope John Paul II at the Vatican to sign an agreement regarding the future of Jerusalem that warned Israel against any unilateral decision affecting Jerusalem; and

WHEREAS: Bob Jones University has been unjustly slandered for anti-Catholic bias by Senators McCain, Torricelli, and Hollings and the liberal mass media; and

WHEREAS: The House of Representatives of the U.S. Congress has just appointed a Roman Catholic priest as its chaplain for the first time, March 23, 2000; and

WHEREAS: Pope John Paul II has declared the year 2000 a "Great Jubilee Year" for Roman Catholics that establishes the restoration of granting indulgences, THE VERY ISSUE THAT PROMPTED MARTIN LUTHER TO DRAFT THE 95 THESES IN OCTOBER OF 1517: papal spokesman, Monsignor Timothy Shugrue states, "The indulgence is one of the spiritual privileges extended during Jubilee. It is a way of applying the merits of the good deeds of the saints and the Virgin Mary and Christ Himself to the rest of us.";

THEREFORE: The South Atlantic Presbytery of the Bible Presbyterian Church, at its Spring meeting in the Bible Presbyterian Church of Charlotte, N.C., March 25, 2000, resolves and warns that the Roman Catholic Church, Mystery, Babylon the Great, Mother of Harlots and abominations of the Earth (Rev. 17:5), constitutes the great threat to fundamental Christianity in the 21st century! The Roman Catholic Church has long since forsaken the Bible alone; grace alone; faith alone; and Christ alone. There should be no confraternity with this apostate church in ministerial associations, community Easter sunrise services, Thanksgiving services, mass evangelism or common social endeavors. We admonish devout believers to lovingly and firmly win Roman Catholics to Christ and urge the new converts to obey Rev. 18:4, "And I heard another voice from heaven, saying, Come out of her, my people, that ye be not partakers of her sins, and that ye receive not of her plagues."

Resolution South Atlantic Presbytery Church, March 25, 2000
images note 18

While it seems safe to say that not all Protestants have wandered from the stalwart stance of the reformation, not many are as true as the Faith Presbytery. Some Lutherans like the Missouri synod have remained consistent to their values; others like the Evangelical Lutheran denomination have left biblical Christianity to even support homosexual clergy. While many modern Lutherans seek to distance themselves from it, *The Book of Concord* still contains the *Smalcald Articles* and the *Treatise on the Primacy of the Pope.* Accordingly, many orthodox Lutherans still affirm the veracity of those documents. However, in the 1860s the Iowa Synod refused to grant doctrinal status to the teaching that the Papacy is the Antichrist. They listed this teaching under the category of "open questions." The Iowa Synod later became part of the American Lutheran Church, and its teaching on the Antichrist persisted in the new union. Since 1930, the ALC taught that it is only a "historical judgment" that the Papacy is the Antichrist. In 1938, this view was officially sanctioned in the ALC "Sandusky Declaration." It stated:

> We accept the historical judgment of Luther in the Smalcald Articles…that the Pope is the Antichrist…because among all the antichristian manifestations in the history of the world and the Church that lie behind us in the past there is none that fits the description given in 2 Thess. 2 better than the Papacy…
>
> The answer to the question whether in the future that is still before us, prior to the return of Christ, a special unfolding and a personal concentration of the antichristian power already present now, and thus a still more comprehensive fulfillment of 2 Thess. 2 may occur, we leave to the Lord and Ruler of Church and world history.[355]

In a sharp rebuttal, the Missouri Synod's "Brief Statement" of 1932 renounced the teaching that the identification of the papacy as the

Antichrist is only a historical judgment. It professed, "The prophecies of the Holy Scriptures concerning the Antichrist...have been fulfilled in the Pope of Rome and his dominion." It subscribed, "to the statement of our Confessions that the Pope is 'the very Antichrist.'" It argued that the doctrine of Antichrist is "not to be included in the number of open questions."[356] However, their position has softened since.

In 1951, the Report of the Advisory Committee on Doctrine and Practice of the Lutheran Church—Missouri Synod stated:

> Scripture does not teach that the Pope is the Antichrist. It teaches that there will be an Antichrist (prophecy). We identify the Antichrist as the Papacy. This is an historical judgment based on Scripture. The early Christians could not have identified the Antichrist as we do. If there were a clearly expressed teaching of Scripture, they must have been able to do so. Therefore the quotation from Lehre und Wehre [in 1904 by Dr. Stoeckhardt which identifies the Papacy as Antichrist] goes too far.[357]

This view was endorsed at the Missouri Synod Convention in Houston in 1953. Even so, many still struggle with their traditions. A Lutheran scholar, Charles Arand, wrote an article to help contemporary Lutheran's deal with the cognitive dissonance they feel when they want to applaud the pope's position against abortion and other moral issues. While he never denies the classic Lutheran position, he claims, "The identification of the papacy as the Antichrist in the Confessions takes place in an apocalyptic climate in which the Reformers also considered other candidates for the title of Antichrist, the most prominent of which were the Turks (Ap XV, 18)."[358] The text he refers to is this one: "For the kingdom of the Antichrist is a new kind of worship of God, devised by human authority in opposition to Christ, just as the kingdom of Mohammed has religious rites and works, through which it seeks to be justified before God."[359]

Indeed, one could infer a Muslim antichrist from this one statement. But, in truth, his use of this reference is obfuscation because
the very next sentences in *Apology of the Augsburg Confession* XV, 18
say:

> It does not hold that people are freely justified by faith
> on account of Christ. So also the papacy will be a part of
> the kingdom of the Antichrist if it defends human rites as
> justifying. For they deprive Christ of his honor when they
> teach that we are not freely justified on account of Christ
> through faith but through such rites, and especially when
> they teach that such rites are not only useful for justification
> but even necessary.[360]

This issue of elevating their rites above the salvific power of the
Gospel has never been recanted by the Church of Rome. He goes on
to argue that as part of the "already but not yet" paradigm, the papacy
was a manifestation of Antichrist during the time of the reformation
but not necessarily the ultimate one. Nevertheless, this confession
clearly says they will be a part of Antichrist's kingdom. He maintains
to be dogmatic that the papacy is the only antichrist precludes awareness and vigilance toward new manifestations, yet to relativize the
confessions as only historical is equally an error.[361]

This seems wise. Perhaps the Vatican will mediate the Jerusalem
conflict and tie together traditionally disparate interpretations? Maybe
the Petrus Romanus will fill the role of the false prophet by supporting a false Jewish Messiah? While agreeing with the pope on moral
issues like abortion is non-controversial, it is important to remember
that the good is often the enemy of the best. It also seems prudent to
recall Paul's warning to the Corinthians, "And no wonder, for even
Satan disguises himself as an angel of light" (2 Cor 11:14).

12 | Historicism: Back to the Future

And now what means the Present and the Past,
This Roman story, Pagan, Papal, fast
Nearing its end? How points the tale thus told?
What moral mystery doth it unfold?
Two aspects of one volume are revealed,
WITHOUT 'tis written, and WITHIN, and sealed.
—HENRY GRATTAN GUINNESS[362]

So what are we to make of all of these great men of God who believed and taught that the papacy satisfied the prophecies of the Antichrist? We tend to agree with Mr. Gsell from the previous chapter that the pope is an antichrist, but not necessarily *the* Antichrist. It was for that reason that we offered the chapter on the Antichrist and false prophet earlier in the book. We believe that the reformation position has merit but lacks adequate explanatory scope for what we read in Scripture. As a result, we are suggesting that a hybrid approach adopting elements from the historicist and futurist view has great potential. We assume that the vast majority of our readers are in the futurist camp and that some of this history is new or perhaps even shocking to them. There are five interpretive schools to the book of Revelation:

preterist, historicist, futurist, idealist, and eclectic. There are sincere Christians in each category but most biblical inerrantists are within the first three. The subject of this chapter, the historicist approach, posits that the book of Revelation provides a detailed accounting of Daniel's prophecy and supplies a synopsis of Church history from the first century until the second coming of Christ.

In the twelfth century, a mystic named Joachim of Fiore reasoned that because God is a Trinity (Father, Son, and Holy Spirit), then history itself is also a trinity of three ages. Martin Luther first struggled with the book of Revelation writing in his first German Bible that "Christ is neither taught nor known in it."[363] Only a few years later in 1530, Luther changed his mind and wrote of it as a map of history. This quickly became the dominant view. Since the reformation, there has been a large body of biblical scholarship which posits the events in the books of Revelation as milestones in Church history. Many think the shift away from this paradigm is a product of the Jesuit Counter Reformation. After all, the destiny of the Church as the bride of Christ is arguably God's primary focus in the book. Even so, it is important to recognize that although it was written for us, it was not originally *to* us. It was first meant to encourage the first-century churches that were enduring persecution and discouragement. Now, two thousand years later, we still can be encouraged that Christ will return to make things right. Where the seals, trumpets, and vials have been progressing since the first century in historicism, the futurist approach places the majority of the book of Revelation's judgments in the seven year Great Tribulation scenario. Traditionally, futurism and historicism are viewed as opposing camps but we think that is a drastic oversimplification. It seems that eschatology is best held with a loose grip.

With exception of the heterodox full preterist view, all interpretations are futurist to one degree or another. Even historicists are necessarily futurists in regard to Christ's return and the battle of Armageddon. Also many (like Spurgeon) are premillennialists who allow for a future restoration of Israel. On the other side, even staunch dispensationalists like John Walvoord have historicist elements in their hermeneutic. Concerning the letters to the seven churches in chapters two and three of the book of Revelation, he writes:

> Many expositors believe that in addition to the obvious implication of these messages the seven churches represent the chronological development of church history viewed spiritually. They note that Ephesus seems to be characteristic of the Apostolic Period in general and that the progression of evil climaxing in Laodicea seems to indicate the final state of apostasy of the church. This point of view is postulated upon a providential arrangement of these churches not only in a geographical order but by divine purpose, presenting also a progress of Christian experience corresponding to church history. As in all scriptural illustrations, however, it is obvious that every detail of the messages addressed to these particular churches is not necessarily fulfilled in succeeding periods of church history. What is claimed is that there does seem to be a remarkable progression in the messages. It would seem almost incredible that such a progression should be a pure accident, and the order of the messages to the churches seems to be divinely selected to give prophetically the main movement of church history. [364]

Whereas Walvoord places the events of the rest of the book into the seventieth week of Daniel (a future seven-year tribulation period), the historicist school sees the seals, trumpets, and bowls as the unraveling of history stretched out until Christ's return. So the issue is not really whether one is a futurist or historicist, it is where one draws the dividing line. Because it is not possible to know where this line is with certainty, we suggest there is plenty of room to allow for elements of both views.

Daniel: A Model of Historicist Interpretation

We believe there is ample warrant for the historicist interpretation to be found in the prophecy of Daniel. In fact, Daniel chapter 11 so precisely predicted specific historical events that liberal commentators cannot accept it as prophecy and have late-dated the book to explain it away. The discovery of Daniel fragments in the Dead Sea Scrolls collection suggests that the Qumran community had accessed the book of Daniel for long enough to consider it part of their cannon. This is revealing because scholars date that Qumran sect as having separated from regular Judaism between 171 and 167 BC, *before* the proposed late date for Daniel.[365] It does seem likely that they would accept a new book as canonical just a few years after they had split. If one holds to biblical inerrancy, late-dating Daniel is not an option because the book claims to be written at the beginning of the Babylonian captivity and corresponds to the dawn of the sixth century BC. If it is late as some argue then it is dishonest. Daniel's prophecy described the fate of second temple period Israel with great precision in similar apocalyptic language to what is found in the book of Revelation. It follows that if one can accept Daniel, then the historicist approach is not so farfetched; perhaps it is difficult to make certain, but not at all improbable.

Recall Nebuchadnezzar's dream (Dan. 2:1) of a great statue that predicted four kingdoms which were represented by the four metals composing the statue. The most important feature is that at the end of the dream the statue is destroyed by a great stone (Dan. 2:44–45). Whereas Romanists believe the stone is Rome, this is what the Jews were expecting then (and still now) and this is what Christians understand to be the promise of the Second Advent. Because of the mention of King Belshazzar, Nabonidus' son and co-regent, we can determine that the book moves chronologically from chapters one to six and then at chapter seven backs up in time to a point somewhere before chapter five. What is important is that Daniel's vision in chapter seven parallels the dream in chapter two albeit, as we will argue below, from the divine perspective rather than a human perspective.

In biblical prophecy, a "vision" is frequently the vehicle employed by God to reveal the future to His prophets. Whether earthbound or through mystical ascension to heaven, apocalyptic visions serve as means to encourage God's people that the Kingdom of God will certainly come. Usually the symbolic images are interpreted to the visionary by an angel. The ancients recognized both dreams and visions but frequently used the terms interchangeably.[366] If one accepts the inspiration of Scripture, an apocalyptic vision should be interpreted as what the prophet actually saw, not merely a genre of literature. Daniel chapter 7 begins with the prophet lying in bed and seeing "a dream and visions of his head" (v.1). Scholars universally agree that this vision parallels the four kingdoms from Nebuchadnezzar's dream in chapter two.[367] However, between chapters 2 and 7, there is a juxtaposition of imagery that speaks to a divine commentary on the vainglory of man.

Daniel saw four great beasts rise out of the sea that later we are told represent "four kings, which shall arise out of the earth" (Da 7:17). Conservative scholars unanimously agree that the kingdoms are Babylon, Medo-Persia, Greece, and Rome.[368] While there are alternate interpretations postulating Babylon, Median, Persia, Greece, only those bent by anti-supernatural bias relegate the vision to the Maccabean era by late-dating the text and ascribing pseudepigraphical status. They must violate the historical record by splitting Medo-Persia into two separate empires. They then proceed to violate holy inspiration by assigning the fourth beast to the Greek Empire. They make the book a clever forgery. Because Jesus, Himself, authenticated Daniel as the author (Mat. 24:15) this is a non-starter for true Christians.

Due to our first principles, we dismiss such naturalistic conjecture outright. However, we will demonstrate that the traditional view is far more coherent with the prophetic symbolism and the historical record, while the liberal critic's position appears *ad hoc* and disingenuous. We also agree with H.A. Ironside, who, commenting on the parallel with the chapter two statue dream, writes, "In what we have already gone over we have been chiefly occupied with prophetic history as viewed from man's standpoint; but in the second half of the book we have the same scenes as viewed in God's unsullied light."[369] Daniel's vision is illustrative of God's view of imperialism and temporal ambition. Contemplate the kingdom values expressed by Christ in His sermon on the mount. Then consider Nebuchadnezzar when Daniel first encountered him: proud, fierce, and ambitious. How aggrandizing it was to be represented as a head of pure gold or perhaps even by wearing a golden tiara?

Pope Benedict XVI's Golden Crown
images note 19

The first beast that looked like a ferocious lion and represents Babylon corresponds to Nebuchadnezzar's golden head. However, in this second vision, additional details make for an apt description of Nebuchadnezzar, himself. In view of chapter four's events, the tearing off of the beast's wings seems to symbolize Nebuchadnezzar's humbling. When the lion-like beast is given the heart of a man, his restoration and testimony about God come to mind. The parallel is compelling. On a more earthbound note, in Nebuchadnezzar's time, the Babylonian Ishtar Gate entrance was lined with yellow lions in relief on blue-glazed brick.[370] The winged lion of Babylon was a well-established emblem. One would be hard-pressed to find a more fitting symbol.

The second beast is a great, blood-thirsty bear raised up on one side which represents the Medo-Persian Empire. The description is subtly appropriate for a federation in which one nation dominates the other. In fact, the historical record is clear that the Persian contingent did dominate the Median. The liberal view that this beast is Median singular fails in this regard. Furthermore, the bear is divinely commanded to devour three ribs, corresponding nicely with the major three conquests made by King Cyrus and his son Cambyses: the Lydian (546 BCE), Chaldean (539 BCE), and Egyptian (525 BCE).[371] Chapter 6 of Daniel is very plain that the kingdom at that time was the kingdom of the "Medes and Persians" (vv. 8, 12, 15). Thus, the book of Daniel itself states that this was the Medo-Persian Empire at this time.[372] The Maccabean hypothesis is incoherent in light of the evidence. This level of correspondence with verifiable history authenticates the traditional interpretation and speaks to the prophetic veracity of the vision. Yet it is a ghastly, bloody scene, far removed from the shining silver of Nebuchadnezzar's dream.

The four-winged leopard with four heads represents the Greek empire won by Alexander the Great. Like a swift and agile leopard, Alexander was famous for his expeditious conquest of the known world. Of particular interest to the biblical perspective, Josephus records that Alexander had intended to destroy Jerusalem until he recognized the purple-robed high priest from his own dream about conquering Asia. The priest handed him the scroll of Daniel:

And when the book of Daniel was showed him, wherein Daniel declared that one of the Greeks should destroy the empire of the Persians, he supposed that himself was the person intended; …He granted all they desired: and when they entreated him that he would permit the Jews in Babylon and Media to enjoy their own laws also, he willingly promised to do hereafter what they desired.[373]

Leniency aside, Alexander died at the young age of thirty-two, leaving his four generals Antipater, Lysimachus, Seleucus, and Ptolemy to squabble over the empire. The biblical writers used the term "head" as a symbol for leadership and ruling authority and this neatly explains the leopard's four heads.[374] Again the traditional interpretation is supported by the data and the liberal view fails. Also we get a glimpse from the heavenly perspective, a carnivorous monster rather than the cast bronze of man-centered majesty.

The fourth and final terrible beast of Daniel's night visions is one unlike any known creature. It corresponds to the iron legs, feet, and toes of Nebuchadnezzar's statue and represents Rome. Several details tie the statue and dreadful beast together. The legs of the statue are iron like the teeth of the animal. The animal has ten horns paralleled in the ten toes of the statue, presumably representing ten kingdoms. However, a unique element not present in the dream of the statue is introduced in the vision of the four beasts: the appearance of "another horn, a little one," which replaced three of the horns of the last and terrible beast. While the horns and toes seem to be kingdoms, this eleventh horn has eyes like a man and supplants three others. This appears to be the first biblical reference to the individual later described in the New Testament as the Antichrist. Of course, many historicists see this character as the pope.

Holding a high view of inspiration, we feel compelled to make much out of the sharp contrast between the vision given to the godly prophet and the impious king. It runs deeper than first appearance. In chapter 2, the interpreter is a man, Daniel. In chapter 5, the interpreter is a holy angel from the divine council scene. World history from man's perspective is triumphal idolatry, while from God's perspective it is beastly carnage. Miller admits, "there may be truth to it."[375] Walvoord concurs, "…world history from God's standpoint in its immorality, brutality, and depravity."[376] This undeniably matches the character of papal Rome and it is inescapable that the prophecy referred to the Roman Empire. With this in mind it is not too difficult to envision the book of Revelation from a historicist perspective. In the economy of Jesus Christ where the meek "shall inherit the earth" (Matt. 5:5), it should not be dismissed as fanciful.

Classic Historicism

As a classic representative example of the historicist approach to the book of Revelation, Irish Protestant preacher, astronomer and author, Henry Grattan Guinness, is good place to begin. He was a popular evangelist in the Evangelical awakening preaching to thousands during events like the Ulster Revival of 1859. He was responsible for training and sending hundreds of missionaries all over the world. He also wrote extensively on the historical interpretation of prophecy. He preferred to call it the presentist interpretation:

> The second or PRESENTIST interpretation, is that historic Protestant view of these prophecies, which considers them to predict the great events to happen in the world and in the church, from St John's time to the coming of the Lord; which sees in the Church of Rome, and in the Papacy, the fulfillment of the prophecies of Babylon and of the Beast, and which interprets the times of the Apocalypse on the year-day system. This view originated about the eleventh century, with those who even then began to protest, against the growing corruptions of the Church of Rome.[377]

Alternately, Spurgeon called it the "continuist" approach.[378] A more modern description of this approach comes from J. L. Haynes at Historicism.com:

Historicism is the view that most of Revelation describes history as it has been unfolding over the last 20 centuries. Historicists see in the prophecies concerning the Dragon, the Beast, the False Prophet, and the Whore of Babylon, references to the pagan Roman Empire, papal Rome (that is, Roman Europe under the rule of the popes), the Papacy, and the Roman Catholic Church. The majority of Historicists also identify the symbols of the smoke rising from the Abyss and the invasion of locusts as descriptions of the rise and spread of Islam. This view united all Protestants throughout the Reformation and has largely been replaced by Futurism as the dominant eschatology (belief about the end-times) of evangelical Christians.[379]

His website provides a lot of information about the historicist approach as well as links to free downloads of many classic works by Guinness and others. While we do not necessarily agree on all points, we recommend it as a valuable resource. The work of Guinness merits further investigation.

While we lean strongly toward the futurist school, we acknowledge that there is merit to the historicist approach. It seems like a mistake to just dismiss centuries of scholarship with a hand wave. However, there are many criticisms. Biblical scholar, G.K. Beale, characterizes historicism in this way, "Typically this view identifies parts of the Apocalypse as prophecies of the invasions of the Christianized Roman Empire by the Goths and the Muslims. Further, the corruptions of the medieval papacy, the reign of Charlemagne, the Protestant Reformation, and the destruction wrought by Napoleon and Hitler have been seen as predicted by John."[380] He also explains why the approach has fallen out of favor since the nineteenth century. He argues that it usually limits itself to Western Church history while neglecting the worldwide church. For instance, there are millions of Asian Christians, but they are not mentioned. Another characteristic weakness is that it tends to be myopic by limiting symbols to the expositors own contemporary situation. Accordingly, when one compares historicist commentaries from different eras, they seldom agree with one another. While speculations on the identity of the Antichrist have run the gamut from Nero through Muhammad to Napoleon, arguably, until very recently, the dominant opinion since the reformation has been the pope, albeit not a single pope rather the office of the papacy.

However, it seems to us that some of this criticism is not valid. Daniel's interpretation of Nebuchadnezzar's dream and his vision of four beasts predict that Rome is the final kingdom which will be destroyed by the Christ's return (as the stone of Dan. 2:44). That being the case, we would expect the ten toes to be parts of Rome and the Antichrist to emerge from part of what once was the Roman Empire. If we interpret Revelation in harmony with Daniel then it seems fair to limit it largely to church history as it corresponds to Rome. We agree that it is a weakness that a historicist commentator will usually believe his own period is the final one. But that is a very real part of the tension, which is inherent for Christians living in the already/not yet paradigm. Though it is also a weakness that historicists seldom agree, the fact that these interpretations are divergent on many details makes the areas where they do converge on even more compelling. It is inescapable that they all converge on Rome and the papacy.

An often-heard criticism from historicists is that modern evangelicals who hold a futurist or preterist view have been influenced by the Jesuit Counter Reformation effort to discredit the historicist view of the reformers. We believe there is some truth to this conspiracy because the Romanists have vested interest in protecting the papacy. It is true that during the Counter Reformation, Spanish Jesuit Luis De Alcazar wrote a commentary called *Investigation of the Hidden Sense of the Apocalypsea* which advocated preterism. However, this does not mean that all modern persons holding that opinion are under Rome's influence. Partial preterist R. C. Sproul is taking one of the staunch-est stands against Roman Catholic theology in evangelicalism today. A lot of the criticism we have read coming from historicists seems unfair.

Truth be told, one could argue that historicism is also a Catholic invention. The dominant Catholic interpretation after Augustine's *City of God* in the fifth century was allegorical. It was only after a mystic monk, Joachim of Fiore (1130–1202), introduced a chron-ological division based on three ages corresponding to the Trinity that the historical interpretation gained traction. According to Larry Richards, "He divided all of history into three ages: the Age of the Father (Creation to Christ), the Age of the Son (Christ to his own day), and the Age of the Spirit (his time, until final judgment). When the Reformation came, this chronological approach was fastened on by Luther, Calvin, and others."[381] So it really is not fair for historicists to charge everyone who disagrees with them as being influenced by Rome. Furthermore, it is a logical fallacy known as the genetic fallacy to deny the truth of a proposition based solely on its origin.[382] The futurist interpretation is judged unfairly in a similar fashion.

A Jesuit named Francisco Ribera published a Revelation com-mentary, *In Sacrum Beati Ioannis Apostoli, & Evangelistiae Apocalypsin Commentarij*, advocating the futurist view in 1590. Another Jesuit, Laconza, wrote under the name Ben-Ezra teaching the premillen-nial advent and literal restoration of Israel. As a means of criticism, strict historicists trace this through to John Nelson Darby, the Moody Bible Institute, and the Scofield Reference Bible. In other words, they argue that nineteenth-century dispensationalists fell for a counter-reformation propaganda campaign. They claim that the teachings of the reformers have been suppressed, drowned in a sea of Jesuit propa-ganda, i.e., futurism. Yet, it seems that even for a Jesuit, the imagery of Revelation 17 is too persuasive to deny. In fact, the Jesuit, Lacunza, actually wrote:

Rome, not idolatrous but Christian, not the head of the Roman empire but the head of Christendom, and centre of unity of the true church of the living God, may very well, without ceasing from this dignity, at some time or other incur the guilt, and before God be held guilty of fornication with the kings of the earth, and amenable to all its consequences. And in this there is not any inconsistency, however much her defenders may shake the head. And this same Rome, in that same state, may receive upon herself the horrible chastisement spoken of in the prophecy.[383]

While we argue that they were already apostate in 1592, we do find it interesting that even these Jesuits identified papal Rome as the woman who rides the beast. Although acknowledging that Rome certainly has an interest in obfuscating the classic historicist view, we are not under Rome's spell in holding futurist views. The futurist interpretation is based on sound exegesis and the historical grammatical hermeneutic.

For instance, the reason we do not agree that the papacy is the ultimate realization of 2 Thessalonians' "man of Sin" is purely exegetical. "Let no man deceive you by any means: for that day shall not come, except there come a falling away first, and that man of sin be revealed, the son of perdition" (2 Th 2:3). Paul was instructing his first-century readers that the judgment of God had not arrived because "the man" had not yet appeared. The Greek language is much more precise that English and the second declension noun, *anthropos* (man), is in the singular form. Paul's teaching would be meaningless if he was referring to an institution lasting hundreds of years that had not yet appeared. For it to be helpful in identifying the day of the Lord he necessarily meant one man. Thus, if one accurately accounts for grammar and context, this is necessarily an individual on the scene when Jesus returns.

Similarly, most historicists argue that the "temple of God" is the

Church (2 Thes 2:4). As we said before, it is an error to impose Paul's other analogies onto 2 Thessalonians. The author's intent to his original readers is always the truest interpretation. Paul's Thessalonian readers had no reason to think he meant anything other than the still-standing temple in Jerusalem. For them, there was no New Testament to compare his letter with and since they were hiding in house-churches, they would have never understood the temple of God to mean the Christian Church or believer. It is simply not sound exegetically to impose a developed New-Testament theology onto 2 Thessalonians' primitive, first-century context. Paul wanted his readers to understand his letter. One should allow Paul's intent be the guiding factor.

It is an epistle written as a pastoral correction to a false teaching. It is not apocalyptic literature written in symbols which can be stretched to represent the institution of the papacy. It seems that the historicist reading of 2 Thessalonians is a product of theological presuppositions rather than exegesis. Paul's readers would have never understood it to mean the institution of the papacy. For them, it was very clearly an individual of whom it says the Lord "shall destroy with the brightness of his coming" (2 Th 2:8). This clearly speaks of one man who is present when Jesus returns. However, Paul taught them about the "mystery of iniquity." It seems more coherent that this mystery, already at work, then explains the development of the papacy and its syncretism of pagan and Christian theology.

Strictly historical interpretations seem inadequate, but a hybrid of historical with a still-yet ultimate realization offers more promise. Another inadequate element of most historicist interpretations is that the text says the Antichrist and false prophet are both individuals who are thrown into the lake of fire (Rev 19:20). Institutions, kingdoms, and offices cannot be cast into Hell. There are two end-time characters: One seems to be a political figure, whereas the other is religious. As we argued earlier, the papacy is more coherent with the latter. Even so, it seems prudent that futurists not be so dogmatic as to ignore the wealth of scholarship generated between the time of Luther throughout the nineteenth and the early part of the twentieth century. It seems wise to keep a loose grip on ones eschatology and to "hold fast to what is good" (Romans 12:9b). Prophecy is often fulfilled in surprising and unexpected ways.

Another reason the historicist approach is not as widely known today is that it requires a great deal of study and knowledge of history. One can pick up the basic framework of dispensationalism fairly quickly. We commend its overarching theology as biblically sound without debating the minutia. A popular marriage of the historicist view of Rome with dispensationalism is Dave Hunt's *A Woman Rides the Beast*. We think his view has promise but we suggest holding eschatology with a loose grip. Without a thorough command of history it is impossible to properly evaluate historicism. The difficulty of a task communicates nothing about its truth value. Even so, very few people are going to invest the time to study the historicist interpretations.

Take the massive eschatological study written by Edward Elliott in the nineteenth century called *Horae Apocalypticae* ("Hour of the Apocalypse").[384] At over 2,500 pages split into four volumes with copious footnotes, charts, and illustrations, Spurgeon called it "the standard work on the subject."[385] Elliot argued Revelation was both the unrolling of a sealed scroll and the continuing drama of salvation history. He saw the first six seals as broken with the empire, decline, and fall of pagan Rome around AD 395. The six trumpets were various attacks by the Goths, Saracens, and Muslims with the Protestant Reformation ensuing at trumpet six. Because Daniel describes the Roman Empire, in terms of legs of iron (Dan 2:33), the split of Rome into Eastern and Western legs is evident in prophecy. He explained the two beasts of Revelation 17 in this way:

> At the same time that in the particular symbolizations contained in this subsidiary Part of the Prophecy, viz. those of the *ten-horned Beast itself*, its chief minister the *two-horned Beast*, and the *Image of the Beast*—explained respectively of the *Papal Empire*, *Papal Priesthood*, and *Papal Councils*, together with the symbolized *name* and *number of the Beast*, construed accordingly

with Ireanus early teaching as *Lateinos*, then were found tens and twenties of particulars wherein to compare the symbols and the supposed things symbolized; and, I think, a fitting proved between them, one after another, unequivocally."[386]

We also see he agreed with Irenaeus that "*Lateinos*" is gematria for the number of the beast and the name of Daniel's fourth empire (as we explained in chapter 2, "Prophecy of the Popes and the Year 2012"). Accordingly, he believed the vial judgments were God's wrath on papal Rome which was in progress as he wrote. Many of the ideas presented within are still compelling but are rarely read anymore.

A major component in *Horae Apocalypticae* and most historicist readings is that the 1260 days in Revelation 12 are years in which the Church is subjected to persecution by the Antichrist in papal Rome. Elliot argued, "on the hypothesis of the Beast symbolizing Antichrist and Antichristendom, we contend that the 1260 days predicted of the *Beasts being in power*, were meant to signify 1260 years as the duration of the *supremacy* and *power* of *Antichrist*."[387] There is of course substantial warrant for this reading found in Daniel's seventy-weeks prophecy, which uses the day/year exchange as well as Ezekiel 4:6, "…I have appointed thee each day for a year." This is another area where nearly all historicists find agreement, but where they disagree is when the 1260 year-long period began. In fact, the death knell of Elliot's gargantuan work of scholarship was that it set a date which came and went.

Unfortunately, Elliot placed the beginning of the 1260 years in AD 606 when the emperor Phocas rubberstamped Pope Boniface III's claim for the primacy of Rome. We discussed this papal milestone in chapter 9, "Donation of Constantine and the Road to Hell." Concerning this, Elliot wrote: "At the same time that the fall and complete commencement of the period appeared on strong and peculiar historic evidence (especially that of the then risen ten diademed Romano-Gothic Papal horns) to have about synchronized with the epoch of Phocas' decree A.D. 606; and the corresponding epoch of end with the year 1866."[388]

Of course, 1866 came and went and the papacy under Pius IX even got bolder by claiming infallibility in 1870. However it is interesting in the same year, Napoleon's advance led the Italian government to raid the Vatican and take the Papal States from the pope. However, the loss of temporal power was brief as Pius XI signed a pact with the fascist dictator Mussolini on February 11, 1929, restoring papal governing power to Vatican City. Even so, Elliot's grand historical scheme was undone when 1866 passed with no second advent. This is another characteristic weakness of the historicist approach. It has this track record of failed date-setting.

Another famous failure was when a Baptist preacher, William Miller, predicted the imminent return of Jesus Christ. On the basis of Daniel 8:14, "Unto two thousand and three hundred days; then shall the sanctuary be cleansed." Miller became convinced that the twenty-three-hundred-day period started in 457 BC with the decree to rebuild Jerusalem by Artaxerxes I of Persia. Then using the day/year principle favored by historicists he calculated Christ's return to occur in 1843. It is now famously called the Great Disappointment of 1844. Many folks had sold everything they owned because of this belief. Other groups resorted to rather pitiable lengths to preserve the date. Reaching for straws, they speculated that Miller's assumption that the sanctuary to be cleansed represented the earth was the problem and that it represented the sanctuary in heaven.

Accordingly, the October 22, 1844 date was modified to denote when Christ entered the Holy of Holies in the heavenly sanctuary, not the Second Coming. This group became the Seventh-day Adventist Church of today and this modification is called the doctrine of the pre-Advent Divine Investigative Judgment.[389] Frankly, it seems like an excuse to us. Miller was simply wrong. The lesson to be learned here is that it is perfectly fine and even commendable to be fascinated by prophecy and to study various interpretations, but always follow Paul's teaching in 2 Thessalonians. The purpose of that letter leads many interpreters to infer that some of the Thessalonians were so sure that the day of the Lord was upon them that they had quit their jobs. Paul admonished them in chapter 3 to remain steadfast maintaining their lives and testimonies. We encourage you to do the same. We want to be upfront that the ideas in this book concerning the Malachy prophecy with dates and times are speculative. We are only pointing out what others have written. It is always wise to be prepared, but we certainly do not recommend selling all of your possessions like the Millerites! Here is an elaborate chart which was popular prior to 1844 showing many historical events in the Millerite historical framework:

images note 20

Suggesting a Hybrid Approach

In light of the Savior's meekness and love, the voluminous record of faithless fraud and apathetic atrocity perpetrated by Rome is heart breaking. The historical survey we offered was not meant to be balanced; rather it was meant to prove a point about Rome. That there have been honorable and holy men within the Roman Catholic Church is beside the point. Because the Romanists make a claim to infallible and exclusive spiritual authority, we have sought to provide counter examples. Our assessment of Church history is by no means unique. Clarence Flick, history and political science professor at Syracuse University, has reached similar conclusions:

> The mighty Catholic Church was little more than the Roman Empire baptized. Rome was transformed as well as converted. The very capital of the old Roman Empire became the capital of the Christian empire. The office of Pontifex Maximus was continued in that of the pope. The deeply religious character of the Romans on the one hand, and the inadequate and degenerate religion which they held on the other, were positive and negative forces enabling the Christian Church to make rapid conquests in territory and numbers. Even the Roman language has remained the official language of the Roman Catholic Church down through the ages. Christianity could not grow up through Roman civilization and paganism, however, without in turn being coloured and influenced by the rites, festivities, and ceremonies of old polytheism. Christianity not only conquered Rome, but Rome conquered Christianity.[390]

Because a great deal of deception and injustice has been masked behind the name of Christ, this research has proven a daunting task. The apostle Paul warned us two millennia ago that "Satan himself is transformed into an angel of light" (2 Corinthians 11:4). The wolves in sheep's clothing have gone to great lengths to obfuscate and conceal history. Even so, the written documents of times gone by speak louder than the contemporary propagandists. We believe we made the case. Rome crossed the line and sealed her identity as a non-Christian religion and, because her policy is one of infallibility, she is incapable of correcting it.

Along with the likes of Guinness, Elliot, Edwards, Spurgeon, and the reformers, we have also suggested to the reader that the Roman Catholic Church most likely appears in the book of Revelation as the leading constituency of the great harlot (17:5). The esteemed Protestant theologian and church historian Philip Schaff has stated, "Where God builds a church the devil builds a chapel close by."[391] Regrettably, we submit to the reader that perhaps this statement should be modified to read something like, "Where the devil builds a cathedral, God builds a little chapel close by." There have always been small groups of true Bible-believers, but it seems followers of Christ are increasingly rare among Christians. While we concede the Church of Rome was basically sound for the first few centuries, we have suggested that there was a point when the Roman Church crossed the line and fell incorrigibly under Satan's influence.

It seems fair to ask, "what if the past failures of the historical interpretation picked the wrong starting place?" It is for that reason that we briefly surveyed the rise of papacy up until the reformation and detailed the reformers unanimous charge that the papacy fulfilled the Antichrist prophecies. In the previous chapter, we revealed that the leader of the first Great Awakening in America,[392] Jonathan Edwards, was open to two possible dates for the rise of the papal Antichrist, 606 and 756. We showed how in AD 756, Pope Stephen used the fraudulent document, *The Donation of Constantine*, to convince King Pepin to go to war for the Vatican to take various lands which became the Papal States. According to contemporary historians: "In 756 a Frankish army forced the Lombard king to surrender his conquests, and Pepin officially conferred the Ravenna territory upon the pope. Known as the 'Donation of Pepin,' the gift made the pope a temporal

ruler over the Papal States, a strip of territory that extended diago-
nally across Italy from coast to coast. Peter recovered his sword."[393]

This collusion with worldly power definitely set a new precedent
in papal apostasy as it was blatantly fraudulent and it crossed a line
drawn in the sand by Christ himself (John 18:36). We demonstrated
from the historical record that this was the impetus for the blackest
night of the dark ages in what was known as the papal pornocracy.
We are not claiming with any certainty that this date will vindicate
the classic historicist interpretation, but we find it odd that nothing
much is being said about the possibility.

Jonathan Edwards and 2016

We first learned that Edwards was open to this date in a *Church
History* journal article which stated, "Edwards considered that the
most likely time for the end of the reign of Antichrist was 1260 years
after either A.D. 606 (the recognition of the universal authority of
the bishop of Rome), or A.D. 756 (the acceding of temporal power
to the pope)."[394] We sought to verify this by examining a collection of
Jonathan Edward's voluminous writings and we found this within a
series of sermons, preached at Northampton, Massachusetts in 1739,
on how history and prophecy coincide:

> I am far from pretending to determine the time when the
> reign of Antichrist began, which is a point that has been so
> much controverted among divines and expositors. It is certain
> that the twelve hundred and sixty days, or years, which are so
> often in Scripture mentioned as the time of the continuance
> of Antichrist's reign, did not commence before the year of
> Christ four hundred and seventy-nine; because if they did,
> they would have ended, and Antichrist would have fallen
> before now. The rise of Antichrist was gradual. The Christian
> church corrupted itself in many things presently after
> Constantine's time; growing more and more superstitious in

its worship and by degrees bringing in many ceremonies into the worship of God, till at length they brought in the worship of saints, and set up images in their churches. The clergy in general, and especially the bishop of Rome, assumed more and more authority to himself. In the primitive times, he was only a minister of a congregation; then a standing moderator of a presbytery; then a diocesan bishop; then a metropolitan, which is equivalent to an archbishop; then a patriarch. Afterwards he claimed the power of universal bishop over the whole Christian church; wherein he was opposed for a while, but afterwards was confirmed in it by the civil power of the emperor in the year six hundred and six. After that he claimed the power of a temporal prince, and so was wont to carry two swords, to signify that both the temporal and spiritual sword was his. He claimed more and more authority, till at length, as Christ's vice-regent on earth, he claimed the very same power that Christ would have done, if he was present on earth reigning on his throne; or the same power that belongs to God, and was used to be called *God on earth*, to be submitted to by all the princes of Christendom.[395]

The suggestions we have made in previous chapters are right in line with what Mr. Edwards taught, so we rest secure being in agreement with such a seminal figure in Christian theology. We also found this letter by Edwards which addresses the 1260 days specifically:

To the Rev. Mr. M'Culloch.
Northampton, Oct. 7, 1748.
Rev. and Dear Sir,
[edited out first section]
    With respect to your very ingenious conjectures, concerning the period of *forty-two months*, or *one thousand two hundred and sixty days*, of the outer court and holy city's being trodden

under-foot of the Gentiles; you know, Sir, that that forty-two months, or one thousand two hundred and sixty days, spoken of Rev. xi. 2. has been universally understood, as being the very same period with the 1260 days of the witnesses prophesying in sackcloth, spoken of in the next verse; and the one thousand two hundred and sixty days of the woman's being led in the wilderness, chap. xii. 6. and the time, times, and half a time, of her being nourished in the wilderness from the face of the serpent, ver. 14. and the forty-two months of the continuance of the beast, chap. xiii. 5. But it does not appear to me probable that these forty-two months of the continuance of the beast, means the sum of the diverse periods in which the *plat of ground*, whereon the ancient literal Jerusalem stood, was under the dominion of the Romans, Saracens, Persians, and Turks; but the space of time during which the reign of antichrist or the popish hierarchy continues; and as to the particular time of the downfall of antichrist, you see my reasons in the forementioned pamphlet, why I think it certain that it will not be known till it be accomplished: I cannot but think that the Scripture is plain in that matter, and that it does, in effect, require us to rest satisfied in ignorance till *the time of the end* comes.

However, I should be very foolish, if I were dogmatical in my thoughts concerning the interpretation of the prophecies: especially in opposition to those who have had so much more opportunity to be well acquainted with things of this nature. But since you have insisted on my thoughts, I conclude you will not be displeased that I have mentioned them, though not altogether agreeable to yours. I am nevertheless greatly obliged to you for your condescension in communicating your thoughts to me. If we do not exactly agree in our thoughts about these things, yet in our prayers for the accomplishment of these glorious events in God's time, and for God's gracious presence with us, and his assistance in

endeavours to promote his kingdom and interests, in the meantime, we may be entirely agreed and united. That we may be so, is the earnest desire of, dear Sir,
Your Affectionate Brother and Servant,
In Our Common Lord,
Jonathan Edwards[396]

As we endeavored to demonstrate in earlier chapters, the pope's rise to temporal power began when the pope Stephen began courting Pepin around 751 and then became a reality in 756 with the expulsion of the Lombards. We quickly broke out our calculators and saw that 756 placed the target sometime in 2016 which can also be thought of as in the range of three and a half years from 2012. Perhaps it seems we are mixing up our eschatological systems? It may seem a bit odd as the futurist view gets seven years from Daniels seventieth week, but usually bifurcates it into two, three-and-a-half-year periods with the latter representing the Great tribulation (the part with the severe trumpet and vial judgments). Of course, the three and a half years is the same as the 1260 days (Rev. 11:3; 12:6) or "times time and half a time" (Dan 7:25; 12:7) that the historicist view uses to span 756 to 2016. Is it possible that the year/day theory and the literal three and half years could *both* be true? The idea is not without precedent.

In the early twentieth century, Reverend Michael Paget Baxter published a newspaper called the Christian Herald and a Bible prophecy magazine called "Signs of the Times."[397] He was passionate about spreading the Gospel because he had a real sense of urgency driven by his belief that the time was short. In one of his many books on prophecy, we came across this statement:

The deepest expositors of prophecy generally admit that the Seals, Trumpets, Vials, and other prophecies in Revelation relating to the 1,260 days, have a double fulfillment—yearday and literalday—first during somewhat more than 1,260 years as the chief period of the Papal and Mahomedan Antichrists, and again more literally during somewhat more than 1,260 days as the chief period of the last Anarchist Antichrist.[398]

Well at least we are not alone in considering a hybrid approach. Another scholar of biblical prophecy who took a hybrid historical approach was Sir Isaac Newton.

Isaac Newton and the Six-Day War

We came across this interesting discovery while studying Newton's work in conjunction with a new book called *2012–2015: The Season of the Return* by T. W. Tramm. If you have ever spent any time studying Daniel's seventy-weeks prophecy you might have been somewhat annoyed by the first seven weeks. Frankly, it seems to just be dangling there without a purpose. "Know therefore and understand, that from the going forth of the commandment to restore and to build Jerusalem unto the Messiah the Prince shall be seven weeks, and threescore and two weeks: the street shall be built again, and the wall, even in troublous times" (Da 9:25). Most prophecy teachers simply add the two together to make sixty-nine weeks without saying much about why it is "seven and threescore and two (62)." Well, this bothered Newton too. He explained the odd seven weeks as the referring to the second coming, after a future restoration of Israel which had not yet occurred! He explained the verse in this way:

> *Know also and understand, that from the going forth of the commandment to cause to return and to build Jerusalem, unto the Anointed the Prince, shall be seven weeks.*
>
> The former part of the Prophecy related to the first coming of Christ, being dated to his coming as a Prophet; this being dated to his coming to be Prince or King, seems to relate to his second coming. There, the Prophet was consummate, and the most holy anointed: here, he that was anointed comes to be Prince and to reign. For Daniel's Prophecies reach to the end of

the world; and there is scarce a Prophecy in the Old Testament concerning Christ, which doth not in something or other relate to his second coming. If divers of the antients, as Irenæus, Julius Africanus, Hippolytus the martyr, and Apollinaris Bishop of Laodicea, applied the half week to the times of Antichrist; why may not we, by the same liberty of interpretation, apply the seven weeks to the time when Antichrist shall be destroyed by the brightness of Christ's coming?[399]

He puts the first seven in the future after the second rebuilding of Jerusalem. Jerusalem was reclaimed by Israel during the Six Days War in June of 1967. Recall that in the seventy-weeks paradigm, the "seven" is seven *weeks* of years which is (7 x 7) forty-nine years. T. W. Tramm explains a remarkable concurrence:

June 7, 1967 falls in the Hebrew year 5727, adding forty-nine prophetic years to this date we arrive in the Hebrew year 5776, which is 2015 on the Gregorian calendar. Interestingly, if one counts exactly forty-nine (360 day) prophetic years (17,640 days) from the June 7, 1967 date of Jerusalem's recapture, we arrive at September 23, 2015—the Day of Atonement! Coincidence?[400]

We verified this remarkable match but we also noted that if one counts 49 x 365 days for solar years, one lands in 2016 which corresponds nicely with historical approach of AD 756 the acceding of temporal power to the pope plus 1260 derived from Revelation 11:3. There seem to be a few other folks pointing to this general time period so we thought it interesting.

Prominent Presbyterian Predicted 2012 Back in 1876

We offer another startling find by a friend Trey Clark who emailed Tom Horn after doing some of his own digging. This is from a collection titled "Lectures on the Revelation" by the Reverend William J. Reid, pastor of First United Presbyterian Church in Pittsburgh, PA, which were given over a period of time ending in March of 1876. Where there seems to be a little disagreement in the nineteenth-century historical scholarship concerning the date of the Donation of Pepin, his lecture is still astounding. He reached the same conclusions we did, but we only became aware of this document near the end of writing this book. Here is a scan of the document published in 1878 (a link is provided in the notes for a free download).

306   LECTURE XXXVIII.

American Cyclopedia, says : " From this time the popes in all their proceedings assumed the style of temporal sovereigns." If this is correct, then we have discovered the beginning of the Papal system. From the time that the popes began to assume in all their proceedings the style of temporal sovereigns, there was that union of ecclesiastical and temporal authority which constitutes the Papacy. And this time, according to the facts of history which have been mentioned, was about the year 752. Other dates have been fixed upon as the time of the origin of the Papal system, but the ones mentioned are the principal ones. The year 533, when the pope was formally acknowledged as the head of the church ; the year 606, when he was formally declared to be universal bishop, and the year 752, when the pope began to exercise temporal in connection with his spiritual authority. For the reasons which have been given, the last date seems to be the correct one; for then appears for the first time that union between temporal and spiritual authority which constitutes the great peculiarity of the Papal system.

If this is correct, we are prepared to answer the question, When will the Papal system come to an end? If it began in the year 752, and if it is to continue for one thousand two hundred and sixty years, then it is to be destroyed in the year 2012. We would not speak too confidently on this point—not because we have any doubts that these visions refer to the Papal church, or because we have any doubts that the forty-two months symbolize one thousand two hundred and sixty literal years, but because there is a question as to the exact time when the Papal system began. But if it began, as seems altogether most probable, about the year 752, when the popes " assumed in all their proceedings the style of temporal sovereigns," then it will be destroyed about the year 2012.

images note 21

Keep in mind this was published in 1878! What is it about this period of time we have entered? What is it about this period of time inaugurated in 2012 that has caught the attention of so many divergent traditions? What are we to make of Jesuit Rene' Thiabut deriving 2012 from the Prophecy of the Popes along with the above? Is it a mere coincidence? If it is true prophecy, then one would expect Rome to be destroyed. While we do not wish harm to come upon anyone, we shall close with an excerpt from the poem "The City of the Seven Hills," by H. G. Guinness:

> Lo! 'tis the FINAL CONFLICT Rome has stirred!
> Writ is its issue in the Eternal Word—
> THE HORNS SHALL HATE THE WHORE, AND DESOLATE
> AND NAKED SHALL THEY MAKE HER, THOUGH SHE SATE
> IN SPLENDOR MANY AN AGE; FOR HE IS STRONG,
> THE LORD OMNIPOTENT, WHO —WRATH WITH WRONG—
> HER WHOREDOM DOTH AVENGE; AND THEY SHALL BURN
> HER FLESH WITH FIRE, AND SHALL HER GLORY TURN
> TO ASHES; AND HER SMOKE SHALL SLOW ASCEND,
> LIKE NIGHT, STILL DARKENING DARKNESS WITH-OUT END!
> Hark, in the Wilderness a Voice doth cry!
> Lifted shall be the valleys! mountains high
> Brought low! the crooked ways shall be made straight,
> And the rough smooth; no power with pride elate
> Shall bar the glory of the Lord, or stay
> His Kingdom's advent in the appointed day!
> Lifted shall be the valleys! mountains high
> Shall be brought low, and all beneath the sky
> That bars heaven's glory, and its Kingdom nigh![401]

DOCTRINES, DOGMAS, SUPERNATURALISM, AND THE END TIMES

13 | Priestcraft, Sacraments, and Sorcery

Never has something so black and wicked,
gotten away with appearing so holy and
mysteriously beautiful...for so long!

—Musician Keith Green, as quoted by "The Catholic
Chronicles"[402]

We hope Catholics understand that the highest expression of love is grounded in truth. We believe that the Roman Catholic Church is the most fertile mission field in the world. We think this because adherents are frequently so very close to being Christian yet still so very far away. We cannot accept Catholicism as another denomination because it is obviously a completely different religion than New Testament Christianity. Pastor John MacArthur seldom minces words, "In the long war on the truth, the most formidable, relentless and deceptive enemy has been Roman Catholicism. It is an apostate, corrupt, heretical, false Christianity; it is affront for the kingdom of Satan. The true church of the Lord Jesus Christ has always understood this. And even through the Dark Ages from 400 to 1500, prior to the Reformation, genuine Christian believers set themselves apart from that system, and were brutally punished and executed for their rejection of that system."[403] We love Catholic people and we want them to be set free from the bondage of that wicked, evil system. Many are blinded from the light of the true Gospel of grace by a sorcerous system and a heretical priesthood. We believe they are literally under the spell of a coven of sorcerers.

If you think this an outrageous claim, we endeavor to persuade. The historical precedent for occultism has been firmly established, but now we are going to deal with established Catholic theology. First, Webster's defines sorcery as: "1) the use of power gained from the assistance or control of evil spirits esp. for divining: necromancy. 2) Magic."[404] We think our charge will be readily apparent in the second sense but by the end of this chapter, we think the first shall be crystal clear as well. Second, the *Tyndale Bible Dictionary* defines magic as: "Attempt to influence or control people or events through supernatural forces. These forces are called upon by means of ceremonies, the recitation of spells, charms, incantations, and other forms of ritual."[405] That same resource defines necromancy as, "Practice of communicating with the dead; a practice strictly forbidden by the law (Dt 18:11)."[406] So we shall endeavor to answer, "Do Rome's rituals match the definition of magic and necromancy, and do the practices of Roman priests meet the definition of sorcery?"

This might seem like hyperbolic language to some, but we believe that Rome imposes all sorts of unbiblical theology, false worship, heretical rituals and idolatry upon God's people. When we say "imposes," we mean Catholics are told that they must believe these items under coercion. When Rome dogmatizes a doctrine it becomes a demand under threat of being anathematized (cursed). For instance, the council of Trent (which was reaffirmed at Vatican II) Session VII, no. 844 states:

If anyone shall say that the sacraments of the New Law were not all instituted by Jesus Christ our Lord, or that there are more or less than seven, namely baptism, confirmation, Eucharist, penance, extreme unction, order, and matrimony, or even that anyone of these seven is not truly and strictly speaking a sacrament: let him be anathema.[407]

This is a curse meant to damn one to hell. The Authorized Version uses the final phrase literally once, "If any man love not the Lord Jesus Christ, let him be Anathema Maranatha" (1 Co 16:22). The last two terms are transliterated Greek meaning "accursed" and "Our Lord, come!" The way "accursed" is used in Scripture means "to be delivered up to the judicial wrath of God."[408] Paul used the term five times. Two of them refer to Jesus (Gal 3:13; 1 Cor. 12:3). One is in reference to himself on behalf of Israel (Rom 9:23). One is used for a person with no love for God (1 Cor. 16:22), and one is in reference to someone who preaches a false Gospel (Gal. 1:8–9). The latter reference will be addressed near the end of this chapter. The Apostle Paul had this authority but when one typically thinks of a person who frequently practices pronouncing curses on another human being, witchcraft and sorcery comes to mind. The Romanists have pronounced more curses on people who disagree with them than any institution on the face of the earth. We firmly believe that Rome's traditions and rituals are sorcerous.

For instance, prayers for the dead began around AD 300. The title "Mother of God" was first applied to Mary during the Council of Ephesus in 431, but as we will examine in the next chapter, Rome took this much further. Prayers to Mary (a deceased human woman), other dead humans (saints), and angels were widely approved of and practiced by 600. Around 850, the ritual of sprinkling holy water with a pinch of salt in it and blessed by a priest was widespread. Canonization of saints was commenced in 995 by Pope John XV. It is important to understand that during the first step in that process, beatification, the papal authorities allegedly supernaturally endow the dead person with the capacity to intercede on behalf of individuals

who pray in his or her name. The papists believe they have jurisdiction over the dead and regularly communicate with the dead.
Although its roots go back further, the doctrine of transubstantiation
was officially proclaimed as dogma by Pope Innocent III in 1215 and
we will handle it thoroughly shortly. But it is important to note that
as the Romanists promulgated these unbiblical practices, in an effort
to squash dissent, they increasingly concealed God's revealed Word
from the common man.

Of course, one of the most transparent offenses occurred when the
Bible was actually banned in the vernacular language. For instance,
the Synod of Toulouse dictated in 1229, "We forbid lay persons to
have books of the Old and New Testament."[409] Pope Sixtus V is infamous for dogmatizing a grossly errant translation due to his own
incompetence. After his demise, this poorly translated version of the
Vulgate was an error his predecessors attempted to cover up with a
revised version, blaming the voluminous mistakes on the printer.[410]
While the pope was at liberty to botch the job, great men of God like
William Tyndale were burned at the stake for translating the Bible
into the vernacular. If one thinks back to the medieval period, the
priests had a virtual stranglehold on biblical truth. Before heroic men
like Huss, Erasmus, Luther, Wycliffe, and Tyndale began to translate, and before Gutenberg's celebrated Bible was mass-produced, it
was simply not possible for a peasant in a hinterland village to read
and study God's word. Peasants were largely illiterate, but even if
they could read, they likely had no comprehension of Latin, much
less Hebrew and Greek. According to a source on occultism, "Books
were viewed with suspicion or superstition. The Bible, as the physical
manifestation of the word of God, was held in awe and reverence, like
some kind of icon or talisman."[411] Ordinary people were necessarily
at the complete mercy of the priests.

Although taught by Gregory I in 593, purgatory was promulgated
as dogma by the Council of Florence in 1439. Purgatory is effectually
the safety net that keeps Rome's works-oriented theology alive. The

Church instills great fear to keep parishioners enslaved to rituals, but one always has the cushion of purgatory to lean on when works inevitably fail. Purgatory has also been extremely lucrative, as the building of St. Peter's was financed on the sale of disingenuous indulgences and horrific relics (human bones and body parts allegedly endowed with magical power). In this regard, Johann Tetzel was particularly offensive to Luther for his famous enticement, "As soon as the coin in the coffer rings, the soul from purgatory springs."[412] In this way, the Romanists exploit the grief of the mourning for profit. While in revised forms like the sale of mass cards, these exploitive practices still continue today. The heinously heretical immaculate conception of Mary (the belief that Mary was born without original sin) was proclaimed by Pope Pius IX in 1854 and the infamous infallibility of the pope in 1870. Astonishingly, there are new unbiblical dogmas being imposed long into the modern era, like the Assumption of Mary (the doctrine that Mary ascended bodily into heaven) which was finally promulgated as a teaching orthodox Catholics *must* believe in 1950. These notions are not simply dreamed up by creative papists, these ideas are often dictated to them by the demonic spirit world. Today the phantom posing as Mary is demanding official elevation to status as "coredemptrix" in an effort to further displace Christ's incomparable role.

These sorts of talismans, dogmas, and rituals have *much* more in common with ritual magic and sorcery than the teachings of Jesus Christ and the apostles. Of course the Romanists argue that these traditions have the same authority as sacred Scripture. They support all of this nonsense on the tall tale of apostolic succession, the controverted claim of the *Petrine Doctrine* which we endeavored to lay bare in chapter 7. Because the *Petrine* logic fails, they really have no basis for any of this and when examined against the Scripture, the whole dogmatic house of cards tumbles into a ruined heap.

While we have gone to great lengths to demonstrate the pope sits absolute in Rome's hierarchy, the claimed power for the priesthood is not as widely known. Rome contends that, as an institution, it alone possesses salvific power and that only a Catholic priest can dispense God's grace, one share at a time, through the seven sacraments. The operative concept is the assertion that they control the distribution of grace through the seven sacraments: baptism, confirmation, Eucharist, penance, extreme unction, holy order, and matrimony. We will look at a few of them as we examine the priesthood. An official source of Catholic Dogma states:

> The Sacraments are the means appointed by God for the attainment of eternal salvation. Three of them are in the ordinary way of salvation so necessary, that without their use salvation cannot be attained. Thus, for the individual person, Baptism is necessary in this way and after the commission of a grievous sin, Penance is equally necessary, while for the Church in general, the Sacrament of Holy Orders is necessary. The other Sacraments are necessary in so far as salvation cannot be so easily gained without them. Thus Confirmation is the completion of Baptism, and Extreme Unction is the completion of Penance, while Matrimony is the basis for the preservation of the Church commonwealth, and the Eucharist is the end (finis) of all the Sacraments.[413]

Because the Eucharist is the central focus of the mass and "the end" of the sacramental system, we begin with it, and especially the priest's role.

Hocus Pocus and the Eucharist

Turning to an official Catholic systematic theology text for its definition, "The Eucharist is that Sacrament, in which Christ, under the forms of bread and wine, is truly present, with His Body and Blood, in order to offer Himself in an unbloody manner to the Heavenly Father, and to give Himself to the faithful as nourishment for their souls."[414] The Council of Trent made this more precise, "by the consecration of the bread and wine a conversion takes place of the whole substance of bread into the substance of the body of Christ our Lord, and of the whole substance of the wine into the substance of His blood. This conversion is appropriately and properly called transubstantiation by the Catholic Church."[415] That this priestly act seems like sorcery is superficially illustrated by the etymology of the common phrase "hocus pocus" often employed by stage magicians. It is thought to be derivative of the Latin used in the mass, "*Hoc est enim corpus meum*," which translates to "this is my body."[416] While this connection to stage magic seems quaint, sanctioned Catholic apologists remove all doubt as to the priest's appalling role in the Eucharist.

John O'Brien's popular Catholic apologetics work, *The Faith of Millions: The Credentials of the Catholic Religion*, is considered a classic defense and accurate explanation of Roman Catholic faith and practice. What follows is a thorough explanation of the priest's role in the Eucharist:

> The supreme power of the priestly office is the power of consecrating. "No act is greater," says St. Thomas, "than the consecration of the body of Christ."[417] In this essential phase of the sacred ministry, the power of the priest is not surpassed by that of the bishop, the archbishop, the cardinal or the pope. Indeed it is equal to that of Jesus Christ. For in this role the priest speaks with the voice and the authority of God Himself.
>
> When the priest pronounces his tremendous words of consecration, he reaches up into the heavens, brings Christ down from his throne, and places Him upon our altar to be offered up again as the Victim for the sins of man. It is a power greater than that of monarchs and emperors: it is greater than that of saints and angels, greater than that of Seraphim and Cherubim.

Indeed it is greater even than the power of the Virgin Mary. While the Blessed Virgin was the human agency by which Christ became incarnate a single time, the priest brings Christ down from heaven, and renders Him present on our altar as the eternal Victim for the sins of man—not once but a thousand times! The priest speaks and lo! Christ, the eternal and omnipotent God, bows his head in humble obedience to the priests command.[418]

We find this description to be utterly flabbergasting. This is no archaic relic of the medieval period, it was published in 1974 and by reading the reviews at Amazon you will encounter the widely held sentiment that this book will lead "you to believe that the Roman Catholic faith is more logical and reasonable than that of other Christian denominations or groups."[419] To the contrary, it makes us want to vomit. It is so transparently demonic. It has the prideful imprint of Satan written all over it. *The sheer unmitigated gall* it takes to conceive of ordering the sovereign Lord down from heaven in head-bowed obedience is beyond comprehension. It reeks of evil.

The quote above is outrageously blasphemous on a number of levels. Recalling the aforementioned definition of magic as the "Attempt to influence or control people or events through supernatural forces. These forces are called upon by means of ceremonies, the recitation of spells, charms, incantations, and other forms of ritual,"[420] we ask: "In the Mass, is the priest said to influence events, people, and things with ceremonies and the recitation of incantations to control supernatural forces?" Indeed, the priest is said to be even more powerful than angels and to have the authority of God, Himself! Not only does he control people or events, *he allegedly controls Christ.* The priest ostensibly reaches up into the heavens, knocks Him off His throne, and offers Him up on "our altar as the eternal Victim." Of course, we deny that any of this really occurs; it is a satanic lie. In reality, Christ triumphed by the onetime event of the cross (cf. Col 2:15). Satan must relish this most blasphemous ritual's characterization of the victorious Lord as an eternal victim. Even so, the most tangible act of sorcery is the mental manipulation performed on the unfortunate millions who are led by the apostate priests.

Although we find it very offensive, our opinion of the Eucharist is not merely emotional, it profanes everything we hold to be sacred. The apostle Paul made an erudite assertion with, "All scripture is given by inspiration of God, and is profitable for doctrine, for reproof, for correction, for instruction in righteousness" (2 Tim 3:16). Speaking of Christ, the Bible says, "For such an high priest became us, who is holy, harmless, undefiled, separate from sinners, and made higher than the heavens; Who needeth not daily, as those high priests, to offer up sacrifice, first for his own sins, and then for the people's: for this he did <u>once</u>, when he offered up himself" (Heb 7:26–27; underline added). The comparison in Hebrews is with the Old Testament priesthood who offered up animals for sin. The Bible could not be much clearer than "needeth not daily" and "for this he did *once.*" Once is the operative term which the Holy Spirit inspired repeatedly throughout Hebrews.

Rome's theology is a one-hundred-and-eighty-degree inversion of what Hebrews unequivocally teaches, because the Eucharist is a sacrifice that is repeated day after day all over the world. Please consider another passage from Hebrews 9 (and just in case one might think there is a Protestant bias in the Authorized Version, this time we will quote from Rome's sanctioned NAB translation):

> For Christ did not enter into a sanctuary made by hands, a copy of the true one, but heaven itself, that he might now appear before God on our behalf. Not that he might offer himself repeatedly, as the high priest enters each year into the sanctuary with blood that is not his own; if that were so, he would have had to suffer repeatedly from the foundation of the world. But now once for all he has appeared at the

end of the ages to take away sin by his sacrifice. Just as it is appointed that human beings die once, and after this the judgment, so also Christ, offered once to take away the sins of many, will appear a second time, not to take away sin but to bring salvation to those who eagerly await him. (Hebrews 9:24–28, NAB)[421]

Oh, how we do eagerly await him! The passage speaks for itself and we only cited the NAB version to show that they are without excuse. It really could not be any clearer that the Roman mass is a disgraceful sacrilege. It really seems that God anticipated the apostasy of the Eucharist because yet again in Hebrews we read, "But this one offered one sacrifice for sins, and took his seat forever at the right hand of God; now he waits until his enemies are made his footstool. For by one offering he has made perfect forever those who are being consecrated" (Heb 10:12–14). If you accept the authority of the Bible, there really is no possible way to reconcile the Roman sacrificial system. It is a deception by which they instill fear to keep the real victims, the parishioners, coming back for more. Do you disagree with the Roman mass as a sacrifice? Well if you do, Rome has a word for you, "If anyone says that in the Mass a true and real sacrifice is not offered to God, or that the act of offering is nothing else than Christ being given to us to eat: let him be anathema."[422]

Heretical Priesthood

"Beloved, when I gave all diligence to write unto you of the common salvation, it was needful for me to write unto you, and exhort you that ye should earnestly contend for the faith which was once delivered unto the saints. For there are certain men crept in unawares, who were before of old ordained to this condemnation, ungodly men, turning the grace of our God into lasciviousness, and denying the only Lord God, and our Lord Jesus Christ" (Jude 2–4).

How do the papists justify such audaciously irreverent claims? With the Eucharist, the Romanists have basically revived the Jewish priesthood of the Hebrew Bible, framed it in Christian terminology, added a big dose of paganism and exchanged the animals for, in their own deluded words, "the eternal Victim."[423] They assert that the Old Testament priesthood is carried forth into a New Testament priesthood on the basis of the following: "For the priesthood being changed, there is made of necessity a change also of the law" (Heb 7:12). But the assertion of a new-covenant priesthood is obviously not found in the passage. On the contrary, Hebrews is actually revealing that both the law and the priesthood are disposed of by Christ's *one-time* sacrifice. The priesthood was dismantled, "For there is verily a disannulling of the commandment going before for the weakness and unprofitableness thereof" (Heb 7:18). Even the Catholic NAB version makes this clear, "On the one hand, a former commandment is annulled because of its weakness and uselessness" (Heb 7:18; underline added).

The formal priesthood is inseparable from the law. Paul handles the inadequacy of the law exhaustively in the book of Romans (cf. Rom. 8). Disagreeing with Catholic claims, Christ did not bring Aaron's priesthood into the New Testament context. To the contrary, the force of this chapter in Hebrews is to show that Christ fulfilled what the Aaronic priesthood prophetically prefigured. It is perplexing that this is used to support the Catholic priesthood because according to the reasoning in the passage, the office of priest is finished. To be emphatic, Hebrews explicitly argues that, because of Jesus' sacrifice, *there are no more legitimate priests*. He replaced them with His own high priestly office, after the order of Melchizedek. In terms of New Testament theology, claiming the title of "priest" in the sense of a special mediator between God and man is a doctrine of demons. In the broadest sense, every believer is now a priest.

In the New Testament, leaders are only called elders or bishops (overseer), but *never* priests. The law and priesthood have been replaced by the Gospel of grace and the priesthood of all believers under a new covenant. Hebrews 8 says, "Now every high priest is appointed to offer gifts and sacrifices; thus the necessity for this one also to have something to offer. If then he were on earth, he would not be a priest, since there are those who offer gifts according to the law" (Heb 8:3–4). Paul argues, "Therefore we conclude that a man is justified by faith without the deeds of the law" (Rom 3:28). The priesthood of all believers is based on the truth that Jesus as our great High Priest cleared our record once and for all. We now enjoy the privilege to "with confidence draw near to the throne of grace" (Heb. 4:14–16). We do not need priestcraft and rituals to approach the throne of God! It is all a lie. Furthermore, because Jesus is our Priest always, all who draw near to God through Him are saved.

Charles Spurgeon preached the following within a sermon entitled, "Jesus, the Delight of Heaven":

> When a fellow comes forward in all sorts of curious garments, and says he is a priest, the poorest child of God may say, "Stand away, and don't interfere with my office: I am a priest; I know not what you may be. You surely must be a priest of Baal, for the only mention of the word vestments in Scripture is in connection with the temple of Baal." The priesthood belongs to all the saints. They sometimes call you laity, but the Holy Ghost says of all the saints, "Ye are God's *cleros*"— ye are God's clergy. Every child of God is a clergyman or a clergywoman. There are no priestly distinctions known in Scripture. Away with them! Away with them forever![424]

Doctrines of Demons

"Now the Spirit expressly says that in later times some will depart from the faith by devoting themselves to deceitful spirits and teachings of demons, through the insincerity of liars whose consciences are seared, who forbid marriage and require abstinence from foods that God created to be received with thanksgiving by those who believe and know the truth. For everything created by God is good, and nothing is to be rejected if it is received with thanksgiving, for it is made holy by the word of God and prayer" (1 Tim 4:1–5).

So what is in sight in this passage? Is it paganism; perhaps New-Age spirituality based on Buddhist asceticism? While those things surely fall under the broad heading of demonic teaching, they are probably not what Paul had in sight. Most biblical scholars concur that, "Paul is not concerned here with paganism per se, but with false teaching within the church. These false teachers have 'abandoned the faith' they once embraced in order to follow demonic doctrines."[425] It is not hard to find this demonically inspired false teaching in the church that forbids marriage. Rome has said: "It is decided that marriage be altogether prohibited to bishops, priests, and deacons, or to all clerics placed in the ministry, and that they keep away from their wives and not beget children; whoever does this, shall be deprived of the honor of the clerical office."[426]

In contrast, God said, "It is not good that the man should be alone" (Gen 2:18a). The apostle Paul predicted in the passage above that in the latter times marriage would be forbidden in response to the teachings of demons. Recent scandals in the news make Paul's fulfilled prophecy a self-evident truth.

While we must oppose them vehemently, we do feel great compassion for the priests. Surely many of them began with noble intentions. They are also victims of a most cruel and demonic system. In an earlier chapter, we mentioned that priestly celibacy has been an albatross around the neck of Rome. It is not a new problem. John Calvin commented on it in his Institutes: "In one thing they are more than rigid and inexorable—in not permitting priests to marry. It is of no consequence to mention with what impunity whoredom prevails among them, and how, trusting to their vile celibacy, they have become callous to all kinds of iniquity."[427] Unfortunately, the Roman system encourages and invites perversion. While we already covered

Pope Benedict XVI's role in covering up and protecting the pedophiles, here we offer some explanation. Number one, it is important to note that no one starts out as a pedophile. Pedophilia is at the end of a long-term addiction which continuously escalates requiring more and more bizarre perversions to titillate and satisfy. The problem for Rome is that it will never stop because enslavement to sexual sin is inherent in the design of the priesthood.

Priests are forced into the impossible (for most) demand of lifetime celibacy. The vast majority, of course, fail in one form or another. In regard to sexual desire, Paul also taught, "But if they cannot contain, let them marry: for it is better to marry than to burn" (1 Co 7:9). But the celibacy rule makes it much easier to sin. If he commits a sexual sin like fornication, all that is required for absolution is confession to a fellow priest(s). All he has to do is tell one of his peers. It is easy to imagine a tit-for-tat arrangement: you forgive me of mine, I'll forgive you of yours. However, if a priest were to engage in the only God-ordained means for sexual fulfillment—that is, within the bounds of a marriage covenant—then he is in big trouble. In fact, the only way to get absolution for getting married is directly from the pope. If they do not get absolution, they believe they will suffer in hell. Can you see how they are virtually enslaved into a world of sinful, sexual pursuit? If they fornicate, they can easily gain absolution. If they marry, they risk excommunication. In this way, the system encourages them to pursue illegitimate perversions outside of God's design. It is no wonder that Catholics with sexual attraction disorders flock to the seminaries. This is widely known and there even street names for seminaries like "Notre Flame."[428] We are forced to conclude that the system itself is inherently wicked.

The evidence for its wickedness abounds. The full extent of the pedophile problem cannot be accurately estimated due to millions of dollars in pay-offs the Church has paid out to keep the victims quiet. Jason Berry, in his new book *Render Unto Rome*, uncovered some appalling financial practices. It seems likely that funds collected for charitable purposes are being diverted toward pedophile pay-offs. He

cites a case in Cleveland where donors are very concerned that charitable contributions are diverted to dubious discretionary funds for
ambiguous purposes.[429] In the end, categories are academic because
the Church is paying out untold millions in hush money, and that
means that faithful Catholics are funding the conspiracy and keeping
pedophiles in the community. When one looks to the behavior of
some of the leadership, it is actually even more dismal.

In October of 2011, the media reported that German bishops
are the full owners of one of the largest and most profitable publishing houses in Germany: Wetbild. In addition to offering titles on
religion, it also garners huge profits from pornography and occult literature. A Lifesite News expose reported, "Its 2,500 porn titles (with
covers too sexually explicit to reproduce) include perverse sexual fantasy of every type. WELTBILD also sells books promoting Satanism,
the occult, esoterism, and anti-Christian atheist propaganda."[430] This
was despite over ten years of protest by German Catholics so it could
hardly be an oversight. It was not only intentional, they fought against
reform. The bishops had all received over seventy pages of documentation in 2008 but they chose to completely ignore the fact they were
profiting from smut and satanic literature. When the Archdiocese of
Munich did reply to those expressing moral outrage, the response
was described as "arrogant and spiteful."[431] The only reason Rome
has issued any corrective measures at all is the widespread media
exposure. It is always important to keep up appearances. However,
facts are facts and the evidence is clear that Rome deliberately made
huge profits from smut, Satanist, and atheist books. Would a truly
Christian organization possibly do such a thing?

Necromancy

On January 20, 2012 a military escort marched down the street in
Bogota Columbia wearing full-dress regalia. The bright red cuffs on
the navy dress blues catch the eye as the four men hoist a flower-
laden litter holding a glass case with a silver vial. The Catholic News

Agency reports that John Paul II arrived in Columbia...well actually only his blood:

> Relics of Blessed John Paul II have arrived in Colombia and will be on display for veneration January 2–22 in the cities of Bogota and Cartago.
>
> The relics consist of a small vile of the late pontiff's blood which was extracted by medical officials before his death in April of 2005.
>
> "His blood is the symbol of life, life given for God and for others and its presence reminds us of the Christian vocation to spend one's life loving God and neighbor," said Father Slawomir Oder, postulator of John Paul II's cause for canonization and custodian of the relic.[432]

The article goes on to promote a Marian prayer service and a special mass where the vial of blood will be venerated. In fact, the blood has been on a whirlwind tour of South America hitting hundreds of locations. The vial of blood's traveling companion is a wax figurine of the deceased pontiff. Thousands upon thousands of worshippers come out to just get a glimpse of a vial of blood. This is not an aberration. It is common practice.

John Paul's Blood on Tour 2012
images note 22

Honestly, we have been living in blissful ignorance to the extent that Roman Catholicism is overtly occult and sorcerous. Right out in the open they proudly worship idols, use talismans made from human body parts and conjure up the dead. According to Edward McNamara, professor of liturgy at the Regina Apostolorum Pontifical University, "The General Instruction of the Roman Missal, No. 302, contains the following statement: The practice of placing relics of Saints, even those not Martyrs, under the altar to be dedicated is fittingly retained. Care should be taken, however, to ensure the authenticity of such relics."[433] The Catholic Encyclopedia confirms that under the altar in each church, relic(s) of the saint or person in which the church is named are inserted.[434] Thus, if a Catholic church is named after John the Baptist, then there is allegedly a piece of John's body or something similar stored in the altar cavity. This macabre practice is still the norm and although they stipulate that great care should be taken to ensure the hacked cadaver pieces are genuine, this is demonstrably not the case as there are more than two churches which claim to have John the Baptist's hand.[435] There are three completely preserved right hands and index fingers claimed to be John's. It is a safe bet to assume that all of them are probably fakes.

The fact that the ghoulish relics stored in nearly all Catholic churches are largely the stolen body parts of unknown individuals is still not the most unsettling aspect of the practice. In truth, it is a necromantic rite forbidden by God's word. According to a standard academic source, the Gale Encyclopedia of Religion:

> Relics may loosely be defined as the venerated remains of venerable persons. This should be taken to include not only the bodies, bones, or ashes of saints, heroes, martyrs, founders of religious traditions, and other holy men and women but also objects that they once owned and, by extension, things that were once in physical contact with them.
>
> According to the principles of contagious magic, any personal possession or part of a person's body can be thought

of as equivalent to his whole self, no matter how minute it may be, or how detached in time and space. Thus a bone, a hair, a tooth, a garment, a footprint can carry the power or saintliness of the person with whom they were once associated and make him or her "present" once again.[436]

These are the first two paragraphs and we think it is noteworthy how the encyclopedia immediately talks in terms of magical practices. Indeed, relics are classified as supernatural items. These occult practices can be traced back to the cults that arose around the tombs of the early Christian saints and martyrs. Today, it is not at all unusual to see hundreds of Catholics gathered around the severed finger of a Saint in worship. Of course, they will argue it is not really idolatry as they plead there is a qualification between the *veneratio* paid to the saints and their relics and the *adoratio* espoused for God and Christ. In practice, there is no discernible difference and the distinction is arbitrary.

The whole affair is ghoulish. For many centuries now, Catholics have been digging up the dead bodies of individuals, chopping up the cadavers and making various charms and talismans. However, many of them are not pieces of Saints at all but simply the stolen remains of unknown individuals. The Church has made untold sums of cash by robbing graves and selling relics over the centuries. As disgusting as it may seem, they even marketed Mary's breast milk by the quart:

In the case of the Virgin, these relics tended to emphasize her maternal, nurturing, and domestic characteristics. Thus vials of her breast milk (spilled on various occasions) could be found in countless churches throughout Christendom, later causing Calvin to comment that, had she been a cow all her life, she could not have produced such a quantity.[437]

Undeniably, Protestants are appalled by the macabre practices of the Romanists. There is certainly nothing in Scripture that supports these morbid practices.

In Israelite religion the tomb and the corpse were thought to be unclean, and contact with them was defiling (Lev 21:1–4; Num 19:11–16). Jesus clearly held this worldview which is clear from how he made an example of the Pharisees hypocrisy, "Woe unto you, scribes and Pharisees, hypocrites! for ye are like unto whited sepulchres, which indeed appear beautiful outward, but are within full of dead men's bones, and of all uncleanness" (Mat 23:27). A Catholic authority on relics irreverently offered, "Even unusual relic traditions, like the supposed foreskin of Jesus, have a deep spiritual significance representing the first blood he shed, giving special meaning to the devotion of the precious blood of Christ…"[438] No! They do not have deep significance because they are obvious fakes and they are a disgusting sacrilege. The Bible clearly views dead bodies and body parts as something to be mourned and entombed, not put in a glass case and taken on tour for idolatrous purposes. If it walks like a duck, then…

The Encyclopedia of Religion also discusses a broader use of the term *necromancy* than simple divination, "More generally, necromancy is often considered synonymous with black magic, sorcery, or witchcraft, perhaps because the calling up of the dead may occur for purposes other than information seeking, or because the separation of divination from its consequences is not always clear."[439] We ask, "How is the Catholic use of relics to experience the presence of the dead, and how the ritualized communication with Saints is, any different?" After all, saints are simply dead human beings; it follows deductively that communicating with them is a necromantic practice. The Bible gives absolutely no indication that any deceased person can hear our prayers. No matter how righteous and holy a person was on earth they are not made to be omniscient and omnipresent. How could they possibly hear the simultaneous prayers of millions of Catholics? Whenever the Bible mentions praying to or speaking with the dead, it is always negative. The practice is exclusively relegated to sorcery, witchcraft, necromancy, and divination which are explicitly condemned (Lev. 20:27; Deut. 18:10–13). It also follows that prayers not offered to God are necessarily offered to idols. *Only the triune God merits prayer.*

The Sacraments are Sorcery

Grace is allegedly dispensed by the priest through the seven sacraments: baptism, confirmation, Eucharist, penance, extreme unction, holy order, and matrimony. Even more, they are said to be necessary for salvation. In the same manner we exposed the Eucharist for the supreme blasphemy that it is, we shall now address the nature of the system as a whole. By way of example, Catholic theology holds that salvation is obtained through infant baptism rather than faith in the Gospel. The priest through baptism confers grace *ex opere operato*, the sacrament works of itself, to a naïve infant.

> If anyone shall say that infants, because they have not actual faith, after having received baptism are not to be numbered among the faithful, and therefore, when they have reached the years of discretion, are to be rebaptized, or that it is better that their baptism be omitted than that they, while not believing, by their own act be baptized in the faith of the Church alone: let him be anathema. (Council of Trent no. 869)[440]

Accordingly, unbaptized infants who die are consigned to a place called *limbus infantium* and can never enter heaven.[441] Where they come up with this stuff from is a mystery because it is nowhere in Scripture. Roman Catholic Theology even teaches justification by baptism:

> If anyone denies that by the grace of our Lord Jesus Christ, which is conferred in baptism, the guilt of original sin is remitted, or even asserts that the whole of that which has the true and proper nature of sin is not taken away, but says that it is only touched in person or is not imputed, let him be anathema. (Council of Trent no. 792)[442]

In contrast, Christian theology teaches justification by faith alone, *Sola Fide*. "For by grace are ye saved through faith..." (Eph 2:8a). (We will return to this important reformation doctrine of *Sola Fide* at the close of this chapter.)

The sacramental system is simply a means to enslave the parishioner to priestcraft. For instance, ritualistic confession and penance are allegedly necessary to receive forgiveness from God. Pope John Paul II lamented, "It is being undermined by the sometimes widespread idea that one can obtain forgiveness directly from God, even in a habitual way, without approaching the sacrament of reconciliation."[443] He clearly opposes the idea that people can approach God directly which is taught explicitly in Hebrews in no uncertain terms, "Let us therefore come boldly unto the throne of grace, that we may obtain mercy, and find grace to help in time of need" (Heb 4:16). Christ came to set people free but the pope wants to enslave them to his false, fear-driven system.

With the working definition of using rituals and ceremonies as a means of controlling supernatural forces to achieve a desired end, the sacramental system meets the definition of sorcery. We are not alone in this assessment. The Christian Apologetics and Research Ministry (CARM) has taken a similar line of argument in this three step proof:

1. The sacraments contain grace. (Trent, Session 7, Canon 6)
2. The sacraments confer grace. (Catholic Catechism 1127)
3. The sacraments work by simply being done. (Catholic Catechism 1128)[444]

Representing CARM, Matt Slick argues this way, "Isn't it exerting control of spiritual forces through ritual(s) with the goal of affecting certain, precise results in the physical realm? Let me say it a different way. Sorcery is the attempt to control the physical realm by invoking a ritual that affects the spiritual realm—every time it is done."[445]

We think this is a valid argument. Furthermore, we believe the eternal lifesaving Gospel has been compromised within the Roman Catholic Church. In so doing, it has necessarily anathematized itself by biblical standards. The Apostle Paul warned the Galatians against preaching any other gospel than the apostolic Gospel. He declared that if anyone, even an angel from heaven, preached any other gospel, then that person should be accursed. Rome has a demonstrably different Gospel than Paul's. We affirm the reformation edict of *Sola Fide*, "faith alone" as a nonnegotiable and essential component of the Gospel. We do allow that there are saved Christians in the Roman Catholic Church, believers who believe the biblical Gospel and trust solely in Christ for their salvation. However, they are necessarily undercover *Sola Fideists* who believe the Gospel in spite of their institution's accursing of it. With that being said, frankly, we ardently and unapologetically oppose the Roman Catholic Church with its idolatrous traditions and false gospel but certainly *not its people*, who we view sympathetically as the victims of a most cruel deception.

We sincerely hope that Catholics will heed the warning in the Prophecy of the Popes whether it pans out or not and more importantly the warnings in sacred Scripture. If the prophecy is indeed correct then the overdue divine chastisement is most imminent. We suggest that the papists have blatantly subverted and openly opposed the true Gospel. While the Roman Catholic Church certainly appears orthodox in some of its positions on Christology and the Trinity, it is a matter of public record that its official dogma declares war on the biblical Gospel of Jesus Christ. It is specifically Cannon 9 of the Council of Trent's decree on justification that officially curses the biblical Gospel of justification by faith alone in no uncertain terms.

> Canon IX: If any one shall say, that by faith alone the impious is justified; so as to mean that nothing else is required to co-operate in order unto the obtaining the grace of justification, and that it is not in any respect necessary that he be prepared

and disposed by the movement of his own will; let him be anathema.[446]

Of course, Scripture stands in sharp relief declaring, "For by grace are ye saved through faith; and that not of yourselves: *it is* the gift of God: Not of works, lest any man should boast" (Ephesians 2:8–9). This is the primary proof text for the famous reformation doctrine *Sola Fide* which is supported by a preponderance of the biblical data (Romans 3:20, 24, 28, 4:30; 5:1; Titus 3:5). Justification by grace through faith alone is alien to demonically inspired, man-made religions like that of Romanism. While some evangelical theologians have compromised with Rome, reformed theologian R.C. Sproul extends a charitable yet firm explanation:

> Surely the Catholic Church of the sixteenth century did not consciously and intentionally condemn the gospel. I trust that the churchmen of Rome condemned what they believed was heresy. If in fact *sola fide* is a heresy, then Rome did the right thing. If, on the other hand, *sola fide* is the very essence of the gospel, then in her misguided zeal Rome condemned the gospel. If the true gospel is condemned after careful deliberation, then that condemnation, intentional or not, is an act of apostasy.[447]

Charity aside, Sproul unequivocally concludes it was apostasy. We agree with Sproul that *Sola Fide* is the essence of the Gospel and that Rome has apostatized. While Rome will give lip service to justification by faith, it is always faith plus works or faith plus the sacramental system. Adding works and rituals is the tell-tale trademark of all cults and heretical sects. Frankly, it is overtly satanic. Satan as the adversary and accuser always adds works. He schemes to create doubt. After all, he is the cosmic grand inquisitor (Job 1:9–11). Accusation is the means he uses to undermine assurance and bring one to hopeless despair and fear. Unfortunately, it is also a defining characteristic of Rome:

> Canon XXIX: If any one shall say, that the justice received is not preserved, and also increased in the sight of God through good works; but that the said works are merely the fruits and signs of justification received, but not a cause of the increase thereof; let him be anathema.[448]

They have unabashedly cursed the apostolic Gospel for all to see. It is not new; the mystery of iniquity has been at work to undermine the Gospel all along. The Holy Spirit through the apostle Paul anticipated this error and providentially recorded it in sacred Scripture, "O foolish Galatians, who hath bewitched you, that ye should not obey the truth, before whose eyes Jesus Christ hath been evidently set forth, crucified among you? This only would I learn of you, Received ye the Spirit by the works of the law, or by the hearing of faith? Are ye so foolish? having begun in the Spirit, are ye now made perfect by the flesh?" (Ga 3:1–3). The subversion of grace through faith alone is epistemic of Rome's theological tradition. The New Testament presents a very simple path to salvation: "And brought them out, and said, Sirs, what must I do to be saved? And they said, Believe on the Lord Jesus Christ, and thou shalt be saved, and thy house. And they spake unto him the word of the Lord, and to all that were in his house. And he took them the same hour of the night, and washed *their* stripes; and was baptized, he and all his, straightway. And when he had brought them into his house, he set meat before them, and rejoiced, believing in God with all his house" (Acts 16:30–34).

"In contrast, Rome requires much more for a new convert. In fact, due to the sheer length of this process we cannot reproduce it without a copyright infringement. We think this illustrates our point that Rome has added so much unbiblical tradition to the apostolic

Gospel to qualify as a unique non Christian religion. Please follow the footnoted link to examine 'How to become a Catholic.'"[449]

Upon examination we are confident that you will conclude, as we have, that this exorbitantly extended process is certainly no good news to the sinner and it is prohibitively laborious for the heavy-laden. After employing this example, evangelical apologist, Eric Svendesen, appropriately remarked, "Choose which gospel you will embrace, for they are clearly not the same."[450] This gospel faux is not an aberration. It is explicitly advocated and celebrated at web-sites like Catholic.com.[451] Some Catholics might tell you that all the anathemas cited from the Council of Trent are historical relics of the reformation that have been superseded by the softer characterizations of separated brethren at Vatican II. But this is disingenuous sophistry or ignorance because during Vatican II, Pope John XXIII stated that the precepts of the Council of Trent continue to the modern day, a position that was confirmed by Pope Paul VI.[452]

What else has Rome added to the Gospel? You might find this shocking but we must return to the serpent's enticement of Eve in the garden. The serpent offered apotheosis, "For God doth know that in the day ye eat thereof, then your eyes shall be opened, and ye shall be as gods, knowing good and evil" (Gen 3:5). In Isaiah 43:10 the Lord lays this bare with, "…I am he: before me there was no God formed, neither shall there be after me." Where most Christians are aware that Mormons and other strange cults teach that their adherents achieve godhood, we wonder how many of you are aware it is also part of the Catechism of the Catholic church? Indeed, it is, what follows is a direct citation from the Vatican's website:

> 460 The Word became flesh to make us "partakers of the divine nature": "For this is why the Word became man, and the Son of God became the Son of man: so that man, by entering into communion with the Word and thus receiving divine sonship, might become a son of God." "For the Son

of God became man so that we might become God." "The only-begotten Son of God, wanting to make us sharers in his divinity, assumed our nature, so that he, made man, might make men gods."[453]

It seems to us that the Catholic profession of faith echoes the serpent's lie in no uncertain terms.

One marvels at how the papists, ostensibly identifying as Christian, can curse the Gospel on one hand and then promise apotheosis while kissing the Koran on the other.[454] The cognitive dissonance must be painful. Even so, despite some liberal readings of Vatican II, the papists are not backing down. On July 10, 2007, Pope Benedict XVI released a decree which restated his conviction that the Roman Catholic Church is the only true Church and that other churches are not true Churches at all.[455] It should be clear that Roman Catholicism certainly falls under the curse of Galatians 1:6–9 in reference to another Gospel. Subversion of the Gospel is enough to qualify as antichristian but the papists have gone much further by institutionalizing all sorts of sorcery and occult rituals under the guise of Christianity. The Catechism of the Catholic Church, section 2117 states:

All practices of magic or sorcery, by which one attempts to tame occult powers, so as to place them at one's service and have a supernatural power over others—even if this were for the sake of restoring their health—are gravely contrary to the virtue of religion. These practices are even more to be condemned when accompanied by the intention of harming someone, or when they have recourse to the intervention of demons. Wearing charms is also reprehensible. Spiritism often implies divination or magical practices; the Church for her part warns the faithful against it. Recourse to so-called traditional cures does not justify either the invocation of evil powers or the exploitation of another's credulity.[456]

Besides being disgusting, how is using the butchered, putrefied hand of a deceased human as a "hotline to heaven"[457] not occultic? How is praying to Mary or a Saint (as if they can hear you) for healing any different? How is wearing a Saint Christopher medallion for protection not a charm? The only difference is the magisterium endorses some magical practices over others but in the end they are all sorcery. The Bible excludes them all. There is no reason to think deceased individuals hear prayers but there are good reasons to think the demons do. It is a choice between God's revealed Word in the Bible, and Roman tradition. We think this passage applies, "And I heard another voice from heaven, saying, Come out of her, my people, that ye be not partakers of her sins, and that ye receive not of her plagues. For her sins have reached unto heaven, and God hath remembered her iniquities" (Rev 18:4–5).

14 | The Occult Queen of Heaven

On January 1, 2012, Pope Benedict XVI audaciously declared, "Mary is the mother and model
of the Church"; later he added, "Like Mary, the
Church is the mediator of God's blessing for the world."[458] This
followed on the heels of his December 8, 2011 message, when he
emphasized Mary's role as the "woman of the Apocalypse" in reference to the biblical symbolism of "a woman clothed with the sun
and the moon under her feet and upon her head a crown of twelve
stars" (Rev 12:1). The pope's apocalyptic allusion was part of a message delivered for the Feast of the Immaculate Conception where he
pronounced, "And this is manifest in the two great mysteries of her
life: in the beginning, having been conceived without original sin,
which is the mystery that we are celebrating today; and, at the end,
being taken up body and soul into Heaven, into God's glory."[459]
The pope was affirming Mary's preservation from original sin, the
dubious dogma of Mary's sinless perfection which was formally

instituted by Pope Pius IX in 1854. Incidentally, Pius IX was the same pope who confirmed Mary as the patroness of the United States in 1847. Benedict proclaimed, "First of all the 'woman' of the Book of Revelation is Mary herself." While this is true on a superficial level, in our opinion, this statement reflects an ironic hubris. The symbol in Revelation primarily represents Israel which we shall pick up in the next chapter. While we agree that Marian apparitions likely play a pivotal role in the end-time scenario, we assert they have nothing to do with the humble mother of Christ presented in the New Testament.

Perhaps the clearest evidence that the Catholic view of Mary is legendary rather than historical is how the Marian mythology has evolved over time. Whereas the doctrine of Christ has remained stable since the early creeds, Marian dogma continues to evolve: 1) in 431, she was called the "Mother of God"; 2) by 600, prayers were officially offered to Mary; 3) in 649, Pope Martin I stressed the perpetual nature of Mary's virginity declaring her the "blessed ever-virginal and immaculate Mary"; 4) in 1854 came the dogmatic assertion of the Immaculate Conception (that she was born sinless); 5) in 1950, we have the Assumption of Mary (her body was taken to heaven); 6) as recently as 1965, she was proclaimed "Mother of the Church"; 7) currently there is an earnest campaign to proclaim Mary as "Co-Redemptrix Mediatrix of All Graces" and "Advocate for the People of God." (The latter is widely accepted and taught but has not been dogmatized due to the potential negative repercussions for ecumenism.) While number one can be uncontroversial when interpreted within the constraints of biblical theology, the dogmas of perpetual virginity, sinlessness, Immaculate Conception, bodily assumption, and mediatorship, along with the veneration of Mary and her images, are wholly inconsistent with Scripture. Before making that case, we shall first examine Mary as presented in the Bible.

The biblical portrait of Mary is of a pious Jewish girl who was, not surprisingly, flabbergasted by her role as the Messiah's mother.

While a few Old Testament prophecies refer to her (Gen. 3:15; Jer. 31:22; Mic. 5:2–3; Isa. 7:14), the Apostle Paul mentions Mary obliquely and only once (Gal. 4:4). All that can really be known of her is in the Gospels and even there she is a very minor character. In those historical narratives, Mary is presented as a simple young virgin who, much to her own amazement, is chosen by God to birth the long awaited Jewish Messiah (Mt. 1:18–25; Lk. 1:27–32, 39–41). In Luke's narrative, the most thorough account, after being informed by the angel of her role, she is "troubled at his saying, and cast in her mind what manner of salutation this should be" (Luke 1:29). In awestruck bewilderment, she meekly submits to her role as, "the handmaid of the Lord" (Luke 1:37). After Jesus was born and the shepherds came, "Mary kept all these things, and pondered them in her heart" (Luke 2:19). The picture we get from the biblical text is one of astonished obedience rather than supernatural exaltation. Most telling is the incident when she visited her relative Elizabeth and heard her prophesy that her Son was to be the promised Messiah. Mary exclaimed, "…my spirit hath rejoiced in God <u>my Savior</u>" (Lk 1:47; underline added). The biblical Mary acknowledged her need of a savior. It seems quite fair to conclude that an immaculately sinless being, privileged by soaring up to be crowned as Queen of Heaven, would not require a redeemer. Mary was a normal human woman blessed with a special calling.

Perpetual Virginity

Protestants and Catholics agree that Jesus was conceived of a virgin (Is.7:14; Matt 1:18; Luke 1:26). But the papists deceive their followers into believing Mary was a flawlessly sinless lifelong virgin. Where Protestants simply believe the Scripture cited above, Catholics are bound by threat of damnation to the mythology created at the Lateran Synod of AD 649 when Pope Martin I decreed, "blessed ever-virginal and immaculate Mary" and that, "she conceived without seed, of the

Holy Ghost, generated without injury (to her virginity), and her virginity continued unimpaired after the birth."[460]

While this seems self-evidently incoherent, to demonstrate its error, we refer to the occasion recorded in sacred Scripture when Jesus was near His home town and the people asked, "Is not this the carpenter, the son of Mary, the brother of James, and Joses, and of Juda, and Simon? and are not his sisters here with us? And they were offended at him" (Mk 6:3; underline added). Even their officially sanctioned English translation, the New American Bible, renders this as "brother" and "sisters." One can readily see that while Rome teaches that Mary was a perpetual virgin,[461] the Scripture teaches she had at least six other children (cf. Mt. 13:55–56). What makes the Catholic doctrine of perpetual virginity even more perplexing is that Matthew 1:25 explicitly implies that Mary had sexual relations with Joseph after Jesus was born. Again, even the NAB translation reads that Joseph, "had no relations with her until she bore a son, and he named him Jesus" (Mt 1:25, NAB; underline added). On the issue of perpetual virginity, one cannot simultaneously believe the inspired Word of God and the legends of the papists, they are contradictory revelations. So what about the issue of sinlessness?

Perpetual Sinlessness

Official Roman literature states, "In consequence of a Special Privilege of Grace from God, Mary was free from every personal sin during her whole life."[462] The only ostensibly scriptural argument given for this is from the Latin Vulgate rendering of Luke 1:28 when the Angel addresses her, "Hail, full of grace!" Farfetched as it seems, this is the basis from which they argue, "since personal moral defects are irreconcilable with fullness of grace"[463] then she must be sinless. While the Latin term *non sequitur* seems sufficient, we also argue that the phrase "full of grace" is an erroneous Latin rendering that is even corrected in the NAB to read simply "favored one." The Vulgate's distorted translation was the entire basis for the mistaken notion that sinless grace defined Mary's entire life. Exegetically, it is also quite clear in the context of the passage that it is only a reference to her state at that moment when the Angel spoke.

Although leaders of the Catholic Church pretend acceptance of biblical authority, we find in Scripture over and over again just the opposite of what the Romanists teach their followers about Mary. She was a sinner like the rest of us (Lk. 1:47; Rom. 3:23). When reading the Gospels, this makes the most sense of her astonished and humble posture in the narratives. Unfortunately, the Romanists make an absurd assertion that, "Mary gave birth in miraculous fashion without any opening of her womb and injury to her body and without pain."[464] While this is biologically impossible, it is also not at all what the Gospels reveal. In the Levitical law of the Jews, a woman who has just given birth is considered unclean and defiled because of the loss of blood (Lev. 12). After Jesus; birth, recognizing her defilement, Mary presented an offering to the Jewish priest arising out of her sinful condition in accordance to that law (Luke 2:22–24). Of course, this would not have been necessary if her womb fantastically never opened and she was incorruptibly sinless.

While it is completely understandable, it is painfully clear that Mary humanly struggled with her role. Can you imagine how you would feel if one of your relatives claimed to be God? While we certainly affirm it happened to be true in this one case, it was an utterly unique situation amongst a sea of megalomaniacs. This is precisely the exceedingly difficult position Jesus' family was thrust into. In light of these unique circumstances, it is completely understandable that Mark's Gospel records an incident when His family tried to "lay hold on him" because they though He was "beside himself" (Mk. 3:21). This word *krat sai* that was rendered "lay hold of" is used of arresting someone for a crime elsewhere in Mark's Gospel in (6:17; 12:12; 14:1). The language, "beside himself" comes from the Greek, *existemi,* which means "to not be in one's right mind."[465] In other words, his family thought He was crazy. Whereas the Authorized Version rendered it simply as "his friends" the Greek *ho para autos* is a well-known Greek idiom which translates literally as "those beside him" meaning the associates of a person, including family, neighbors, and friends.[466] While Mary is not specially named in this verse it seems most probable that she would be included. But we need not simply speculate. As with any passage of Scripture, it is essential to interpret it in light of the entire chapter.

Indeed, just a few verses later there is another incident. "There came then his brethren <u>and his mother</u>, and, standing without, sent unto him, calling him. And the multitude sat about him, and they said unto him, Behold, <u>thy mother</u> and thy brethren without seek for thee. And he answered them, saying, <u>Who is my mother,</u> or my brethren? And he looked round about on them which sat about him, and said, Behold my mother and my brethren! For whosoever shall do the will of God, the same is my brother, and my sister, <u>and mother</u>" (Mk 3:31–35; underline added). In other words, *anyone* who does the will of the God is equivalent to Mary. According to the papists, "Mary has by grace been exalted above all angels and men to a place second only to her Son."[467] But Jesus denied this Mariolatry, teaching that those who obey God are actually blessed the same as Mary. In the Authorized Version we read, "And it came to pass, as he spake these things, a certain woman of the company lifted up her voice, and said unto him, Blessed is the womb that bare thee, and the paps which thou hast sucked. But he said, Yea rather, blessed are they that hear the word of God, and keep it." Note also, the NAB translation: "While he was speaking, a woman from the crowd called out and said to him, 'Blessed is the womb that carried you and the breasts at which you nursed.' He replied, '<u>Rather,</u> blessed are those who hear the word of God and observe it.'"(Lk 11:27–28; underline added). Jesus is saying that any Christian that hears the word of God and obeys it is as blessed as His mother. So how do Rome's theologians purpose to get away with their sophistry?

Immaculate Conception

The Immaculate Conception is the basis from which it is asserted Mary was sinless. Contrary to what any reasonable person would deduce from Scripture, this doctrine has nothing to do with the birth of Jesus, rather it is about the *birth of Mary*. Of course, the Bible is silent concerning Mary's birth. Nevertheless, Pope Pius IX promulgated the following doctrine as an infallible and divine revelation that all Catholics are absolutely required to affirm: "The Most Holy Virgin Mary was, in the first moment of her conception, by a unique gift of grace and privilege of Almighty God, in view of the merits of Jesus Christ, the Redeemer of mankind, preserved free from all stain of original sin."[468] This is quoted directly from the papal bull "Ineffabilis" which was delivered on December 8, 1854. Ineffable means it so sacred, divine, and transcendent that it is hard to express in words. This document is even called *ineffabilis deus* meaning God's ineffable declaration.

While the biblical evidence for Mary's very human sin nature presented above conclusively refutes the Pope's error, he went much further than purposing a fanciful doctrine. Pius IX also infallibly declared that you are excommunicated and damned to hell if you even think to question this dubious doctrine. He pronounced, "Hence, if anyone shall dare which God forbid to <u>think otherwise</u> than has been defined by us, let him know and understand that he is condemned by his own judgment, that he has suffered shipwreck in the faith, that he has separated from the unity of the Church and that furthermore by his own action he incurs the penalties established by Law if he should dare to express in words or writing or by any other outward means the error he thinks in his heart" (underline added).[469] If one were to accept its authority, this unambiguous damnation necessarily implies that St. Thomas Aquinas and St. Augustine are now in hell by papal decree. Aquinas argued, "Therefore the Blessed Virgin was not sanctified before her birth from the womb" and he also cites

Augustine, "The sanctification, by which we become temples of God, is only of those who are born again. But no one is born again, who was not born previously. Therefore the Blessed Virgin was not sanctified before her birth from the womb."[470] Thomas presents four objections and refutes them all. He was decidedly opposed to the Immaculate Conception as heresy. Accordingly, it appears that, in his Mariloatorus zeal, Pope Pius IX infallibly damned two of the Roman churches most exceptional and venerated theologians to eternal hell. The sinless Mary of myth is decidedly disparate to the fallible yet actual mother of the Lord.

Assumption of Mary

On November 1, 1950, Pope Pius XII promulgated the "Munificentissimus Deus" as divinely revealed doctrine that: "Mary, the immaculate perpetually Virgin Mother of God, after the completion of her earthly life, was assumed body and soul into the glory of Heaven"[471] Because there is no historical or theological evidence whatsoever for this, the arguments offered by Catholic theologians seem to be wholly based on emotion. For instance, "Since our Redeemer is the Son of Mary, surely, as the most perfect observer of divine law, He could not refuse to honor, in addition to His Eternal Father, His most beloved Mother also. And, since He could adorn her with so great a gift as to keep her unharmed by the corruption of the tomb, it must be believed that He actually did this."[472] It seems that the papist's preferred theological methodology is to proclaim and then try to explain. Historically, this seems to be a clear case of pagan goddess legends which infiltrated the Roman Church. The oldest manuscript fragments of the legend are in Syriac, dating to the fifth century, and the oldest quotation is a sentence in a homily of Eusebius of Alexandria from the late fourth century.[473] It was then rightfully denounced as heresy and the various apocryphal books were never taken seriously. Here is an abbreviated sample of an English rendering of one such text just to give you the flavor of how unhistorical and fantastic they are:

There were thunderings and lightnings. Jesus came on a chariot of light with Moses, David, the prophets, and the righteous kings, and addressed Mary. (There is a refrain to the speech, 'O my beloved Mother, arise, let us go hence'.) Mary spoke comfort to the apostles. Jesus spoke of the necessity of death. If she were translated, "wicked men will think concerning thee that thou art a power which came down from heaven, and that the dispensation (the Incarnation) took place in appearance".

He turned to the apostles—to me Peter and to John—and said that Mary should appear to them again. "There are 206 days from her death unto her holy assumption. I will bring her unto you arrayed in this body."

When the 206 days were over, on the evening of the 15th, that is the morning of the 16th of Mesore, we gathered at the tomb and watched all night.

At the tenth hour there were thunderings, and a choir of angels was heard, and David's harp. Jesus came on the chariots of the Cherubim with the soul of the Virgin seated in his bosom, and greeted us.

He called over the coffin and bade the body arise...[474]

As the typical version of the legend goes, the Virgin is visited by Jesus who informs her of her impending death. The apostles assemble from various locations around the world to assist her and to hear her final words. She dies and Christ descends taking her soul back to heaven. Of course, this is surrounded in high otherworldly drama as the angels, prophets, and patriarchs assemble singing praise to Mary. Tension builds as the apostles must quickly hide her corpse in the tomb of Gethsemane. She must be hidden from the Jews, portrayed as the agents of Satan, who want to destroy her body. The endings vary as in some versions the apostles pray for three days and on the third day, angelic choirs announce that the Virgin has been assumed bodily to heaven. Alternately in the Coptic version presented above, the body was hidden from the hostile Jews in a tomb for some 206 days, and then her body was believed to have been taken to heaven simultaneously with the celebration of the Jewish destruction of the temple on August 9.[475] This has all the earmarks of a fairy tale and yet it became official infallible Roman dogma in 1950.

Mariolatry

Bishop Mark A. Pivarunas representing "The Religious Congregation of Mary Immaculate Queen" states emphatically that, "Catholics do not, as Protestants falsely believe, worship the Blessed Virgin Mary."[476] While a brief look around his website will convince most folks of how disingenuous that is, Catholic apologists engage in quite a lot of sophistry when they argue that Mary is not worshipped. They attempt to obfuscate their blatant idolatry by means of artificial and contrived distinctions. First, there is *lateria*, the sacrificial worship of God. This is a legitimate use of the Greek term, as *latreia* is used in Scripture for worship, ministry, or service to God.[477] Second, there is *douleia* which ostensibly refers to the worship of saints and angels. Both of these practices are explicitly condemned in Scripture (Lev 20:6; Col 2:18). But far above saints and angels they certainly do worship Mary. This constitutes the third category, *hyperdouleia*, which is the enhanced exclusive worship of Mary. Interestingly, the word *douleia* in the New Testament is always used for slavery, bondage, or subservience.[478] While enslavement seems particularly apt in this case, the superficial system of distinction only serves as a red herring for Rome's apologists. In practice, they idolatrously worship Mary and saints (dead humans) and angels (cf. Rev. 22:9). Regardless of the seemingly endless stream of rationalizations, Mary is believed to hold the sovereign authority of God. Of course, they also claim to worship God. But God has spoken, "I am the LORD: that is my name: and my glory will I not give to another, neither my praise to graven images" (Is 42:8). Idolatry by a thousand qualifications is still idolatry. God does not accept such syncretistic worship.

Ask yourself, does this prayer by Pope Pius XII sound like worship?

Enraptured by the splendor of your heavenly beauty, and impelled by the anxieties of the world, we cast ourselves into your arms, O Immaculate Mother of Jesus and our Mother, Mary, confident of finding in your most loving heart appeasement of our ardent desires, and a safe harbor from the tempests which beset us on every side.

Though degraded by our faults and overwhelmed by infinite misery, we admire and praise the peerless richness of sublime gifts with which God has filled you, above every other mere creature, from the first moment of your conception until the day on which, after your assumption into heaven, He crowned you Queen of the Universe.

O crystal fountain of faith, bathe our minds with the eternal truths! O fragrant Lily of all holiness, captivate our hearts with your heavenly perfume! O Conqueress of evil and death, inspire in us a deep horror of sin, which makes the soul detestable to God and a slave of hell!

O well-beloved of God, hear the ardent cry which rises up from every heart. Bend tenderly over our aching wounds. Convert the wicked, dry the tears of the afflicted and oppressed, comfort the poor and humble, quench hatreds, sweeten harshness, safeguard the flower of purity in youth, protect the holy Church, make all men feel the attraction of Christian goodness. In your name, resounding harmoniously in heaven, may they recognize that they are brothers, and that the nations are members of one family, upon which may there shine forth the sun of a universal and sincere peace.

Receive, O most sweet Mother, our humble supplications, and above all obtain for us that, one day, happy with you, we may repeat before your throne that hymn which today is sung on earth around your altars: You are all-beautiful, O

Mary! You are the glory, you are the joy, you are the honor of our people! Amen.[479]

Perhaps consider if this officially sanctioned work *The Glories of Mary* by St. Alphonse Liquori, qualifies as worship:

HAIL, holy Queen, Mother of mercy.
Hail, our life, our sweetness, and our hope!
To thee do we cry, poor banished children of Eve;
To thee do we send up our sighs,
mourning and weeping in this vale of tears.
Turn then, most gracious advocate,
thine eyes of mercy toward us.
And after this our exile show unto us
the blessed fruit of thy womb, Jesus.
O clement, O loving, O sweet Virgin Mary.
V. Pray for us, O holy Mother of God.
R. That we may be made worthy of the promises of Christ.[480]

We cannot imagine how the Roman apologist can conceivably argue the above does not constitute worship. The Bible forbids us to bow down in adoration before any created being, even angels (Col. 2:18; Rev. 22:8–9). The Bible is explicit that it is idolatrous to turn to them in spiritual devotion (Exod. 20:4–5). To the biblically literate, it is utterly horrifying that Mary is identified as "Queen of Heaven," when that title denotes a demonic entity that Israel was severely punished for worshipping (Jer. 7:18). But it seems to us that the level of idolatry is much more virulent than these extravagantly misplaced affections.

Mediatrix & Coredemptrix

Mary was given the title "Mediatrix" in the above cited bull "Ineffabilis" of Pope Pius IX, the same document that proclaimed her immaculate conception. In 2012, Pope Benedict XVI affirmed this blasphemy in the statement quoted at the beginning of this chapter when he referred to her as "the mediator of God's blessing for the world." Rome's theologians argue it is an inference from her role in the incarnation of the God-man Christ Jesus. They further claim she had a role in His sacrifice on the cross to God the Father for the sake of the redemption of mankind. While there is nothing in the Bible to support it, they extend the role to the more demanding sense that, after her death, "Mary's intercessory co-operation extends to all graces, which are conferred on mankind, so that no grace accrues to men, without the intercession of Mary."[481] This is untenable and idolatrous. Let's compare a few more Scriptures with Rome's increasingly Marian mythology.

SACRED SCRIPTURE (underline added)	ROMAN DOGMA (underline added)
"Jesus saith unto him, <u>I am the way</u>, the truth, and the life: no man cometh unto the Father, but by me" (John 14:6). "Come <u>unto me</u>, all ye that labour and are heavy laden, and <u>I will</u> give you rest" (Mt 11:28).	"From that great treasure of all graces, which the Lord has brought, nothing, according to the will of God, comes to us <u>except through Mary</u>, so that, as nobody can approach the Supreme Father except through the Son, similarly nobody can approach Christ <u>except through the Mother.</u>" —Pope Leo XIII[482]
"And I will put enmity between thee and the woman, and between thy seed and her seed; it [He] shall bruise thy head, and thou shalt bruise his heel" (Ge 3:15). "And the God of peace shall bruise Satan under your feet shortly. The grace of our Lord Jesus Christ be with you. Amen" (Ro 16:20).	"All our hope do we repose in the most Blessed Virgin—in the all fair and immaculate one who has crushed the poisonous head of the most cruel serpent and brought salvation to the world: in her who is the glory of the prophets and apostles, the honor of the martyrs, the crown and joy of all the saints." —Pope Pius IX[483]

SACRED SCRIPTURE (underline added)	ROMAN DOGMA (underline added)
"For it pleased the Father that <u>in him</u> should all fulness dwell; And, having made peace through the blood of his cross, <u>by him</u> to reconcile all things unto himself; <u>by him</u>, I say, whether they be things in earth, or things in heaven" (Col 1:19–20).	"In the power of the grace of Redemption merited by Christ, Mary, by her spiritual entering into the sacrifice of her Divine Son for men, made atonement for the sins of men, and (de congruo) merited the application of the redemptive grace of Christ. In this manner she co-operates in the subjective redemption of mankind."[484]
"For there is one God, and <u>one mediator</u> between God and men, the man Christ Jesus" (1 Ti 2:5).	"Mary is the Mediatrix of all graces by her intercession in Heaven (Mediatio in speciali). Since her assumption into Heaven, Mary co-operates in the application of the grace of Redemption to man."[485]

While the last example is particularly offensive, according to Walter Martin, official Catholic sources have formulated it in even more blasphemous language as, "There is one Mediator between Christ and men, the Holy Mother Mary. Mary is the way, the truth and the life. No man comes to Jesus but by Mary."[486] This phrasing has the earmark of the demonic as it is deliberately designed to mock 1Timothy 2:5 and John 14:6 by usurping Christ's unique role and authority. No matter what visions, emotional passions, and physical healings are associated with the Marian paranormal phenomenon, it is not from God.

As if this is not bad enough, the majority of Romanists now position the imposter as "Coredemptrix," implying that she is involved in the task of saving sinners. While savvy Catholic theologians are hesitant to sign on, the title is tacitly approved by the Catholic Magisterium. In a 1918, Pope Benedict XV wrote:

As the blessed Virgin Mary does not seem to participate in the public life of Jesus Christ, and then, suddenly appears at the stations of his cross, she is not there without divine intention. She suffers with her suffering and dying son, almost as if she would have died herself. For the salvation of mankind, she gave up her rights as the mother of her son and sacrificed him for the reconciliation of divine justice, as far as she was permitted to do. Therefore, one can say, she redeemed with Christ the human race.[487]

This is a blatant *non sequitur*. Mary did not *allow* Christ to die on the cross; she certainly would have prevented it if she could have. In John 19, Jesus speaks to Mary Magdalene, Mary the mother of Cleophas, the Apostle John, and His mother Mary. I'm sure it was terrible for the others as well. Does it follow that they all suffered for our sins as well? She did not give up her rights as mother, the Roman authorities arrested Jesus, she had no choice in the matter and *she certainly did not redeem anyone.* Do Catholic leaders not see the fallacious special pleading in this sophomoric reasoning? It is hard to believe an alleged intellectual would publicly advance such poor argumentation. It seems, in the stupefying spirit of antichrist, the pope went to extravagantly inept lengths to diminish Christ's redemptive work.

Unfortunately, it has only festered since. According to a 1997 Newsweek cover story, Pope John Paul II had "received 4,340,429 signatures from 157 countries—an average of 100,000 a month—supporting the proposed dogma. Among the notable supporters are Mother Teresa of Calcutta, nearly 500 bishops and 42 cardinals, including John O'Connor of New York, Joseph Glemp of Poland and half a dozen cardinals at the Vatican itself."[488] The Marian phenomenon has increased significantly since then and it seems the only reason the title has not been officially dogmatized is in deference to ecumenism. The apparition that appears to thousands now calls itself the "Coredemptrix."[489] Clearly, this phantom femme fatale is an ambitious usurper of Christ's unique and incomparable role. This is unmistakably in the spirit of antichrist.

Marian Apparitions

It cannot be reasonably denied that a very real paranormal phenomenon is inspiring the Marian cult. These manifestations are increasing in frequency and heretical boldness. While the Church's official dogma evolves over time, the deceiving entity has been a constant in Roman theology for over a thousand years. As "Queen of Heaven," she ostensibly rules with Christ as the King of Heaven. Regrettably, the Queen of Heaven worshipped by the Roman Catholic religion is completely alien to the New Testament although she may find an analog in the Hebrew Scriptures in the book of Jeremiah (7:18; 44:17, 18, 19, 25), where her cult is condemned as one of spiritual harlotries committed by the populace of Judah. Another likely candidate from ancient lore is the goddess Roma, the deity of the city of Rome, who was also seen as the mother goddess, the Queen of Heaven. In reference to the Revelation 12 woman claimed as Mary by the popes, Eugene Boring has noted, "A grateful citizen of the Roman world could readily think of the story as a reflection of his or her own experience, with the following cast: the woman is the goddess Roma, the queen of heaven."[490] While this is certainly not what the apostle John intended, it is interesting that this is likely what a Roman pagan might think. When examining the Jeremiah passages, we see that they made cakes for the Queen of Heaven in the seventh century BC (Jer. 7:18). Astonishingly, over a thousand years later in the fourth century AD, the Eastern Church Father, Epiphanius, criticized women from Thracia, Scythia, and Arabia, for worshipping the Virgin Mary as a goddess and offering to her a certain kind of cake.[491] While none of this conclusively identifies the apparition, it suggests intriguing possibilities when viewed through the lens of the Deuteronomy 32 worldview discussed in a previous chapter.

Today it seems the Marian phantasm dictates Rome's new dogma as the pressure continues to mount for her official exaltation as "Coredemptrix." In some circles, the Marian phantom is worshipped far more than Christ and this can be demonstrated to have evolved tactically. The poseur presents herself as the immaculate sinless Coredemptrix "Queen of Heaven" endowed with incomparable compassion for sinners. She beguiles would-be Christians with a feminine gentleness they find irresistible. This clever feminine ruse seemingly makes her more approachable, motherly, and merciful than the holy sovereign Father and Lord. Pastor John MacArthur has taught exhaustively on this issue is a series of sermons available free on the internet. To this matter he commented, "The Roman Catholic view of Mary calls into question the compassion, the sympathy, the lovingkindness of God. It places in the people's minds doubt about God's care, concern, sympathy, compassion and interest in their plight. Nothing could be further from the truth."[492] People rightfully fear God but make a fatal error by directing prayer to the femme-phantom. Jesus is the only intercessor with the Father and people are being deceived into bypassing His care. This appears to be a deliberate strategy which has played out over centuries as Catholics have been trained to use the rosary, ritually chanting ten "hail Marys" for each "our Father."[493] At a ten-to-one ratio, the phantasm-matron has a prescriptively engrained advantage in the Romanized psyche. When Pope John Paul II was shot, he credited Mary as saving him in accordance with the Fátima messages. He was known as Mary's pope. All apologies aside, Mary is often the de facto Catholic deity. Accordingly, elaborate cultic shrines have been erected and millions upon millions of faithful worshippers arise to "Hail Mary."

Marian apparitions appear all over the world affirming Rome's unbiblical mythology. Every year, nearly 6 million pilgrims visit the site where "Our Lady of Lourdes" appeared to a fourteen-year-old girl in Lourdes, France.[494] The impressionable teenager, Bernadette Soubirous, was canonized as a saint in 1933, heralded as a mystic and was even given her own feast day on the sixteenth of April. Fátima,

Portugal boasts nearly 5 million worshippers a year and controversy rages concerning the cryptic apocalyptic messages actual content. In war-ravaged Bosnia-Herzegovina, over 30 million pilgrims have visited Medjugorje since the apparitions began in 1981.[495] Even so, the "spiritual leader" of the six channeler children, a Franciscan monk, Father Tomislav Vlasic, allegedly impregnated a nun and then abandoned her for a new mistress at his Marian cult compound and is described by the press as a "modern-day Rasputin with a taste for sex and séances."[496] Poland's "Our Lady of Czestochowa" shrine hosts over 5 million travelers a year.[497] "Our Lady of Knock" in Knock, Ireland has been endorsed by four recent popes and draws millions to visit the "Apparition Gable."[498] In Amsterdam, "Our Lady of the Nations" has demanded the pope declare her "Coredemptrix" with support of prominent Cardinals, bishops, priests, and thousands of devotees from over seventy countries.[499] While she heralds from Rome, the phantasmal dogma-matrix is not limited to Europe.

Mariolatry has a virtual stranglehold on Latin America as each year, some 15 to 20 million devotees visit a single shrine in Guadalupe, Mexico.[500] In Sabana Grande, Puerto Rico, "Our Lady of the Rosary" draws one hundred thousand pilgrims each year prompting plans to build a Mystical City complex boasting a gargantuan statue of Mary said to exceed the statue of Liberty in size. The Puerto Rican faithful have been described as a cult whose leaders advocate extreme acts of penance such as kneeling on pieces of sharp corrugated metal during prayer.[501] In America, a chapel in Wisconsin where the entity self-identified as the "Queen of Heaven" in 1861 was approved by Rome as an officially recognized Marian site.[502] Accordingly, attendance has, "grown tenfold, growing from an average 75 to 100 visitors a day to between 500 to 800, including daily bus tours."[503] In Conyers, Georgia, Marian channeler Nancy Fowler has received up to one hundred thousand visitors to her farm on a single day.[504] Emmitsburg, Maryland hosts the "Grotto of Our Lady of Lourdes" attracting in excess of five hundred thousand per year and is referred to as a National Shrine and hosts Mount St. Mary's University and

Seminary.[505] These are a mere sampling; it is beyond the scope of this work to catalog the full scope of the cult. It is enormous.

It is also conclusive this entity is leading people ever-so-subtly astray. It is for this reason that we first systematically examined all of the major doctrines of Roman Mariology and demonstrated their incoherence and sometimes blatant opposition to Scripture. What makes breaking this spell so particularly difficult are the alleged healing miracles and intensified devotional lives associated with the apparitions. As far as healings go, consider that if someone is already suffering from a demonic oppression, then it is trivial for demonic entities to simply cease their efforts in order to attribute a miraculous healing to the femme-phantom. As to devotion, it is quite telling that the majority of visionaries are suggestible children. For those not grounded in Scripture, mystical experience and emotional reactions lead them to accept anything supernatural as from God. They are far too immature to "try the spirits whether they are of God: because many false prophets are gone out into the world" (1 Jn 4:1), and the Roman priests who are supposed to help them are the false proph-ets the verse warns of. Of course, to the biblically literate, this is a known satanic stratagem. The apostle Paul warned, "And no marvel; for Satan himself is transformed into an angel of light" (2 Co 11:14). Jesus warned of increasing deceptive paranormal phenomenon as His return approaches, emphasizing, "if *it were* possible, they shall deceive the very elect" (Mt 24:24). The femme-phantom seems to be doing just that.

This is not simply a conclusion arrived at by our investigation, rather it is supported by peer-reviewed university research. The *Social Science Journal* published a study in 2000 by Sara Horsfall Ph.D., "The Experience of Marian Apparitions and the Mary Cult." The abstract follows:

Since the earliest visions of Mary in the 4th century, there have been an estimated 21,000 sightings of Mary in the eastern and western Christian worlds. Centered on youth from the lower economic strata, the visions spawn a considerable following. Millions visit the well-known vision sites such as Lourdes, Fátima, and Guadalupe. Many healings were reported, a proportion of which were verified as miracles by authorities. Visions have become increasingly common in the 20th century, with reports from so many places it is hard to keep track of them all. Modern visions tend to be serial, or recurring, as well as public-witnessed by hundreds or thousands of others. Phenomenological examination reveals 16 characteristics of the Marian Apparitions spiritual life world.[506]

While the visual phenomena are witnessed by thousands of people, the actual messages themselves are communicated through visionaries who go into a trance state. After a careful study of many accounts, a pattern emerged with sixteen common characteristics: 1) when they see Mary, they are still aware of their surrounding environment; 2) the visionary life world seems as real as the physical world, Mary seems to occupy real, three-dimensional space; 3) the Marian apparition has a force of its own, and the visionaries are powerless to stop it (including Pope Pius XII); 4) it includes visions of otherworldly realms like heaven, hell, and purgatory; 5) the experience often entails a progressive growth; 6) some visionaries seem to have control over it; 7) the visionary world breaks known laws of physics (i.e. the dancing sun at Fátima); 8) the trance state is hard to describe with materialistic language; 9) people are drawn to the experience and the visionaries; 10) the visionary world includes conflict and dichotomy (it is not an escapist fantasy); 11) it seems to parallel the real world even offering knowledge of future events; 12) lives are often changed; 13) the visionaries display increased knowledge; 14) the experience appears to be universal, occurring all over the planet to varying persons; 15) there is mystical union with Mary that can block the external world; 16) the apparitions are communal in that hundreds or thousands of people come to witness the vision.[507]

Most telling from this academically rigorous study is the final conclusion that, "Marian apparitions appear to be the Catholic equivalent of New Age spirituality."[508] Prophecy scholars have long puzzled over what sort of lying signs and wonders could lead the entire world to embrace a one-world religion as predicted by the book of Revelation. In light of recent events, it seems probable these phantasms are an instrumental component of the "strong delusion" the apostle Paul warned of in 2 Thessalonians. It just cannot be denied that the Marian apparitions appear to be leading the world down the primrose path to the prophesied one-world spirituality. For instance, the phantom-femme announced at Medjugorje, "Tell this priest, tell everyone, that it is you who are divided on earth. The Muslims and the Orthodox, for the same reason as Catholics, are equal before my Son and I. You are all my children."[509] This message of unity has great sentimental appeal to the postmodern pluralistic worldview but it offers little as to how such contradictory religions can all be true.

This universal appeal makes the "Our Lady of Nations" message of global peace a prime piece in the end-time puzzle. Pastor Charles Dickson expresses this colorfully in his book *A Protestant Pastor Looks at Mary:*

> A Muslim student visiting Rome wants especially to see the Church of Santa Maria Maggiore. Surprised? The poetry of a Syrian mystic is replete with Marian devotion. Surprised? Martin Luther recommended prayer to Mary. Surprised? An American Pentecostalist minister begins to visit shrines of Marian apparitions. Surprised? Muslims refer to Mary as il-Sittneh, or Our Lady. Surprised? A chapter in the Koran is named after her. Surprised? Mary's deep kindness as a mother is portrayed in Chinese art. Surprised? And now a presbyterian minister has written a book recommending praying the rosary. Still surprised? …a closer investigation of both past history and current events points out that Mary has a universal appeal that transcends our cultural, geographical, and even religious boundaries.[510]

While Mary certainly covers a lot of ground in religious circles, the strong delusion would need to embrace the world view of skeptics as well. While materialists lack belief in the supernatural, they are open to the fantastic. There seem to be indications that several areas of formally disparate thought are converging.

The mechanism of the Marian messages is eerily similar to that of the alleged alien communications delivered by New Age channelers, Buddhists, Taoists and occult mystics of the past who similarly call for humanistic unity always in opposition to biblical Christianity. Many have pointed to the UFO phenomenon and the increasing embrace of belief in benevolent alien overlords. The world has certainly been primed to accept such a revelation through the media, and the speculations of prominent scientists like Carl Sagan, Richard Dawkins, and Stephen Hawking. The scientific theory of directed panspermia has elevated a once-certifiable lunacy into respectable science. Similarly, the Darwinian-based transhumanist eschatology offered by the likes of Ray Kurzweil promises a technological utopia and radical life extension. While at first glance these are incompatible visions, coherence has never been an essential quality of Roman Catholic theology. The Roman Catholic Church has officially endorsed belief in Darwinian evolution, space aliens, and Marian apparitions. It seems entirely possible that these pseudoscientific ideas which appeal to atheists will converge with the Marian apparition to form an all-encompassing mystic spirituality under Rome…and the Prophecy of the Popes suggests the likelihood that it will be led by Petrus Romanus.

15 | The Woman Clothed with the Sun and the Red Dragon

I n Vatican City, on October 10, 2010, Pope Benedict XVI opened the Synod of Bishops' Special Assembly for the Middle East at St. Peter's Basilica. The synod took place at the Vatican from Oct. 10–24 under the theme: "The Catholic Church in the Middle East: Communion and Witness." Speaking as the alleged Vicar of Christ, the *pontifex maximus* said the Promised Land is "not of this world" and that Israel is not an earthly kingdom. His words are not surprising as the Roman Catholic Church has historically led the way in promoting supercessionism (replacement theology) by denying ethnic Israel's place in God's plan. According to the pope's biblical eisegesis, "He reveals Himself as the God of Abraham, Isaac and Jacob (cf. Ex 3:6), who wants to lead his people to the 'land' of freedom and peace. This 'land' is not of this world; the whole of the divine plan goes beyond history, but the Lord wants to build it with men, for men and in men, beginning with the coordinates of space and time in which they live and which He Himself gave them."[511]

While it is true that God's plan ultimately transcends time and space, it simply cannot be denied that the Lord meant a literal land in His promises to the patriarchs. However, the pope is not so naïve; rather, he is promoting an agenda by painting the Promised Land as a metaphysical abstraction. His political and theological overtones reflect the Vatican's consistent position that "Jerusalem cannot belong to one state."[512] Rome ostensibly pleads the case of Palestinians and Catholics who want to make pilgrimage but in truth, there is a wealth of evidence that the Vatican wants to possess Jerusalem as its own. Even more, there are high-level Jewish officials waiting in the wings to hand it over. We will examine that case thoroughly, but first we will address some foundational, historical, and theological issues.

Supercessionism (or replacement theology) is the idea that the New Testament Church has completely superseded the ethnic Hebrew nation in God's prophetic plan. No matter who endorses it, this idea is fundamentally unscriptural. Jesus in Luke 19:42 and Paul in Romans 11:25 explain, "that blindness in part is happened to Israel, until the fullness of the Gentiles be come in" (Ro 11:25b). The word "until" means they are temporarily blinded, not replaced. In Romans 9, 10, and 11 Paul's purpose was to explain Israel's future. If you have doubts, simply reading that sequence of chapters makes replacement theology absurd. The Gentile Church is clearly described as "grafted into," not *replacing* Israel. Even opposition to the Gospel is accounted for, "As concerning the gospel, they are enemies for your sakes: but as touching the election, they are beloved for the fathers' sakes. For the gifts and calling of God are without repentance" (Ro 11:28–29). In the interest of clarity, more contemporary translations render "without repentance" as "irrevocable." We wonder how Paul could have made it any clearer than that... Perhaps he did say it even stronger in Romans 11:1?

Furthermore, the pope's homily is harbinger of the coming tribulation or "time of Jacob's trouble" (Jer. 30:7). Like Paul, Jesus also said that Jerusalem would be occupied by gentiles *until* the times of the gentiles are fulfilled, just prior to His Second Coming. "And they shall fall by the edge of the sword, and shall be led away captive into all nations: and Jerusalem shall be trodden down of the Gentiles, until the times of the Gentiles be fulfilled" (Lk 21:24). Several important points can be derived from this statement by Jesus. First, it is a prophecy of the diaspora, which occurred in AD 70. The Romans spread the Jews all over the known world, selling many as slaves. Jesus' prophecy could have been easily falsified but its fulfillment is verifiable. Second, the text uses the Greek term *achri*, rendered "until," that clearly implies one day Jerusalem will be back in Jewish hands.[513] Thus, it is also an inferred prophecy about the reclamation of Jerusalem which began in 1967 and is still being contested by the Romanists. Jerusalem certainly was under Gentile control until 1967, and today it is the most fiercely contested piece of real estate on the planet. This should give skeptics pause because there are existing copies of Luke's Gospel dated to the second century.[514] The fact that Jerusalem is ostensibly in Jewish hands speaks to the lateness of the hour in God's prophetic plan.

A Woman Clothed with the Sun

There is wide agreement amongst biblical scholars that the key to the book of Revelation is chapter 12. There is also little doubt that it describes a historical sequence because Jesus' birth and ascension are conspicuous anchor points (vv.4–5). Previously, we suggested a hybrid approach that could reconcile the historicist interpretation. In light of those suggestions, we would like to make it clear that in suggesting those possibilities, we are not distancing ourselves from what we believe to be the principle meaning of the passage. The woman clothed in the sun is primarily meant to symbolize Israel. This is made very clear by the allusion to Joseph's dream seen in her crown of twelve stars (Gen 37:9). Contemporary New Testament scholar, Leon Morris, concurs, "In this symbolism we must discern Israel, the chosen people of God… The *twelve stars* will be the twelve patriarchs or the tribes which descended from them."[515]

As discussed in chapter 14, "The Occult Queen of Heaven," Pope Benedict's recent statements about the ghostly imposter's role as "woman of the Apocalypse" also relate to Israel. For millennia, this entity impersonating the Virgin Mary has been appearing and delivering sacrilegious messages to gullible children and credulous Catholic mystics. This phantom apparition also explicitly claims to be the woman in Revelation 12. She has said, "In the Apocalypse, I have been announced as the Woman Clothed with the Sun who will conduct the battle against the Red Dragon and all his followers. If you want to second my plan, you must do battle, my little ones, children of a Mother who is Leader."[516] But in the biblical text, the symbolic woman flees to the desert and hides for 1,260 days while the Archangel Michael and his forces engage in battle. The "woman" is the victim of Satan's persecution, not a military leader. This so-called Marian entity trades on biblical illiteracy. The figurative woman in the biblical text is not a warmongering phantom; rather, she is a symbol for the nation of Israel.

Pope Benedict offers lip-service that the woman symbolizes Israel, but twists it back toward Marian spiritualism, "In the vision of the Book of Revelation there is a further detail: upon the head of the woman clothed with the sun there is 'a crown of twelve stars'. This sign symbolizes the 12 tribes of Israel and means that the Virgin Mary is at the center of the People of God, of the entire communion of saints."[517] We can agree with the pope that the crown of twelve stars is an allusion to Joseph's prescient dream that predicted his future role in Egypt but prompted his brothers' treacherous jealously (Gen 37:9). Of course, Joseph was one of the twelve sons of Jacob who was renamed "Israel" from whom all Jews descend. While the deceiving entity seeks to associate with the apocalyptic symbol for the nation, the biblical Mary was simply a humble Israelite.

The symbolic woman is properly decoded by Isaiah's prophecy speaking of Israel: "Before she travailed, she brought forth; before her pain came, she was delivered of a man child" (Is 66:7). It is important to note that, contrary to the normal birthing sequence, the pain comes *after* the birth of the man-child, Jesus. For clarification, the ESV renders, "Before she was in labor she gave birth; before her pain came upon her she delivered a son" (Is 66:7). This pain speaks to the constant persecution Israel has endured since the time of Jesus and, as we shall examine, it was largely at the hands of Roman Catholicism. In Isaiah's oracle, the "she" is inarguably the nation of Israel, and this same prophecy continues to predict the remarkable rebirth of a nation in one day, which we believe represents the events of May 14, 1948. The next line reads, "Who hath heard such a thing? who hath seen such things? Shall the earth be made to bring forth in one day? or shall a nation be born at once? for as soon as Zion travailed, she brought forth her children" (Is 66:8). These "children" are Israel's spiritual offspring, Christians, who are also mentioned as "her seed" in Revelation 12. This prophecy of "a nation born at once" appears to have been fulfilled to the letter in 1948 which leads many to conclude that the time before Jesus' return is very short.

It is strangely ironic that the femme phantom of Romanism claims that she leads the battle against the Red Dragon, because it has always been Rome that has persecuted the symbolic woman, the nation of Israel. In our chapter on historicism, we also allowed for the woman's persecution by the dragon to symbolize papal Rome's war against biblical Christianity. Again, we want to be clear, that this was allowing for multiple typological layers of prophetic realization. The woman is principally ethnic Israel because the Church did not yet exist in order to give birth to the man-child, "who was to rule all nations with a rod of iron: and her child was caught up unto God, and to his throne" (Rev 12:5). The Church only came after His birth, so this symbol is necessarily Israel, and true Christians are her offspring who are visible in verse 17: "And the dragon was wroth with the woman, and went to make war with the remnant of her seed, which keep the commandments of God, and have the testimony of Jesus Christ" (Rev 12:17). The Church as "her seed" is now grafted into Israel. But chapter 12 speaks of an ongoing persecution of Israel beginning at the ascension of Jesus, "the time caught up unto God, and to his throne" (Rev 12:5) onward. The evidence that Rome led by its phantasm is allied with the mission of the red dragon in this vision is simply overwhelming.

The Red Dragon Pursues Israel

Few scholars have explored the relationship between Israel and the Church as deeply Dr. Arnold Fruchtenbaum. In his seminal work, *Israeology the Missing Link in Systematic Theology,* he writes, "Theologically, Satan is the cause of anti-Semitism."[518] Most Christians are generally uninformed as to the extent of Rome's record of anti-Semitism because most Church history books neglect or tone down its disgraceful prevalence. In contrast, Jews are deeply cognizant of this historical hatred and persecution. It is arguable that for Jews, the most blinding obstacle to the truth of the Gospel has been the actions of so-called Christians. Within a brief period following the Jewish Messiah's death, resurrection, and ascension, many of the Early Church fathers seem to have completely forgotten that their Savior, His family, Paul, the twelve apostles, and the majority of the Early Church *were Jews.* Very early, many of the fathers began teaching that God had eternally cursed the Jews for rejecting the Messiah. They taught that the Church was the new Israel. As time went on, Rome capitalized on this eisegesis declaring it authoritative. Because there seems to be some ambiguity surrounding the term "Israel," it is important to look at its use in the New Testament.

In the modern world, the word "Israel" is unambiguous. For instance, when we hear it on the nightly news we automatically think of the modern Jewish nation located in the Middle East. This is the accepted definition of the word for a good reason. Even though

Gentiles are now partakers of the covenant blessings of God, in New Testament usage the term "Israel," with one possible exception, refers exclusively to the Jewish nation. First, it was used as the new name for Jacob, the son of Isaac. It was given to him after his wrestling match with God and subsequent blessing (Gen 32:8). The second use of the term derives from when the united Davidic monarchy was divided into the northern kingdom called Israel and the southern kingdom called Judah. In 721 BC, that northern kingdom, Israel, was sacked by the Assyrians; the ten tribes residing there were dispersed and its existence as a nation ended. However, because there were representatives from all of the twelve tribes still residing in Judah, the southern kingdom, there really are no lost tribes. Only a short time later, the Babylonians did much the same to Kingdom of Judah, although they preserved their identity as a people-group.

A third use of the word ensued when those Babylonian exiles returned to the Promised Land and referred to it as Israel (Ezra, 2:2, 70; 4:3; 6:16; Neh 1:6; 2:10; Zech 12:1; Mal 1:1). This is unmistakably the way it is used by Jesus and the various New-Testament writers. It is often used to refer to the physical descendants of Abraham especially in light of God's covenant promises (c.f. Matt 2:20–21; 10:6; Luk 1:68; John 1:31; Rom 9:4). The fourth use of the name is a more specific instance of the third. Whereas the third sense is ethnic and political, the fourth refers to the elect remnant as argued by Paul in Romans chapter 9. In that chapter, Paul defines it as those who are specifically chosen by God. For instance, in verses 6–13, he notes that Abraham's son Isaac was chosen over Ishmael so it wasn't just simply a descendent of Abraham, but the one that God chose. He uses Esau and Jacob as another example, "that the purpose of God according to election might stand, not of works, but of him that calleth" (Rom 9:11b).While he said in verse 3 that his kinsmen according to the flesh were Israelites, Paul contended that, in spite of unbelief, God's Word had not failed because they are not all Israel who are descended from Israel. Thus, in this narrower use of the term, Paul referred to the remnant of believing Jews within the larger ethnic group of Israel, albeit they are still ethnic Jews.

The fifth and final way is the one possibility where "Israel" could obliquely refer to believing Gentiles. In Galatians 6:16, Paul prays for the "Israel of God." It seems that in this letter, Paul is making a distinction between the "Jerusalem which now is" (Gal 4:25) and "Jerusalem which is above" (Gal 4:26). He also argues that, "they which are of faith, the same are the children of Abraham" (3:7). Even so, it is still possible to take this in the same sense as Romans 9: ethnic Jews who come to faith in Jesus. Hebrew Christian scholar, Arnold Fruchtenbaum, argues, "Paul did not view the Church as a continuation of Old Testament Israel, but rather a new entity altogether. Finally, Galatians 6:16 does not refer to all New Testament believers as *the Israel of God*, but only to the Jewish believers who are the believing remnant."[519] While this one reference is debatable, gentiles are elsewhere clearly described as unnatural branches grafted into Israel (Rom 11:24). In the Authorized Version of the New Testament, the term "Israel" appears seventy-five times in seventy-three verses and, without a doubt, the vast majority of occurrences fall under the first, third, and fourth uses. Considering the conspicuous absence of a single unambiguous application, there is no sound exegetical reason to believe the term "Israel" should apply broadly to the Church. Nonetheless, this was the dominant dogma imposed by the Roman magisterium for millennia.

It is rather perplexing that many of the Church fathers seemed to deny that any Jews ever trusted Jesus to be their Savior. The Scripture is full of examples like: "And the word of God increased; and the number of the disciples multiplied in Jerusalem greatly; and a great company of the priests were obedient to the faith" (Ac 6:7). Also, Luke 23:48 records that many of the Jewish witnesses deeply regretted Jesus' crucifixion, beating their chests as a sign of mourning. Of course, Nicodemus, a leading Pharisee, had earlier confessed to Jesus that many of his associates were impressed enough by His works to know "thou art a teacher come from God: for no man can do these miracles that thou doest, except God be with him" (Jn 3:2). This same Nicodemus also helped supply at the tomb and dress Jesus' dead body after the crucifixion (Jn 19:39). The Church fathers largely portrayed the Pharisees and priests as exclusively evil and hostile to the Gospel. They cherry-picked statements from the Gospels and from Paul's writings to justify their racist attacks while ignoring Paul's own testimony to his Jewish heritage including his being a Pharisee (Phil 3:5). If anything, the Early Church served to drive Jews further from the truth. Could this be Satan's primary means of blinding them, through the very ones who were supposed to be ministers of reconciliation (2 Cor 5:20)? It seems to be so.

They accused the Jews of having murdered Jesus. This charge has been repeated over and over again by racist groups throughout history and is still promoted today. Of course, Jesus left no room for such heresy, "Therefore doth my Father love me, because I lay down my life, that I might take it again. No man taketh it from me, but I lay it down of myself. I have power to lay it down, and I have power to take it again. This commandment have I received of my Father" (Jn 10:17–18). In sharp opposition to Christ, the canonized Roman Catholic Saint and Doctor of the Church with his own feast day, John Chrysostom, accused the Jews of the worst of crimes imaginable. According to him, God eternally hates the Jews who would never again be a sovereign nation nor rebuild the Temple. In one sermon, he raged, "You did slay Christ, you did lift violent hands against the Master, you did spill his precious blood. This is why you have no chance for atonement, excuse, or defense."[520] Apparently, along with ignoring Jesus, he did not obey Paul's teaching that Gentile Christians should not behave arrogantly toward the broken off Jewish branches (Rom 11:18). Unfortunately, this moral failing was characteristic.

Origen wrote, "And therefore the blood of Jesus falls not only on the Jews of that time, but on all generations of Jews up to the end of the world."[521] This was more the virulent rhetoric as it touched lives in tangible ways. In AD 306, Spanish church leaders issued a decree absolutely forbidding Christians and Jews to marry. In 325, after Constantine had allegedly become a Christian, he ordered all Jews to leave Rome. The Nicaean Council also ruled that Christians could have nothing in common with Jews. In fact, this was the rationale behind disassociating the date for Easter from the Passover as it is in Scripture (Mark 14:16; Luke 22:15; John 19:14). This sort of thinking caught on and the Council of Antioch passed an ordinance prohibiting Christians from celebrating Passover with their Jewish neighbors in AD 341. Later, the Council of Laodecia (434–481) officially banned Christians from keeping the Jewish Sabbath.

In AD 438, Roman Emperor Theodosius banned all Jews from holding any form of public office. This early law was the legal precedent on which centuries of later anti-Semitic legislation was founded. Jews were also forbidden to work in many occupations but they were encouraged to be money lenders and pawn brokers. This was because charging interest was not allowed for Catholics, a practice condemned as usury at the Council of Nicea in 345 and the Council of Aix in 789. Jews were tolerated usurers when their lending was to the advantage of the Church or secular authorities. While many popes and councils condemned the practice, Nicholas V (1452), Sixtus IV (1478), and Innocent VIII (1489) all granted absolutions to promote it in the Jewish community.[522] Thus, it is demonstrable that the ubiquitous conspiracy theory that "Jews control all the money" is simply a derivative of the Catholic Church's past decrees.

Things only digressed as Jews were forced out of their homes and banned from living in certain cities. In the seventh century, Gaul, Burgundy, and Lombardy in northern Italy ordered all Jews to leave their territories. Evangelism took the form of a choice between conversion and death. Under those terms, many chose death. Ferguson's history text notes, "In 721–22 emperor Leo III decreed the forced conversion of Jews, a decree repeated by later emperors, all unsuccessful."[523] Jewish children were taken from their parents to be reared as Roman Catholics. Also during this time in Spain, the religion of Judaism was officially outlawed. Later, they were forcibly expelled from the Kingdom of Granada. Even with persecution on the rise, there was still a flourishing Jewish community in Spain. Unfortunately, the ninth-century invasion of Spain by Muslims resulted in massive Jewish casualties. Of course the Muslim invasions led to widespread European support for the crusades. Even so, the rationale for the crusades reflects apostate Roman Catholic theological traditions rather than biblical theology or "just war" theory.

There was certainly justification for defending Europe against the Muslim invaders, but Pope Urban II's rationale for the first Crusade in 1095 was to defend pilgrims going to to the Holy Land. You might ask, "What is wrong with protecting tourists?" It was not tourism. Rome's tradition was that by making a pilgrimage to Jerusalem, one could gain special favor with God, obtain absolution from particularly bad sins, or even spring deceased relatives from purgatory. While this reflects Rome's proclivity for ritual magic, God is not manipulated by vacations to special locations. Nevertheless, this theologically erroneous concept of pilgrimage is demonstrably what drove the crusades. According to Ferguson:

> Some went on pilgrimage to a holy site as a penance imposed by a confessor, some as an act of devotion (often to fulfill a vow), and some went to Jerusalem in their old age in order to die there. Pilgrims to Jerusalem had at first been forbidden to carry arms. Then they carried them for self-defense. Finally, the "pilgrims" took the offensive against the Muslims. The Crusades combined the language of pilgrimage and of a military expedition. Pilgrimage to Jerusalem was one of the motifs inspiring the zeal of the crusaders.[524]

This period near the height of the papal pornocracy marked a new low in hatred and racism. For the next few hundred years Jews were treated worse than animals throughout Europe and the Middle East. Even though the crusaders seemingly believed that they were doing the will of God, they viciously slaughtered Jews in the most horrid ways imaginable. The women were often raped and even babies were killed. In 1099, when Jerusalem was conquered ostensibly "in the name of Christ," the crusaders rounded up what was left of Jesus' ethnic brethren into a synagogue and set it ablaze to raucous, celebratory praise. Unfortunately, these practices were not limited to the Middle East and the horrors of war.

Across Europe, Jews were increasingly falsely accused of triggering plagues and similar ludicrous charges like using children's blood in Passover celebrations. This period marks the initial time when Jews were forced to wear distinctive yellow patches (a practice the twentieth-century *Führer* of Germany, Adolf Hitler, would also adopt). As the mythos about plagues and other nonsense spread, Jewish quarters were razed all over France, Germany, and England. One notable example occurred in 1189 at the coronation of King Richard I when the Jewish quarter of London was intentionally set ablaze incinerating many Jews who were simply sleeping in their homes.[525] The celebration day of the resurrection is dreaded by Jews because of the long history of violent Easter riots against "the Christ killers." Apparently, the fact that it was actually the *Roman* authorities that crucified Jesus escaped the ignorant masses. Even so, it was human sin that made His death necessary. Jesus said that He laid His life down and that no one took it from Him. He came to die for Jews as well as racist gentiles.

During the fourth Lateran Council of 1215, the papists enacted strict legislation mandating that all Jews wear the yellow badge.[526] Also the council of Arles in 1234 decreed, "male Jews from the age of 13 and up, when outside their homes, except when on a journey, must wear upon the outer garment, upon the breast, a round badge of three or four fingers in width."[527] Similarly, females twelve and older were required to wear veils. As incredible as it seems, this legislation was justified largely to prevent accidental sexual liaisons between Catholics and Jews, a practice which merited the death penalty. One marvels at how such an "accident" could occur amongst so-called Christians who held to biblical morals. Obviously, it couldn't, so this rationale is another product of Rome's maladroit theology. This new papal legislation led to unprecedented expulsions and persecutions across Europe.

In 1290, Jews were systematically purged from England and Wales, then Paris and surrounding areas of France. Pope Gregory IX wrote, "If what is said about the Jews…is true, no punishment would be sufficiently great or sufficiently worthy of their crime."[528] Later, in 1306, they were expelled from the Rhineland, a few years later from Hungary, and then from the south of France in 1394. A date that every grade school kid knows is when Columbus sailed the ocean blue in 1492; what they aren't told is that he set sail just as the Jews were being forced from Spain and then from Portugal a few years later. According to historian Cushing B. Hassell, "In 1492, persecution was begun against the Jews, of whom 500,000 were expelled from Spain and their wealth confiscated. In seventy years the population of Spain was reduced from 10,000,000 to 6,000,000 by the banishment of Jews, Moors and Morescoes ('Christianized' Moors), the most wealthy and intelligent of the inhabitants of that country."[529] It was also during this era that the plague known as the Black Death wiped out nearly a third of Europe's population including Jews. Even so, they were blamed for poisoning the water supply with human hearts and body parts. The resulting backlash resulted in hundreds of Jewish communities being completely wiped out.

As if things couldn't get any worse, Pope Sixtus IV instituted the Inquisition, which specifically targeted Jews as heretics. The death toll of the inquisition is difficult to ascertain largely because of Rome's penchant for revisionist history. According to Wylie, "under that bull commenced that system of juridical extermination which is said to have cost Spain upwards of five millions of her citizens, who either perished miserably in the dungeon, or expired amid the flames of the public *auto da fe*."[530] While it is probably not possible to get a precise number, many protestant historians place the number of Jews exterminated by Rome in the neighborhood of two million.[531] The inquisition truly merits the term "holocaust." The untold horrors and variety of injustice visited on the Jewish people are simply beyond the scope of our brief survey, but we hope the point is sinking in as to the identity of symbols in Revelation 12.

Pope Paul IV stated that the Jews' "own guilt has consigned them to perpetual slavery"[532] when he officially decreed in his 1555 bull *Cum Nimis Absurdum* that all Jews must live in walled ghettos. Really, this was only the official decrial of what had long been in practice. The Council of Basel (1431–1449) had already advised that all Jews live apart from Christians but this new papal pronouncement in the sixteenth century put them under literal lock-and-key. According to Catholic historian, Edward Flannery, "Patterns varied, but usually the ghetto was located in a poorer region of the city and enclosed by high walls, its gates guarded by Christian gatekeepers, paid by the confined. Some of the most famous ghettos were those in Prague, Venice, Frankfurt-on-Main, and Rome. Most were unbelievably overcrowded, often comprising of a single street of abnormally tall houses, crammed with people who lived ever in dread of plagues and fires that frequently struck."[533] For centuries, Jews were forced to live like caged rats for no other reason than their ethnicity. One can readily see that the later German concentration camps were simply an ideological extension of the ghettos.

At the dawn of the Protestant reformation, many Jews found respite from the barbarism of the papists. While it was short-lived, in 1523, Martin Luther wrote, "I would request and advise that one deal gently with the Jews…if we really want to help them, we must be guided in our dealings with them, not by Papal Law, but by the Law of Christian love."[534] Unfortunately, when this did not result in the mass conversion of Jews, his frustration got the best of him. He published a pamphlet in 1543 called, "On the Jews and their Lies," expressing his outrage at Jesus being portrayed as a bastard. But he went way too far; he advocated the burning of synagogues, books, expelling Jews from their homes and seizing assets. It is indefensible, but then again, Luther never claimed infallibility. Even though this pamphlet is deplorable, Luther confessed that he was too harsh. It is important to note that despite his failings, Luther did not err theologically in the grievous manner of the shameful "Saint" Chrysostom or outrageous Origen. His 1544 revised edition of the Bible allowed, "There are always a few Jews who will be saved,"[535] and his hymn "O, You Poor Judas, What Did You Do" (published the same year) reflects his more reasonable convictions:

> T'was our great sins and misdeeds gross
> Nailed Jesus, God's true son, to the cross
> Thus you, poor Judas, we dare not blame
> Nor the band of Jews; ours is the shame.[536]

In 1751, Pope Benedict XIV issued the Encyclical, *A Quo Primum*, "On Jews and Christians Living in the Same Place," which is as an astonishing a statement of racial bigotry as any you are likely to find in a neo-Nazi propaganda mill. In it, he cites popes Nicholas IV, Paul IV, Paul V, Gregory VIII, and Clement VIII forbidding Christians from living in the same cities with Jews. He was deeply troubled that polish Jews were becoming more successful in business than Roman Catholics and even more outraged that Jews were hiring Catholics as servants. After issuing a string of recommendations to the Polish bishops about not allowing their people to associate with or work for Jews, he encourages them to set a proper example: "You will be able to give these orders and commands easily and confidently, in that neither your property nor your privileges are hired to Jews; furthermore you do no business with them and you neither lend them money nor borrow from them. Thus, you will be free from and unaffected by all dealings with them."[537] We wonder how anyone can buy into the notion that the pope speaks for Christ when there are so many glaring examples of papal bigotry against Christ's own race.

A couple hundred years later, a baptized Roman Catholic who had served as a communicant and altar boy waxed eloquent about his childhood dream to be a papist, "I had excellent opportunity to intoxicate myself with the solemn splendor of the magnificent church festivals. As was only natural the position of the abbot seemed to me, as the village priest had once seemed to my father, the highest and most desirable ideal."[538] But this man never achieved that childhood ideal… Instead, he pushed the ideological precedent of the crusades, ghettos, and inquisition to their logical extremes. In receiving the blessing of two popes, he became the *Führer* of the Third Reich and enforcer of the Final Solution that sent over 6 million Jews to their deaths. While it is not fair to pin all of Hitler's madness on Roman Catholicism, it seems even more unjust to argue it was unrelated. We mentioned the Faustian concordats signed by two popes, Pius XI and XII, which for all intents and purposes endorsed the Nazi regime in the eyes of German-Roman Catholics. Also, one of Hitler's favorite propaganda items was the sham called, *The Protocols of the Learned Elders of Zion.* While we will not explore it here, there is a solid case that it was a Jesuit creation (see link).[539] Ultimately, conspiracy *theories* are not really necessary because there is ample evidence in the historical record.

At the outset of World War II, *Time Magazine* ran an article which revealed that the Vatican, in allegiance with the fascist dictator Benito Mussolini (called Il Duce), had it its sights on gaining control over Jerusalem in the spoils of war:

VATICAN CITY: Pope to Get Jerusalem?

Monday, July 08, 1940
In a Rome clinic last week lay Myron Charles Taylor, 66, slowly convalescing from his second gallstone operation in

a twelvemonth. Despite his efforts as special ambassador to Pope Pius XII, World War II had spread further than ever. Reports were persistent that Mr. Taylor would resign when he was well enough.

Mr. Taylor started with a strike against him when U. S. Protestants hotly protested his appointment, cried that it encroached on the historic separation of Church & State. Last week the U. S. Evangelical and Reformed Church added its official outcry to those of the Methodists, Presbyterians, Lutherans, Baptists and Seventh Day Adventists. Strike two was Italy's entry into the war, which fouled the Pope's peace efforts, left Mr. Taylor no one with whom to cooperate.

Third strike and out on Mr. Taylor—the Catholic Church's tacit participation in the spoils of Fascist victory—last week became a distinct possibility. To Il Duce went a telegram from 30 Italian Bishops, urging him to crown "the unfailing victory of our Army" by planting the Italian flag over Jerusalem. In England, the Manchester Guardian reported that the Axis powers plan to turn Palestine over to the jurisdiction of the Vatican and transport Palestine's Jewish population to Ethiopia.

Under the plan, said the Guardian, the Pope will care for the holy places in Palestine, let Italy run the country.[540]

They saw this as the quick way to gain sovereignty over Jerusalem and Temple Mount from the British and the Muslims. As you can see, early on, when it looked like the Fascists would be conquering Europe, the Vatican was behind them. After centuries of political gamesmanship, they are masters of shifting allegiances to position themselves favorably. As the war progressed and the tides shifted, they expediently associated themselves with the allies and later the United Nations, hoping to reach their goals that way. French journalist, Edmond Paris, contends, "The public is practically unaware of the overwhelming responsibility carried by the Vatican and its Jesuits in the start of the two world wars—a situation which may be explained in part by the gigantic finances at the disposition of the Vatican and its Jesuits, giving them power in so many spheres, especially since the last conflict."[541] The cold, hard historical facts reveal that none of Hitler's ideas about Jews were original, and nearly all of them find ample precedent in the practices of papal Rome. There is simply no denying that the papal endorsements encouraged Hitler to write, "And so I believe to-day that my conduct is in accordance with the will of the Almighty Creator. In standing guard against the Jew I am defending the handiwork of the Lord"[542] and most likely, he honestly believed it. If Roman Catholicism truly wants to disassociate from his legacy, we wonder why they have never excommunicated Adolf Hitler and Benito Mussolini like they did countless innocents who simply disagreed with them. We can only suppose in their twisted system, after a few coins in coffer ring, Hitler's soul from purgatory springs.

After the war, the Vatican, escaped Nazis, and western intelligence community formed an unholy alliance against communism that employed what can only be described as acts of terrorism across Europe. Frankly, it is extremely difficult to determine who is telling the truth. While we do not endorse all the opinions within, the books *Unholy Trinity* and *The Secret War Against the Jews* by Mark Aarons and John Loftus provide quite a bit of damning evidence, including the "rat lines" which helped Nazi war criminals escape via the Vatican amongst other things. Perhaps the only positive thing the Second World War did for the Jews was provide the impetus for the establishment of their homeland in Canaan. We use the biblical term Canaan because that was what it was called before the Israelites first moved there. The term "Palestine" is actually an anti-Semitic slur created by the Romans to belittle the Jews after they sacked Jerusalem in AD 70 and put down the revolt of AD 135. As they auctioned Jews off as slaves, the emperor Hadrian determined to rename the Promised Land after King David's classic foes, the Philistines. The Latin name *Provincia Syria Palaestina* was later shortened to *Palaestina* and this is where the anglicized "Palestine" comes from. Thus, the name "Palestine" was Rome's original way of rubbing in the seizure of the Jewish homeland. Today, the term is so common that few people are sensitive to its original demeaning purpose. But we digress.

At this point, we cannot imagine that there is much doubt as to the identity of the Red Dragon's principle agent in Revelation 12:13–17. What other agency consistently blamed Israel for killing Christ? What other power has pursued the Jews from the ascension onward? Who instituted purging them from their homes and seized their assets? Who first forced them to wear badges and live in camps? Who instituted the inquisition that killed millions? Who inspired and endorsed of the leader of National Socialism? With this in mind, consider Messianic theologian Arnold Fruchtenbaum's explanation:

Satan's war against the Jews between Abraham and the first coming was to try to thwart the first coming (Rev. 12:1–5). His present and future war against the Jews is to thwart the second coming (Rev. 12:12–14). It has been pointed out earlier that the basis of the second coming is Israel's national salvation and Jesus will not come back until the Jewish people ask Him to. If Satan can ever succeed in destroying the Jews before there is a national salvation, then Satan's career is eternally safe. For this reason he has had a perpetual, unending war against the Jew.[543]

The symbol of the woman in Revelation 12 is Israel as pursued by the Red Dragon symbolizing Satan. Consciously or not, there has been only one establishment so persistently inclined against the Jews from the ascension onward, and it has been Rome.

So, where does that leave the supreme replacement theologian Benedict XVI? We surmise that he lives in a state of blissful denial more than malevolence. Either way, the stage is set for Petrus Romanus. As we shall see in the following chapter, the Vatican is actively maneuvering to take control of the Old City of Jerusalem and has gained a foothold. This seems to be bringing biblical prophecy to a head. The eminent theologian and longtime President of Dallas Theological Seminary, Louis Sperry Chafer, wrote concerning Rome's ambitions: "Christendom expands its influence even to governments, which governments must yet be judged for their misleading professions. Though inexplainable [*sic*] to the finite mind, it is nevertheless certain that God brings every unholy assumption, which He has permitted His creatures to advance, to an experimental test and to the end that all may be judged in its reality. Even the purpose of the Church of Rome to gain political ascendency is allowed to come to fruition for a brief period preceding the judgment which is to fall upon her."[544]

It seems that judgment is forecast in the Prophecy of the Popes. If so, then it will be sooner rather than later. One wonders how the description of the Antichrist who shall "divide the land for gain" (Dan 11:39) escapes the attention of Catholic exegetes. Even more, the many prophetic warnings about dividing God's land like in Joel 3:2. Note that "those days and that time" clearly refers to the "day of the Lord" that Christians understand as the second coming of Jesus Christ. It is also noteworthy that God refers to it is as *His* land.

"For, behold, in those days, and in that time, when I shall bring again the captivity of Judah and Jerusalem, I will also gather all nations, and will bring them down into the valley of Jehoshaphat, and will plead with them there for my people and for my heritage Israel, whom they have scattered among the nations, and parted my land" (Joel 3:1–2).

16 The Burdensome Stone

And in that day will I make Jerusalem a
burdensome stone for all people: all that burden
themselves with it shall be cut in pieces, though
all the people of the earth be gathered together
against it.

—ZECHARIAH 12:3

On December 15, 2011, this story ran on the *Israeli
Arutz Sheva 7* website:

Exposé: The Vatican Wants to Lay its Hands on Jerusalem

Peace negotiations in the Middle East must tackle the issue
of the status of the holy sites of Jerusalem", Cardinal Jean-
Louis Tauran, head of the Vatican's Council for Interreligious
Dialogue, declared several days ago in Rome.

The Vatican's former foreign minister asked to place
some Israeli holy places under Vatican authority, alluding to
the Cenacle on Mount Zion and the garden of Gethsemane
at the foot of the Mount of Olives in Jerusalem.

The first site also houses what is referred to as King David's tomb.[545]

The Significance of Jerusalem

Serving as bookends for all of redemptive history, "Jerusalem" is first mentioned when Melchizedek, a prophetic type of Jesus Christ, is called the "king of Salem" (Gen 14:18), and then finally, the book of Revelation closes with the "New Jerusalem" coming down from heaven (Rev 21). It is undoubtedly holy ground. God was once present in Jerusalem in a special way above and beyond His usual omnipresence. The Hebrew Bible records that God's presence manifested physically as the "Shekinah" described as a radiant cloud (1 Kgs 8:10–11). During Ezekiel's ministry, when God became fed up with His people's sin, His glory departed Jerusalem (Eze 10). Shortly thereafter, just as the prophets predicted, the Babylonians captured and destroyed Jerusalem (2 Kgs 25; Jer. 52). This marked the inauspicious end of the first temple period.

The Jews rebuilt the second temple in Jerusalem but things did not happen as they expected. They might have known because the prophet Daniel not only predicted the second temple's destruction, he told them the Messiah would come prior (Dan 9:24–26). This should lead all Jews to the inescapable conclusion that because only Jesus meets that requirement, their Tanakh (Hebrew Bible) demands that Jesus was the Messiah. Isaiah had even written that the Messiah would be rejected and suffer for the sins of the people (Isa 53:5). Jesus marked the return of God to the temple in the first century and just as before, when He was rejected it was again destroyed. Although it has taken centuries, some Jews have begun to acknowledge this. Even the late Rabbi Yitzchak Kaduri (a popular kabbalist, who died in 2006 prompting three hundred thousand people to march in his funeral procession) came to this truth. In what can only be described as a bizarre twist of fate, he left a sealed message with strict orders for it to be opened one year after his funeral. That message named Yeshua as the Messiah and said He would return shortly after Ariel Sharon dies.[546] Sharon is alive but has been preserved in a permanent vegetative state since suffering a stroke in January of 2006. Whether this comes to pass or not, more and more Jews are beginning to acknowledge that Jesus must be the Messiah for the Torah to hold true.

The Torah promised the nation blessings under obedience (Deu 28: 1–14) and it promised they would be cursed and uprooted from the land if they were not (Deu 28:15ff). The Torah was not broken because, as we examined in the last chapter, the latter condition is exactly what has happened from AD 70 onward. God's permissive will toward the centuries of satanic persecution and even the holocaust only make sense in light of Deuteronomy 28:15 onward. But the prophets also spoke of a time beyond those two temples to a glorious future and their descriptions feature Jerusalem prominently. A representative example is, "Thus saith the LORD; I am returned unto Zion, and will dwell in the midst of Jerusalem: and Jerusalem shall be called a city of truth; and the mountain of the LORD of hosts the holy mountain" (Zec 8:3). Indeed, this is the ultimate destiny of Jerusalem and it also explains why the leaders of Judaism, Islam, and Romanism want to claim it as their own. Christians are, for the most part, unconcerned because they expect Jesus to claim it for Himself upon His return.

Considering that the tiny nation of Israel is about the size of Rhode Island, isn't it rather amazing that it is the primary focus for the foreign policy experts of the world? How can it be that such a seemingly insignificant minority has such a major impact on the world? The truth might be unpalatable to the replacement theologian, but the answer is very simple: God. We learn from the Bible that God often deals with mankind in terms of nations and "For the LORD'S portion is his people; Jacob is the lot of his inheritance" (Deu 32:9). It is not because they deserved it. The awesome Creator and Sustainer of all life, space, and time *condescended* to have Israel function as His mechanism for His purposes on earth and they still have unfinished business. Ultimately, it has nothing to do with politics or race. It is not that Jews are better people or genetically superior. It is only because God keeps His word.

One reason many Bible interpreters fail to see the significance of modern Israel is that they are not aware that the prophets spoke of a two-stage gathering associated with the Day of the Lord. Messianic scholar Arnold Fruchtenbaum explains, "First, there was to be a regathering in unbelief in preparation for judgment, namely the judgment of the Tribulation. This was to be followed by a second worldwide regathering in faith in preparation for blessings, namely the blessings of the messianic age."[547] The initial gathering in unbelief ensued in force during the twentieth century for the purpose of judgment as explained by Ezekiel (20:33–38). In addition, the prophet Amos forecast a time in which God would gather them for judgment just prior to restoring the Davidic King, "For, lo, I will command, and I will sift the house of Israel among all nations, like as corn is sifted in a sieve, yet shall not the least grain fall upon the earth" (Am 9:9). The same passage goes on to explain that God will restore them to *never* again be taken from the land (Amos 9:7–15). This necessarily refers to the current restoration or a future one.

According to the Hebrew Scriptures, it is only after this initial gathering and tribulation that the nation of Israel will acknowledge Jesus as the Messiah, a requirement for His Second Coming. That prerequisite derives from Jesus' pronouncement to the leaders of Israel, "Behold, your house is left unto you desolate: and verily I say unto you, Ye shall not see me, until the time come when ye shall say, Blessed is he that cometh in the name of the Lord" (Lk 13:35). The Old Testament contains a vivid prophecy of that eventuality, "And I will pour upon the house of David, and upon the inhabitants of Jerusalem, the spirit of grace and of supplications: and they shall look upon me whom they have pierced, and they shall mourn for him, as one mourneth for his only son, and shall be in bitterness for him, as one that is in bitterness for his firstborn" (Zec 12:10). The Hebrew term, *dāqar*, which is rendered "pierced," is derivative of *madqārâ* which appears ten times in various forms and always denotes a puncture wound. *The Theological Wordbook of the Old Testament* states, "The weapon associated with *dāqar* is usually the sword, though a spear is the instrument in Num 25:8."[548] So according to the Hebrew prophet Zechariah, God was pierced and only Jesus Christ meets that characteristic. Tensions in the Middle East seem to forecast this prophesied national repentance sooner rather than later. Recalling the end-time markers "the fullness of the gentiles" (Ro 11:25) and "times of the Gentiles" (Lk 21:24) which were qualified by "until," we now examine the current state of affairs.

The Imminent Terminus of the Times of Gentiles

One way to examine that "until" is to look at the spread of the Gospel, and there are many competent sites like the *The Joshua Project* doing that.[549] One rather astonishing indicator is the success of the Gospel in China where it is reported that there are currently sixteen thousand, five hundred new converts *per day*![550] Africa reports similar numbers where sixteen thousand Muslims leave Islam *per day* for Christianity.[551] (While these numbers are exciting, there are still many unreached people-groups and languages with no Bible translation. To that end, we strongly encourage Christians to support missions.)

Still yet, another way to quantify that "until" might be to look at Israel and see if there is any movement in that sector. There were no more than a dozen or so Messianic believers in the Jewish homeland when they declared statehood in 1948 and only around 250 when they retook Jerusalem in 1967. Writing in the year 2000, Brent Kinman reported that, "Now there are in the neighborhood of six thousand believers in more than fifty congregations."[552] Has this trend continued? As of May 26, 2011 The Baptist Press reported: "Now there are an estimated 150 Jewish congregations around Israel meeting in different languages. The number of believers is estimated to be around 20,000, growing exponentially from 1948 when 12 Jews who believed in Jesus could be counted, to 1987 when there were 3,000 and 1997 where there were 5,000."[553]

If you know anything about exponential growth then this strongly implies an event horizon when the line goes vertical, meaning that the time of national repentance and recognition is close-at-hand. Even so, some people seem to have difficulty accepting God's longsuffering disposition toward the Jewish people.

The Dry Bones Come to Life

God gave the prophet Ezekiel the reason why He would restore the ethnic nation even while they are still denying their Messiah: "Therefore say unto the house of Israel, Thus saith the Lord GOD; I do not this for your sakes, O house of Israel, but for mine holy name's sake, which ye have profaned among the heathen, whither ye went" (Eze 36:22). Because God made irrevocable promises to Jewish people concerning the land (Gen 13:14–15) the real issue is *His name.* We believe He is gathering them now despite their unbelief and that this infers that the hour is late on the prophetic time clock. This can be seen in the prophecy of the dry bones by Ezekiel which seems to prefigure the aftermath of the holocaust and the subsequent rebirth of the Jewish homeland.

> Thus saith the Lord GOD; Behold, O my people, I will open your graves, and cause you to come up out of your graves, and bring you into the land of Israel. And ye shall know that I am the LORD, when I have opened your graves, O my people, and brought you up out of your graves, And shall put my spirit in you, and ye shall live, and I shall place you in your own land: then shall ye know that I the LORD have spoken it, and performed it, saith the LORD. (Eze 37:12–14)

Once the horrors of the holocaust were widely known, worldwide sentiment carried enough influence over the power elites in the United Nations to evoke support for a Jewish homeland in the Promised Land. The Zionist movement, which had begun in the nineteenth century, inspired Jews to return to the land even before the war. After the holocaust, this movement gained traction and the UN recommended partitioning the land into Jewish and Arab states and all the major powers the United States, Great Britain, and Soviet Union agreed to the plan. As we will see below, the Vatican never supported the deal. But they are quick to remind us that part of the original plan was to make Jerusalem an international city, according to UN Resolution 181 issued on November 29, 1947, "The City of Jerusalem shall be established as a corpus separatum under a special international regime and shall be administered by the United Nations. The Trusteeship Council shall be designated to discharge the responsibilities of the Administering Authority on behalf of the United Nations."[554]

A few months later on May 14, 1948, David Ben Gurion declared the new state of Israel. This was a historic moment that, as we mentioned in the previous chapter, fulfilled Isaiah's prophecy about a nation being born in a day in surprising detail (66:8). In so doing, Ben Gurion offered the Arabs an olive branch:

We extend our hand to all neighboring states and their peoples in an offer of peace and good neighborliness, and appeal to them to establish bonds of cooperation and mutual help with the sovereign Jewish people settled in its own land. The State of Israel is prepared to do its share in a common effort for advancement of the entire Middle East.[555]

The day after this peaceful offer, the Red Dragon responded through his current instrument of war: radical Islam. Israel was attacked from all sides by Syria, Egypt, Iraq, Lebanon, and

Trans-Jordan. Against all odds, the tiny fledgling nation not only defended its borders, it acquired new territory. There was another war in 1956 and yet two more in 1967 and 1973. It has been reported that, "A West Point general once remarked that though the US Military Academy studies wars fought throughout the world, they do not study the Six Day War—because what concerns West Point is strategy and tactics, not miracles."[556] The six-day war of 1967, which marked the reclamation of Jerusalem, is nothing short of legendary and reminds one of Old Testament accounts of the Lord's hand being with them.

While we certainly have sympathy for the Arab refugees (some of whom are Christians), they are largely the end result of the Arab assault in 1948, not Jewish aggression. The managed corporate media is as one-sided as the Vatican in presenting a skewed version of history. In 1948, only six hundred fifty thousand Jews lived in the region. Over the next decade, through war and discrimination, the surrounding Arab nations expelled close to seven hundred thousand Jews who subsequently were welcomed into the Jewish homeland. But on the other side of the coin, the Arab refugees (now called Palestinians) who also numbered around seven hundred thousand were *not* allowed to be absorbed into the surrounding Arab nations (incidentally most of whom still refuse to acknowledge Israel's existence). The poor "Palestinians" are stuck in the middle but it seems that the media (and the Vatican) pins all of the blame on the Jews when the Arabs are much more culpable. We think the evidence shows the papists are using the refugees as political pawns to advance their Jerusalem ambition. The problem with Rome's current reiteration of UN Resolution 181 is that the Arab's nullified the UN agreement by attacking in 1948. There seems to be little hope for a lasting peace. While the pope promotes the two-state solution, we believe the only political answer is the Davidic monarchy (Lk 1:32), and that all of the current posturing is a manifestation of the spiritual warfare prefigured in Revelation 12.

Jerusalem: The Burdensome Stone

The idea that tribulation is inevitable is visible in that today the tiny little nation of Israel is still surrounded on all sides by people who have literally sworn to wipe it off the map. We certainly believe they have the right to protect themselves. Even so, supporting the nation's right to exist is a far cry from endorsing all of its politics and actions. Many aspects of modern Israel do disturb us (and those that we do not support), but even so, we think that the Jews have a right to their historic homeland and that it is prophetically significant. The bottom line is that if you take the Bible seriously, Jerusalem has a prophesized future as the spiritual capital of the world. The Hebrew prophets all spoke of a golden age, a righteous reign of the Messiah, and in those oracles they often included references to Jerusalem (Isa. 44:26–28; 52:1–10; Joel 2:28–3:21). Of course before that happens, we expect a usurper to sit in a rebuilt third temple declaring that he is God. As we will examine, there seems to be evidence that the Vatican wants to participate in building that temple. We now come full-circle to the bombshell we ended the chapter on the Antichrist and False Prophet with.

We closed the discussion of the biblical false prophet (who we suspect is one and the same as Petrus Romanus) with a tease from a 2008 leaked, classified US State department memo which recorded this exchange between Secretary of State Condoleezza Rice (CR) and Dr. Saeb Erekat (SE), a Palestinian representative:

> **CR:** I understand that there is no agreement without Jerusalem 1967 as a baseline. But if we wait until you decide sovereignty over the Haram or the Temple Mount... Your children's children will not have an agreement! Sometimes in international politics you need to have a device to solve the problem later. When it comes to holy sites, no one will argue the sovereignty of the other—leave it unresolved [i.e. both Palestine and Israel could simultaneously claim sovereignty over the Haram].

SE: And actually in life?

CR: There are two other issues—who will administer? Make sure that the sewer system, the municipal issues are resolved [notes that this was a problem in Berlin], safe access to all the holy sites for all. I understand that this worked well before 2000. Some kind of custodians appointed by the world, possibly religious figures, non-governmental people… One problem is that under the Dome is crumbling. Every time Israel tries to fix it, you call it excavations! (brackets in original)[557]

While Condoleezza Rice's relationship with the Vatican is murky, her suggestion that "religious figures" become custodians of the Old City of Jerusalem is in line with the exposes by Israeli journalists. In August of 2007, Rice met with Cardinal Tarcisio Pierto Bertone (a leading candidate for Petrus Romanus) who said of the American Secretary, "If the angels did not accompany her, then she would not be able to knit back together all of these relationships that have been so fragile."[558] Could this strange coalescence of diplomacy and prophecy be leading toward the final manifestation of apostate ecumenical faith predicted in Revelation 17 headquartered in Jerusalem? We think there is compelling evidence suggesting just that.

Prophecy scholars have long suspected that the Antichrist will seemingly resolve the Middle East conflict, which will drive his meteoric rise to fame and adoration. This idea is drawn from Daniel's seventy-weeks prophecy which predicts that in the final week, "And he shall confirm the covenant with many for one week: and in the midst of the week he shall cause the sacrifice and the oblation to cease, and for the overspreading of abominations he shall make it desolate, even until the consummation, and that determined shall be poured upon the desolate" (Da 9:27). We think this interpretation must be correct because the "consummation" is rendered from the Hebrew term kālâ which carried the basic idea, "to bring a process to completion." The beginning of the seventy-weeks prophecy listed things like, "to bring in everlasting righteousness" (9:24b), which simply have not yet occurred. Furthermore, the same term is used in Daniel 12:7, rendered as "end," unambiguously referencing the Day of the Lord. This firmly places the initial covenant at the beginning of the final seven years prior to Armageddon and Jesus' return. Another problem with interpretations that place this final week in the past is that Jesus spoke of the "abomination of desolation" as a future event occurring just prior to His return, "When ye therefore shall see the abomination of desolation, spoken of by Daniel the prophet, stand in the holy place, (whoso readeth, let him understand)" (Mt 24:15). The seventieth week includes "the overspreading of abominations he shall make it desolate" and Jesus mentions Daniel explicitly so one cannot take Jesus seriously while arguing that the events of the seventieth week are previous history. Furthermore, the context of this prophecy was Daniel's people, the Jews, and the covenant violation is interference of the temple sacrifice. Accordingly, we believe that the "covenant with many" speaks to the two-state solution for the Israel/Palestinian issue and forecasts the tribulation temple being built in Jerusalem.

It was suggested in *Apollyon Rising 2012* that secret occult societies have long been conspiring to rebuild the Jewish Temple. In that work it is revealed:

Due to the occult value or sacredness then of the numerous elements surrounding the story of Solomon's Temple in mystical literature, there has been an idea for some time that groups from among the Freemasons and illuminated fraternities intend to rebuild or to participate in the rebuilding of a glorious New Temple in Jerusalem fashioned after the one built by Solomon. Disclosure of this has occasionally reached the public's ear. The Illustrated London News, August 28, 1909 ran a spectacular supplement in which they detailed this goal. The article was titled, "The Freemason's Plan To Rebuild Solomon's Temple At Jerusalem". Three years later,

September 22, 1912, The New York Times published an outline by Freemasons to rebuild the Temple under the title "SOLOMON"S TEMPLE: Scheme of Freemasons and Opinions of Jews on Rebuilding". By 1914, some publishers had begun adding unprecedented details, including a report that the land on which the Dome of the Rock now stands was secretly purchased and plans were already under design for the construction of the Third and Final Temple. Researchers since have produced intelligence that a hushed collaboration was firmly in place, held back only against the right time, opportunity and circumstances when exalted Freemasons and their associates would move with haste to reconstruct a New Temple, from which their "earthly representative" would reign.

In addition to occultists, groups including the Temple Mount Faithful and the Temple Institute in Jerusalem are busy restoring and constructing the sacred vessels and vestments that will be used for service in the New Temple at the arrival of their "Messiah." Students of Bible prophecy recognize the importance of such plans as signaling the arrival of Antichrist. Old and New Testament scriptures explain that a false Jewish Messiah will appear, enthroning himself as God in the Temple in Jerusalem, but afterward he will defile the holy place by setting up a sacrilegious object in the Temple and ordering the sacrifices and offerings to cease (see Dan. 9:27; II Thess. 2:3–4). For any of this to occur, it is necessary for the Temple to be rebuilt, thus making claims by Freemasons or other groups interested in fulfilling this monumental task highly suspect with regard to unfolding end-times events.[559]

It has also been reiterated in this present work that the design of Washington DC in the likeness of Vatican City with its proportionate Dome and Obelisk was no accident, but rather the product of an arcane science ostensibly related to apotheosis. These parallel apotheotic sites seem poised to spawn the beast from the bottomless pit (Rev 11:7) and the beast from the earth (Rev 13:11). While it is speculative, this seems to suggest a Washington figurehead will be the one who initiates the covenant spoken of in Daniel 9. Whereas this figure could be a Jew, it is not really necessary. The late Messianic Christian author, Zola Levitt, wrote, "It is an outsider that has to sign a legal covenant with the Jewish people, not one of their own… They wouldn't need a special covenant drawn up between them and one of their own citizens."[560] In fact, while it is possible, there is no direct evidence that the Antichrist will be accepted as the Jewish Messiah. Rather, he could simply be the one who facilities the building of the tribulation temple like the Persian King Cyrus who was designated a *mashiyach* (anointed one) for freeing the Jews to build the second temple (Isa 45:1).

In fact, Orthodox Jews are not likely to be fooled by the Antichrist. Midrash tradition, including works like *Sefer Zerubbavel,* contains warnings about a character named Armilus who will deceive the whole world into false idolatrous worship. He is said to come to power when ten kings fight over Jerusalem and after emerging victorious he rules the entire world for a brief time before Messiah comes. According to Randall Price, "Other sources describe Armilus as rising from the Roman empire, having miraculous powers, and being born to a stone statue of a virgin."[561] This sounds remarkably congruent with Roman Catholic Mariolatry where stone statues feature prominently. Other traditions say he is offspring of Satan and a virgin which sounds eerily similar to the pedophilic rite described by Malachi Martin which occurred on June 29, 1963 at the parallel enthronement site in Charleston, SC. Furthermore, this stone statue aspect of the Jewish tradition could find some sort of bizarre realization in the image of the beast which seemingly comes to life (Rev 13:4, 15). While a minority of religious Jews are aware of these traditions, the secular Jews probably are not. Still, with the centuries of papists corralling Jews into ghettos and mandating yellow badges, one wonders how they could be persuaded by a future pope leading an ecumenical religion in Jerusalem.

Mystery Babylon's Ecumenical Jihad

In addition to the satanic enthronement ceremony, other events in Rome during the 1960s paved the way for Petrus Romanus to take the world's stage. The third millennium zeitgeist has primed the world for pluralism. In 1962, despite two millennia of anathematizing everyone with whom they disagreed, the second Vatican council (concurrent with the enthronement ceremony), began paving the way for the final, one-world, ecumenical faith prophesied in Revelation 17. One product of this era was a document called *Nostra Aetate* (Our Age), defined as "the declaration on the relation of the church to non-Christian religions."[562] While there is an inherent fallacy in equating Romanism with Christianity, this document likely lays the ideological underpinnings for the religion of the great prostitute in Revelation 17. One can readily see the Vatican's ambition of reconciling world religions in the document's equating the god of Islam with the god of Romanism and with special pleading like, "Since in the course of centuries not a few quarrels and hostilities have arisen between Christians and Moslems, this sacred synod urges all to forget the past and to work sincerely for mutual understanding and to preserve as well as to promote together for the benefit of all mankind social justice and moral welfare, as well as peace and freedom."[563] Of course, Rome is always very eager for others to forget the past while holding a long memory of her own. Perhaps papists and Muslims are praying to the same god, but then that would necessarily *not* be the God of the Bible albeit the "god of this world" (2 Cor 4:4).

Of course it all sounds so peaceful and well-intentioned that it is hard to criticize without sounding like a bully. We love all people but hold that the highest expression of love is always grounded in truth. Whispering platitudes to a man who is on fire is not as helpful or loving as a blunt bucket of cold water. *Nostra Aetate* acknowledges truth in Hinduism with its millions of gods and even atheistic Buddhism:

> Thus in Hinduism, men contemplate the divine mystery and express it through an inexhaustible abundance of myths and through searching philosophical inquiry. They seek freedom from the anguish of our human condition either through ascetical practices or profound meditation or a flight to God with love and trust. Again, Buddhism, in its various forms, realizes the radical insufficiency of this changeable world; it teaches a way by which men, in a devout and confident spirit, may be able either to acquire the state of perfect liberation, or attain, by their own efforts or through higher help, supreme illumination.[564]

We cannot be so charitable as to call eastern mediation a path to "illumination" along with the pope, rather something more along the lines of *offering yourself up to be possessed*. Paul put it this way, "But I say, that the things which the Gentiles sacrifice, they sacrifice to devils, and not to God: and I would not that ye should have fellowship with devils" (1 Co 10:20). Furthermore, Jesus taught explicitly that He came to divide, "Think not that I am come to send peace on earth: I came not to send peace, but a sword" (Mt 10:34). The Vatican's ecumenical jihad is an inversion of that of Christ.

This was all seeded into the public consciousness by papist philosopher and apologist Peter Kreeft's 1996 book, *Ecumenical Jihad*. While Kreeft is a respected academic philosopher who normally rails against the evils of relativism, his book promotes a radical inclusivism which contradicts the teaching of Jesus (Jn 14:6; Mt 7:13). He claims to have had a mystical experience in Hawaii where he soul-surfed to an ethereal beach. On this beach, he had a conversation with Moses,

Buddha, Confucius, and Mohammed, all of whom had converted to Romanism post mortem. Coherence does not seem to trouble Kreeft because the newly converted Mohammed asserts the Koran as divinely inspired while Kreeft raises no objections.[565] Even more astonishing is that Kreeft infers that all of this inclusivist nonsense is in some bizarre way "true."[566] The cognitive dissonance must be painful but one can see this sort of thought is blazing the trail toward the one-world religion of Revelation 17. A sampling of which was witnessed in John Paul II's 2002 "prayer meeting" with Muslim clerics, Jewish rabbis, Buddhists, Sikhs, Bahais, Hindus, Jains, Zoroastrians, voodoo priests, and witch doctors.[567] It has also made significant headway toward their Jerusalem ambitions.

That distancing themselves from their complicity with Hitler and Mussolini was part of the real agenda behind all of this can be seen in that the first draft of *Nostra Aetate* was entitled "*Decretum de Judaeis*" (Decree on the Jews), completed in November 1961 (but it never saw the light of day). The fourth section of *Nostra Aetate* addresses the Jewish question when it speaks of the "bond that spiritually ties the people of the New Covenant to Abraham's stock."[568] It seeks to mitigate the millennia of accusation and persecution with, "Although the Church is the new people of God, the Jews should not be presented as rejected or accursed by God, as if this followed from the Holy Scriptures." The document goes a long way in what it says but falls short of admitting the gross errors of past popes. It is for that reason the laborious survey of history offered in the previous chapter is so important. Rome should never be taken at face value. While they will offer up platitudes and apologies when it serves them, they never admit the centuries of gross doctrinal errors and the obvious ineptitude of countless pontiffs. They still claim infallible authority. Even so, the ruse is working.

Rabbis Bemporad and Shevack authored a book in 1996 called, *Our Age: The Historic New Era of Christian Jewish Understanding*, that celebrated Rome's new agenda. While we find the title *Our Age* to be prophetically significant, again we protest the equivocation of Romanism with Christianity. The two Rabbis write, "*Nostra Aetate* was the seed of a whole new relationship with the Jews. The beginning of the end of Catholic anti-semitism. The beginning of the end of the theologically justified anti-semitism."[569] While everyone can applaud the improved relations, we suspect it is purely agenda-driven. Even so, it is not necessary to accuse the Romanists of intentional disingenuousness. The Bible tells us, "For we wrestle not against flesh and blood, but against principalities, against powers, against the rulers of the darkness of this world, against spiritual wickedness in high places" (Eph 6:12). Rome can have the best of intentions while still unwittingly leading the world to ride the beast along with her. It is also quite telling that the Vatican has always opposed the formation of the Jewish state in 1948 and waited *forty five years* until 1993 to establish official diplomatic relations.

The Jerusalem Agenda

There is ample evidence that Rome is merely self-interested and duplicitous. For instance, just prior to the formation of the Jewish state, the word coming from the Vatican's Apostolic Delegate to Washington D.C., Amleto Giovanni Cicognani, did sound nearly as benevolent as the sympathetic tones found in *Nostra Aetate*:

> If the greater part of Palestine is given to the Jewish people, this would be a severe blow to the religious attachment of Catholics to this land. To have the Jewish people in the majority would be to interfere with the peaceful exercise of these rights in the Holy Land already vested in Catholics. It is true that at one time Palestine was inhabited by the Hebrew Race, but there is no axiom in history to substantiate the necessity of a people returning to a country they left nineteen centuries before.[570]

Of course, the Jews were slaughtered *en masse* and sold as slaves by the *Romans*. The fiction that they simply left on their own accord is a colossal affront in and of itself. With this sort of dishonest rhetoric in recent history, it seems prudent to assume that Rome's posturing for improved relations and diplomacy is driven only by self-interest, namely the desire to control the holy sites in the old city of Jerusalem, the city of David, what diplomats refer to as the "holy basin."

The Vatican's establishment of full diplomatic relations with Israel in 1993 has been credited as an overdue political consequence to the theological changes reflected in *Nostra Aetate*. However, in truth, there is much more going on than meets the eye. As early as April 15th, 1992, Cardinal Joseph Ratzinger visited Israel and met exclusively with Jerusalem Mayor Teddy Kollek. The Jerusalem mayor was quoted previously as saying, "The Israeli government should meet the Vatican's demand to apply special status for Jerusalem."[571] An Israeli journalist, Barry Chamish, has been working fearlessly for over two decades to expose a conspiracy which includes the current President of Israel, Shimon Peres, and his aid, Yossi Beilin. In his 2000 book, *Save Israel*, Chamish wrote:

> In March 1994, the newspaper Shishi revealed a most remarkable secret of the Middle East "peace" process. A friend of Shimon Peres, the French intellectual Marek Halter, claimed in an interview that in May 1993, he delivered a letter from Peres to the pope. Within, Peres promised to internationalize Jerusalem, granting the UN political control of the Old City of Jerusalem, and the Vatican hegemony of the holy sites within. The UN would give the PLO a capital within its new territory and East Jerusalem would become a kind of free trade zone of world diplomacy.
>
> Halter's claim was backed by the Italian newspaper *La Stampa*, which added that Arafat was apprised of the agreement and it was included in the secret clauses of the Declaration of Principles signed in Washington in September 1993.[572]

We took pains to fact-check Chamish's claims, and to the extent that we were able, they checked out. Below is the original article which ran in the Italian paper *La Stampa*:

The headline reads " 'Now Jerusalem' Secret Plan: to entrust it to the Pope"; the text below and to left of John Paul II's photo reads, "The old town, under the auspices of the Vatican would be administered by the Palestinians Arafat told me: 'I'm going to Jericho.' " The small print below that reads, "Mark Halter, French Israeli writer who, like other Jewish intellectuals played a mediating role in the difficult question, said here, the Pope would have the 'spiritual sovereignty' of the old town."

It seems that the timing of the Vatican's long overdue recognition of the state of Israel was motivated more by ambition than repentance. The major players on the Israeli side are the current President Shimon Peres (the Israeli representative at Oslo) and his aid, left-wing politician Yossi Beilin, a former Knesset member, Deputy Foreign Affairs Minister, and Justice Minister. The secret deal was allegedly meant to sweeten the pot as a clandestine portion of the Oslo Accords. The Oslo Accords were an attempt (likely engineered by the Council on Foreign Relations) to resolve the conflict through face-to-face meetings between the leaders of Israel and the Palestine

Liberation Organization. The secret meetings completed on August 20, 1993 were held at the Fafo institute in Oslo, Norway. Once presented in Israel, the left wing supported these surreptitious accords while the right wing opposed. The Knesset vote was close: sixty-one in favor, fifty opposed, and eight abstained.

According to another Israeli journalist, Joel Bainerman, New World Order think-tank, the Council on Foreign Relations was behind the deal all along and was encouraging a turnover of Jerusalem to the Vatican:

> The plan was originally discussed in November 1992 (the same time the first meetings in London took place to discuss an agreement between Israel and the PLO which was probably arranged by Council on Foreign Relations executive, Edgar Bronfman) when then Foreign Minister Shimon Peres met with Vatican officials in Rome. Under the plan, Jerusalem will stay the capital of Israel but the Old City will be administered by the Vatican. Arafat agreed not to oppose the plan. *The plan also calls for Jerusalem to become the second Vatican of the world with all three major religions represented but under the authority of the Vatican.*[573] (emphasis added)

The last line is particularly intriguing in light of the imminent pontificate of Petrus Romanus. While these revelations sparked a whirlwind of controversy in Israel, most Americans have no idea about Rome's Jerusalem ambitions. The prophetic implications of the "peace" negotiation are not reported by the managed corporate media in the United States.

The Oslo Accords were officially signed with great fanfare featuring President Bill Clinton in Washington, DC on September 13, 1993. At that time the Vatican had still never established diplomatic relations with Israel. On September 25 of that year, the *San Antonio Express-News* ran a story which reported, "Israel could gain an elusive, long-desired side benefit from its recent agreement with the Palestine

Liberation Organization, Jewish leaders hope. The agreement could be a giant step toward diplomatic recognition of Israel by the Holy See, which Israeli and Jewish leaders have been seeking since the state of Israel was established in 1948."[574] This article telegraphs the connection between Oslo's clandestine promises and the Vatican's change of heart. Just a few months later in December of 1993, "Fundamental Agreement Between The Holy See And The State Of Israel" was signed and the Vatican finally recognized the Jewish homeland the after forty-five years of stonewalling.[575]

In retrospect, the timing vindicates the claims of Israeli journalists Bainerman and Chamish. By all appearances, the Vatican only recognized Israel because they thought they were going to gain sovereignty over the old city of Jerusalem. This conspiracy has surfaced several times since Oslo. In *Save Israel*, Chamish continues:

> In March 1995, the Israeli radio station Arutz Sheva was leaked a cable from the Israeli Embassy in Rome to Peres' Foreign Ministry in Jerusalem confirming the handover of Jerusalem to the Vatican. This cable was printed on the front page of the radical leftwing Israeli newspaper Ha'aretz two days later. A scandal erupted and numerous rabbis who had invited Peres for Passover services cancelled their invitations in protest of his treachery. Peres reacted by claiming that the cable was real, but that someone had whited out the word, "not;" the cable really said that Israel would "not" hand Jerusalem over to the holy pontiff.[576]

For that to be true, we would have to believe that no one noticed the gaping hole in the sentence: "We plan to hand Jerusalem over to the Vatican." The implausibility of a simple white-out trick not being noticed renders the excuse laughable. The Vatican almost always sides with the Palestinians over Israel which carries weightier spiritual implications than political ones. On February 14, 2000, Pope John Paul II met Arafat in Rome to sign an accord to encourage relations between the Palestinian Authority and Romanist institutions in Jerusalem. Shortly afterward, Arafat's spokesperson Nabil Abu Rudaineh was reported to say, "Arafat had been lobbying for the idea of sharing undivided Jerusalem, and for creating Vatican-style sovereignty in the Old City."[577] This incident seems to support the notion that the PLO is used by the Vatican as means of squeezing the Israelis.

As we examined in the previous chapter, the Roman Catholic Church has had designs on owning Jerusalem since the time of the crusades. While those bloody expeditions were largely in defense of the dubious theology behind pilgrimage, the Vatican's ambitions today seem more concrete. They want political control over the Old City of Jerusalem in the same manner as the old Papal States and Vatican City today. As we saw above with Arafat, the Arab refugees appear to be nothing more that useful pawns in the hands of Vatican operatives. When Israel does not cooperate, the Vatican uses the "Palestinian" issue to put the pressure on. A probable example of this can be seen in the recent reports that Israel was dragging its feet over Rome's request for special tax status and other privileges in Jerusalem.

A 2005 *Catholic News Agency* article bemoaned, "In what has become a familiar pattern, Israel has once again delayed negotiations with the Holy See over the legal rights and tax status of church properties in Israel."[578] This stalemate continued for a few years. And then there is a seemingly "unrelated" public outburst by one Archbishop Cyrille Bustros who scorned in full view of the media, "The Holy Scriptures cannot be used to justify the return of Jews to Israel and the displacement of the Palestinians." He huffed, "We Christians cannot speak of the promised land as an exclusive right for a privileged Jewish people," adding "This promise was nullified by Christ. There are no longer a chosen people—all men and women of all countries have become the chosen people."[579] After all the hubbub died down, the pope reprimanded him, but within a few months, in January 2011, we read in the news, "Jerusalem and the Vatican have made significant progress in the ongoing negotiations between the sides after a breakthrough on the issue of taxation of the Holy

See's property in Israel. According to conclusions reached Tuesday at the Bilateral Permanent Working Commission taking place in the Vatican, religious institutions owned by the Holy See in Israel will be exempted from tax, in the same manner synagogues and mosques are."[580] Is it mere coincidence? The timing is remarkable and seems to defy coincidence. That same article reported that, "While Israel remains firm in its refusal to relinquish ownership over the Cenacle and other sites, certain gestures might be made to provide the Holy See with leeway."[581] Recent developments seem to show the fruit of that "leeway."

While the papal power play is likely to progress by the time this book returns from the printer, on February 4, 2012, an op-ed piece ran on the Israeli news site *Ynet News* titled, "Don't Bow to the Vatican." The editorial by Italian journalist Giulio Meotti opposes the Vatican's designs on Jerusalem, and speaks in the *past tense* referencing the sovereignty over the Cenacle (which houses the Hall of the Last Supper and King David's tomb):

Don't Bow to the Vatican

Israel reached an historical agreement with the Vatican to give up some sort of sovereignty over the "Hall of the Last Supper" on Mount Zion in Jerusalem. The Vatican will now have a foothold at the site: Israel agreed to give the Vatican first priority in leasing opportunities and access to it.

This was the culmination of a long campaign by the Roman Catholic Church to regain religious stewardship over the place where Jesus broke bread and drank wine with his disciples on the eve of his crucifixion, and where the Holy Spirit descended on the disciples at Pentecost. [582]

As this book goes off to the printer we have not been able to verify the past-tense phrasing "Israel reached an historical agreement with the Vatican" with a concrete piece of documentation, but it appears that the Vatican has reached its long-sought goal of sovereignty over at least one site on Mount Zion. This comes as no surprise to many journalists like Barry Chamish, with whom we have corresponded and read several of his books. Chamish wrote an article in 2005 covering the history of this same site on Mount Zion, which is not only the purported site of the last supper, but also allegedly houses the tomb of King David.

Hagia Maria Sion Abbey is a Benedictine abbey in Jerusalem on Mt. Zion just outside the walls of the Old City near the Zion Gate. The present day "Hall of the last Supper" within its structure is what remains of a twelfth-century building built by the crusaders. After the crusaders retreated from the Muslims, the structure was taken over by monks. The last German Emperor Kaiser Wilhelm II who was king or the German Empire before World War I bought the land from the Ottoman Sultan Abdul Hamid II. He built the Abbey of the Dormition of the Virgin Mary over the site (incorporating the older remains and tomb) and presented it to his country as the *Deutscher Verein vom Heiligen Lande* (German Union of the Holy Land). While there are distinctions between Greek Orthodox and Roman Catholic beliefs, the term "dormition" refers to the "falling asleep," as in the death of the Virgin Mary, and this site is alleged to be the spot where her body was hypothetically "assumed" to heaven. In 1998, the name was changed from the Abbey of the Dormition of the Virgin Mary to the Hagia Maria Sion Abbey.

Barry Chamish interviewed the German historian, Dr. Asher Edar, concerning the Vatican's sudden interest in obtaining legal ownership of this site on Mount Zion. Dr. Edar argued that there was nothing sudden at all about the Vatican's ambition, but that it traces all the way back to King Charlemagne a Carolingian who was the Vatican's principle agent in creating "The Holy Roman Empire." This was directly on the heels of the infamous pact in AD 756 between Charlemagne's father King Pepin and Pope Stephen (based on the fraudulent Donation of Constantine) which we discussed in chapter 9, "Donation of Constantine and the Road to Hell." At first Chamish did not see the relationship until Dr. Edar connected the dots (AE=Dr. Asher Edar; BC=Barry Chamish):

AE: Kaiser Wilhelm II came to Jerusalem in 1898 to build two churches, a modest Lutheran Church of minor religious significance and a magnificent Catholic structure on Mount Zion. In 1898, the ruler of a nation didn't make such a difficult journey to a diplomatic backwater unless it was extremely important. The Vatican was worried that the British had an operating church in Jerusalem and its presence could solidify and spread. The Vatican provided much of the funds for the trip and the bribe to the Turkish Sultan, Khamid. Since Wilhelm had a Protestant population to appease, he put up a smaller Lutheran church as well, but the real prize was Mount Zion.

BC: Why all the money and trouble if the Vatican gets the real estate? What was in it for Germany?

AE: Germany has never given up its dream of reviving the Holy Roman Empire. At the height of that empire, their greatest king, Frederick the Great, marched into Jerusalem and became the city's king. Jerusalem was once part of the Holy Roman Empire and the dream is that it will be again. In this empire, the delineation of powers was strict. The pope was the spiritual leader, but the political leader was whoever ruled Germany. This dream led straight to World War I.

BC: Where do the Jews fit in all this?

AE: Nowhere. Herzl tried to get a role for the Jews and met with Wilhelm in Jerusalem. Wilhelm would have nothing to do with him. His goal was to save Jerusalem for a Christendom led politically by Germany and spiritually by Rome. Nothing has changed except now the pope is a determined German. The Vatican wanted the Jews out of the

Old City and apparently our government is agreeing with them.[583]

Aachen Cathedral
images note 23

Hagia Maria Abbey Mt. Zion
images note 24

World Wars I and II did not fare well for German ambitions, and Rome's chameleon-like diplomats quickly assumed new allegiances. The Vatican's Jerusalem dream was frustrated by the Muslims until the British took control from the Ottoman Empire in 1917. Furthering frustration, the English gave it to the Zionists. Can this centuries-old ambition be simply for promoting pilgrimages and manufacturing dubious relics? Or could it really be for the revival of the Holy Roman Empire? We do believe there is an unspoken agenda and that it might be related to the prophecy of the pope's apocalyptic ending.

The Great City Called Sodom and Egypt

So, we come full-circle and ask, "What does the Vatican have in mind for Jerusalem?" The Bible not only predicts that a great apostasy will occur there just prior to Christ's return, it predicts that God's two witnesses will be killed there. "And their dead bodies shall lie in the street of the great city, which spiritually is called Sodom and Egypt, where also our Lord was crucified" (Re 11:8). That characterization symbolically describes the nature of the coming third-temple faith. In the interest of demonstrating how transparent Rome's ambitions have become, and rather than simply asserting our own scenario based on Bible prophecy, we defer to the secular Israeli journalist Joel Bainerman who wrote:

First, you have to realize that for centuries The Vatican has attempted to obtain control of Jerusalem, which started with the Crusades. For them to convince the world that the Messiah they put on the world's stage is going to be accepted as genuine, they need to perform this play in the Old City. The story of this production is that this "Messiah" will merge the three monotheistic religions, usher in peace and harmony in the world, and solve the Middle East conflict. The location for this "production" will be in none other than the Old City of Jerusalem.

This so-called "Messiah" that will be proclaimed, will be a false one and it will insist that by having a "world government" (i.e., the United Nations) the world peace and harmony will be ushered in. This will be a lie, and a fraud, but never mind. In our world, reality isn't important. Public perceptions are. The end result is the stripping of Israel's sovereignty as an independent nation giving way to a "regional bloc of nations" in the Middle East. Israel will be pressured to accede to these demands by all world bodies and the superpowers on the claim that "this is the only way to solve the Middle East conflict". In order to the Jews to go along they will convince them that with the "Messiah" having appeared for the Jews, it is time to start rebuilding the Third Temple—what they call "Solomon's Temple". This version of events is widely available through a simple search on the Internet as there are many Christian groups and organizations (the majority of which who are very pro-Israel) who don't buy into these beliefs and thus are against them. I didn't come up with the theory—I am just bringing it to the attention of the Israeli public.

Make no mistake about it. The Old City of Jerusalem, as well as most of the eastern half of the city, is what The Vatican is after.[584]

This is certainly astounding coming from a secular reporter but we do suspect the Vatican has something like this in mind. They have a revisionist version of history and a track record of deception, which speaks louder than words. Again, it is not even necessary to assert that they are intentionally planning this sham as they are being directed by the blinding "god of this world" (2 Cor 4:4). Also, the Marian phantasm is leading the way for reconciliation with Islam and promoting itself as coredemptrix "Our Lady of the Nations." This lying sign and wonder could serve to unite world religions under Rome's iron fist. One way or another, Rome is the pied piper for the "strong delusion" mentioned in 2 Thessalonians 2:11.

This brings us around again to the apocalyptic coda of Malachy's Prophecy of the Popes. While there have been many Jesuit critics, Rome ostensibly believes the prophecy as it has never been officially denounced after centuries of circulation. How are the Romanists planning to deal with it? Do they fear Rome's destruction? One internet site is speculating that Iran will fire a missile at Rome, instigating World War III.[585] This seems unlikely since Iran is threatening Israel whom Rome usually opposes. While we do not think that scenario is very likely, we would not put it out of the reach of possibility that Rome might perpetrate a ruse that would seemingly satisfy the Malachy prediction while serving other interests such as...a permanent move to Jerusalem? On the *Noise of Thunder Radio* podcast, award-winning filmmaker and researcher, Christian J. Pinto, speculated the following concerning the Malachian apocalypse that caught our attention:

According to the Malachy prophecy the next pope is Peter the Roman and after that is supposedly the destruction of the city of Rome, that's what it says literally, Peter the Roman, his pontificate will end in the destruction of the city of Rome. What does that tell us about what is coming up in 2012? Well we don't know... *the Lord knows...* I don't buy into Catholic prophecies, I don't buy into the prophecies of Fátima, I think if anything God is going to make sure that He is glorified and not the false prophets of Romanism. God is ultimately going to defend His glory and His name and the word of the Lord is going to prevail and all things are going to happen as God sees fit, not necessarily as these Catholic prophecies are foretelling. However, is it possible that these things are being intentionally manipulated by the Vatican, by the Jesuits because they have some plan in mind and they are going to use these things to try and validate the faith of Romanism and the idea of their Saints and so on? Could they possibly destroy the Vatican and from the ashes thereof, through that, try to create some ecumenical one world system in its place? Will they destroy the Vatican in conjunction with rebuilding the temple in Jerusalem and make that the new palace for the next pope or the one world leader?[586]

We have a lot of respect for Chris and, as you can see, he was mirroring some of our own concerns as well as those expressed by Joel Bainerman. What if the papists are planning to intentionally fulfill this prophecy? In light of Rome's transparent designs on Jerusalem, we believe that this possibility deserves serious consideration. We have already seen evidence that popes like Pius XII went to extravagant lengths (the "Pastor Angelicus" documentary) to bring about a sense of fulfillment. But then again, there have been fulfillments like *Religio Depopulata* and *De labore solis* that seem to defy human influence. The prophecy has shown remarkable accuracy; shouldn't we expect something to happen in Rome? However, even if elements conspiring within the Vatican believe they are manufacturing a fulfillment, it effectively still comes to pass. It seems in the realm of possibility that they would engineer a false flag attack as a rationale to move to Jerusalem. Even more, there is surprising evidence to support it.

We have examined Jesuit René Thibaut's many derivations of the year 2012 for the arrival of *Petrus Romanus* from the Latin text. However, we have not discussed what he wrote about the apocalyptic ending and demise of Rome, which necessary falls within the pontificate of Petrus Romanus. It is important to reiterate that fact because, for Thibaut's cryptographic work to be substantiated, all that is necessary to occur in 2012 is a change of pope. The tribulation and judgment of Rome is not really connected to a specific timeframe other than within his reign. The year 2012 has been a viral cultural meme, which has even inspired a few Hollywood movies. Accordingly, we are also mystified as to why this book, *The Mysterious Prophecy of the Popes*, which predicts 2012 so prominently has remained so obscure. Why has it not garnered attention? Since Thibaut was a professor in Belgium and respected member of the Jesuit order, they are surely aware of his work. Have the Jesuits kept this astonishing tome out of public view? Is it possible that his book reveals *too much*? In light of all that has been discussed in this chapter, consider Thibaut's justification for the destruction of Rome:

> This is obviously a judgment of God but by what right will we see it as the last trial? No doubt, the judgment in question follows the "last" persecution, but does it follow from this that the trial is similarly "last"? Doesn't the book of Revelation point to a long period of peace between the "last" persecution and the last judgment? Can we call this "persecution" the supreme burst of hell that will reach the City of Saints before Christ breaks it by his sudden coming? And, assuming there is still persecution after that mentioned in the conclusion of our prophecy; would this new test necessarily hit the Roman Church? That would require him to be of faith that the true

Church will be judged through its center in Rome. Or could it be that with Rome destroyed, the Papacy will seek a residence elsewhere. We believe that this change in the papal residence is precisely what the Prophecy of the Popes saw happen after the 111th Roman papacy. In the year 2012, we will cease to call "Roman" the Catholic Church. God's judgment will happen then, far from putting an end to the history of the Church, it will mark the beginning of a new era.[587]

SECTION FOUR

THE FINAL CONCLAVE

17 | The United States, the Vatican, the New World Order, and the Coming of the Antichrist

S hould the world continue, historians will undoubtedly record how the messianic fervor surrounding
the election of the forty-fourth president of the
United States reflected not only widespread disapproval for Bush
administration policies, but how, in the aftermath of September 11,
2001, the American psyche was primed to accept expansive alterations in political and financial policy with an overarching scheme for
salvation from chaos. Among these historians, a few will undoubtedly also argue that, as National German Socialists did in the years
following World War I, Barack Hussein Obama appealed to the
increasingly disenfranchised voters among American society by playing on their understandable fears in order to posture himself as the
essential agent of change.

What most of these historians are not likely to record, however, is the involvement before and after the US presidential election by unseen shapers of the New World Order. If they did, the vast numbers of people would not believe it anyway, the idea that behind the global chaos that gave rise to Obama's popularity was a secret network, a transnational hand directing the course of civilization. Yet no account of history including recent times is complete or even sincere without at least acknowledging the behind-the-scenes masters who manipulate international policy, banking and finance, securities and exchange, trade, commodities, and energy resources. Numerous works, including scholarly ones, have connected the dots between this ruling "superclass" and the integration of policy—especially that of the United States—handed down to governing bodies of nation-states and supra-national organizations.

The Economist newspaper in April 2008 pointed to research by academic David Rothkopf, whose book, *Superclass: The Global Power Elite and the World They Are Making*, documented how only a few thousand people worldwide actually dictate the majority of policies operating at a global scale. *The Economist* described this comparatively small number of elites as being "groomed" in "world-spanning institutions…[who] meet at global events such as the World Economic Forum at Davos and the Trilateral Commission or…the Bilderberg meetings or the Bohemian Grove seminars that take place every July in California."[588] Long-time radio host and author of *Brotherhood of Darkness*, Stanley Monteith, says such persons are part of an "occult hierarchy" that rules the world and directs the course of human events. "The movement is led by powerful men who reject Christianity, embrace the 'dark side,' and are dedicated to the formation of a world government and a world religion," he writes. "They control the government, the media…many corporations, and both [US] political parties."[589]

Interestingly, Pope Benedict XVI may have referred to the same group when, in 2008, he warned United Nations diplomats that multilateral consensus needed to solve global difficulties was "in crisis" because answers to the problems were being "subordinated to the decisions of the few." His predecessor, Pope John Paul II, may have acknowledged the same, believing a One-World Government beneath the guidance of a ruling superclass in league with spiritual influences (whether they perceived it that way or not) was inevitable. If researchers like Dr. Monteith are correct, and world governments are to this day influenced by such dark angelic powers, the elite who head the current push to establish a New World Order are directly connected with an antichrist system currently unfolding.

Signs and evidence of such supernatural immersion in the present move towards worldwide totalitarian government have been increasing in political commentary, occult symbolism, and numerological "coincidences" in the United States over the past decade. As public opinion has been engineered toward final acceptance of international subordination, "mirrors" of occult involvement have produced so many open semiotic messages (visible signs and audible references that communicate subliminal ideas) that it is starting to feel as if the "gods" are mocking us, challenging whether or not we will willingly admit their connection. This has been exponentially true since the election of US President Barack Hussein Obama, whom news services (and church services) around the globe had hoped would become the "President of the World." While the antichrist-sounding title granted Obama by euphoric crowds on election night remains to be prophetic, the glorified ideal behind it reflects the global hunger for and movement toward the arrival of "the one" who represents the invisible agencies mentioned above and who, for a while, will appear to be the world's answer man. The book *Apollyon Rising 2012* (Defender Publishing, 2009) documented this development and foresaw how this was preparing the world for the coming of Petrus Romanus and the Antichrist.

On pages 93–96 it states:

Consider the unprecedented messianic rhetoric that reporters, politicians, celebrities, and even preachers used in celebrating the "spiritual nature" of Obama's meteoric rise from near obscurity to U.S. president, and how this reflected people's strong desire for the coming of an earthly savoir. *San Francisco Chronicle* columnist Mark Morford characterized it as "a sort of powerful luminosity." In Morford's opinion, this was because Obama is "a Lightworker, that rare kind of attuned being who has the ability to…help usher in a new way of being on the planet."[590] The dean of the Martin Luther King Jr. International Chapel, Lawrence Carter, went further, comparing Obama to the coming of Jesus Christ: "It is powerful and significant on a spiritual level that there is the emergence of Barack Obama…. No one saw him coming, and Christians believe God comes at us from strange angles and places we don't expect, like Jesus being born in a manger."[591] Dinesh Sharma, a marketing science consultant with a PhD in psychology from Harvard, appraised Obama likewise: "Many… see in Obama a messiah-like figure, a great soul, and some affectionately call him Mahatma Obama."[592] It would have been easy to dismiss such commentary as the New Age quiverings of loons had it not been for similar passion on the lips of so many people. The following is a brief list of like expressions from a variety of news sources:

> Barack's appeal is actually messianic…he…communicates God-like energy…. What if God decided to incarnate as men preaching "hope and change"? And what if we…let them slip away, not availing ourselves…to be led by God! —Steve Davis, *Journal Gazette*[593]

> This is bigger than Kennedy…. This is the New Testament! I felt this thrill going up my leg. I mean, I don't have that too often. No, seriously. It's a dramatic event. —Chris Matthews, *MSNBC*[594]

Does it not feel as if some special hand is guiding Obama on his journey, I mean, as he has said, the utter improbability of it all? —*Daily Kos*[595]

Obama, to me, must be not just an ordinary human being but indeed an Advanced Soul, come to lead America out of this mess. —Lynn Sweet, *Chicago Sun Times*[596]

He is not operating on the same plane as ordinary politicians...the agent of transformation in an age of revolution, as a figure uniquely qualified to open the door to the twenty-first century. —Former U.S. Senator Gary Hart, *Huffington Post*[597]

He is not the Word made flesh [Jesus], but the triumph of word over flesh [better than Jesus?].... Obama is, at his best, able to call us back to our highest selves. —Ezra Klein, *Prospect*[598]

Obama has the capacity to summon heroic forces from the spiritual depths of ordinary citizens and to unleash therefrom a symphonic chorus of unique creative acts whose common purpose is to tame the soul and alleviate the great challenges facing mankind. —Gerald Campbell, *First Things First*[599]

Obama was...blessed and highly favored.... I think that...his election...was divinely ordered.... I'm a preacher and a pastor; I know that that was God's plan.... I think he is being used for some purpose. —Janny Scott, *New York Times*[600]

He won't just heal our city-states and souls. He won't just bring the Heavenly Kingdom—dreamt of in both Platonism and Christianity—to earth. He will heal the earth itself. —Micah Tillman, *The Free Liberal*[601]

The event itself is so extraordinary that another chapter could be added to the Bible to chronicle its significance. —Rep. Jesse Jackson Jr., *Politico*[602]

Though he tried to keep it subtle himself, Obama encouraged such public perception of him as an "anointed" one whose time had come. Officially produced Obama campaign advertising consistently used such words as "faith," "hope," and "change." Republican nominee John McCain picked up on this during his run for office and put out a cynical video called *The One*. Using some of Obama's own words against him, the video mocked Obama's play as a Christ-like figure, showing him in New Hampshire saying, "A light beam will shine through, will light you up, and you will experience an epiphany, and you will suddenly realize that you must go to the polls and vote for Barack!" The video failed to mention that having an "epiphany" actually means the sudden realization or comprehension of an appearance of deity to man. Another part of the video included Obama during his nomination victory speech in St. Paul, Minnesota, saying, "This was the moment when the rise of the oceans began to slow and our planet began to heal." Anybody who followed the presidential campaign would have picked up the same nuances: angelic children organized to sing about Obama; logos depicting rays of sunlight beaming out from his O-shaped hand sign (a gesticulation Hitler used as well); books such as Nikki Grimes' *Barack Obama: Son of Promise, Child of Hope* (Simon & Schuster); comparisons to Plato's "Philosopher King," without whom our souls will remain broken; comparisons to the "spiritually enlightened" Mahatma Gandhi; comparisons to the solar hero Perseus; comparisons to Jesus Christ; and even comparisons to God Himself.[603]

Though at the time we are writing this chapter it appears likely Obama will only assist in the rise of the superhuman superstar the world has been hoping for, if symbolic gestures are any indication, there certainly were plenty of religious folks during his march into the White House that were ready to accept *him* as "The One." Dozens of churches and faith groups, including mainline Protestants, organized activities to mark Obama's inauguration as a "spiritual" event. Randall Balmer, professor of religion in American history at Columbia University, admitted he had never seen anything like it before.[604] *CNN* went so far as to compare Obama's inauguration to the Hajj—the journey by Muslims to the holy city of Mecca, an obligatory pilgrimage that demonstrates their dedication to Allah.[605] In Des Moines, Iowa, an inaugural parade for Obama included a simulation of the triumphant entry of Christ in which a facsimile of Obama rode upon a donkey. As the reproduction made its way down the streets, palm branches were handed out to onlookers so that they could wave them like Christ's adorers did in the twenty-first chapter of Matthew.[606] Several ministries, including the Christian Defense Coalition and Faith and Action, came together to perform what was heralded as a first for US presidential inaugurations—applying anointing oil to the doorposts of the arched doorway that Obama passed through as he moved to the platform on the West Front of the Capital to be sworn in. Congressman Paul Broun (Georgia) was part of the ritual, joining Rev. Rob Schenck, who said, "Anointing with oil is a rich tradition in the Bible and…symbolizes consecration, or setting something apart for God's use."[607] Even the conventional inaugural prayers, which have been historically offered during US presidential installation ceremonies, carried an unparalleled New Age flavor this time around. Rick Warren, considered America's Christian pastor, rendered a blessing in the name of the Muslim version of Jesus (Isa), while the bishop of New Hampshire, Gene Robinson, invoked the "God of our many understandings."

While all this was highly unusual, even unprecedented, it was not surprising. Obama had spent significant time during the campaign distancing himself from conservative Christians, evangelicals, and especially the Religious Right (which had held prominent sway over Republicans since Ronald Reagan held office), countering that his faith was more universalist and unconvinced of Bible inerrancy. In a five-minute video available on YouTube, a pre-election speech by Obama was highly cynical of Bible authority and even derided specific Old and New Testament Scriptures. "Whatever we once were," Obama says on the video, "we're no longer a Christian nation." He then adds, "Democracy demands that the religiously motivated translate their concerns into universal, rather than religion-specific values.... This is going to be difficult for some who believe in the inerrancy of the Bible, as many evangelicals do."[608] Consequently, the conscious effort by Obama to reorient America away from conservative Christianity was widely embraced by people who identified with the man who carried a tiny idol of the Hindu god Hanuman in his pocket—whose blessings he sought in the race to the White House—together with a Madonna and child.

For Obama, who grew up in a household where the Bible, the Koran, and the Bhagvat Gita sat on a shelf side-by-side, organized religion was best defined as "closed-mindedness dressed in the garb of piety," but a useful political tool nonetheless. And so he used it masterfully, and earned a cult following while doing so. In February 2009, Obama temporarily replaced Jesus Christ as America's favorite hero according to a Harris poll, and dedication to his come-one, come-all mysticism was spreading like wildfire in esoteric circles, with evangelists of the new religion calling for the "tired" faith of our fathers to be replaced with a global new one. Terry Neal, writing for the *Hamilton Spectator*, proclaimed boldly: "The faiths of our fathers are tired now…only a global world view will suffice. The marriage of a believable faith with the husbandry of government [dominionism] is the union that must be contracted, for only then will there be peace on earth and goodwill toward all."[609]

Although it is more difficult to understand the broad appeal of Obama's New-Age philosophy to the many evangelical and Catholic voters who supported him, the phenomenon can be explained to some degree as the result of a changing culture. Over the past fifty years, and especially as baby boomers listened attentively to pastors telling them to focus on human potential and the "god within us all," eastern philosophies including monism, pantheism, Hinduism, and self-realization grew, providing Americans with an alluring opportunity to throw off the "outdated ideas" of fundamental Christianity and to espouse a more "enlightened," monistic worldview (all is one). Aimed at accomplishing what the builders of the Tower of Babel failed to do (unify the masses of the world under a single religious umbrella), God was viewed as pantheistic, and humans were finally understood to be divine members of the whole "that God is." Pagans argue this principle of inner divinity is older than Christianity, which is true. Even so, the gospel according to the Roman Catholic catechism[610] and such New-Age concepts—a gospel of "becoming god"—is as old as the fall of man. It began when the serpent said to the woman, "ye shall be as gods" (Genesis 3:5), and it will zenith during the reign of the Man of Sin.

In the lead-up to his election, even Obama seemed secretly attuned to the esoteric "antichrist" underpinning people were applying to his destiny as president and god-king. An extraordinary example of this was when Obama gave his speech titled, "The World that Stands as One" in Berlin, Germany, on July 24, 2008. More than a few students of occult history took notice of the symbolism and location of the event, even causing some who until then had rejected any "antichrist" labels hurled at Obama to reconsider their position. This included well-known Catholic writer Michael O'Brien, best known for his apocalyptic novel, *Father Elijah*. O'Brien had received numerous letters and emails from subscribers and visitors to his website wondering if Obama was the Antichrist. At first, O'Brien wrote that this was not possible. Then a friend who had seen Obama's speech in Berlin called him, talking about how mesmerizing the speech was, and stating that an announcer over German radio had said: "We have just heard the next president of the United States...*and the future President of the World.*" By now, Obama was conveying an unusual likeness to the Antichrist character of his novel. After watching the Berlin speech several times for himself, O'Brien sent out a newsletter in which he admitted that while he still doubted Obama was the prophesied ruler of the end times, he had come to believe he was "a carrier of a deadly moral virus, indeed a kind of anti-apostle spreading concepts and agendas that are not only anti-Christ but anti-human as well." O'Brien finally conceded Obama could be instrumental in ushering in the dreaded Great Tribulation period, and worse, that he was "of the spirit of Antichrist."[611] Because it is true that any significant public political event requires both forethought and symbolic meaning, the location where Obama gave his Berlin speech in front of Berlin's Victory Column contributed to O'Brien's conclusions. The site was offensive to educated Germans as well as to Christians and Jews because of its ties to the modern antichrist Adolf Hitler and the Nazis. It was nevertheless oddly appropriate, for it was upon this exact location that Hitler had planned to enthrone himself as the King of the World in the Welthauptstadt Germania—the new "World Capital" upon winning World War II.

During the 1930s, Hitler commissioned Albert Speer, "the first architect of the Third Reich," to design the new capital. As part of the plans, the *Siegessäule*, or Berlin Victory Column—a 226-foot monument topped by a golden-winged figure representing Borussia, the female personification of Prussia, and Victoria, the cult goddess of military victory—was removed from its location in front of the Reichstag building in 1939 and relocated to its current location in the Tiergarten, a 495-acre park in the middle of Berlin where Obama gave his speech in front of the Nazi symbol.

Rainer Brüderle, deputy leader of the liberal political party Free Democrats in Germany, complained to the newspaper *Bild am Sonntag*: "The Siegessäule in Berlin was moved to where it is now by Adolf Hitler. He saw it as a symbol of German superiority and of the victorious wars against Denmark, Austria and France." This represented a serious question in Brüderle's mind as to "whether Barack Obama was advised correctly in his choice of the Siegessäule as the site to hold a speech on his vision for a more cooperative world."[612] Another German politician named Andreas Schockenhoff was equally disturbed, saying, "It is a problematic symbol."[613]

Evidently it was not problematic for Obama, who stood in front of it and saluted the German audience in a way eerily similar to what Adolf Hitler used to do, followed by thousands returning the salute, which is against German law. When Obama ended his speech in front of the war goddess, he said, "With an eye toward the future, with resolve in our hearts, let us remember this history, and answer our destiny, and remake the world once again." This is exactly what Hitler had promised to do and exactly where he had planned to memorialize it.

Of greater significance and not far from where Obama delivered his rousing speech is the Great Altar of Zeus in the Pergamon Museum. According to several reports, Obama visited the Great Altar while in Berlin, which is especially important, given what he did on returning to the United States. Before we examine Obama's revealing actions, consider carefully what the Bible says about the Altar of Zeus in the letter to the church in Pergamos (Pergamum, Pergamon):

And to the angel of the church in Pergamos write; These things saith he which hath the sharp sword with two edges; I

know thy works, and where thou dwellest, even where Satan's
seat is: and thou holdest fast my name, and has not denied
my faith, even in those days wherein Antipas was my faithful
martyr, who was slain among you, where Satan dwelleth.
(Revelation 2:12–13)

The Greek, the phrase, "where Satan's seat is," literally means,
"where a throne to Satan is." Scholars identify this throne or "seat"
as the Great Altar of Zeus that existed in Pergamos at that time. So
important was the worship of Zeus in ancient Pergamos that perpetual sacrifices were offered to him upon the towering and famous
forty-foot-high altar. Antipas, the first leader and martyr of the early
Christian Church, is believed to have been slain on this altar, slowly
roasting to death inside the statue of a bull, the symbol and companion of Zeus. The phrase in Revelation 2:13, "wherein Antipas was my
faithful martyr, who was slain among you, where Satan dwelleth," is
considered a citation of this event.

Approximately two thousand years after Revelation 2:13 was written, German archeologists removed the massive altar of Zeus from
the ruins of Pergamos and took it to Berlin, where it was restored as
the centerpiece of the Pergamon Museum. It is here that Hitler first
adored it, later building an outdoor replica of it from which he gave
a series of speeches that mesmerized many Germans.

"Fast forward about another seventy-five years," says blogger
El Gallo. "Another charismatic young politician mesmerizes huge
German crowds with a rousing speech in Berlin. Barack Hussein
Obama…[and] did Barack Obama visit…the Great Altar of Zeus…?
Presumably he did."[614]

Whether Obama received inspiration from the throne of Satan
while in Berlin or not, what he did next was astonishing. Upon
returning to the United States, he immediately commissioned the
construction of a Greek-columned stage from which he made his
acceptance speech for his party's nomination. Because Greek temples

such as those built to honor Zeus were thought to house the patron deity, the GOP ridiculed Obama, mocking him as playing Zeus of "Mount Olympus" and accusing his supporters of "kneeling" before the "Temple of Obama." *The New York Post* ran an enlightening "Convention Special" supplement on August 28, 2008, with the telling headline: "'O' My God: Dems Erect Obama Temple" blazoned across the front cover. But it was not until blogger Joel Richardson pointed out how the design of Obama's stage was a dead ringer for the Great Altar of Zeus[615] that Obama's campaign managers tried to explain away the design as being a conglomeration representing the portico of the White House with the US capitol building. "But experts agreed with Richardson," Gallo wrote. "It was a replica of the Great Altar of Pergamum."[616]

Thus incredibly, like Hitler, Obama honored the goddess Victoria with his presence before ordering a replica of the biblical throne of Satan, upon which he accepted his date with destiny.

An unusual discovery that may cast light on why Obama seemed fascinated with such anti-Christian symbolism in the lead-up to his election involves a Hadith (tradition) sacred to Shiite Islam from the seventeenth century. It contains a prophecy from Ali ibn Abi-Talib, which predicts that just before the coming of the Mahdi (who some believe to be the Antichrist), a "tall black man will assume the reins of government in the West." This leader will command "the strongest army on earth" and will bear "a clear sign" from the third imam, *Hussein.* The prophecy concludes that: "Shiites should have no doubt that *he is with us.*"[617]

Does this Islamic prophecy identify Obama as the "promised warrior" who comes as a facilitator to set in motion world events that ultimately help the savior of Shiite Muslims (or an antichrist) conquer the world? Amir Taheri asked this very question for *Forbes Magazine* in October 2008, pointing out how "Obama's first and second names—Barack Hussein—mean 'the blessing of Hussein' in Arabic and Persian" while his "family name, Obama, written in the

Persian alphabet, reads O Ba Ma, which means 'he is with us,' the magic formula in Majlisi's tradition."[618]

Leap forward to 2009, and Barack Hussein Obama on June 4 gave an unprecedented speech to the Muslim world from Cairo, Egypt, declaring that he was launching a new era between the United States and the Muslim world. For the first time, Obama was forthright about his Muslim heritage and stated that the United States—which he is on record as saying is "no longer a Christian nation"—is now "one of the largest Muslim countries in the world." *Newsweek* editor Evan Thomas followed the president's speech with a declaration, reflected in the passion of so many regarding their hopes for a global leader and the clear signal as to how ready the world is for the Antichrist, that "Obama is standing above the country, above the world, he is a sort of God."[619]

The Secret Destiny of America

It would be pleasant to think that using the Bible during the US presidential oath of office actually means something to those who place their hand on it and swear to "faithfully execute the office of president of the United States...so help me God." But Obama, who had to repeat his swearing-in ceremony after the word "faithfully" was garbled by Chief Justice John Roberts during the inauguration, did so the following day in the Map Room of the White House before a press pool and a small group of aides. This time, the oath was administered without the use of a Bible, insinuating to some that the Good Book was only public "eye-candy" in the first instance, and also that the timing of the Bible-less oath of Barack Hussein Obama held deep, secret, occult meaning. Though it might be tempting to disregard that statement as a rush to judgment or even over-conspiratorial, it could be a serious mistake to do so. What oaths of office mean to secret orders is very consequential.

Groups such as Masons who marked the date of passage by honoring Obama with the first-ever Masonic inaugural ball in Washington, DC, January 20, 2009, esteem rituals, gestures, the use of books such as the Bible, and oaths taken by heads of state to be of the highest mystical importance. This is why everything they do is administered through appropriate rituals, initiations, and incitations. Ethereal power—including supernatural agents—can be manipulated, bound, and released to execute blessings or curses as a result of proper oaths. Breaking an oath can likewise result in dire repercussion, in their opinion. Because this is not taken lightly by occultists, members of the Craft would have a difficult time believing the oath of office of the president of the US—one of the most hallowed American traditions—was so easily flubbed. The very beginning of the oath, "I do solemnly swear," is a spiritual petition. The word "solemn" means "an invocation of a religious sanction" or entreaty before deity to witness, sanction, and bless the binding nature of the ceremony to carry out the office or duty. The oath also binds the individual before "God" to faithfully execute a covenant. Thus, government representatives make an oath before taking public office, and witnesses in a court of law take an oath to "swear to tell the truth" before offering testimony. These principles are deeply rooted in the Judeo-Christian faith as well as most other religions. Though there is no way of knowing what the presidential oath of office deeply means to Obama, or whether the blunder and redo of the swearing-in ceremony was anything more than an accident, the unprecedented gaffe was suspicious to some as denoting important hidden meaning, *as in symbolically representing that moment in history when the United States passed from its biblical moorings to the Secret Destiny of America—a time when Masons believe what was lost in Atlantis (known to the Greeks as the "Golden Age of Osiris" and to the Egyptians as "Zep Tepi") is finally to be reclaimed.*

To understand the significance of these statements one must also comprehend America's designed place in history by Founding Fathers whose dedication to setting aside the new continent according to an Atlantian scheme had been carefully concealed from the colonists,

farmers, shopkeepers, and soldiers that made the long and dangerous journey from England to the New World in their little ships to
help settle the west. For this, one must look to Sir Francis Bacon,
an English philosopher and author whose Rosicrucian novel *New
Atlantis* (published in 1624) portrayed a specific utopian vision—one
that the European secret societies were obsessed with—wherein a
world government and a new world order would be established based
on the "enlightened" grandeur of ancient Atlantis. At the time, secret
but powerful intellectuals had set their eyes on America as the New
World where Bacon's strategy could be unimpeded by political reali-
ties entrenched in his own homeland. According to Manly P. Hall
(widely considered Freemasonry's "greatest philosopher" and a 33rd-
Degree Freemason), Bacon had garnered an impressive following of
wealthy men who were as dedicated as he was to the task of building
"The New Atlantis" in America.

> Bacon quickly realized that here in the new world was the
> proper environment for the accomplishment of his great
> dream, the establishment of the philosophic empire. It must
> be remembered that Bacon did not play a lone hand; he was
> the head of a secret society including in its membership the
> most brilliant intellectuals of his day. All these men were
> bound together by a common oath to labor in the cause
> of a world democracy. Bacon's society of the unknown
> philosophers included men of high rank and broad influence.
> Together with Bacon, they devised the colonization scheme.
> Among the colonizers were some who belonged to the Order
> of the Quest [who helped establish] Bacon's secret society
> [in] America before the middle of the 17th Century. Bacon
> himself had given up all hope of bringing his dream to fruition
> in his own country, and he concentrated his attention upon
> rooting it in the new world. Through carefully appointed
> representatives, the machinery of democracy was set up at

least a hundred years before the period of the Revolutionary War… Alchemists, Cabalists, Mystics, and Rosicrucians were the incisive instruments of Bacon's plan. Representatives of these groups migrated to the colonies at an early date and set up their organization in suitable places.[620]

Hall continues:

By this time most of the important secret societies of Europe were well represented in this country. The brotherhoods met in their rooms over inns and similar public buildings, practicing their ancient rituals exactly according to the fashion in Europe and England. These American organizations were branches under European sovereignty, with the members in the two hemispheres bound together with the strongest bonds of sympathy and understanding. The program that Bacon had outlined was working out according to schedule. Quietly and industriously, America was being conditioned for its destiny…the New Atlantis was coming into being, in accordance with the program laid down by Francis Bacon a hundred and fifty years earlier. The rise of American democracy was necessary to *a world program.*[621] (emphasis added)

Whereas Bacon's utopian vision for the enlightened democracy imagined in *New Atlantis* underlined the social scheme of many secret societies, including American Freemasonry and even Jamestown colonists under Captain John Smith, another of Bacon's works, *De Sapientia* (The Wisdom of the Ancients), revealed to his "invisible college" where the hidden wisdom, philosophy, and even theology that would guide their mission would come from. The root of the purest mystery knowledge, Bacon taught, came long before Homer and Heisod, when in the remote past, uncorrupted by Hellenism, the gods dwelled with man during a "Golden Age" and shepherded hand-picked individuals with endowed empirical knowledge of spirit and nature. The loss of this ancient wisdom happened after a "fall" and the subsequent destruction of ancient man and Atlantis. Quoting Walter Leslie Wilmshurst (considered one of the world's greatest Masons and deepest mystics), Jim Marrs explains how, in Masonry, this "fall" is different from the biblical "fall from grace" in that it was not due "to any individual transgression but to 'some weakness or defect in the collective or group-soul of the Adamic race' so that 'within the Divine counsels' [the pantheon of divine beings or angels who, beginning at the Tower of Babel, were to administer the affairs of heaven and earth, as discussed elsewhere in this book] it was decided that 'humanity should be redeemed and restored to its pristine state,' a process which required... 'skilled scientific assistance' from 'those gods' and angelic guardians of the erring race of whom the ancient traditions and sacred writing tell"[622] (brackets added).

In a lecture by Manly P. Hall titled "What the Ancient Wisdom Expects of Its Disciples," we learn that Wilmshurst was not speaking to his Masonic students metaphorically. In the remote past, Hall outlines, these "instructor gods" literally walked with men "and while the instructors from the invisible planes of Nature were still laboring with the infant humanity of this planet, they chose from among the sons of men the wisest and the truest. These they labored with, preparing them to carry on the work of the gods after the spiritual hierarchies themselves had withdrawn into the invisible worlds. With these specially ordained and illumined sons [Atlantian forefathers of the Masons] they left the keys of their great wisdom, which was the knowledge of good and evil. They ordained these anointed and appointed ones to be priests or mediators between themselves (the gods) and... humanity [in order to develop] what we now know as the Ancient Mysteries [the secret teachings of Freemasonry]."

"So one inner Masonic secret has to do with their awareness of prehistoric 'gods' who left their knowledge to certain individuals, thus illuminizing them," continues Marrs. "This knowledge was passed down through ancient Mystery Schools to the founders of…the Knights Templar and brought to the inner core of Modern Freemasonry [and this] transition from ancient secret societies to more modern secret organizations was invigorated by the introduction of this 'Illuminized' Freemasonry in the late eighteenth century, itself a blending of elder esoteric lore with Cabalistic traditions. These secrets continue to lurk at the inner core of Freemasonry even as its unknowing millions of members enjoy its outward philanthropy and fellowship."[623]

The belief that man's evolution on Earth and in the beyond is thus part of a cosmic evolution overseen and guided by a hidden Spiritual Hierarchy was effectively promulgated in Helena Blavatsky's 1888 magnum opus, the *Secret Doctrine*. According to Blavatsky, so-called Masters of the Ancient Wisdom (whose upper echelons consist of advanced spiritual beings) inspire the Hierarchy of an earthly infrastructure (such as the Theosophical Society) with "truths" found in all the world's religions. Besides occult organizations such as Freemasonry, similar ideas turn up in institutions like the Liberal Catholic Church, whose doctrine advocates "a communion of Saints or Holy Ones, who help mankind, also a ministry of Angels."[624] Such teachings corresponding between the esoteric traditions include the Roman Catholic veneration of the seven archangels where, for instance, Pope Gregory I lists Gabriel, Michael, Raphael, Uriel (or Anael), Simiel, Oriphiel, and Zachariel. In the ninth century, Auriolus issued a prayer to "all you patriarchs Michael, Gabriel, Cecitiel, Oriel, Raphael, Ananiel, Marmoniel, who hold the clouds in your hands."[625]

While there has been obfuscation of the angelic names instituted by papal decree, these seem to be one and the same as the seven planetary star angels worshipped by occultists under various secret names. The veneration of the "Seven Angelic Princes" was instituted by Pope Pius IV during his dedication of the Basilica of St. Mary of the Angels and the Martyrs after the rigorous campaign of a Sicilian friar Antonio del Duca who had been personally petitioned by the entities. According to Occultist H. P. Blavatsky, "The Archangels were now urging the Popes through him [del Duca] to recognize them, and to establish a regular and a universal worship in their *own names*, just as it was before Bishop Adalbert's scandal."[626] She was referring to a previous controversy in which Pope Clement XII had ordered the mystery names of the seven spirits concealed. In the papal bull dated July 27, 1561, Pius IV ordered the church "built," to be dedicated to the *Beatissimae Virgini et omnium Angelorum et Martyrum* ("the Most Blessed Virgin and all the Angels and Martyrs").

The Roman Catholic worship of angels aside, Francis Bacon, like other medieval thinkers, including Descartes and his close associate, John Dee (the court astrologer for Queen Elizabeth I and a sorcerer who summoned demonic spirits via Rosicrucian magic to obtain secret knowledge, as did Bacon, who often contacted the demon goddess Pallas Athena, whom he claimed as his inspirational muse), was interested in sharing with adepts occult and mystical knowledge obtained from these invisible "gods." He practiced alchemy and exhibited an enduring interest in the philosophy and rituals of secret societies, especially as it involved ciphers, symbols, and cryptic communication as tools for concealing "in plain sight" archetypes that only metaphysicians would be able to decipher. History connects these works of Bacon to the founding American Freemasons and Rosicrucians including Benjamin Franklin, some of whom believed he was an Ascended Master of Wisdom (Mahatmas), or reincarnated, "spiritually enlightened being" of the theosophical concept who had come to bestow hidden knowledge.

Designing the New City of Atlantis

As many as forty-four (though probably a lower number) of the fifty-six signers of the Declaration of Independence were Freemasons dedicated to the secret destiny of America as the New Atlantis. Numerous US presidents were part of this Craft, including Washington, Monroe, Jackson, Polk, Buchanan, A. Johnson, Garfield, McKinley, T. Roosevelt, Taft, Harding, F. Roosevelt, Truman, L.B. Johnson, and

Ford. Additional elites in the Order included Benjamin Franklin, Paul Revere, Edmund Burke, John Hancock, and more, while John Adams, Alexander Hamilton, Thomas Jefferson, and numerous others were accounted friends of the brotherhood.

That these Rosicrucian-Masonic brothers engineered the US city named after America's first president according to an occult design is indisputable today. David Ovason, who became a Mason after writing *The Secret Architecture of our Nation's Capital: The Masons and the Building of Washington, D.C.*, argues effectively that the city's layout intentionally incorporated the esoteric belief system of Freemasonry, especially as it involved astrologically aligning the capital with the constellation Virgo (Isis). In 1793, when George Washington sanctioned the laying of the capitol building's cornerstone, he did so wearing a Masonic apron emblazoned with the brotherhood's symbols. For occult expert Manly P. Hall, this made perfect sense. "Was Francis Bacon's vision of the 'New Atlantis' a prophetic dream of the great civilization, which was so soon to rise upon the soil of the New World?" he asked. "It cannot be doubted that the secret societies… conspired to establish [such] upon the American continent."[627] Hall continued that city streets, building designs and even statues were laid out in the United States clearly bearing "the influence of that secret body, which has so long guided the destinies of peoples and religions. By them nations are created as vehicles for the promulgation of ideals, and while nations are true to these ideals they survive; when they vary from them, they vanish like the Atlantis of old which had ceased to 'know the gods.'"[628]

For those unfamiliar with this secret American-Masonic history, involvement by Freemasons in the development of early America and the symbolic layout of Washington, DC as the capital for the New Atlantis has been so well-documented over the last two decades that even most Masons have ceased denying the affiliation. In fact, daily Masonic tours through services devoted to this history are now offered of the city's landmarks to illustrate the connection. For a fee, a guide will help you visit locations such as the George Washington

Masonic National Memorial or the House of the Temple, the headquarters building of the Scottish Rite of Freemasonry. Designed in
1911, the House of the Temple hosts the Freemason Hall of Fame,
an enormous collection of Freemason memorabilia including various artworks important to Masons, a library of two hundred fifty
thousand books, and is the location for the Rite's Supreme Council
33rd-degree meetings. Upon leaving, you can exit the House of the
Temple, walk down the street, and take pictures of the enormous
Masonic Obelisk (phallic Egyptian symbol of fertility) in the distance
known as the Washington Monument.

For obvious reasons, while modern Masons may openly admit
these days to involvement by their Jacobite ancestors toward establishing the foundation for a utopian New World Order in Washington,
DC, most vigorously deny that the talisman-like street designs, government buildings, and Masonic monuments were meant for what
researcher David Bay calls an "electric-type grid" that pulsates "with
Luciferic power twenty-four hours a day, seven days a week."[629]

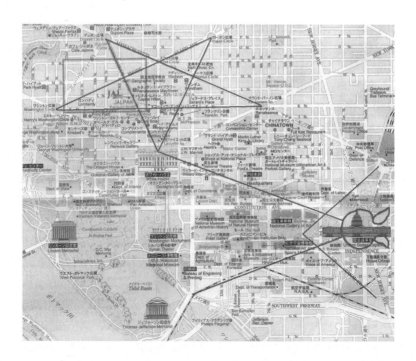

Notwithstanding this denial, the government's own records explain otherwise, clearly stating that the capital city's design was "shepherded" by those who wanted it to reflect dedication to those ancient "pagan gods" that Bacon and his followers sought wisdom from. For instance, the article, "The Most Approved Plan: The Competition for the Capitol's Design," on the Library of Congress's website tells how, after advertising a competition for the design of Government Center in DC, "Washington, Jefferson, and the Commissioners of the District of Colombia" rejected the public entries, and a design based on "The Roman Pantheon—the circular Domed rotunda *dedicated to all pagan gods*—was suggested by Jefferson, who later shepherded it through several transformations [emphasis added]."[630] Freemason David Ovason, whose published research into these matters has been highly praised and endorsed by the likes of Fred Kleinknecht, Sovereign Grand Commander of the 33rd-Degree Supreme Council of Freemasons in Washington DC, adds that when the cornerstone of the US Capitol building was laid, it was done through Masonic ritual meant to procure *approval of the pagan gods.* As recorded in two bronze panels on the Senate doors of the Capitol, George Washington is seen standing in front of a Mason who holds two versions of the Masonic square, while he, himself, uses a Masonic trowel on the cornerstone. The apron Washington so famously wore that day bears specific Masonic symbolism, which Ovason explains was designed to please the "invisible agencies" who watched over the event. "Undoubtedly, invisible agencies were present at the cornerstone ceremony," he says, "but they were made visible in the apron's symbolism. The radiant eye represented the invisible presence of the Great Architect—the high Spiritual Being who had been invited by prayer and ritual to oversee the ceremonial. The radiant eye was…the 'sun-eye,' or Spiritual Sun [Horus/Osiris/Apollo]."[631]

Ovason goes on to document how the dedication of the US Capitol building cornerstone in particular had to be done at a certain astrological time related to the zodiacal constellation Virgo (Isis), while Jupiter was rising in Scorpio, because "the cornerstone ceremonial was designed not only to gain the approval of the spiritual beings, but also to ensure that these were content that the building was being brought into the world at the right time."[632] Ovason later adds more directly, "Whoever arranged for Virgo to be so consistently operative during foundation and cornerstone ceremonies, must have been alert to the fact that *they were inviting some archetype, or spiritual being, to direct the destiny of the city*" (italics in original).[633]

As a result of this alignment of the Capitol buildings and streets in Washington DC with this constellation, every August 10, an astrological event reoccurs in the sky above Washington, tying the city to the pagan Virgo—known in ancient Egypt as the goddess Isis. "At dusk, as golden light turns brick facades a dusty rose, the shimmering sun floats a few degrees just to the left of Pennsylvania Avenue, gradually inching to the right until it sets directly over the famous street," writes Julie Duin. "If the horizon remains cloudless, three stars are visible in a straight line from the Capitol to the White House to the skies in the west. Known as Regulus, Arcturus and Spica, the stars form a right-angled triangle framing the constellation of Virgo."[634]

Such mysticism incorporated into the layout of Washington DC by Freemasons for summoning the timing, presence, and approval of these "invisible agents" was a formula perfected in pagan Rome. John Fellows explains why:

> They consulted the gods, to know if the enterprise would be acceptable to them, and if they approved of the day chosen to begin the work…they invoked, besides the gods of the country, the gods to whose protection the new city was recommended, which was done secretly, because it was necessary that the tutelary gods should be unknown to the vulgar.[635]

Freemason Foster Bailey adds that these symbols intentionally hide "a secret…which veils mysterious forces. These energies when released can have a potent effect."[636] Scottish philosopher Thomas Carlyle once famously added: "By symbols, accordingly, is man guided and commanded, made happy, made wretched." Masons, as a result, are under oath never to reveal the true meaning of these symbols guiding the destiny of America, and when somehow they are compelled to offer explanation, they falsify the statement, even to lower-degree Masons, as explained by Sovereign Grand Commander Albert Pike in the Masonic handbook *Morals and Dogma*:

> Masonry, like all the Religions, all the Mysteries, Hermetic, and Alchemy, conceals its secrets from all except the Adepts and Sages, or the Elect, and uses false explanations and misinterpretations of its symbols to mislead those who deserve only to be misled; to conceal the Truth, which it calls Light, from them, and to draw them away from it.[637]

Substantial reasons exist for why the designers of Washington's Government Center would have wanted to obscure the meaning behind the occultic layout of America's capital. If the public in general had been prematurely convinced of the end-game prophesied in the DC symbolism—what Manly Hall went on to call *The Secret Destiny of America*—it would have been beyond the acceptance of prior generations who likely would have demanded change in leaders and facilities. But as time has moved forward and increasingly it has become necessary for public understanding of America's heritage and intended purpose, little by little—either by providence, promotion, or even resistance—a clearer picture has emerged as to who, what, and why the United States capital and the Vatican City are designed the way they are. What might this have to do with Petrus Romanus and the coming of Antichrist? We deal with that in the next chapter, but meanwhile, the book *Apollyon Rising 2012* explains:

> According to the symbolism in Washington DC, the secret destiny of America includes future national and global subservience to the god of Freemasonry, a deity most Americans would not imagine when reciting the pledge of allegiance to "one nation under *God*." In fact, the idea by some that the United States was established as a monotheistic, "Christian nation" by those who designed Washington DC, and that the "God" referred to on American currency is a Judeo-Christian one, is a puzzling conclusion when reflected against the deistic beliefs of so many of the founding fathers (as perpetually viewed in the "Supreme Architect" deism of Freemasons and in the "Supreme Judge of the world" and "Divine Providence" notations in the Declaration of Independence) and the countless pagan icons that dominate the symbols, statues, buildings, and seals carefully drafted under official government auspices. The Great Seal of the United States, which Hall rightly called "the signature" of that exalted body of Masons who designed America for a "peculiar and particular purpose," bears rich symbolism forecasting anything but Christianity. In fact, when Christians in the 1800s argued that a hypothetical annihilation of the

U.S. would lead to "antiquaries of succeeding centuries" concluding that America had been a heathen nation based on symbolism of the Great Seal, Congress was pushed to create something reflecting the Christian faith of so many of its citizens. U.S. President and Freemason Theodore Roosevelt strongly opposed this idea, while other Masons were not as frustrated with the plan. Given the ambivalence of the term "God" and the axiom that, interpreted within the context of the Great Seal symbolism, this would certainly not infer a traditional Christian God, the slogan "In God We Trust" (whomever you believe that is) was accommodated by Masons and other illuminatus and so approved as the official U.S. motto.

To illustrate the point that one would not determine the "God" in America's official motto refers to the Father of Jesus Christ or a biblical Trinity, imagine yourself as a space traveler who visits earth in a fictional, post-apocalyptic world. Digging through the rubble of the once-thriving planet, you come across a copy of a U.S. one-dollar bill with the two-sided Great Seal of the United States joined in the middle by the phrase, "IN GOD WE TRUST."

Upon consideration, you ask yourself, "What *god* did this refer to?" With no preconceptions, you allow the symbolism on the seal to speak for itself, from which you quickly determine that this had been a great culture who worshipped

Egyptian and Greek deities, especially a particular solar one whose all-seeing eye glared from atop an unfinished Egyptian pyramid. Upon further investigation into the specific beliefs of the strange group whose members had influenced the Great Seal, you discover from their highest masters, including one "illustrious" Albert Pike, that the sun god they venerated so highly had been known to them at various times in history by the names *Apollo, Osiris,* and *Nimrod.*

Then, you decode something even more important—a hidden divination in the Great Seal that prophesied a time when this "god" would return to earth in a physical body. His coming, according to the information you gleaned from the draftsmen of the Great Seal, would herald a New World Order. In retrospect, you wonder: *Was this prophesied advent on this Great Seal the fomenter of destruction that annihilated what at once was so beautiful a world?*[638]

18 | Mystery Babylon

The Mother of Harlots Gives Birth Again

The arrival of Petrus Romanus as the final pope presages a very near future in which a man of superior intelligence, wit, charm, and diplomacy will emerge on the world scene as a savior. He will seemingly possess transcendent wisdom that enables him to solve problems and offer solutions for many of today's most perplexing issues. His popularity will be widespread, and his fans will include young and old, religious and non-religious, male and female. Talk show hosts will interview his colleagues, news anchors will cover his movements, scholars will applaud his uncanny ability to resolve what has escaped the rest of us, and the poor will bow down at his table. He will, in all human respects, appeal to the best idea of society. But his profound comprehension and irresistible presence will be the result of an invisible network of thousands of years of collective knowledge stemming from his embodiment of a very old, super-intelligent spirit. As Jesus Christ was the "seed of the woman" (Genesis 3:15), he will be the "seed of the serpent." Moreover, though his arrival in the form of a man was foretold by numerous Scriptures, the broad masses will not immediately recognize him for what he actually is—paganism's ultimate incarnation; the "beast" of Revelation 13:1.

It's been assumed for centuries that a prerequisite for the coming of Petrus Romanus and his Antichrist master would be the sudden or contrived emergence of a new world order—an umbrella under which national boundaries dissolve and ethnic groups, ideologies, religions, and economics from around the world orchestrate a single and dominant sovereignty. At the head of the utopian administration, the Antichrist will surface. At first, he will appear to be a man of distinguished character, but will ultimately become "a king of fierce countenance" (Daniel 8:23) who makes the combined depravities of Antiochus Epiphanes, Hitler, Stalin, and Genghis Khan, all of whom were types of the Antichrist, look like child's play. With imperious decree, he will facilitate a One-World Government, universal religion, and global socialism. Those who refuse his New World Order will inevitably be imprisoned or destroyed until finally he raises his fist, "speaking great things...in blasphemy against God, to blaspheme his name, and his tabernacle, and them that dwell in heaven" (Revelation 13:5–6). Exalting himself "above all that is called God, or that is worshiped," he enthrones himself "in the temple of God, showing himself that he is God" (2 Thessalonians 2:4).

For many years in the United States, the notion that such an Orwellian society could arise wherein One World Government oversees the smallest details of our lives and in which human liberties are abandoned was considered anathema. The idea that rugged individualism would somehow be sacrificed for an anesthetized, universal harmony was repudiated by America's greatest minds. Then, in the 1970s, things began to change. Following a call by Nelson Rockefeller for the creation of a "New World Order," presidential candidate Jimmy Carter campaigned, saying, "We must replace balance of power politics with world order politics." This struck a chord with international leaders, especially Masonically approved men like President George Herbert Walker Bush, who in the 1980s began championing the one-world dirge, announcing over national television that the time for a "New World Order" had arrived. The invasion into Kuwait by Iraq/Babylon provided perfect cover for allied forces to engage the Babylonian "prince" by launching Desert Storm against Saddam Hussein's forces, an effort Bush made clear was "to forge for ourselves and for future generations a New World Order…in which a credible United Nations can use its…role to fulfill the promise and vision of the U.N.'s founders." Following this initial statement, Bush addressed the Congress, adding:

> What is at stake is more than one small country [Kuwait], it is a big idea—a New World Order, where diverse nations are drawn together in common cause to achieve the universal aspirations of mankind…. Such is a world worthy of our struggle, and worthy of our children's future…the long-held promise of a New World Order.[639]

Ever since the president's astonishing newscast, the parade of political and religious leaders in the United States and abroad pushing for a New World Order has multiplied. Britain's Prime Minister, Tony Blair, in a speech delivered in Chicago, April 22, 1999, said frankly, "We are all internationalists now, whether we like it or not." Blair could barely have imagined how quickly his doctrine would catch on. By December 9, 2008, respected chief foreign affairs columnist for *The Financial Times*, Gideon Rachman (who attended the 2003 and 2004 Bilderberg meetings at Versailles, France, and Stresa, Italy), admitted, "I have never believed that there is a secret United Nations plot to take over the U.S. I have never seen black helicopters hovering in the sky above Montana. But, for the first time in my life, I think the formation of some sort of world government is plausible." The United Kingdom's Gordon Brown not only agreed, but in an article for *The Sunday Times*, March 1, 2009, said it was time "for all countries of the world" to renounce "protectionism" and to participate in a new "international" system of banking and regulations "to shape the twenty-first century as the first century of a truly global society." On January 1, 2009, Mikhail Gorbachev, the former head of state of the USSR, said the global clamor for change and the election of Barack Obama was the catalyst that might finally convince the world of the need for global government. In an article for the *International Herald Tribune*, he said:

> Throughout the world, there is a clamor for change. That desire was evident in November, in an event that could become both a symbol of this need for change and a real catalyst for that change. Given the special role the United States continues to play in the world, the election of Barack Obama could have consequences that go far beyond that country....
>
> If current ideas for reforming the world's financial and economic institutions are consistently implemented, that would suggest we are finally beginning to understand the important of global governance.

Four days later, on January 5, 2009, the chorus call for a New World Order was again ramped up by former Secretary of State Henry Kissinger while on the floor of the New York Stock Exchange. A reporter for CNBC asked Kissinger what he thought Barack Obama's first actions as president should be in light of the global financial crises. He answered, "I think that his task will be to develop an overall strategy for America in this period, when really a New World Order can be created." Kissinger followed on January 13 with an opinion piece distributed by Tribune Media Services titled "The Chance for a New World Order." Addressing the international financial crises "inherited" by Barack Obama, Kissinger discussed the need for an international political order (world government) to arise and govern a new international monetary and trade system. "The nadir of the existing international financial system coincides with simultaneous political crises around the globe," he wrote. "The alternative to a new international order is chaos." Kissinger went on to highlight Obama's extraordinary impact on the "imagination of humanity," calling it "an important element in shaping a New World Order."[640] Kissinger—a Rockefeller functionary and member of the Bilderberg group and Trilateral Commission who routinely turns up in lists among senior members of the Illuminati—peppered his article with key phrases from Masonic dogma, including the comment about the "alternative to a new international order is chaos," a clear reference to "*ordo ab chao*" from ancient Craft Masonry, a reference to the doctrine of "order out of chaos." Like the mythical phoenix firebird, Kissinger visualized the opportunity for a New World Order to be engineered from the ashes of current global chaos, exactly the point he had made years earlier at the Bilderberger meeting in Evian, France, on May 21, 1991, when describing how the world could be manipulated into willingly embracing global government. He said:

> Today Americans would be outraged if UN troops entered Los Angeles to restore order; tomorrow they will be grateful! This is especially true if they were told there was an outside threat from beyond, whether real or promulgated, that threatened our very existence. It is then that all peoples of the world will plead with world leaders to deliver them from this evil. The one thing every man fears is the unknown. When presented with this scenario, individual rights will be willingly relinquished for the guarantee of their well being granted to them by their world government.[641]

The once anathematic idea of surrendering national and individual rights in order to embrace a single geopolitical authority under the pretense of global civil and economic security (as envisioned by Henry Kissinger and others) was confirmed by the Vatican as an objective goal on October 24, 2011, when the Pontifical Council for Justice and Peace published their document, "Toward Reforming the International Financial and Monetary Systems in the Context of a Global Public Authority."

In this new unsettling directive, Pontifical Council members cited social, political, and economic instability as a "moral" mandate for establishing "a global public authority" and "a central world bank" that would provide oversight for individual and world pecuniary institutions. "The economic and financial crisis which the world is going through calls everyone, individuals and peoples, to examine in depth the principles and the cultural and moral values at the basis of social coexistence," the report said. It then condemned "the idolatry of the market" and promoted what sounded like socialism as an "ethic of solidarity" against "selfishness, collective greed and hoarding of goods on a great scale." In calling for the establishment of a "supranational authority" with worldwide clout, it contended the need for "universal jurisdiction" should be housed inside the United Nations. The most telling statement made by the Pontifical Council was when it acknowledged how "one can see an emerging requirement for a body that will carry out the functions of a kind of 'central world bank' that regulates the flow and system of monetary exchanges similar to the national central banks." This was followed by a startling if not altogether prophetic formula, which outlined how subjugation to the new global power would be made *"at the cost of a gradual, balanced transfer of a part of each nation's powers to a world authority and to regional authorities"*[642] (emphasis added).

In 1990, former Jesuit Malachi Martin warned that such a plan by political authorities, transnational bankers, and the Vatican was secretly being devised toward establishment of a world government and global economic system. A decade after Malachi's disclosure, on the eve of the G8 Summit in Italy (and perhaps not coincidently just before the Holy Father met with President Barack Obama), Pope Benedict XVI published his third encyclical (July 7th, 2009) *Caritas in Veritate* ("Charity in Truth") that proposed what Father Martin had alleged was coming. Almost immediately, *Forcing Change Magazine* chief editor Carl Teichrib wrote of the encyclical: "While Pope Benedict's perspective on the global economy was a perplexing blend of free-market and social welfare ideals, what raised eyebrows were his thoughts on international politics. In section 67 of Caritas in Veritate, the Pope dropped an ideological bombshell—a world authority to 'manage the economy,' bring about 'timely disarmament,' and ensure 'food security and peace.'"[643] Teichrib noted how the reference to a "world political authority" was a very clear signal and that Benedict wanted the global authority's power of enforcement to have "real teeth." The portion of Caritas in Veritate in question reads:

> In the face of the unrelenting growth of global interdependence, there is a strongly felt need, even in the midst of a global recession, for a reform of the United Nations Organization, and likewise of economic institutions and international finance, so that the concept of the family of nations can acquire real teeth.
>
> One also senses the urgent need to find innovative ways of implementing the principle of the responsibility to protect and of giving poorer nations an effective voice in shared decision-making. This seems necessary in order to arrive at a political, juridical and economic order which can increase and give direction to international cooperation for the development of all peoples in solidarity.
>
> To manage the global economy; to revive economies hit by the crisis; to avoid any deterioration of the present crisis and the greater imbalances that would result; to bring about integral and timely disarmament, food security and peace; to guarantee the protection of the environment and to regulate

migration: for all this, there is urgent need of a true world political authority, as my predecessor Blessed John XXIII indicated some years ago.[644]

The month following the publication of Caritas in Veritate, in an article for Accuracy in Media titled "Who Will Probe the U.N.-Vatican Connection," journalist Cliff Kincaid wondered why "the leader of the worldwide Catholic Church, considered by Catholics the personal representative of Jesus Christ, has become an advocate for one of the most corrupt organizations on the face of the earth—the United Nations." Combined with the more recent (and similar-sounding) Pontifical Council document advocating for a new global political authority and world banking system to be housed within the United Nations, Mr. Kincaid may have understood that a much older blueprint for structuring the world's political and economic authorities into a centralized World Government had been concealed inside the Holy See for hundreds of years. This is true, especially given that Kincaid finally admitted, "This has prophetic implications for Christians who fear that a global dictatorship will take power on earth in the 'last days.'"[645]

Enter Peter the Roman's Useful Evangelicals—Dominionists and Their Quest for a Revived Church State

During his second inaugural address, US President George W. Bush similarly envisioned the specter of a Babylonian-like, one-world monetary and political authority. With an almost religious tone, he cited Masonic script, saying, "When our Founders declared a new order of the ages…they were acting on an ancient hope that is meant to be fulfilled."[646] New Age guru Benjamin Creme was clearer still on how the marriage of politics and religion would epitomize the New World Order when he added some years ago, "What is the plan? It includes the installation of a new world government and a new world religion under Maitreia" (Maitreia is a New Age "messiah").[647]

Five-time United States senator from Arizona and Republican presidential nominee in 1964, Barry Goldwater, likewise foresaw the union of politics and religion as a catalyst for global government. In writing of the efforts of behind-the-scenes groups, including international bankers, to bring about a New World Order, he said it would occur through consolidating "the four centers of power—political, monetary, intellectual, and ecclesiastical." As the managers and creators of the new (prophetic) system, this power elite would "rule the future" of mankind, he believed.[648] So concerned was Goldwater with the consolidation of government policy and religious creed that on September 16, 1981, he took the unique position of warning political preachers from the floor of the US Senate that he would "fight them every step of the way if they [tried] to dictate their [religious ideas] to all Americans in the name of conservatism."[649] The increasing influence of the Religious Right on the Republican Party was bothersome to Goldwater in particular because of his libertarian views. It should have concerned theologians as well, and we say this as writers sometimes associated with the Religious Right.

Combining religious faith with politics as a legislative system of governance is exactly the formula upon which Antichrist will come to power. Thousands of years ago, in the books of Daniel and Revelation, the picture was drawn of the *political* figure known as Antichrist who derives ultra-national dominance from the world's *religious* faithful through the influence of an ecclesiastical leader known as the False Prophet (whom we believe may be Petrus Romanus). Neither Jesus nor His disciples (who turned the world upside down through preaching the Gospel of Christ, the true "power of God," according to Paul) ever imagined the goal of changing the world through supplanting secular government with an authoritarian theocracy. In fact, Jesus made it clear that His followers would not fight earthly authorities purely because His kingdom was "not of this world" (John 18:36). While every modern citizen—religious and non-religious—has responsibility to lobby for moral good, combining the mission of the Church with political aspirations is not only unprecedented in New

Testament theology—including the life of Christ and the pattern of the New Testament Church—but, as Goldwater may have feared, a tragic scheme concocted by sinister forces to defer the Church from its true power while enriching insincere bureaucrats, a disastrous fact that too many churchgoers are soon to learn.

As we write this book, we head into the 2012 political season with many of the nationally known talking heads for the Religious Right ravenously postulating—and being supported to do so by their followers—a marriage between politics and religion as the ideal scheme for curing what ails the US and the world. Seemingly unaware of the New Testament's revolutionary stance on composite rather than sacral societies, this ancient occult concept, known in modern times as *dominionism*, was reincarnated through hyper-Calvinism (though supported by both reconstructionists and nonreconstructionists) and seeks to establish the Kingdom of God on earth through the union of politics and religion: exactly what many Catholic and Evangelical prophets have long believed is described in ancient apocalyptic literature as the engine of power for the rise of Antichrist.

It was among conservative Calvinists in 1973, after R. J. Rushdooney ignited the modern dominionist movement with his book, *The Institutes of Biblical Law* (followed by a horde of copycats from Pentecostals, Fundamentalists, conservative Roman Catholics and Episcopalians) that the concept caught on as an ideology.[650] Unlike so many other occult-based doctrines which faded over time, something about the notion that churchgoers could easily fulfill their Christian duty through simply pulling a voting lever and electing the latest Saul-in-the-line appealed to modern believers. Michelle Goldberg, author of the article "A Christian Plot for Domination?" points out how, as a result, we now have the most theocratic-mad "Republican field in American history" and that "the concept of Dominionism is reaching mainstream audiences." Michelle goes on to reveal some important history about Mr. Rushdooney, the father of Christian Reconstructionism:

...while Rushdoony was a totalitarian, he was a prolific and influential one—he... consistently defended Southern slavery and contrasted it with the greater evils of socialism: "The law here is humane and also unsentimental," he wrote. "It recognizes that some people are by nature slaves and will always be so... Socialism, on the contrary, tries to give the slave all the advantages of his security together with the benefits of freedom, and in the process, destroys both the free and the enslaved."

Rushdoony's most influential idea was the concept of Dominionism, which spread far beyond the Christian Reconstructionist fringe. "'Dominion theologians,' as they are called, lay great emphasis on Genesis 1:26–7, where God tells Adam to assume dominion over the animate and inanimate world," wrote the scholar Garry Wills in his book *Under God: Religion and American Politics*, describing the influence of the ideology on [certain national religious leaders who believe] "When man fell, his control over creation was forfeited; but the saved, who are restored by baptism, can claim again the rights given Adam."[651]

The dominionist concept "that some people are by nature slaves and will always be so" and that others should have the authority as overseers of the world and Vicar's of Christ to rule over them is especially consistent within historical Roman Catholicism. After all, it was Pius IX who, in 1873 "...attached an indulgence to a prayer for the 'wretched Ethiopians in Central Africa that Almighty God may at length remove the curse of Cham [Ham] from their hearts.'" [652] A statement he made referring to Genesis 9:22–27 which was later used by Romanists to justify the enslavement of Africans. As internationally known author and lecturer, Dave Hunt, points out, "the separation of church and state is a concept of recent origin, and one which the Roman Catholic Church, as the religious continuation of the Roman

Empire, has continuously and even viciously opposed."[653] Numerous ancient and modern Catholic scholars not only agree with this assessment, but have stated unequivocally that no secular government can correctly regulate the affairs of mankind without the oversight and approval of the Roman Catholic Church. The highly esteemed nineteenth-century Catholic philosopher, essayist, and reviewer, Orestes Augustus Brownson articulated it this way: "No civil government, be it a monarchy, an aristocracy, a democracy...can be a wise, just, efficient, or durable government, governing for the good of the community, without the Catholic Church; and without the papacy there is and can be no Catholic Church."[654] Dave hunt puts this in historical context, writing:

> The Vatican has consistently fought every democratic advance from absolute monarchies toward government by the people, beginning with England's Magna Carta (June 15, 1215), "the mother of European Constitutions." That vital document was denounced immediately by Pope Innocent III [who was responsible for the death of more Christians than all Roman Caesars combined] (1198–1216) who "pronounced it null and void and excommunicated the English barons who obtained it" and absolved the king of his oath to the barons. Encouraged by the pope, King John brought in foreign mercenaries to fight the barons, bringing great destruction upon the country. Subsequent popes did all in their power to help John's successor, Henry III, overturn the Magna Carta...
>
> Pope Leo XII reproved Louis XVIII for granting the "liberal" French Constitution, while Pope Gregory XVI denounced the Belgian Constitution of 1832. His outrageous encyclical, *Mirari vos*, of August 15, 1832 (which was later confirmed by Pope Pius IX in his 1864 *Syllabus Errorum*), condemned freedom of conscience as "an insane folly" and

freedom of the press as "a pestiferous error, which cannot be sufficiently detested." He reasserted the right of the Church to use force and like countless popes before him demanded that civil authorities promptly imprison any non-Catholics who dared to preach and practice their faith. One eminent historian of the nineteenth century, commenting upon the Vatican's denunciation of the Bavarian and Austrian constitutions, paraphrased its attitude thus:

> Our absolutist system, supported by the Inquisition, the strictest censorship, the suppression of all literature, the privileged exemption of the clergy, and arbitrary power of bishops, cannot endure any other than absolutist governments...[655]

And yet, as the Spanish philosopher George Santayana once so famously noted, "Those who cannot remember the past are condemned to repeat it." This is interesting in light of the Prophecy of the Popes and what some believers say is indicative of the title "Petrus Romanus" (Peter the Roman) and the relationship between pontifical authority predating Vatican II and earlier—a time when the iron of secular authority and the gold of religious authoritarianism were more outwardly bonded by human clay than today—and that which will be reasserted by the final pope. In this regard, Catholic experts say the title "Peter the Roman" is potent in that it indicates the last pope may satisfy the desires of Rome and its dominionist pals in America by reviving an authoritarian Babylonian State Religion. On this order, the man who in 2002 correctly predicted that the pope succeeding John Paul II would be named Benedict XVI, Ronald L. Conte Jr., believes the next pope will take the name Pius XIII, and that "Peter the Roman" implies this pope "will reaffirm the authority of the Roman Pontiff over the Church" and "will emphasize the supremacy of the Roman Catholic Faith and the Roman Catholic

Church above all other religions and denominations, and its authority over all Christians and all peoples of the world." To this, Conte adds, "During the reign of Pope Peter the Roman, the great apostasy begins" and this pope will mark "the first part of the tribulation, during our generation."[656]

Cardinal Manning, the Pope, and the Antichrist

Dr. Henry Edward Cardinal Manning was Lord Archbishop of Westminster from 1865–1892. Before conversion to Catholicism he was an influential Anglican cleric but lost faith in the Church of England in 1850, when, "in the so-called Gorham judgment, the Privy Council successfully ordered the Church to institute an Evangelical clergyman who denied that the sacrament of baptism had an objective effect of baptismal regeneration. The denial of the objective effect of the sacraments was to Manning and many others a grave heresy." This contradicting of tradition within the church by order of a civil, secular court was too much for Manning, who viewed it as evidence the Anglican Church "was merely a man-made creation of the English Parliament."[657]

After departing the Church of England, Manning converted to Catholicism and entered the seminary. He was ordained a priest June 14, 1851, and by 1865, had risen to Archbishop of Westminster. He was a significant presence in setting the direction of the modern Catholic Church, and achieved particular fame for his doctrine of papal infallibility (the dogma that the pope is preserved from even the possibility of error when he speaks "ex cathedra"), which became dogma during the First Vatican Council of 1870. Manning's unrelenting emphasis on the prerogatives and powers of the pope, including authority over local temporal and spiritual hierarchies such as local bishops, defined *ultramontanism* in his day—the idea that papal superiority should exist even over councils and kings.

Historians view the nineteenth-century revival of ultramontanism as progressing through three distinct stages:

- 1814. The revival of the Jesuit Order, which was always the mainstay of curial as opposed to local authority.
- 1864. The issuing by Pius IX of the *Syllabus*, in which Catholicism and any form of liberalism were held to be incompatible.
- 1870. The declaration by the First Vatican Council that the Pope is infallible when he makes, by virtue of his office, a solemn pronouncement on faith or morals. This declaration, though not conceding the claim of administrative infallibility which many Ultramontanes would have wished, marked a substantial triumph for their point of view.[658]

These facts make Manning all the more remarkable given how during the 1800–1900s a series of scholarly opinions were published outlining how events in the Roman Catholic Church combined with long-time anti-papist goals by secret Masonic infiltrators would give rise in the last days to great apostasy in Rome and the advent of Antichrist. Among the strongest proponents of this eschatology was Cardinal Manning himself, who delivered a series of lectures in 1861 under the title "The Present Crises of the Holy See Tested by Prophecy" (later incorporated into a larger study entitled "The Temporal Power of the Vicar of Jesus Christ") in which Manning foresaw a future crises in the Roman Catholic Church initiated by the type of ecumenism and flexible dogma that many modern conservative Catholics have loathed following the Second Vatican Council (October 1962 through December 1965). Manning believed this change to orthodoxy would undermine the authority of the Church and finally result in a departure of the profession of Catholic faith by the nations together with the displacement of the true pope by

440 I Petrus Romanus

a false prophet, thus ushering in the Antichrist and global apostasy. Manning also believed secret societies like the Freemasons were part of this conspiracy. "The secret societies have long ago undermined and honeycombed the Christian society of Europe, and are at this moment struggling onward towards Rome, the center of all Christian order in the world,"[659] he wrote. But when he looked at the prophecy in Revelation 18 concerning the end-time destruction of Mystery Babylon, Manning saw it was the hand of God in judgment of worldwide apostasy emanating from Rome:

> We read in the Book Apocalypse, of the city of Rome, that she said in the pride of her heart, "I sit as a queen, and am no widow, and sorrow I shall not see. Therefore shall her plagues come in one day: death, and mourning, and famine; and she shall be burned with fire, because God is strong who shall judge her." Some of the greatest writers of the Church tell us that…the great City of Seven Hills…the city of Rome will probably become apostate…and that Rome will again be punished, for he will depart from it; and the judgment of God will fall…[660]

Thus, just as the Prophecy of the Popes and numerous other Catholic visionary conveyances do, Manning foresaw the destruction of the city of Rome as a result of its partnership with the Antichrist. This doctrine would have been unfamiliar to most Catholics in those days, so Manning explained how Catholicism's greatest theologians agreed with this point of view:

> The apostasy of the city of Rome…and its destruction by Antichrist may be thoughts so new to many Catholics, that I think it well to recite the text of theologians, of greatest repute. First, Malvenda, who writes expressly on the subject, states as the opinion of Ribera, Gaspar Melus, Viegas, Suarez,

Bellarmine, and Bosius, that Rome shall apostatize from the faith, drive away the Vicar of Christ, and return to its ancient paganism. Malvenda's words are:

> But Rome itself in the last times of the world will return to its ancient idolatry, power, and imperial greatness. It will cast out its Pontiff, altogether apostatize from the Christian faith, terribly persecute the Church, shed the blood of martyrs more cruelly than ever, and will recover its former state of abundant wealth, or even greater than it had under its first rulers.

Lessius says: "In the time of Antichrist, Rome shall be destroyed, as we see openly from the thirteenth chapter of the Apocalypse;" and again: "The woman whom thou sawest is the great city, which hath kingdom over the kings of the earth, in which is signified Rome in its impiety, such as it was in the time of St. John, and shall be again at the end of the world." And Bellarmine: "In the time of Antichrist, Rome shall be desolated and burnt, as we learn from the sixteenth verse of the seventeenth chapter of the Apocalypse." On which words the Jesuit Erbermann comments as follows: "We all confess with Bellarmine that the Roman people, a little before the end of the world, will return to paganism, and drive out the Roman Pontiff."

Viegas, on the eighteenth chapter of the Apocalypse says: "Rome, in the last age of the world, after it has apostatized from the faith, will attain great power and splendor of wealth, and its sway will be widely spread throughout the world, and flourish greatly. Living in luxury and the abundance of all things, it will worship idols, and be steeped in all kinds of superstition, and will pay honor to false gods. And because of the vast effusion of the blood of martyrs which was shed under the emperors, God will most severely and justly avenge them, and it shall be utterly destroyed, and burned by a most terrible and afflicting conflagration."[661]

Throughout history including recent times, numerous Catholic priests have built on the foundation laid by Cardinal Manning and have often been surprisingly outspoken on their agreement regarding the inevitable danger not only of apostate Rome but of the False Prophet rising from within the ranks of Catholicism itself as a result of secret satanic "Illuminati-Masonic" influences. (The term "Illuminati" as used here is not strictly a reference to the Bavarian movement founded May 1, 1776, by Jesuit-taught Adam Weishaupt, but as indicative of a modern multinational power elite, an occult hierarchy operating behind current supranatural and global political machinations.) According to Catholic priests such as Father E. Sylvester Berry, whose book *The Apocalypse of Saint John* foretold the usurpation of the Papacy by a false prophet; Father Herman Bernard Kramer, whose work *The Book of Destiny* painted a terrifying scenario in which Satan enters the church and assassinates the true pope (possibly during conclave) in order that his false pope can rise to rule the world; as well as similar beliefs by priests like Father John F. O'Connor, Father Alfred Kunz, and Father Malachi Martin, this will happen because secret-society and sinister false Catholic infiltrators understand the geopolitical influence of Rome in the world is indispensable for controlling future global elements in matters of church and state. The Roman Catholic Church represents one-sixth of the world's population and over half of all professing Christians, has its own diplomatic corps of ambassadors posted in industrialized nations globally, and over one hundred eighty nations of the world send their ambassadors to the capital city, the Vatican.

In a two-hour presentation (available on DVD), Father O'Connor gave a homily titled "The Reign of the Antichrist," in which he described how changes within society and in the institution were already at work before his death to provide for the coming of Antichrist. In this sermon and elsewhere, O'Connor outlined the catalyst for this scheme unfolding as a result of "Masonic Conspirators" within the organization whose plan, called "Alta Vendita," would essentially take control of the papacy and help the False Prophet deceive the world's faithful (including Catholics) into worshipping Antichrist.

The Permanent Instruction of the Alta Vendita (or simply the Alta Vendita) is a nineteenth-century Italian document, allegedly written by the highest lodge of the Italian Carbonari—a secret revolutionary society associated with Freemasonry—both of which had been publically condemned by Rome. The document clearly maps out a blueprint for infiltrating the Catholic Church in order to slowly turn it into an instrument of propaganda for the society's principles and goals, ultimately seeking to produce Catholic laity, clergy, and finally a pope who would be warm to the ideas of the Enlightenment—the eighteenth-century philosophical view of man as held by naturalists, atheists, deists, and Freemasons, who sought to reform society by elevating science and intellect over religion.

In the nineteenth century, Pope Pius IX and Pope Leo XIII both asked for the Alta Vendita to be published. In 1859, Jacques Crétineau-Joly did so in his book, *L'Église romaine en face de la Révolution*, and in 1885 it was published in English by Monsignor George F. Dillon in *The War of Anti-Christ with the Church and Christian Civilization*. Due to its importance to this chapter, we have provided a significant portion of the text below:

PERMANENT INSTRUCTION OF THE ALTA VENDITA

The Papacy has at all times exercised a decisive action upon the affairs of Italy. By the hands, by the voices, by the pens, by the hearts of its innumerable bishops, priests, monks, nuns and people in all latitudes, the Papacy finds devotedness without end ready for martyrdom, and that to enthusiasm.

Everywhere, whenever it pleases to call upon them, it has friends ready to die or lose all for its cause. This is an immense leverage which the Popes alone have been able to appreciate to its full power, and as yet they have used it only to a certain extent. Today there is no question of reconstituting for ourselves that power, the prestige of which is for the moment weakened. Our final end is that of Voltaire and of the French Revolution, the destruction forever of Catholicism and even of the Christian idea which, if left standing on the ruins of Rome, would be the resuscitation of Christianity later on. But to attain more certainly that result, and not prepare ourselves with gaiety of heart for reverses which adjourn indefinitely, or compromise for ages, the success of a good cause, we must not pay attention to those braggarts of Frenchmen, those cloudy Germans, those melancholy Englishmen, all of whom imagine they can kill Catholicism, now with an impure song, then with an illogical deduction; at another time, with a sarcasm smuggled in like the cottons of Great Britain. Catholicism has a life much more tenacious than that. It has seen the most implacable, the most terrible adversaries, and it has often had the malignant pleasure of throwing holy water on the tombs of the most enraged. Let us permit, then, our brethren of these countries to give themselves up to the sterile intemperance of their anti-Catholic zeal. Let them even mock at our Madonnas and our apparent devotion. With this passport we can conspire at our ease, and arrive little by little at the end we have in view.

Now the Papacy has been for seventeen centuries inherent to the history of Italy. Italy cannot breathe or move without the permission of the Supreme Pastor. With him she has the hundred arms of Briareus, without him she is condemned to a pitiable impotence. She has nothing but divisions to foment, hatreds to break out, and hostilities to manifest themselves from the highest chain of the Alps to the lowest of the Appenines. We cannot desire such a state of things. It is necessary, then, to seek a remedy for that situation. The remedy is found. The Pope, whoever he may be, will never come to the secret societies. It is for the secret societies to come first to the Church, in the resolve to conquer the two.

The work which we have undertaken is not the work of a day, nor of a month, nor of a year. It may last many years, a century perhaps, but in our ranks the soldier dies and the fight continues.

We do not mean to win the Popes to our cause, to make them neophytes of our principles, and propagators of our ideas. That would be a ridiculous dream, no matter in what manner events may turn. Should cardinals or prelates, for example, enter, willingly or by surprise, in some manner, into a part of our secrets, it would be by no means a motive to desire their elevation to the See of Peter. That elevation would destroy us. Ambition alone would bring them to apostasy from us. The needs of power would force them to immolate us. That which we ought to demand, that which we should seek and expect, as the Jews expected the Messiah, is a Pope according to our wants…. Do you wish to know the reason? It is because by that we should have no more need of the vinegar of Hannibal, no more need of the powder of cannon, no more need even of our arms. We have the little finger of the successor of St. Peter engaged in the plot, and that little finger is of more value for our crusade than all the Innocents, the Urbans, and the St. Bernards of Christianity.

We do not doubt that we shall arrive at that supreme term of all our efforts; but when? but how? The unknown does not yet manifest itself. Nevertheless, as nothing should separate us from the plan traced out; as, on the contrary, all things should tend to it – as if success were to crown the work scarcely sketched out tomorrow – we wish in this instruction which must rest a secret for the simple initiated, to give to those of the Supreme Lodge, councils with which they should enlighten the universality of the brethren, under the form of an instruction or memorandum. It is of special importance, and because of a discretion, the motives of which are transparent, never to permit it to be felt that these counsels are orders emanating from the Alta Vendita....

It is to the youth we must go. It is that which we must seduce; it is that which we must bring under the banner of the secret societies....

Now then, in order to secure to us a Pope in the manner required, it is necessary to fashion for that Pope a generation worthy of the reign of which we dream. Leave on one side old age and middle life, go to the youth, and, if possible, even to infancy. Never speak in their presence a word of impiety or impurity. Maxima debetur puero reverentia. Never forget these words of the poet for they will preserve you from licences which it is absolutely essential to guard against for the good of the cause. In order to reap profit at the home of each family, in order to give yourself the right of asylum at the domestic hearth, you ought to present yourself with all the appearance of a man grave and moral. Once your reputation is established in the colleges, in the gymnasiums, in the universities, and in the seminaries – once that you shall have captivated the confidence of professors and students, so act that those who are principally engaged in the ecclesiastical state should love to seek your conversation. Nourish their souls with the splendours of ancient Papal Rome. There is always at the bottom of the Italian heart a regret for Republican Rome. Excite, enkindle those natures so full of warmth and of patriotic fire. Offer them at first, but always in secret, inoffensive books, poetry resplendent with national emphasis; then little by little you will bring your disciples to the degree of cooking desired. When upon all the points of the ecclesiastical state at once, this daily work shall have spread our ideas as the light, then you will be able to appreciate the wisdom of the counsel in which we take the initiative.

Events, which in our opinion, precipitate themselves too rapidly, go necessarily in a few months' time to bring on an intervention of Austria. There are fools who in the lightness of their hearts please themselves in casting others into the midst of perils, and, meanwhile, there are fools who at a given hour drag on even wise men. The revolution which they meditate in Italy will only end in misfortunes and persecutions. Nothing is ripe, neither the men nor the things, and nothing shall be for a long time yet; but from these evils you can easily draw one new chord, and cause it to vibrate in the hearts of the young clergy. That is the hatred of the stranger. Cause the German to become ridiculous and odious even before his foreseen entry. With the idea of the Pontifical supremacy, mix always the old memories of the wars of the priesthood and the Empire. Awaken the smouldering passions of the Guelphs and the Ghibellines, and thus you will obtain for yourselves the reputation of good Catholics and pure patriots.

That reputation will open the way for our doctrines to pass to the bosoms of the young clergy, and go even to the depths of convents. In a few years the young clergy will have, by the force of events, invaded all the functions. They will govern, administer, and judge. They will form the council of the Sovereign. They will be called upon to choose the Pontiff who will reign; and that Pontiff, like the greater part of his contemporaries, will be necessarily imbued with the Italian and humanitarian principles which we are about to put in circulation. It is a little grain of mustard which we place in the earth, but the sun of Justice will develop it even to be a great power, and you will see one day what a rich harvest that little seed will produce.

In the way which we trace for our brethren there are found great obstacles to conquer, difficulties of more than one kind to surmount. They will be overcome by experience and by perspicacity; but the end is beautiful. What does it matter to put all the sails to the wind in order to attain it. You wish to revolutionize Italy? Seek out the Pope of whom we give the portrait. You wish to establish the reign of the elect upon the throne of the prostitute of Babylon? Let the clergy march under your banner in the belief always that they march under the banner of the Apostolic Keys. You wish to cause the last vestige of tyranny and of oppression to disappear? Lay your nets like Simon Barjona. Lay them in the depths of sacristies, seminaries, and convents, rather than in the depths of the sea, and if you will precipitate nothing you will give yourself a draught of fishes more miraculous than his. The fisher of fishes will become a fisher of men. You will bring yourselves as friends around the Apostolic Chair. You will have fished up a Revolution in Tiara and Cope, marching with Cross and banner – a Revolution which needs only to be spurred on a little to put the four quarters of the world on fire.

Let each act of your life tend then to discover the Philosopher's Stone. The alchemists of the middle ages lost their time and the gold of their dupes in the quest of this dream. That of the secret societies will be accomplished for the most simple of reasons, because it is based on the passions of man. Let us not be discouraged then by a check, a reverse, or a defeat. Let us prepare our arms in the silence of the lodges, dress our batteries, flatter all passions the most evil and the most generous, and all lead us to think that our plans will succeed one day above even our most improbable calculations.[662]

In the wake of Vatican II, traditionalist Roman Catholic groups see evidence that the Alta Vendita has indeed succeeded "above even the most improbable calculations." As a result, some have developed a critical attitude toward church hierarchy in the belief that post-Vatican II teachings contradict and infect solemn Catholic dogmas with modernism, ecumenism, collegiality, and religious liberty, which are clearly reminiscent of the secret society's objectives. Such secessionists point to examples like John Paul II's 1982 prayer meeting at Assisi with over one hundred religious leaders including pagans, his meetings with the Dalai Lama (who placed a Buddhist statue on the altar in the Church of St. Francis), his receiving the mark of the adorers of the Hindu god Shiva, his meetings with devil worshipping voodoo high-priests (during which he even justified voodoo as possessing "truth and good, seeds of the Word") and so on, all in accordance with the principles of Vatican II. Radical Catholic groups like the Sedevacantists (Latin: *sede vacante*, "the seat being vacant") consider such activity evidence that the popes following Vatican II are illegitimate heretics and that the Holy See of Rome has been technically "vacant" since the death of either Pope Pius XII in 1958 or Pope John XXIII in 1963 (with some classifying John XXIII a Modernist antipope).

Some believe this has even paved the way for a showdown during the next period of vacancy in the papal office that could witness frustrated traditionalists among the College of Cardinals desperate to elect a sitting Bishop of Rome as apostolic successor of Saint Peter (Petrus Romanus) who will institute a vigilant revival and reinstitution of pre-Vatican II authoritarianism. This conflict seems to be boiling under the surface, largely unknown to the public, but seen by such mystics as Father Herman Bernard Kramer (mentioned earlier) in his work, "The Book of Destiny." During a strange interpretation he made of the twelfth chapter of the Book of Revelation concerning "the great wonder" mentioned in verse one, Father Kramer writes: "The 'sign' in heaven is that of a woman with child crying out in her travail and anguish of delivery. In that travail, she gives birth to some definite 'person' who is to RULE the Church with a rod of iron (verse 5). It then points to a conflict waged within the Church to elect one who was to 'rule all nations' in the manner clearly stated. In accord with the text this is unmistakably a PAPAL ELECTION, for only Christ and his Vicar have the divine right to rule ALL NATIONS... But at this time the great powers may take a menacing attitude to hinder the election of the logical and expected candidate by threats of a general apostasy, assassination or imprisonment of this candidate if elected."[663]

Although we disagree with Kramer's interpretation of the book of Revelation, the idea that a specific "person" was born and is now of the appropriate age to fulfill the incarnation of St. Malachy's Prophecy of the Popes, is without question. Whatever one makes of the Petrus Romanus prediction, the pope following Benedict XVI is the last on the list. Furthermore, Kramer's fear that "great powers may take a menacing attitude to hinder the election of the logical and expected candidate" echoes the sentiment of priests mentioned elsewhere in this book (and others unmentioned) who see a crises for the Church coming, and the Man of Sin rising as a result.

Petrus Romanus

The Final Pope is Here

From Christians to New Agers, skeptics to historians, the world is presently enthralled with what will happen during and following the year 2012. In general, the excitement (or dread, as the case may be) surrounds a variety of predictions made by ancient and modern sources concerning a portentous moment in time. Mankind has entered a period of unprecedented global upheaval, according to these experts, when the earth and all life on it will undergo apocalyptica marked by the end of the "thirteenth baktun" of the Mesoamerican Mayan Long Count. The exact end date of this calendar is December 21, 2012, when during the winter solstice at 11:11, GMT (Greenwich Mean Time), the New Age crowd says the sun will align with the galactic center of the Milky Way galaxy, an event that occurs only every thirteen thousand years. The precession of the equinoxes will conclude a twenty-six-thousand-year cycle, bringing the astrological

Age of Pisces to an end and introducing the beginning of Aquarius, when the next cycle begins and the sun rises out of the mouth of the Ouroboros (great serpent of the Milky Way). This is the sun rising in Sagittarius, the centaur with a bow—the symbol for Nimrod coming out from the mouth of Leviathan and the sun "god" rising again—Apollo/Osiris. The Mayans predicted this conjunction, interpreting it as a harbinger of the end of the world as we know it and the beginning of a new "enlightened" pagan age. People from the world's greatest religions including Christianity and Islam also see current global developments as potential omens of an end-times scenario leading to the Apocalypse. This includes catholic mystics who believe in the Prophecy of the Popes.

On this order, the man who in 2002 correctly predicted that the pope succeeding John Paul II would be named Benedict XVI, Ronald L. Conte Jr., believes the next pope will be Cardinal Francis Arinze and that he will take the name *Pius XIII*. This name (Pius) is associated historically with popes who emphasized authoritative doctrine during their pontificates. Cardinal Arinze fits this description, and Conte interprets this qualification as best fulfilling "Peter the Roman" as a pope who "will reaffirm the authority of the Roman Pontiff over the Church; this authority is based on his place as a Successor of Peter" and "will emphasize the supremacy of the Roman Catholic Faith and the Roman Catholic Church above all other religions and denominations, and its authority over all Christians and all peoples of the world." To this, Conte adds, "During the reign of Pope Peter the Roman, the great apostasy begins" and this pope will mark "the first part of the tribulation, during our generation."[664] Conte envisions this apocalypse beginning in 2012 when, as he sees it, Benedict suddenly dies or steps down and is replaced by Petrus Romanus. This is followed by a series of cascading events resulting in World War III, which is triggered when Iranian-backed terrorists explode a nuclear bomb in New York City. The Great Tribulation begins, and by July 2013, Rome is destroyed when it is struck by a nuclear missile.

Elsewhere in this book we have meticulously investigated a French codex entitled, *La Mystérieuse Prophétie des Papes* ("The Mysterious Prophecy of the Popes"), issued in 1951 by a Jesuit priest and mathematician named René Thibaut (1883–1952). Among his astonishing findings—hidden to the modern world until the publishing of our work—Thibaut found concealed in the Prophecy of the Popes a clever number of word plays that form many acrostics and anagrams.[665] An example of one of the linguistic codes may hold cryptic agreement with Ronald L. Conte's conclusion that Petrus Romanus will take the name Pius. The code is discovered in the Latin text "*Peregrinus apostolicus*"[666] which was the prophecy for the ninety-sixth pope on the list, Pius VI. The anagram not only reveals the papal name, it does so twice: *PpereglinUS aPostolIcUS*. This appearance of the name "Pius" is rather astounding considering we have a published copy dated almost two hundred years before Pius VI was elected. But Thibaut suggests the repetition serves as an even farther-reaching poetic refrain. In other words, "Pius! Pius!" is similar to the excited binary "Mayday, Mayday!" that sailors cry out in dire circumstances[667] and which may have prophetic implications concerning the name of the final pope on the list.

In addition to being associated with Roman authoritarianism and cryptogramed in the Prophecy of the Popes, Conte bolsters his prognostication concerning the name "Pius" by pointing to the electrifying visions of another pope named Pius—Pope Pius X who served as pope from 1903 to 1914 and who saw a papal successor carrying the same name *Pius* fleeing Rome over the bodies of dead priests at the onset of the end times. Pius X is widely reported to have said:

> *What I have seen is terrifying! Will I be the one, or will it be a successor? What is certain is that the Pope will leave Rome and, in leaving the Vatican, he will have to pass over the dead bodies of his priests! Do not tell anyone this while I am alive.*[668]

In a second vision during an audience with the Franciscan order in 1909, Pope Pius X appeared to fall into a trance. After a few moments, he opened his eyes and rose to his feet, announcing:

> *I have seen one of my successors, of the same name [a future pope named Pius], who was fleeing over the dead bodies of his brethren. He will take refuge in some hiding place; but after a brief respite, he will die a cruel death. Respect for God has disappeared from human hearts. They wish to efface even God's memory. This perversity is nothing less than the beginning of the last days of the world.*[669]

The third part of the Secret of Fátima, which was supposedly released in total by the Vatican June 26, 2000, seems to echo the visions of Pius X. A section of the material reads:

> *…before reaching there the Holy Father passed through a big city half in ruins and half trembling with halting step, afflicted with pain and sorrow, he prayed for the souls of the corpses he met on his way; having reached the top of the mountain, on his knees at the foot of the big Cross he was killed by a group of soldiers who fired bullets and arrows at him, and in the same way there died one after another the other Bishops, Priests, men and women Religious, and various lay people of different ranks and positions.*[670]

The conceptual framework of these visions and their validity is volatile among many Catholics who believe Rome is complicit in an intentional cover-up involving the *true* Third Secret of Fátima as well as other suppressed Catholic foresights that are rife with wildly different predictions concerning the future prophetic role of the Roman Catholic Church. Marian apparitions, visions by popes, interpretations by cardinals of the apocalypse, and approved mystical prophecies often stand at odds with recent Vatican publications. Even the "Catechism of the Catholic Church" approved by the Church and promulgated by Pope John Paul II (released in English in 1994, the first catechism in more than four hundred years), which draws on the Bible, the mass, the sacraments, traditions, teachings, and the lives of the saints, states under the section *The Church's Ultimate Trial:*

> 675 Before Christ's second coming the Church must pass through a final trial that will shake the faith of many believers. The persecution that accompanies her pilgrimage on earth will unveil the mystery of iniquity in the form of a religious deception offering men an apparent solution to their problems at the price of apostasy from the Truth. The supreme religious deception is that of the Antichrist, a pseudo-messianism by which man glorifies himself in the place of God and his Messiah who has come in the flesh.[671]

Possibly at the center of this prophecy and a "Vatican cover-up" of the complete vision of Fátima (and related prophecies) is a second and potentially more powerful papal contender for the role of Petrus Romanus or "Peter the Roman"—Cardinal Tarcisio Pietro (Peter) Bertone, who was born in Romano (the Roman) Canavese ("Peter the Roman"). Among other things, Cardinal Bertone is, at the time this book heads to the printer, second in command at the Vatican. As the Secretary of State and the Pope's Camerlengo (Italian for "Chamberlain"), he is responsible during a papal vacancy to serve as acting Head of State of the Vatican City until "the time of agreement" and the election of a new pope. Our interest for the moment is with his 2007 book, *The Last Seer of Fátima* that appears to have accomplished exactly the opposite of its primary objective, mainly, to refute another work by famous Italian media personality, journalist, and author Antonio Socci, whose manuscript *The Fourth Secret of Fátima* claims the Holy See has repressed information concerning the true secrets delivered in Marian apparitions to three shepherd children in the rural Portuguese village of Fátima in 1917. The three young people were Lúcia (Lucy) dos Santos and her cousins Francisco Marto and his sister Jacinta Marto, whose visions—containing elements of prophecy and eschatology—are officially sanctioned by the Catholic Church.

In his uncharacteristically explosive response to Cardinal Bertone—*Dear Cardinal Bertone: Who Between You and Me is Deliberately Lying?*—we first discover how, after significant time and investigation, Mr. Socci concluded the Vatican had withheld an important part of the Fátima revelation during its celebrated press conference and release of "The Message of Fátima," June 26, 2000.

Socci describes in the introduction to his book how at first he truly believed the Vatican's official version of the Fátima Message, prepared at that time by Cardinal Ratzinger (current Pope Benedict XVI) and Monsignor Tarcisio Bertone (possible next and final pope), which with its release to the public claimed to be the final Secret. Then Socci came across an article by Italian journalist Vittorio Messori, entitled "The Fátima Secret, the Cell of Sister Lucy Has Been Sealed," and a series of questions cast suspicions on the Vatican's authorized publication for which Socci had no answers. Why would Messori, whom Socci describes as "a great journalist, extremely precise...the most translated Catholic columnist in the world,"[672] want to challenge the Church's official version of the Third Secret without good cause, he reasoned. Not long after, Socci came across a second similar thesis published in Italy by a young and careful writer named Solideo Paolini, which convinced Socci to begin a probe of his own focusing on the biggest question of them all—was a portion of Lucy's hand-written document, which contained the principal words "of the Blessed Virgin Mother" concerning end-times conditions at Rome, being withheld from public view by the Vatican due to its potentially explosive content?

Socci's suspicions only deepened after he requested an interview (well ahead of his work, *The Fourth Secret of Fátima* which later cast doubts on Rome's official story) with Cardinal Bertone, who, together with Joseph Ratzinger, had coauthored the June 26, 2000 Vatican document that purportedly released the final segment of the "The Message of Fátima."[673]

"I've searched many influential authorities inside the Curia, like Cardinal Bertone, today Secretary of State in the Vatican, who was central to the publication of the Secret in 2000," Socci says. "The Cardinal, who actually favored me with his personal consideration, having asked me to conduct conferences in his former diocese of Genoa, [now] didn't deem it necessary to [even] answer my request for an interview. He was within his rights to make this choice, of course, but this only increased the fear of the existence of embarrassing questions, and most of all, that there is something (extremely important) which needs to be kept hidden."[674]

Though not expecting to uncover such a colossal enigma, in the end Socci was left convinced that two sets of the Fátima Secret actually exist: one which the public has seen, and another, which for reasons yet unknown, the Vatican is keeping buried.

At the beginning of this possible plot was a description of the Third Secret given by Cardinal Angelo Sodano a full five weeks before the June 26, 2000 "Message of Fátima" was delivered by Rome. Sodano's comments came during Pope John Paul II's beautification of Jacinta and Francisco at Fátima, when he surprised many in a speech, saying the vision of a "bishop clothed in white" who makes his way with great effort past the corpses of bishops, priests, and many lay persons, is only "apparently dead" when he falls to the ground under a burst of gunfire.[675]

Using the added language "apparently dead," Cardinal Sodano went on to suggest the Fátima vision had been fulfilled in the 1981 assassination attempt against John Paul II. "It appeared evident to His Holiness that it was 'a motherly hand which guided the bullet's path,' enabling the 'dying Pope' to halt 'at the threshold of death.' "[676]

Though some applauded Sodano's presentation that day, others saw in it, and him, a concerted cover-up, as the Fátima prophecy and the alleged fulfillment in 1981 bore significant differences. The Washington Post was happy to point out these glaring contradictions on July 1, 2000 when under the stinging headline, "Third Secret Spurs More Questions: Fátima Interpretation Departs from Vision" the newspaper opined:

> On May 13, Cardinal Angelo Sodano, a top Vatican official, announced the imminent release of the carefully guarded text. He said the Third Secret of Fátima foretold not the end of the world, as some had speculated, but the May 13, 1981, shooting of Pope John Paul II in St. Peter's Square.
>
> Sodano said the manuscript…tells of a "bishop clothed in white" who, while making his way amid corpses of martyrs, "falls to the ground, apparently dead, under a burst of gunfire."
>
> But the text released Monday (June 26) leaves no doubt about the bishop's fate, saying that he "was killed by a group of soldiers who fired bullets and arrows at him." Everyone with the pontiff also dies: bishops, priests, monks, nuns and lay people. John Paul survived his shooting at the hands of a single gunman, Mehmet Ali Agca, and no one in the crowd was harmed in the attack. [677]

Other facts the Washington Post did not point out is how according to the prophecy the pope is killed in "a big city half in ruins" while walking to the top of a mountain and kneeling at the foot of a cross. John Paul was riding in the pope's car through St. Peter's square, not walking, there was no big mountain or kneeling at a cross, and the city was not half-destroyed. And then there is the contradictory testimony by Cardinal Ratzinger (current Pope Benedict XVI) himself from 1984, which he gave in an interview with the Pauline Sisters' newsletter (Jesus Magazine) and which was re-published a year later in The Ratzinger Report, titled "Here is Why the Faith is in Crisis." In this discussion, Ratzinger, who had read the actual Fátima Secret, said the vision involved "dangers threatening the faith and the life of the Christian and therefore [the life] of the world" as well as marking the beginning of the end times.[678] Additionally, he said, "the things contained in [the] Third Secret correspond to what has been announced in Scripture and has been said again and again in many other Marian apparitions" and that, "If it is not made public, at least for the time being, it is in order to prevent religious prophecy from being mistaken for a quest for the sensational."[679]

Concerned Catholics have since contrasted this 1984 testimony with the more recent report by Ratzinger, and have wondered when, where, and under what circumstance his account changed. The 1981 assassination attempt against John Paul II certainly did not fulfill the published parts of the Fátima vision nor correspond to the "last times" as depicted in the Bible. And then there is the affirmation by the Vatican's most respected scholars who had deduced from years of studying the Fátima prophecy that it concerned an end-time global crisis of faith emanating from the highest echelons at Rome. Celebrated Cardinal Mario Luigi Ciappi (1909–1996) served as the personal theologian to five popes including John Paul II and unreservedly held that in "the Third Secret it is foretold, among other things, that the great apostasy in the Church *begins at the top*" (emphasis added).[680] Cardinal Silvio Oddi added in a March, 1990 interview with Il Sabato magazine in Rome, Italy: "...the Third Secret alluded to dark times for the Church: grave confusions and troubling apostasies within Catholicism itself... If we consider the grave crisis we have lived through since the [Vatican II] Council, the signs that this prophecy has been fulfilled do not seem to be lacking."[681] Even more impressive in his testimony was the late Father Joaquin Alonso who knew Sister Lucy personally, had conversations with her, was for sixteen years the archivist at Fátima, and who before his death in 1981, stated the following concerning the Third Secret:

...the text makes concrete references to the crisis of faith within the Church and to the negligence of the pastors themselves [and the] internal struggles in the very bosom of the Church and of grave pastoral negligence *by the upper hierarchy*... terrible things are to happen. These form the content of the third part of the Secret... [and] like the secret of La Salette, for example, there are more concrete references to the internal struggles of Catholics or to the fall of priests and religious. Perhaps it even refers to the *failures of the upper hierarchy* of the Church. For that matter, none of this is foreign to other communications Sister Lucy has had on this subject.[682]

Perhaps most unvarying among those who actually had access to and read the Fátima message was Jesuit Malachi Martin, a close personal friend of Pope Paul VI who worked within the Holy See doing research on the Dead Sea Scrolls, publishing articles in journals on Semitic paleography, and teaching Aramaic, Hebrew, and Sacred Scripture. As a member of the Vatican Advisory Council and personal secretary to renowned Jesuit Cardinal Augustin Bea, Martin had privileged information pertaining to secretive church and world issues, including the Third Secret of Fátima, *which Martin hinted spelled out parts of the plan to formerly install the dreaded False Prophet (Petrus Romanus?) during a "Final Conclave."* Comparing the conflicting statements between Cardinal Ratzinger and Malachi Martin, Father Charles Fiore, a good friend of the murdered priest Alfred J. Kunz (discussed elsewhere in this book) and the late eminent theologian Fr. John Hardon, said in a taped interview: "We have two different Cardinal Ratzingers; we have two different messages. But Malachi Martin was consistent all the way through."[683]

Wikipedia's entry on the *Three Secrets of Fátima* adds:

On a syndicated radio broadcast, Father Malachi Martin was asked the following question by a caller: "I had a Jesuit priest tell me more of the Third Secret of Fátima years ago, in Perth. He said, among other things, the last pope would be under control of Satan… Any comment on that?" Fr. Martin responded, "Yes, it sounds as if they were reading, or being told, the text of the Third Secret." In a taped interview with Bernard Janzen, Fr. Martin was asked the following question: "Who are the people who are working so hard to suppress Fátima?" Fr. Martin responded, "A bunch, a whole bunch, of Catholic prelates in Rome, who belong to Satan. They're servants of Satan. And the servants of Satan outside the Church, in various organizations; they want to destroy the Catholicism of the Church, and keep it as a stabilizing factor in human affairs. It's an alliance. A dirty alliance, a filthy alliance…" In the same interview, Fr. Martin also said with respect to Lucia [Lucy of Fátima] that, "They've (The Vatican) published forged letters in her name; they've made her say things she didn't want to say. They put statements on her lips she never made."[684]

One thing is certain; something unnerving did seem to be happening around and with Sister Lucy in the lead-up to the release of the so-called Final Secret. After all, the first two parts of the Message of Fátima had been publically issued by her Bishop in 1941, and the Third Secret sent to the Holy See with instructions that it be made public in 1960. That year was chosen according to Lucy because the "Holy Mother" had revealed to her that it would then be when "the Message will appear more clear." And lo and behold it was immediately following 1960 that Vatican II set in motion what many conservative Catholics today believe is a crisis of faith in the form of Roman heresies. And though there could have been much more to the revelation than just a Vatican II warning, and the Secret was not released in 1960 as it was supposed to be anyway (so we may never know), when Pope John XXIII read the contents of the secret, he refused to publish it, and it remained under lock and key until it was supposedly disclosed in the year 2000. If the first two Secrets were any indication of the scope and accuracy of the Third one, they had been amazingly insightful including the "miracle of the sun" that was witnessed "by over 70,000 persons (including non-believers hoping to dispel the apparitions), whereby the sun itself [seemed to be] dislodged from its setting and performed miraculous maneuvers while emitting astonishing light displays; the end of World War I; the name of the pope who would be reigning at the beginning of World War II; the extraordinary heavenly phenomenon that would be witnessed worldwide foretelling of the beginning of World War II; the ascendance of Russia (a weak and insignificant nation in 1917) to an evil monolithic power that would afflict the world with suffering and death."[685]

But something about the Third and Final Secret was different, a phenomenon evidently to be avoided and obfuscated at all costs by the hierarchy of Rome. At a minimum, it spoke of the apostatizing of the clergy and dogma that followed Vatican II. And yet perhaps these were simply devices to lead to something more sinister, elements so dark that it was keeping Lucy awake at night. When she finally had written down the Secret in 1944 under obedience to Rome, she had a hard time doing so because of its terrifying contents. It had taken a fresh visit from the "Holy Mother" herself to convince Lucy it was okay. Then in the years following, she had been ordered by the Vatican to remain silent concerning its disclosure. Visits to her for hours at a time were made by Cardinal Bertone under orders from the pope during which the two of them would go over the diminutive aspects of the vision in private. This happened in 2000, again in 2001, and again in 2003. When at age ninety-seven the Carmelite nun finally passed away (2005), taking whatever secrets remained with her to the grave, her behavior at the last seemed odd to Catholics who understood Roman doctrinal "salvation" implications. Antonio Socci comments on this, pointing out how the long visits with the aged seer were not videotaped or recorded for posterity because viewers would have seen for themselves the psychological pressure that was being exerted on the cloistered Sister. "These thoughts came back to my mind while I was reading a passage of Bertone's book, in which the Cardinal remembers that at one point the seer was 'irritated', and she told him 'I'm not going to confession!'" About this, Socci wonders, "What kind of question could Sister Lucy answer to so strongly? Maybe someone was reminding the old Sister of the ecclesiastical power, and hinting that she would 'not get absolution'? We don't know, because the prelate [Bertone]—who knows and remembers the Sister's (quite tough) answer very well—says he literally 'forgot' what his question was."[686]

It appears in truth that poor Lucy was trapped inside a sinister ring of *Romanita Omertà Siciliani* or "Mafia Code of Silence" imposed by Rome. Yet Socci believes the full truth of Fátima may have gotten out anyway, and based on his investigation he offers a brave theory in his book *The Fourth Secret of Fátima* about what actually transpired in 2000 behind the Vatican's walls. John Vennari summarizes Socci's shocking hypothesis this way:

Socci believes that when John Paul II decided to release the Secret, a power-struggle of sorts erupted in the Vatican. He postulates that John Paul II and Cardinal Ratzinger wanted to release the Secret in its entirety, but Cardinal Sodano, then Vatican Secretary of State, opposed the idea. And opposition from a Vatican Secretary of State is formidable.

A compromise was reached that sadly reveals heroic virtue from none of the main players.

The "Bishop dressed in white" vision, which is the four pages written by Sister Lucy would be initially revealed by Cardinal Sodano, along with his ludicrous interpretation that the Secret is nothing more than the predicted 1981 assassination attempt on Pope John Paul II.

At the same time, at the May 13 2000 beatification

ceremony of Jacinta and Francisco, Pope John Paul II would "reveal" the other part—the most "terrifying part"—of the Secret obliquely in his sermon. It was here that John Paul II spoke on the Apocaplyse: "Another portent appeared in Heaven; behold, a great red dragon" (Apoc. 12: 3). These words from the first reading of the Mass make us think of the great struggle between good and evil, showing how, when man puts God aside, he cannot achieve happiness, but ends up destroying himself... The Message of Fátima is a call to conversion, alerting humanity to have nothing to do with the "dragon" whose "tail swept down a third of the stars of Heaven, and dragged them to the earth" (Apoc. 12:4).

The Fathers of the Church have always interpreted the stars as the clergy, and the stars swept up in the dragon's tail indicates a great number of churchmen who would be under the influence of the devil. This was Pope John Paul II's way of explaining that the Third Secret also predicts a great apostasy.[687]

If Socci is correct in this analysis, Bishop Richard Nelson Williamson, an English traditionalist Catholic and member of the Society of St. Pius X who opposes changes in the Catholic Church brought on by Vatican II, may have verified his hypothesis in 2005 when he related how a priest acquaintance of his from Austria shared privately that Cardinal Ratzinger had confessed: "I have two problems on my conscience: Archbishop Lefebvre and Fátima. As to the latter, my hand was forced." Who could have "forced" Ratzinger's hand to go along with a false or partial statement on the final Fátima Secret? Was it pressure from the papal office, or, as Williamson questions, "Some hidden power behind both Pope and Cardinal?"[688] If Pope John Paul II's sermon at Fátima did in fact speak to the "terrifying part" of the Final Secret—*as in the Dragon's tail sweeping down a third of the clergy to do his bidding*—we are left with the unsettling impression that at least 33 percent (Masonic marker) of the Vatican's hierarchy *are committed to a Satanic Plan.*

The Warning of La Salette

Most people are probably unaware that in addition to the Secrets of Fátima, a second, most renowned Marian apparition from La Salette, France, which was approved by Popes Pius IX and Leo XIII, revealed analogous information about a crisis of faith that would transpire within Roman Catholicism in the last days, during which Rome would become the seat of the Antichrist.

Delivered to Mélanie Calvat and Maximin Giraud on September 19, 1846, while they tended cattle in the mountains, the *Secret of La Salette* reads in part:

> The earth will be struck by calamities of all kinds (in addition to plague and famine which will be wide-spread). There will be a series of wars until the last war, which will then be fought by the ten Kings of the Antichrist, all of whom will have one and the same plan and will be the only rulers of the world. Before this comes to pass, there will be a kind of false peace in the world. People will think of nothing but amusement. The wicked will give themselves over to all kinds of sin…this will be the hour of darkness. The Church will suffer a terrible crisis… Rome will lose the Faith and become the seat of the Antichrist… The Church will be in eclipse, the world will be in dismay.[689]

In *The Plot Against The Pope; Coup dé'tat in the Conclave–1958,* Gary Giuffré discusses how French Masonic influences who had infiltrated the Catholic clergy in the 1800s were working overtime to suppress and discredit the Secret of La Salette, even though its message had been officially favored by two popes. This was because at that time, prophetic references to Rome "becoming the seat of Antichrist" was forming a common eschatology among Catholic scholars like Cardinal Henry Manning (discussed elsewhere in this book), Bishop Salvator Grafen Zola, and Frederick William Helle, who saw in these predictions the work of Masonically infested clergy who plotted the overthrow of the papacy and the use of the Church as a political vehicle for an occult World Order. "These kinds of details, found in the genuine, modern-day, Marian prophecies, would always generate the greatest opposition from the Church's enemies who had infiltrated her structures," wrote Giuffré. "For they threatened to expose the satanic plot and long-time goal of the Masonic Lodge's agents in the Vatican, to usurp and control the papal chair."[690]

And it has to be remembered that the specter of infiltration of the Roman Catholic hierarchy by members of Freemasonry's luciferian "light bearers" was a fairly well-established agenda historically, one which Pope Pius IX called the "Synagogue of Satan." Pope Leo XIII went so far as to issue a damning encyclical (Humanum Genus) on April 20, 1884 against the efforts to invade and corrupt Roman Catholicism by Freemasons, and yet Leo's own Secretary of State, Cardinal Mariano Rampolla del Tindaro was later identified as a secret Freemason of the diabolical Ordo Templi Orientis (O.T.O.) sect of whom Satanist Aleister Crowley belonged and later became leader. When Pope Leo passed away in 1903, it was widely anticipated that Rampolla would replace him as pope, and Rampolla did receive the early votes during conclave. Then something extraordinary happened, and the balloting was interrupted when Prince Jan Maurycy Paweł Puzyna de Kosielsko, a Polish Roman Catholic Cardinal from Kraków, rose on behalf of his Sovereign, Emperor Franz Joseph of Austria, and shocked the assembly by declaring in Latin, "…officially and in the name and by the authority of Franz-Josef, Emperor of Austria and King of Hungary, that His Majesty, in virtue of an ancient right and privilege, pronounces the veto of exclusion against my Most Eminent Lord, Cardinal Mariano Rampolla del Tindaro."[691] This *Jus Exclusivæ* ("right of exclusion" or papal veto) was an ancient rule of order claimed by Catholic monarchs to veto a candidate for the papacy. "At times the right was claimed by the French monarch, the Spanish monarch, the Holy Roman Emperor, and the Emperor of Austria. These powers would make known to a papal conclave, through a crown-cardinal, that a certain candidate for election was considered objectionable as a prospective Pope."[692] It has since been suggested by some historians that the alert Emperor Franz Joseph knew something of Rampolla's masonic connection and saved Rome from usurpation. It is also noteworthy that the official Liber LII Manifesto of the O.T.O. BAPHOMET XI° does indeed list Cardinal Rampolla among its members.[693] But was Rampolla just one of many covert Masons? The answer to that question appears to be *yes* according to experts like the late Canadian naval officer, author, and popular lecturer William James Guy Carr. In addition to his accounts of wartime activity as a Navigating Submarine Officer during World War One, Carr—though a conspiracy theorist—was a noted authority on the history of the Illuminati and its connection to Freemasonry. He chronicled the movement from its founding in 1776 by Adam Weishaupt to its purported penetration of the Vatican. In 1959, Carr published *The Red Fog Over America,* in which he said:

> Weishaupt boasted that the Illuminati would infiltrate into the Vatican and bore from within, until they left it nothing but an empty shell... Since I exposed certain events which indicate that agentur of the Illuminati have infiltrated into the Vatican, I have received a number of letters from priests who have studied in the Vatican... Those who wrote assured me that the fears I express are more than well founded. One priest informed me that the Pope was surrounded by picked "Specialists", "Experts" and "Advisors" to such an extent that he was little better than a prisoner in his own palace. Another priest informed me of the eternal surveillance exercised over

the Pope…those who maintain the surveillance…give him no freedom of action even in the privacy of his own chambers. The priest said 'Those who exercise this surveillance are all hand-picked members of a certain order and they all come from the same institution…where Weishaupt…conspired.' "[694]

Carr's description matches so closely to what Malachi Martin and similar priests have alleged on different occasions concerning a formidable Illuminati-Masonic group inside the Vatican that it is tempting to believe Malachi himself may have been one of Carr's informants. But was this Illuminated council the unseen hand in Rome that "forced" Cardinal Ratzinger and Cardinal Bertone to issue what Antonio Socci thought was *astuzia inganno* (cunning deception) at Fátima? And would this indicate both the current pope and his Secretary of State are clandestinely committed to, or being forced to go along with, the overarching scheme of a secret order inside the Holy See?

The solidarity between Pope Benedict and Cardinal Bertone goes back a long way and it certainly appears to have continued—at least for the first few years of Benedict's papacy—in the time following the "Message of Fátima" controversy. After being elected pope in April, 2005 and taking his place as successor of John Paul II as Sovereign of the Vatican City State and leader of the Roman Catholic Church, Ratzinger as "Pope Benedict XVI" quickly appointed Cardinal Bertone to replace Fátima co-conspirator Angelo Sodano as the Cardinal Secretary of State. On April 4, 2007, Benedict also appointed Bertone as his Camerlengo to administrate the duty of the Pope in the case of a vacancy of the papacy. Benedict has since made decisions that indicate Bertone could be (or once was) his choice for successor, and both men have at times appeared to be stacking and massaging the Red Hats in Bertone's favor for the next (final?) conclave. This was noted in the May 13, 2011 *National Catholic Reporter* article, "A Triptych on Benedict's Papacy, and Hints of What Lies Beyond," when NCR

Senior Correspondent John L. Allen Jr. spoke of the shake-up inside the Roman Curia (the Curia is the administrative apparatus of the Vatican and, together with the pope, the central governing body of the Catholic Church) in which Italian Archbishop Giovanni Angelo Becciu was appointed the Substitute for General Affairs by Pope Benedict XVI. Becciu, who replaced Archbishop Fernando Filoni for the job, seemed at first an odd selection to Vatican insiders. "Given how difficult it is to master the role [of Substitute], many observers found it curious that Filoni would be shipped out after less than four years, to be replaced by someone in Becciu who has no previous experience at all working inside the Vatican," observed the NCR.[695] But then the nail was hit on the head when the news service added, "When the dust settles, the most obvious beneficiary of these moves would seem to be Italian Cardinal Tarcisio Bertone, the Secretary of State, who will not have to be concerned about the new substitute forming a rival center of power."[696] The job of the Substitute for General Affairs has been described as the most complicated and demanding responsibility in the Roman Curia due to the staggering amount of concerns the Substitute must carry on a daily basis. Roughly compared to a White House Chief of Staff, the Substitute meets with the Pontiff usually once per day to administer Vatican affairs and also regularly reports to the Cardinal Secretary of State (currently Cardinal Bertone). The organizational "success or failure of a papacy often rests on his shoulders," adds the NCR. And those who have handled the office well over the years "have been the stuff of legend: Giovanni Battista Montini, for instance, was the substitute under Pius XII from 1937 to 1953, and went on to become Pope Paul VI; Giovanni Benelli, who was Paul's own substitute from 1967 to 1977, was widely understood to be *the power behind the throne*" (emphasis added).[697]

But if positioning a Vatican novice in the role of Substitute in order not to challenge future papal possibilities for the Italian Cardinal Bertone was telling, Pope Benedict even more-so aligned the group-type from which the next pope will come, when on January 6, 2012 he named twenty-two new cardinals, most of them Europeans, primarily Italians already holding key Vatican stations. By elevating these advisors to the Sacred College of Cardinals at a February 18th ceremony in Rome, the German pope certified that "Europeans will now number over half of all cardinal-electors (67 out of 125), and nearly a quarter of all voters in a conclave will be Italian," reported Newsmax.com.[698] As a result, Benedict seemed to put his definitive stamp on an Italian successor and lined up those who could give Bertone the so-called apostolic chair of Saint Peter. And evidently this wasn't Benedict's idea alone. Most Vatican experts "put the large number of Italian appointments down to the influence of the Pope's deputy, Vatican Secretary of State Cardinal Tarcisio Bertone, whose hand in these nominations, they say, is clearly visible."[699]

Also interesting in lieu of recent reports regarding Pope Benedict's health (and news that he might step down in April) was the February timing of the consistory for the new cardinals to receive their red hats, rings, and titular assignments in Rome. As we hope to have this book in print by first quarter 2012, we can only speculate why the February date was chosen. Of course the scheduling around the Feast of the Chair of St. Peter could be cited, but some who work with the pope had been pushing him for a June (Feasts of St. Peter and Paul) or November (Feast of Christ the King) consistory, and more often than not Benedict has held consistories in November (2007 and 2010). So what was the hurry? If Pope Benedict truly is considering a 2012 departure and wants to significantly influence the papal conclave toward an Italian, the date and timing in February made perfect sense as the best and final opportunity to stack the sacred deck.

Of course, just when we thought it couldn't get any more obvi-ous, another—and this time unprecedented—move to consolidate his power (and which also raises the question of a third contender for the throne of St. Peter) was made by Bertone himself. It followed the October 24, 2011, document, "Toward Reforming the International

Financial and Monetary Systems in the Context of a Global Public Authority," which amounted to a call by the Vatican for a World Political and Financial Authority. Published by the Pontifical Council for Justice and Peace, which is headed by Cardinal Peter Turkson, the media was quick—inside and outside Christianity—to see the dark side of socialism raising its head, not to mention prophetic implications of the paper's call for a Global Authority seated inside the United Nations. In a different chapter we explain how this new unsettling directive attempts to devise a "moral" mandate for establishing "a global public authority" and "a central world bank" that would oversee individual and world pecuniary institutions through subjugation to a new global power made *at the cost of a gradual, balanced transfer of a part of each nation's powers to a world authority and to regional authorities*" (emphasis added).[700] The document was addressed at the 2011 G20 Summit in Cannes in comments by President Barack Obama and French President Nicholas Sarkozy, but nothing came of it there due to what Cardinal Bertone did just ten days later. And this is where things start getting interesting, as some soothsayers were already predicting that the author of the document, Peter Turkson of Ghana (Peter the Roman?) could be the next pope, as he is considered papabile by the College of Cardinals.

Following the election of America's first black president in Obama, analysts around the world began speculating that perhaps Rome would follow suit and roll out the red carpet for a black pope, the first in fifteen hundred years, in somebody like Turkson. Cardinal Francis Arinze, whom Ronald L. Conte Jr. believes will be the next pope and fulfill "The Prophecy of the Popes" by taking the name Pius XIII, is also a black man, an Igbo Nigerian considered papabile since before the 2005 conclave that elected Cardinal Ratzinger (Pope Benedict XVI). "The election of Barack Obama as the first African-American US President could pave the way for the election of [a] black Pope, according to a leading black American Catholic," wrote the *Times Online* in 2008. "Wilton Daniel Gregory, 60, the

Archbishop of Atlanta, said that in the past Pope Benedict XVI had himself suggested that the election of a black pontiff would 'send a splendid signal to the world' about the universal Church."[701] *The Associated Press* agreed. "The pope has appointed Cardinal Peter Turkson of Ghana to head the Vatican's justice and peace office, a high-profile post that cements his reputation as a possible future papal candidate... Turkson told reporters three weeks ago there was no reason there couldn't be a black pope, particularly after Barack Obama was elected U.S. president."[702] Given that Turkson is popular in some circles, here is how the *National Catholic Reporter* heralded the release of his document on Reforming the International Financial and Monetary Systems in their October 28, 2011, headline: *A Papal Contender Grabs the Spotlight:*

> Rome saw a striking coincidence this week, which could be either simple luck or a sign of things to come. There were two big-ticket Vatican news flashes, Monday's note on reform of the international economy and Thursday's summit of religious leaders in Assisi. In both cases, the same Vatican official was a prime mover: Cardinal Peter Turkson of Ghana, president of the Pontifical Council for Justice and Peace.
>
> Turkson, still young in church terms at 63, was the chief organizer of the Assisi gathering, just as he was the top signatory on the document blasting "neo-liberal" ideologies and calling for a "true world political authority" to regulate the economy. During Vatican press conferences to present both, Turkson was the star attraction each time.
>
> Can anyone say, papabile?[703]

Only a week following the *National Catholic Reporter* celebration, however, and only ten days after Turkson released his document calling for a global financial authority, an emergency summit at the Vatican was called by...you guessed it...the Secretariat of State—

Cardinal Tarcisio Bertone. And this time he wasn't taking any prisoners. Bertone blasted the document by Turkson and laid down a new set of laws. From that day forward, he ordered, any new Vatican text would have to be authorized in advance by himself. The popular *Chiesa News* in Rome said of the power play:

> Precisely when the G20 summit in Cannes was coming to its weak and uncertain conclusion, on that same Friday, November 4 at the Vatican, a smaller summit convened in the secretariat of state… In the hot seat was the [Turkson] document on the global financial crisis released ten days earlier by the pontifical council for justice and peace… The secretary of state, Cardinal Tarcisio Bertone, complained that he had not known about it until the last moment. And precisely for this reason he had called that meeting in the secretariat of state. The conclusion of the summit was that this binding order would be transmitted to all of the offices of the curia: from that point on, nothing in writing would be released unless it had been inspected and authorized by the secretariat of state.[704]

While Bertone convinced some Vatican watchers that his over-reaching motives had to do with protecting the Holy See from confusion by claiming that he had been in the dark and thus side-swiped by the release of the document (a case *Chiesa News* thoroughly debunked), others saw in it another giant step in Bertone carefully solidifying his powerbase in Rome. They also imagined that old enemy the Freemasons having something to do with it. "It would seem that the dark forces in the Vatican are making their moves to seize control of the Catholic Church," wrote Catholic Jew Aron Ben Gilad. "They are using the recent document of the Pontifical Council of Justice and Peace on the global financial crisis as the excuse to seize autocratic control of all the congregations of the curia and putting them under the control of Cardinal Bertone and the Vatican's Secretariat of State. Whatever the merits or demerits of this document is not the important question, *but its use as an instrument for ecclesiastical masonry to take control of the Roman Curia*" (emphasis added).[705] Top Vatican watcher and journalist Andrea Tornielli had stated as much earlier, documenting how Bertone had been consolidating his influence in the Vatican:

> ...through a number of actions: he appointed bishops who are well known to him and friends in key roles, especially in positions involving the management and control of the Holy See's finances. The last individual appointed, was the Bishop of Alexandria Giuseppe Versaldinew, to the position of President of the Prefecture for Economic Affairs of the Holy See... On the other hand, Bertone has done away with prelates who had moved against him in some way or another, such as Archbishop Carlo Maria Viganò, who had left the Government office to become Nuncio (ambassador) to the United States, or Bishop Vincenzo di Mauro, who left the Office of Economic Affairs to become Archbishop of Vigevano.[706]

Cracks in the Foundation, Dark Horses Appear

Having documented the above, one could think with some certainty that Bertone is a shoo-in for Petrus Romanus. However, as we move into 2012, cracks are suddenly appearing in the foundation of his sand castle, and not everybody in the Curia—including Pope Benedict XVI, himself—may wind up as eager to support him as they once were. As Pope Benedict's health weakens, the sharks smell blood, and claims of mismanagement have been increasing from competing factions in the Church that are more than happy to seize opportunity to cast aspersion on Bertone in order to elevate their own standing among the College of Cardinals. This may include Archbishop Vigano, whose personal letters to Pope Benedict and Cardinal Bertone concerning his reassignment as Nuncio were partially broadcast by an Italian television news program in January 2012. The letters, confirmed by the Vatican as authentic, exposed a blistering relationship between himself and Bertone involving political jockeying and financial deal making including charges of "corruption, nepotism and cronyism linked to the awarding of contracts to contractors at inflated prices."[707] One of the letters to Cardinal Bertone, dated March 27, 2011 (eight days before the letter to Pope Benedict), complained of Bertone removing him from his post and of Bertone "breaking a promise to let the archbishop succeed the then-president of the commission, Cardinal Giovanni Lajolo, upon the latter's retirement. According to the letter, Cardinal Bertone had mentioned unspecified 'tensions' within the commission to explain Archbishop Vigano's reassignment, but [Vigano] suggested that a recent Italian newspaper article criticizing the archbishop [Bertone] as incompetent had contributed to the decision."[708] Most Vatican sources agree that an internal campaign involving Machiavellian manipulation and maneuverings—what Phillip Pullella for Reuters called "a sort of 'mutiny of the monsignors'"[709]—is playing out behind the scenes against the pope's right-hand man, Secretary of State Cardinal Tarcisio Bertone. The same sources say "the rebels have the tacit backing of a former secretary of state, Cardinal Angelo Sodano, an influential power-broker in his own right and a veteran diplomat who served under the late Pope John Paul II for 15 years."[710] If Sodano truly is behind a campaign to undermine papal possibilities for Bertone, suspicions deepen that something may be lingering between Fátima cover-up conspirators Ratzinger, Bertone, and Sodano, as the reader might recall Antonio Socci's belief that when John Paul II decided to release the Third Secret of Fátima, a power-struggle of sorts erupted in the Vatican when future Pope Benedict XVI (Cardinal Ratzinger) wanted to release the Secret in its entirety, but Cardinal Sodano, then Vatican Secretary of State, opposed the idea. Whatever the case may be, the January 26, 2012 headline at *The New York Times* said it all: "Transfer of Vatican Official Who Exposed Corruption Hints at Power Struggle,"[711] and echoed the fact that, just like in American presidential politics, today's rising star at the Vatican can all-to-soon become crushed under the juggernaut of ambitious and motivated men if one does not vigilantly maintain every bit as much cunning as their challengers. Also suddenly blossoming are other dubious movements in Rome that seem to validate a game is afoot. This includes a hasty appointment on January 11, 2012, by Pope Benedict XVI of another Italian, Archbishop Lorenzo Baldisseri, as the new secretary of the Congregation for Bishops (the branch of the Roman Curia that oversees the selection of new bishops). Baldisseri is intriguing because his Principal Consecrator during his 1963 ordination was Bertone predecessor and Fátima deception accomplice, Cardinal Angelo Sodano. And Baldisseri's ordination to priesthood occurred June 29, 1963, eight (8) days after Giovanni Montini (Pope Paul VI) was elected. This is interesting on two levels. First, the number eight (8) is associated with destiny, divinity, occult fertility rites, resurrection, and the incarnation of Jesus (888), as any Bishop of Rome knows. But more importantly, the exact date of Baldisseri's ordination—June 29, 1963—is the very day on which Malachi Martin swore the "enthronement of the fallen Archangel Lucifer" took place in the Roman Catholic Citadel. This *rituale*, as Martin had called it, had two primary objectives: 1) to enthrone Lucifer as the true Prince over Rome; and 2) *to assure the sorcerous inception and embodiment in flesh of that immaterial spirit <u>into a priest</u> was made, one who would later become Petrus Romanus.*

In his book, *Windswept House*, Martin wrote:

> The Enthronement of the Fallen Archangel Lucifer was effected within the Roman Catholic Citadel on June 29, 1963; a fitting date for the historic promise about to be

fulfilled. As the principal agents of this Ceremonial well knew, Satanist tradition had long predicted that the Time of the Prince would be ushered in at the moment when a Pope would take the name of the Apostle Paul [Pope Paul VI]. That requirement—the signal that the Availing Time had begun—had been accomplished just eight days before with the election of the latest Peter-in-the-Line.[712]

The big problem with Baldisseri is that he does not yet appear papabile, so his role may be coincidental or that of a carrier collaborator, for the mystery of the 1963 conclave, which began June 19 and ended June 21 with the election of Pope Paul VI, carries a secret most in the public are completely unaware of but that Malachi Martin most courageously took on. It is called in investigative circles, "The Siri Thesis," and involves whispered evidence that Cardinal Giuseppe Siri of Genoa actually received the majority vote in both the 1958 and 1963 conclaves but under mysterious pressure (presumably from Masonic influences) refused the papal office. When asked twenty years later if in both conclaves he had initially been elected as pontiff, Siri responded, "I am bound by the secret. This secret is horrible. I would have books to write about the different conclaves. Very serious things have taken place. But I can say nothing."[713] Malachi Martin wasn't so silent. He claimed to be an eye-witness of the 1963 Conclave and in his book, *The Keys of This Blood*, said that Siri was in fact elected pope in both 1958 and 1963, but that his election was "set aside" because of "interference" by an "emissary of an internationally based organization" (the Freemasons).[714] Given that our book, *Petrus Romanus: The Final Pope is Here*, is based in part on the prophecy attributed to St. Malachy called "The Prophecy of the Popes," we would be remiss not to also point out how, in 1958, the inevitability of Siri's election was believed so strongly that in Italy, "the prophesy of Saint Malachy, describing Pius' successor as 'Shepherd and Sailor' [#107 in the Prophecy of the Popes] (Pastor et Nauta), was commonly attributed to the illustrious Archbishop of Genoa [Siri]. The maritime city had been his life-long home, where he was born the son of a dockworker. It was the most important seaport in the country, and birthplace of Christopher Columbus. A Genoan newspaper would write: 'No one better than Siri could symbolize this motto: he is a pastor of highest virtues, a captain of the ship, born and raised on the sea.'"[715]

So how and for what purpose could the election of Siri have been set aside and covered up so completely? William G. von Peters, Ph.D., explains in *The Siri Thesis*:

> Most Catholics today, simply cannot comprehend why or how such a crime could have been so successfully carried out almost undetected by the outside world, with the active participation of high princes of the Church, over the span of a generation, as alleged by the "Siri thesis". Surely such a long, drawn-out conspiracy would be beyond the ability of even the most evil of men. But 130 years ago, Pope Pius IX explained that: "If one takes into consideration the immense development which [the]...secret societies have attained; the length of time they are persevering in their vigor; their furious aggressiveness; the tenacity with which their members cling to the association and to the false principles it professes; the persevering mutual cooperation of so many different types of men in the promotion of evil; one can hardly deny that the SUPREME ARCHITECT [the god of Freemasonry] of these associations (seeing that the cause must be proportional to the effect) can be none other than he who in the sacred writings is styled the PRINCE OF THE WORLD; and that Satan himself even by his physical cooperation, directs and inspires at least the leaders of these bodies physically cooperating with them."[716]

Further speculation about the Masonic plot originally spelled out in the Alta Vendita does seem related to what went on in the 1958 and 1963 conclaves because it was under these secret meetings when the popes were "elected" that would implement the Second Vatican Council and its Vendita-like heretical decrees. Of course we could cite once again a plethora of Church Fathers, Marian apparitions, and Catholic seers down through time that had forecast these events as a pre-game for the arrival of Petrus Romanus. Even Saint Francis of Assisi—one of the most venerated religious figures in history—gathered his devotees shortly before his death and prophesied that: "At the time of this tribulation a man, not canonically elected, will be raised to the Pontificate, who, by his cunning, will endeavor to draw many into error and death... Some preachers will keep silence about the truth, and others will trample it under foot and deny it...for in those days Jesus Christ will send them not a true Pastor, but a destroyer."[717] As we write this book, the Vatican enters the Golden Anniversary of Vatican II, a perfect time, Illuminati would say, to install Petrus Romanus and to exact their revenge. But we are left, at least for the moment, with a quandary as to which of the candidates we have discussed in this chapter (or perhaps an as yet unidentified contender) will fulfill the dark augury of the Prophecy of the Popes amidst a showdown that is set to occur among the College of Cardinals inside the Sistine Chapel in the Palace of the Vatican during the next period of papal vacancy. The unpleasant reality is that a conflict over who will become Petrus Romanus is boiling beneath the surface, largely unknown to the public but nevertheless foresaw by Catholic mystics such as Father Herman Bernard Kramer (mentioned in the previous chapter) in his work, "The Book of Destiny." Let us remind the reader of his frightening prophecy and strange interpretation of the twelfth chapter of the Book of Revelation concerning "the great wonder" mentioned in verse one. Father Kramer prophesied:

> The "sign" in heaven is that of a woman with child crying out in her travail and anguish of delivery. In that travail, she gives birth to some definite "person" who is to RULE the Church

with a rod of iron (verse 5). It then points to a conflict waged within the Church to elect one who was to "rule all nations" in the manner clearly stated. In accord with the text this is unmistakably a PAPAL ELECTION, for only Christ and his Vicar have the divine right to rule ALL NATIONS... But at this time the great powers may take a menacing attitude to hinder the election of the logical and expected candidate by threats of a general apostasy, assassination or imprisonment of this candidate if elected."[718]

While we disagree with Kramer's interpretation of the book of Revelation, the idea that a specific "person" was born and is now of the appropriate age to fulfill the incarnation of St. Malachy's Prophecy of the Popes and to produce the Man of Sin, is without question. Kramer's fear that "great powers may take a menacing attitude to hinder the election of the logical and expected candidate" also reverberates the sentiment of other priests, past and present, including Cardinal Archbishop Paolo Romeo, the leader of Sicily's Catholics, who made headlines February 10, 2012 when the Italian newspaper Il Fatto Quotidiano (which is famous for breaking exclusives) published parts of a secret *communique* involving the Cardinal and a criminal conspiracy to assassinate Pope Benedict XVI before the end of 2012.[719] Evidently at the center of the *Mordkomplott* (or contract to kill the pope) is political machinations in Rome involving Vatican Secretary of State Cardinal Tarcisio Bertone, whose growing thirst for power Benedict has come to hate according to the leaked document, and another Italian now favored as successor by Benedict, Cardinal Angelo Scola, currently the Archbishop of Milan. The contract against the pope and the prediction by Cardinal Paola that was allegedly made in secret to his Italian and Chinese business partners in Beijing concerning Benedict not living past the end of 2012 was apparently believed serious enough that somebody among Paola's listeners "suspected that he himself was involved in a specific plot to assassinate Pope Benedict XVI. At least one of those present therefore reported the Cardinal's words to Rome, and a special report on the incident—complied by Cardinal Darío Castrillón Hoyos and written in German in an attempt to stop it from being leaked—was presented to the Pope on 30 December last year."[720]

Whether or not the threat whispered by Paola was actually formulated or will come true, the report illustrates once again how efforts are being made by at least some members of the College of Cardinals to align themselves as candidates for Petrus Romanus. Besides Francis Arinze, Tarcisio Bertone, Peter Turkson, and Angelo Scola, we would round out our top ten candidates for the Final Pope in descending order with Cardinals Gianfranco Ravasi, Leonardo Sandri, Ennio Antonelli, Jean-Louis Tauran, Christoph Schönborn, and Marc Quellet.

With these in mind, a finishing thought each of these papal contenders may want to consider is how many Catholics believe the sixteenth-century seer Nostradamus was actually the author of "The Prophecy of the Popes." If that is so, a point made by the *National Catholic Reporter* earlier in this chapter concerning the popular West African Cardinal Peter Turkson being "young" in terms of electability at age sixty-three may have a way of coming back around. The "dark horse" candidate Turkson—and his ideas for a one-world financial and political authority housed in the United Nations—could become a remarkable and unexpected fulfillment of both the Prophecy of the Popes and Nostradamus's prediction of an end-times "young black pope" who seizes control of the Roman Hierarchy with the assistance of conspirators during times of darkness and war. In Quatrain 6.25 Nostradamus wrote:

> Through Mars adverse [a time of war] will be the monarchy
> Of the great fisherman [the pope] in trouble ruinous
> A young black red [a young black Cardinal] will seize the
>   hierarchy
> The predators acting on a foggy day

The Zohar, the Antichrist, and the Year 2012

Contemporaneous to the arrival of the False Prophet (Petrus Romanus?) is a prophecy from what is widely considered the most important work of Jewish Kabbalah, the *Zohar*, a collection of books written in medieval Aramaic over seven hundred years ago containing mystical commentary on the Pentateuch (five books of Moses, the Torah). In addition to interpreting Scripture, the "Vaera" section (volume 3, section 34) includes "The signs heralding Mashiach," or "The coming of the Messiah." The fascinating date for "his" appearance is set in the Zohar *in late 2012!* Given the rejection of Jesus by orthodox Jews as Messiah, Christians understand this "coming" would herald the unveiling of Antichrist in 2012.

J. R. Church of *Prophecy in the News* called our office a couple years back and led us through verses 476–483 of this part of the *Zohar* to point out what nobody in the 2012 research community had written before—that the time of Jacob's trouble (the Great Tribulation, which some Catholic scholars say begins with the election of Petrus Romanus) will commence according to this ancient text in the year 2012 when the "kings of the earth" gather in Rome, possibly during a papal conclave, and are killed by fiery stones or missiles from the sky.

The prophecy in the Zohar, given by Jews hundreds of years separate from the divination of "the last pope," is amazing when compared with the Catholic prediction. The final pope, "Peter the Roman," whose reign ends in the destruction of Rome, will assume authority during a time of great tribulation, and then *"the City of Seven Hills will be destroyed, and the terrible and fearsome Judge will judge his people."* But Dr. Church pointed out how in the Jewish Zohar, this vision of the destruction of Rome is repeated, though one prophecy connects it to the coming of the False Prophet, and the other, the Antichrist:

> This ancient rabbinical dissertation claims that Rome will be destroyed in the Jewish calendar year 5773, which, in our

calendar begins with the new moon of September 2012 and concludes a year later:

"In the year seventy-three [2012/2013] the kings of the world will assemble *in the great city of Rome, and the Holy One will shower on them fire and hail and meteoric stones until they are all destroyed,* with the exception of those who will not yet have arrived there."

Is he hinting at the destruction of Mystery Babylon? He notes that not all kings will be destroyed. Of those remaining, he says: "These will commence anew to make other wars. From that time the Messiah will begin to declare himself, and round him there will be gathered many nations and many hosts from the uttermost ends of the earth."[721]

Thus the false messiah (antichrist) is predicted in a seven-hundred-year-old Jewish prophecy to appear in 2012. Similarly, the nine-hundred-year-old Prophecy of the Popes looks to be unfolding in parallel fashion to provide Petrus Romanus in 2012. To these, we could add numerous other strange attractors from throughout history that also assigned apocalyptic importance to the year 2012, including:

- The Mayan calendar ends in **2012** with the return of their flying dragon god Kulkulkan.
- The Aztec calendar ends in **2012** and their flying dragon god Quetzalcoatl returns.
- The Cherokee Indian calendar ends in the year **2012** and their flying rattlesnake god returns. The "Cherokee Rattlesnake Prophecies," also known as the "Chickamaugan Prophecy" or the "Cherokee Star Constellation Prophecies," are part of a series of apocalyptic prophecies made by members of the Cherokee tribe during 1811–1812. Like the Maya, the Cherokee calendar ends mysteriously in the

year **2012** when astronomical phenomena related to Jupiter, Venus, Orion, and Pleiades cause the "powers" of the star systems to "awaken."

- According to ancient Mayan inscriptions, in **2012**, the Mayan underworld god Bolon Yokte Ku also returns.

- The Hindu Kali Yuga calendar ends in the year **2012** at the conclusion of the age of "the male demon."

- According to the book, *Apollyon Rising 2012*, the prophecy of the Cumaean Sibyl on the Great Seal of the United States (*novus ordo seclorum*) points to the coming of the Antichrist in **2012**.

- Over two hundred sixty years ago, the leader of the first Great Awakening in America, Jonathan Edwards, tied the arrival of the Antichrist and Great Tribulation period to the timeframe **2012**.

- One hundred thirty years after that, in 1878, Reverend William J. Reid did the same, writing in his "Lectures on the Revelation" concerning the papal system: "…we are prepared to answer the question, When will the Papal system come to an end? [It] will be destroyed in the year **2012**."[722]

- Also of interest is the Web Bot Project, which was developed in the late 1990s for tracking and making stock market predictions. This technology crawls the Internet, much like a search engine does, searching for keywords and following "chatter" in order to tap into "the collective unconscious" of the global community for tipping points regarding past, current, and future buying patterns. In 2001, operators began noticing what looked like more than coincidences, and that the "bot" was taking on a mind of its own, accurately predicting more than just stock market predictions, including June of 2001 when the program predicted that a life-altering event would be felt worldwide and would take place within sixty to ninety days. On

September 11, 2001, the Twin Towers of the World Trade Center fell. The Web Bot also predicted the 2001 anthrax attack on Washington DC; the earthquake that produced the December 26, 2004, tsunami; Hurricane Katrina; and more. The Web Bot has now foretold global devastation for late December **2012**.

- In **2012**, the United States will elect a President.
- In **2012**, the United Nations will get a new leader.
- And in **2012**, Petrus Romanus is predicted to arrive during a Final Conclave.

The Final Conclave

A single, brightly colored starling landed and fluffed his vibrant feathers together against the chilly spring air just atop the outside ledge of a Sistine Chapel window. The wind was barely more than a light breeze, but cold, adding a sense of urgency to the emotionally charged atmosphere below. Proudly, the bird puffed out his chest and belted a chirpy greeting to a group of onlookers before taking flight over the enormous crowd that huddled uncomfortably close in the Piazza San Pietro. Despite their numbers, only a respectful and curious murmur washed between them, their hot breath creating miniature clouds of anxious anticipation as they stood on tiptoe and glanced about restlessly. His usual perch and view obscured by the tall chimney coughing up steady spurts of white smoke, the starling took wing again to the roofs of the basilica in St. Peter's square.

The view was exciting, unsettling, and strangely conflicting all at once. Cameras blinked in a never-ceasing wave of flickering light, bathing the overcast multitudes in a surreal quality reminiscent of an old malfunctioning movie projector. News channels wheeled their machinery about as their crew focused lenses in sweeping motions over the assembly, and reporters spoke in several languages for the benefits of their own local audiences back home. Small children were hoisted to the shoulders of parents and shouted in excitement as others bowed their heads and said silent prayers in the warm folds of their scarves.

And then, just as suddenly as the muted tones had come a short while before, the voices of the people erupted in a thunderous roar, an unwelcome explosion of sound to the beautiful bird, who responded in a clumsy and frantic stumble-into-flight that carried him from the solidity of the rooftops to the vibration-violated air above the masses. Hands stretched out everywhere toward the balcony, pointing and praising, missing him by only inches several times, though nobody seemed to notice. Women cried tears of joy and men swayed to and fro with their eyes to the heavens, as the volume continued to grow: a stark contrast to the usual bird-feeding tourists he was accustomed to.

And then abruptly below, cardinal-red garments emerged in a ritual march from behind the windows and beyond the curtains of the balcony of St. Peter's Basilica. The man recognized as the senior Cardinal Deacon stepped forward, claimed the silence again for a short time, and announced with great enthusiasm:

"Annuntio vobis gaudium magnum!" ("I announce to you a great joy!")

"Habemus Papam!" ("We have a Pope!)"

"Eminentissimum ac reverendissimum Dominum…" ("The most eminent and most reverend Lord…")

A moment later, bringing his brief introductory proclamation to a close, the people ignited into an even more heightened state of commotion than they had been in before. Resolved to being evicted by the mayhem and chaos, the proud bird surrendered, and just as his wings and the gentle wind carried him away from the now-rapid, ethereal Vatican City, he glimpsed sight of the entity whose presence was the cause of everything new.

Petrus Romanus materialized with arms outstretched toward the people as the starling soared out of sight, carrying away on his wings all he had seen and the unusual sense of foreboding that had suddenly fallen over the once-inspirational city.

ALSO AVAILABLE FROM THESE AUTHORS

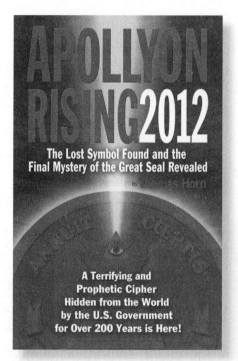

LEARN MORE AT WWW.SURVIVORMALL.COM

ALSO AVAILABLE FROM THESE AUTHORS

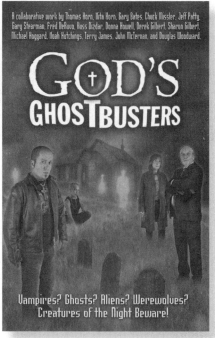

LEARN MORE AT WWW.SURVIVORMALL.COM

Notes

1. D. A. Carson and Douglas J. Moo, *An Introduction to the New Testament*, Second Edition (Grand Rapids, MI: Zondervan, 2005), 733.
2. D. A. Carson and Douglas J. Moo, *An Introduction to the New Testament*, 734.
3. Confraternity of Christian Doctrine. Board of Trustees, Catholic Church. National Conference of Catholic Bishops and United States Catholic Conference. Administrative Board, The New American Bible: Translated from the Original Languages With Critical Use of All the Ancient Sources and the Revised New Testament (Confraternity of Christian Doctrine, 1996, c1986), 1 Jn 5:19.
4. John Hogue, *The Last Pope: The Decline and Fall of the Church of Rome* (Boston, MA: Element Books Inc., 2000), 8.
5. H. J. Lawlor, *St. Bernard of Clairvaux's Life of St. Malachy of Armagh* (New York, NY: The Macmillan Company, 1920), page 19, position 242.
6. Ibid., page 20, position 245.
7. Ibid., page 19, position 245.
8. "Saint Malachy—Our Patron Saint," *StMalachy.org*, last accessed December 15, 2011, http://www.saintmalachy.org/churchpatronsaint.aspx.
9. Hogue, *The Last Pope*, 30.
10. Yves Dupont, *Catholic Prophecy: The Coming Chastisement* (Rockford IL: Tan Publishers, 1973), 15.
11. Hogue, *The Last Pope*, 11.
12. H. J. Lawlor, *St. Bernard of Clairvaux's Life of St. Malachy of Armagh*, page 37, position 326.
13. Ibid., page 37–38, position 329.
14. "Saint Malachy—Our Patron Saint," *SaintMalachy.org*.
15. M. J. O'Brien, *An Historical and Critical Account of the So-Called Prophecy of St. Malachy Regarding the Succession of Popes* (Dublin: M. H. Gill & Son, 1880), 82.
16. "Prophecy of the Popes," *Wikipedia*, last modified, December 27, 2011, http://en.wikipedia.org/wiki/Prophecy_of_the_popes.
17. John Hogue, *The Last Pope*, 178.

18. Anonymous, *La profezia dei sommi pontefici*, FERRARA: 1794, p.30 (translated by CD Putnam).

19. Arthur Devine, "Prophecy," *The Catholic Encyclopedia, Volume 12* (New York: Robert Appleton Company, 1911). (Retrieved online, December 27, 2011 from *New Advent*: http://www.newadvent.org/cathen/12473a.htm.

20. Available free here: http://www.gutenberg.org/ebooks/25761.

21. F. L. Cross and Elizabeth A. Livingstone, *The Oxford Dictionary of the Christian Church*, 3rd ed. rev. (Oxford; New York: Oxford University Press, 2005), 1029.

22. Herbert Thurston, "Prophecies of the Future Popes," *The Month: A Catholic Magazine* vol. XCIII (Jan.–June 1899), 565.

23. John N. Lupia, "Hoax Or Authentic? The Prophecies Of St. Malachy (Part 2)," *Roman Catholic News, Vol. 5* (Issue 67, April 14, 2005), http://groups.yahoo.com/group/Roman-Catholic-News/message/957?l=1.

24. Gordon D. Fee and Douglas K. Stuart, *How to Read the Bible for All Its Worth*, 3rd ed. (Grand Rapids, MI: Zondervan Publishing House, 1993), 135.

25. René Thibaut, *La Mystérieuse Prophétie des Papes* (Paris: J. Vrin, 1951), 23.

26. John N. Lupia, "Hoax Or Authentic?" *Roman Catholic News*, http://groups.yahoo.com/group/Roman-Catholic-News/message/957?l=1.

27. Benito Jerónimo Feijóo, *Teatro Crítico Universal* VI.38, http://www.filosofia.org/bjf/bjft204.htm. (Also corroborated at http://en.wikipedia.org/wiki/Alfonso_Chac%C3%B3n, and http://en.wikipedia.org/wiki/Prophecy_of_the_Popes#Authenticity_and_skepticism.)

28. M. J. O'Brien, *An Historical and Critical Account*, 27.

29. John N. Lupia, "Hoax Or Authentic?" *Roman Catholic News*, http://groups.yahoo.com/group/Roman-Catholic-News/message/957?l=1.

30. M.J. O'Brien, *An Historical and Critical Account*, 97–98.

31. Anonymous, *La profezia dei sommi pontefici*, FERRARA: 1794, p. 180–181 (translated by CD Putnam).

32. John N. Lupia, "Hoax Or Authentic?" *Roman Catholic News*, http://groups.yahoo.com/group/Roman-Catholic-News/message/957?l=1.

33. M. J. O'Brien, *An Historical and Critical Account*, 14.

34. Ibid., 15.

35. Ibid., 109.

36. Compare the antipopes listed in the Catholic encyclopedia (http://www.newadvent.org/cathen/12272b.htm) with the Malachy Prophecy (http://en.wikipedia.org/wiki/Prophecy_of_the_Popes) and this is clearly visible.

37. René Thibaut, *La Mystérieuse*, 23–24 (translation by Putnam).

38. René Thibaut, *La Mystérieuse*, 7.

39. Ibid., 92.

40. Ibid., 93 (translation by Putnam).

41. In the Wion manuscript which reads Peregin' apostolic' the raised ' is a common scribal notation for an "us" ending. It looks similar to a fat comma placed after the letter on the median line represented us or os, generally at the end of the word being the Nominative case affix of the second declension sometimes is or simply s. The apostrophe used today originated from various

marks in sigla, hence its current use in elision, such as in the Saxon genitive. See: http://en.wikipedia.org/wiki/Scribal_abbreviation#Latin_alphabet.

42. René Thibaut, *La Mystérieuse*, 91.

43. Ibid., 22 (translation by Putnam).

44. Ibid., 22–23.

45. See: http://books.google. com/books?id=lzQZAAAAIAAJ&q=2012#search_anchor.

46. Ibid., 97.

47. Ibid., 101.

48. Benedict XIV, Heroic Virtue III, 144:150.

49. Kenneth L. Barker, *Expositors Bible Commentary (Abridged Edition: Old Testament)* (Grand Rapids, MI: Zondervan Publishing House, 1994), 216.

50. *La profezia dei sommi pontefici*, 1794, p. 15. Translation CD Putnam.

51. John Hogue, *The Last Pope*, xviiii.

52. Ibid.

53. See: https://www.google.com/search?q=Rene%E2%80%99+Thibaut%2 C&btnG=Search+Books&tbm=bks&tbo=1#hl=en&tbo=1&tbm=bks&t bm=bks&q=inauthor:%22Ren%C3%A9+Thibaut%22&sa=X&ei=PJ4X T5D4A8O3twewi_XtAg&ved=0CEQQ9Ag&bav=on.2,or.r_gc.r_pw.,cf. osb&fp=f467b2e3ce2319a8&biw=1525&bih=659.

54. Anonymous, *La profezia dei sommi pontefici romani* (FERRARA: 1794), 171, translation Putnam.

55. Joseph Maitre, *La Prophetie des Papes* (Beaune Librairie G. Loireau, 1901), 46.

56. Peter Bander, *The Prophecies of St. Malachy* (IL: Tan Books, 1969), 11.

57. Martin Lings, "St. Malachy's Prophecy of the Popes," *Studies in Comparative Religion* (1984), 148–153, online journal, viewable here: last accessed February 7, 2012, http://www.studiesincomparativereligion.com/Public/articles/St_ Malachy%E2%80%99s_Prophecy_of_the_Popes-by_Martin_Lings.aspx

58. Ibid, 150.

59. Ibid, 150.

60. John Lupia, "Letters to the Editor"; "Hoax or Authentic? The Prophecies of St. Malachy (Part 1)," *Roman Catholic News vol 5* issue 66, last accessed January 30, 2012, http://groups.yahoo.com/group/Roman-Catholic-News/message/956.

61. Romolo Marcellini, director, "Pastor Angelicus," 1942, *IMDb*, last accessed January 30, 2012, http://www.imdb.com/title/tt0035177/.

62. John Hogue, *Last Pope Revised*, ebook, 30.

63. René Thibaut, *La Mystérieuse Prophétie des Papes* (Paris: J. Vrin, 1951), 24.

64. Ibid., 20.

65. Karl Popper, *Conjectures and Refutations* (London: Routledge and Keagan Paul, 1963), 33–39.

66. Guy W. Selvester, "Aspects of Heraldry in the Catholic Church" last accessed January 30, 2012, http://www.coaf.us/AspectsofHeraldry.pdf, page 3.

67. "Pope Leo XIII," *Catholic Encyclopedia*, as quoted by: *New Advent*, last accessed January 30, 2012, http://www.newadvent.org/cathen/09169a.htm.

68. Stephen Skinner, *Millennium Prophecies* (Stamford, CT: Longmeadow

Press, 1995), 75. Also see: http://www.bibliotecapleyades.net/profecias/esp_
profecia01c2b.htm.

69. Yves Dupont, *Catholic Prophecy* (Rockford Il: Tan Books, 1973), 22. Also see:
http://www.bibliotecapleyades.net/profecias/esp_profecia01c2b.htm.

70. Karl Popper, *Conjectures and Refutations,* 33.

71. John Julius Norwich (2011-07-12T04:00:00+00:00). *Absolute Monarchs: A
History of the Papacy* (Random House Digital, Inc.. Kindle Edition), Kindle
locations 7678–7679.

72. R. J. Rummel, "How Many Did Communist Regimes Murder?" last
accessed January 31, 2012, https://www.hawaii.edu/powerkills/COM.ART.
HTM?PHPSESSID=2a47ce24761a818095b37d0dd2e2112c.

73. John Julius Norwich, *Absolute Monarchs: A History of the Papacy,* Kindle
locations 7772–7775.

74. Ibid., Kindle locations 7779–7780.

75. "*intrepidus,*" *Collins Latin Dictionary Plus Grammar,* Includes index (Glasgow:
HarperCollins, 1997).

76. L. Gedda, *18 Aprile 1948: Memorie inedite del'Artefice della Sconfitta del Fronte
Popolare* (Milan, 1998), 74. As Cited in: John Cornwell, *Hitler's Pope: the Secret
History of Pius XII* (New York, N.Y.: Viking Adult, 1999), 271.

77. Yves Dupont, *Catholic Prophecy* (Rockford Il: Tan Books, 1973), 22.

78. "ALLOCUTIO IOANNIS PP. XXIII IN SOLLEMNI SS. CONCILII
INAUGURATIONE," Section 6 final paragraph translated from Latin by CD
Putnam, last accessed February 2, 2012, http://www.vatican.va/holy_father/
john_xxiii/speeches/1962/documents/hf_j-xxiii_spe_19621011_opening-
council_lt.html.

79. Paul VI, Discourse, November 21, 1964. See footnote 503 at http://www.
vatican.va/archive/ccc_css/archive/catechism/p123a9p6.htm.

80. Michel Pastoureau, *Heraldry: Its Origins and Meaning,* Francisca Garvie trans.
(Thames and Hudson 1997), p. 98.

81. Malachi Martin, *Keys of This Blood: Pope John Paul II Versus Russia and the West
For Control of the New World Order,* 1st Ed. (New York: Simon & Schuster,
1991), 632.

82. Paul VI, Speech at the UN October 4, 1965, as quoted in: *The Power Puzzle: A
Compilation of Documents and Resources on Global Governance,* edited by Carl
Teichrib, Copyright 2004, second edition, 43.

83. Chris Summers, "An end to the mystery of God's Banker?" *BBC News Online,*
last updated March 31, 2004, http://news.bbc.co.uk/2/hi/uk_news/3568409.
stm.

84. Georges de Nantes, "POPE JOHN PAUL I OR JOSEPH SOLD BY HIS
BRETHREN," September 2009, last accessed January 23, 2023, http://www.
crc-internet.org/CCR/2009/84-John-Paul-I.php. Freemasons named here:
Catholic Voice, last accessed February 2, 2012, http://www.catholicvoice.co.uk/
fatima4/ch9.htm (chapter from book *The Whole Truth About Fátima*).

85. This can be verified by entering the date August 26, 1978 here: http://stardate.
org/nightsky/moon.

86. John Allen, "He Was a Magnificent Pope Who Presided Over a Controversial Pontificate," *National Catholic Reporter*, last accessed February 2, 2012, http://www.nationalcatholicreporter.org/update/conclave/jp_obit_main.htm.

87. Partial solar eclipse May 18, 1920 http://eclipse.gsfc.nasa.gov/SEdecade/SEdecade1911.html; and his burial was April 8 2005 the day of a hybrid solar eclipse, http://eclipse.gsfc.nasa.gov/SEdecade/SEdecade2001.html.

88. "Saint Benedict Joseph Labre," last accessed January 21, 2012, http://www.bowdoin.edu/~hholbroo/.

89. René Thibaut, *La Mystérieuse Prophétie des Papes*, 97.

90. Philip Pullella, "Vatican Urges Economic Reforms, Condemns Collective Greed" *Reuters*, October 24, 2011, http://uk.reuters.com/assets/print?aid=UKL5E7LO1LS20111024.

91. René Thibaut, *La Mystérieuse Prophétie des Papes*, 44, translation Putnam.

92. Ibid., 45.

93. Verified here: last accessed February 7, 2012, http://jumk.de/wortanalyse/word-analysis.php.

94. "Julian Period," *Encyclopedia Britannica*, last accessed January 12, 2012, http://www.britannica.com/EBchecked/topic/307846/Julian-period.

95. "*Ab urbe condita*," *Collins Latin Dictionary Plus Grammar*, 3:1–2.

96. René Thiabaut, *La Mystérieuse Prophétie des Papes* 45, translation Putnam.

97. Ibid., 64.

98. He cites the date April 29, 2012 twice on page 64.

99. Ibid., 101.

100. Irenaeus, *Against Heresies*, Book 5, Chapter 30, section 3; as quoted in: Alexander Roberts, James Donaldson, and A. Cleveland Coxe, *The Ante-Nicene Fathers Vol.I : Translations of the Writings of the Fathers Down to A.D. 325*, The apostolic fathers with Justin Martyr and Irenaeus, (Oak Harbor: Logos Research Systems, 1997), 559.

101. James I, *The Politial Works of James I: Reprinted from the Edition of 1616*, ed. Charles Howard McIlwain (Medford, MA: Harvard University Press, 1918), 144–45.

102. Irenaeus, *Against Heresies*, Lib. 5.

103. A. D. 897–898.

104. George Downame, *A Treatise Concerning Antichrist*, 1603, viewable here: last accessed January 30, 2012, http://www.iconbusters.com/iconbusters/docs/dname/part6.htm#_ftn1.

105. *ThinkExist.com*, last accessed January 13, 2011, http://thinkexist.com/quotation/patience_is_the_companion_of_wisdom/14659.html.

106. Gordon D. Fee and Douglas K. Stuart, *How to Read the Bible for All Its Worth*, 3rd ed. (Grand Rapids, MI: Zondervan Publishing House, 1993), 145.

107. Chad Brand, Charles Draper, Archie England et al., *Holman Illustrated Bible Dictionary* (Nashville, TN: Holman Bible Publishers, 2003), 1249.

108. L. J. Lietaert Peerbolte, "Antichrist," *Dictionary of Deities and Demons in the Bible,* 2nd extensively rev. ed. K. van der Toorn, Bob Becking, and Pieter

Willem van der Horst (Leiden; Boston; Grand Rapids, Michigan: Brill; Eerdmans, 1999), 62.

109. Leon Morris, *1 and 2 Thessalonians: An Introduction and Commentary Volume 13*, Tyndale New Testament Commentaries (Downers Grove, IL: InterVarsity Press, 1984), 129.

110. William W. Combs, "Is *Apostasia* in 2 Thessalonians 2:3 a Reference to the Rapture?" *Detroit Baptist Seminary Journal*, 3 (Fall 1998), 87.

111. G. K. Beale, *1 and 2 Thessalonians*, 204.

112. "Used in the political sense in 1 Esr. 2:23. It is usually used in the religious sense, Jos. 22:22; Jer. 2:19; 2 Ch. 29:19 (the apostasy of Ahaz); 33:19 (of Manasseh)." *Theological Dictionary of the New Testament Volume 1*, Gerhard Kittel, Geoffrey W. Bromiley and Gerhard Friedrich, electronic ed. (Grand Rapids, MI: Eerdmans, 1964), 513.

113. Stephen R. Miller, *Daniel Volume 18*, electronic ed., Logos Library System; The New American Commentary (Nashville: Broadman & Holman Publishers, 2001), 305.

114. H. A. A. Kennedy, *St. Paul's Conceptions of the Last Things* (New York: A.C. Armstrong & Son, 1904), 49.

115. Paul's use of "labor pains" in 1 Thes 5:3 cf. Mt. 24:8; "thief in the night" 1 Thes 5:2 cf. Mt 24:43–44; the apostasy is seen in Mt. 24:9–11; Richard N. Longenecker, "The Nature of Paul's Early Eschatology," *New Testament Studies* 31 (1985), 91.

116. G. K. Beale, *1-2 Thessalonians*, 207.

117. John Calvin, *Calvin's Commentaries: 2 Thessalonians*, electronic ed. (Albany, OR: Ages Software, 1998), 2 Th 2:4.

118. "In 2 Thess 2:9, 11 (→ also 2) use of the word underlines the demonic power of Satan and the πλάνη caused by him." Horst Robert Balz and Gerhard Schneider, *Exegetical Dictionary of the New Testament*, Translation of: *Exegetisches Worterbuch Zum Neuen Testament* (Grand Rapids, Michigan: Eerdmans, 1993), 1:453.

119. Craig S. Keener, *The IVP Bible Background Commentary: New Testament* (Downers Grove, IL: InterVarsity Press, 1993), 2 Th 2:10.

120. "ELCA Assembly Opens Ministry to Partnered Gay and Lesbian Lutherans," *ELCA News Service*, last accessed December 08, 2011, http://www.elca.org/Who-We-Are/Our-Three-Expressions/Churchwide-Organization/Communication-Services/News/Releases.aspx?a=4253.

121. Eric Marrapodi, "First Openly Gay Pastor Ordained in the PCUSA Speaks," *CNN News*, October 10, 2011, http://religion.blogs.cnn.com/2011/10/10/first-openly-gay-pastor-ordained-in-the-pcusa-speaks/.

122. John MacArthur, "When God Abandons a Nation," *Grace to You*, August 20, 2006, http://www.gty.org/resources/sermons/80-314.

123. John Piper, "The Tornado, the Lutherans, and Homosexuality," *Desiring God*, August 19, 2009, http://www.desiringgod.org/blog/posts/the-tornado-the-lutherans-and-homosexuality.

124. Lauren Green, "Christianity in China," *Fox News*, January 20, 2011, http://www.foxnews.com/world/2011/01/20/christianity-china/.

125. Also see Matt. 7:15; 24:11, 24; Mark 13:22; and 1 John 4:1.

126. *Pseudepigrapha of the Old Testament*, ed. Robert Henry Charles (Bellingham, WA: Logos Research Systems, Inc., 2004), 2:224–225.

127. J. Daniel Hays, J. Scott Duvall, and C. Marvin Pate, *Dictionary of Biblical Prophecy and End Times* (Grand Rapids, MI: Zondervan Publishing House, 2007), 63.

128. Peter Goodgame, "The Biblical False Prophet," *RedMoonRising*, last accessed November 11, 2011, http://www.redmoonrising.com/21Defense/biblicalFP. htm.

129. Ibid.

130. Minutes from Bilateral and Trilateral US-PAL-ISR Sessions Post Annapolis, Tuesday, 29th July 2008: viewable here: *Al Jazeera*, last accessed February 7, 2012, http://www.aljazeera.com/palestinepapers/.

131. Alexander Mitchell, "SCIENTOLOGY: Revealed for the First Time…The Odd Beginning of Ron Hubbard's Career," *The Sunday Times*, October 5, 1969, viewable here: http://www.lermanet.com/scientologynews/crowley-hubbard-666.htm.

132. Aleister Crowley et al, *Magick Book 4 part III* (Chapter 12: Of the Bloody Sacrifice and Matters Cognate) Second one-volume edition (York Beach, ME: Red Wheel/Weiser, LLC, 1997 [2004]), 206–207.

133. Judi McLeod, "Scouting Out Satan," *Canada Free Press*, February 23, 2005, http://www.canadafreepress.com/2005/cover022305.htm.

134. John Daniel, *Scarlet and the Beast*, Vol 1, 3rd edition (Longview, TX: Day Publishing, 2007), 938.

135. Malachi Martin, *Windswept House: A Vatican Novel* (Doubleday, 1996), 492–493.

136. Malachi Martin, *The Keys of This Blood: The Struggle for World Dominion* (New York, NY: Simon and Schuster, Sep 15, 1991), 632.

137. Malachi Martin, *Windswept House*, 7.

138. Day Williams, "Masons and Mystery at the 33rd Parallel" *Hidden Mysteries E-Magazine* last accessed January 19, 2012, http://www.hiddenmysteries.org/themagazine/vol14/articles/masonic-33rd.shtml.

139. Malachi Martin, *Windswept House*, 8.

140. "The Catholic Church in Crisis," *The New American, June 9, 1997, 6–8*.

141. Malachi Martin, *Windswept House*, 600.

142. Chuck Nowlen, "The Devil and Father Kunz: An Easter Tale about Murder, the Catholic Church and the Strange Paths of Good and Evil," *Las Vegas Weekly*, April 12, 2001 (Radiant City Publications), viewable here: http://www.chucknowlen.com/kunz.htm.

143. Ibid.

144. Ibid.

145. Manly P Hall, *The Lost Keys of Freemasonry* (Philosophical Research Society), 1976, 19.

146. Albert Pike, *Morals and Dogma of the Ancient and Accepted Scottish Rite of Freemasonry* (Masonic Publishing Company, 1874), 104.

147. As told to Thomas Horn during a private meeting with a former Freemason.

148. Foster Bailey, *The Spirit of Freemasonry* (New York, NY: Lucis Press, 1957), 20.

149. Manly P. Hall, *Lectures on Ancient Philosophy: An Introduction to Practical Ideals* (Philosophical Research Society, 1984), 433.

150. Manly P. Hall, *The Secret Destiny of America* (Los Angeles, CA: The Philosophical Research Society, Inc., 1991), 26.

151. Mitch Horowitz, *Occult America* (New York, NY: Bantam Books, 2010), 172.

152. John C. Culver and John Hyde, *American Dreamer: The Life and Times of Henry A. Wallace* (W. W. Norton & Company, 2001), 135.

153. Helena Petrovna Blavatsky, *The Secret Doctrine: The Synthesis of Science, Religion, and Philosophy, Volume 1* (New York: NY, Newman, Cowell & Gripper, Ltd., 1893), 332.

154. John C. Culver and John Hyde, American Dreamer, 136.

155. "How the Great Seal Got on the One Dollar Bill," *GreatSeal.com*, last accessed January 23, 2012, http://www.greatseal.com/dollar/hawfdr.html.

156. Mitch Horowitz, *Occult America*, 173.

157. Frederick S. Voss, *The Smithsonian Treasury: Presidents* (Random House Value Publishing, 1991), 72.

158. Henry A. Wallace, *Statesmanship and Religion* (New York, NY: Round Table, 1934), 78–79.

159. John C. Culver and John Hyde, *American Dreamer*, 134.

160. William Henry, *Cloak of the Illuminati: Secrets, Transformations, Crossing the Stargate* (Kempton, IL: Adventures Unlimited, 2003), 13.

161. John Dryden, trans., as published by Georgetown University Online; also appears in: Thomas Horn, *Apollyon Rising 2012*.

162. Peter Goodgame, *The Giza Discovery, Part Nine: The Mighty One*, last accessed January 23, 2012, http://www.redmoonrising.com/Giza/Asshur9.htm.

163. Thomas and Nita Horn, *Forbidden Gates: How Genetics, Robotics, Artificial Intelligence, Synthetic Biology, Nanotechnology, and Human Enhancement Herald the Dawn of TechoDimensional Spiritual Warfare* (Crane, MO: Defender Publishing, 2011), 55.

164. Herodotus, *The history of Herodotus* (The Tandy-Thomas company, 1909), 62.

165. Thomas Horn, *Spiritual Warfare: The Invisible Invasion* (Huntington House Publishers,1998), 23–24.

166. "Growth of a Young Nation," *U.S. House of Representatives: Office of the Clerk*, last accessed January 30, 2012, http://artandhistory.house.gov/art_artifacts/virtual_tours/splendid_hall/young_nation.aspx.

167. "1964–Present: September 11, 2001, The Capitol Building as a Target," *United States Senate*, last accessed January 30, 2012, http://www.senate.gov/artandhistory/history/minute/Attack.htm.

168. See: http://www.gwmemorial.org/tours/2_MemorialHall.html.

169. See: http://www.msa.md.gov/msa/stagser/s1259/121/5847/html/story.html.

170. Thomas Horn, *Apollyon Rising 2012: The Lost Symbol Found and the Final*

Mystery of the Great Seal Revealed (Crane, MO: Defender Publishing, 2009), 287–288.

171. William Henry and Mark Gray, *Freedom's Gate: Lost Symbols in the U.S.* (Hendersonville, TN: Scala Dei, 2009), 3.

172. Ibid., 4.

173. "Sandpit of Royalty," *Extra Bladet* (Copenhagen, January 31, 1999).

174. Manly P Hall, *Secret Teachings*, 104.

175. James Lees-Milne, *Saint Peter's: The Story of Saint Peter's Basilica in Rome* (Little, Brown, 1967), 221.

176. Rebecca Zorach and Michael W. Cole, *The Idol in the Age of Art* (Ashgate, 2009), 61.

177. Rebecca Zorach and Michael W. Cole, *The Idol in the Age of Art*, 63.

178. David Flynn, *Cydonia: The Secret Chronicles of Mars* (Bozwman, MT: End Time Thunder, 2002),156.

179. Albert Pike, *Morals and Dogma: Of the Ancient and Accepted Scottish Rite of Freemasonry*, (Forgotten Books), 401.

180. Albert Mackey, *A Manual of the Lodge* (1870), 56.

181. Dan Brown, *The Lost Symbol* (Anchor; Reprint edition, 2010), 3–4.

182. Manly P. Hall, *Lost Keys*, Prologue.

183. Manly P. Hall, *Secret Teachings*, 116–120.

184. Manly P. Hall, "Rosicrucianism and Masonic Origins," from *Lectures on Ancient Philosophy—An Introduction to the Study and Application of Rational Procedure* (Los Angeles: Hall, 1929), 397–417.

185. Albert Pike, *Morals and Dogma*, 335.

186. Ibid., 16.

187. Ibid., 472.

188. Hope, Murry, Practical Egyptian Magic (New York: St. Martin's Press), 1984 p. 107. Quoted by Fritz Springmeier, The Watchtower & the Masons, 1990, 1992 pp. 113, 114.

189. Thomas Horn, *Apollyon Rising 2012*,, 7-10.

190. Martin Short, *Inside the Brotherhood: Explosive Secrets of the Freemasons* (UK: HarperCollins, 1995), 122.

191. Manly P. Hall, *The Lost Keys of Freemasonry*, 48.

192. Manly P. Hall, *Secret Destiny of America* (Penguin Group, 2008), chapter 18.

193. See: http://en.wikipedia.org/wiki/Hermetic_Order_of_the_Golden_Dawn.

194. See: http://en.wikipedia.org/wiki/Ars_Goetia#Ars_Goetia.

195. *See: http://www.redmoonrising.com/Giza/DomDec6.htm.*

196. "Shemhamphorasch," *Wikipedia*, last modified December 6, 2011, http://en.wikipedia.org/wiki/Shemhamphorasch.

197. Manly P Hall, *The Secret Teachings of All Ages*, 623–633.

198. Ken Hudnall, *The Occult Connection II: The Hidden Race* (Omega Press, 2004), 207.

199. Pedro Sarmiento De Gamboa, *Acosta, Hint of the New World*, Clements Markham, trans. (Cambridge: The Hakluyt Society, 1907), 28–58.

200. Koran, Surah 89: 9–15, 27.

201. Thomas Horn, *Apollyon Rising 2012.*
202. "Discovery of Vast, Prehistoric Works Built by Giants?: The Geoglyphs of Teohuanaco," *Raiders News Network*, February 24, 2008, http://www. raidersnewsupdate.com/giants.htm.
203. "Tenochtitlan," *Wikipedia*, last modified January 16, 2012,http://en.wikipedia. org/wiki/Tenochtitlan.
204. Thomas Horn, *Apollyon Rising 2012*, 278–284.
205. *Vatican Council, Sess. IV, Const. de Ecclesiâ Christi, Chapter 3, as quoted by Global Catholic Network, last accessed December, 18, 2011,* http://www.ewtn. com/library/COUNCILS/V1.HTM#6.
206. Vincent McNabb, *The Decrees of the Vatican Council* (New York, NY: Benzinger Brothers, 1907), 46.
207. Ibid., 47.
208. Augustine, "On the Gospel of John," Tractate 12435; as quoted in James R. White, *Answers to Catholic Claims: A Discussion of Biblical Authority* (Southbridge, MA: Crowne Pubns, 1990), 106.
209. Chad Brand, Charles Draper, Archie England et al., *Holman Illustrated Bible Dictionary* (Nashville, TN: Holman Bible Publishers, 2003), 1282.
210. Ibid., 263.
211. David Noel Freedman, *The Anchor Bible Dictionary* (New York, NY: Doubleday, 1996, c1992), 1:867.
212. Irenaeus, in *Against Heresies* 3.1.1, writes that both Peter and Paul were responsible for "laying the foundations of the Church" at Rome. But this could simply refer to their ministry.
213. Thomas F. X. Noble, "Lecture One: What is Papal History and How Did it Begin?" notes for course, *Popes and the Papacy: A History* (The Teaching Company, 2006), 3.
214. J. C. Walters, "Romans, Jews, and Christians: The Impact of the Romans on Jewish/Christian Relations in First-Century Rome," in *Judaism and Christianity in First-Century Rome*, ed. K. Donfried and P. Richardson (Grand Rapids, Michigan: Eerdmans, 1998), 176–77.
215. Suetonius, *Life of Claudius,* 25.4. (as cited by Habermas in next endnote).
216. Gary R. Habermas, *The Historical Jesus: Ancient Evidence for the Life of Christ*, Rev. Ed. of: *Ancient Evidence for the Life of Jesus* (Joplin, MO: College Press Pub. Co., 1996), 191. (On "Chrestus" as a variant, see Graves, *The Twelve Caesars*, 197; Bruce, *Christian Origins*, 21; Amiot, "Jesus," 8.)
217. F. F. Bruce, *Paul, Apostle of the Heart Set Free* (Milton Keynes, UK: Paternoster, 1977), 251.
218. Tom Mueller, "Inside Job," *The Atlantic Monthly* (October 2003), Last accessed November 10, 2011, http://www.theatlantic.com/past/docs/issues/2003/10/ mueller.htm.
219. Tom Mueller, "Inside Job."
220. Jonathan Wynne-Jones, "St. Peter Was Not the First Pope and Never Went to Rome, Claims Channel 4," *The Telegraph*, March 23, 2008, http://www.

telegraph.co.uk/news/worldnews/1582585/St-Peter-was-not-the-first-Pope-and-never-went-to-Rome-claims-Channel-4.html.

221. F. Paul Peterson, *Peter's Tomb Recently Discovered In Jerusalem* (4th Edition, 1971). (Copies may be obtained from your local bookstore or from the author and publisher, F. Paul Peterson, P.O. Box 7351, Fort Wayne, Indiana; Price $2.00.) Permission is granted to reproduce any part of this book if title, price, and address where it may be purchased are given. (Cris Putnam obtained this information here: http://biblelight.net/peters-jerusalem-tomb.htm; also featured in a documentary: *The Secrets of the 12 Disciples*, BBC Channel 4, transmitted on 23 March 2008. Entire quote is also cited here: Grant R. Jefferey, *Jesus the Great Debate*, [Random House Digital Inc, 1999] no page #, chapter 5, last accessed January 20, 2012, http://books.google.com/books?id=FQgxBy umb1kC&printsec=frontcover#v=onepage&q&f=false. Also portions in an article viewable here: Jean Gilman, "Jerusalem Burial Cave Reveals: Names, Testimonies of First Christians," *Leadership U*, last accessed January 20, 2012, http://www.leaderu.com/theology/burialcave.html.

222. Ibid.

223. Ibid. This quote is only in the originally cited source. http://biblelight.net/peters-jerusalem-tomb.htm

224. Alexander Roberts, James Donaldson, and A. Cleveland Coxe, *The Ante-Nicene Fathers Vol.I: Translations of the Writings of the Fathers Down to A.D. 325*, The Apostolic Fathers With Justin Martyr and Irenaeus (Oak Harbor: Logos Research Systems, 1997), 6.

225. Montague Rhodes James, *The Apocryphal New Testament: Being the Apocryphal Gospels, Acts, Epistles, and Apocalypses* (Bellingham, WA: Logos Research Systems, Inc., 2009), 331.

226. *The First Apology of Justin* XXVI in Philip Schaff and David Schley Schaff, *History of the Christian Church* (Oak Harbor, WA: Logos Research Systems, Inc., 1997) 1.1.6.1.0.26.

227. David Noel Freedman, *The Anchor Bible Dictionary* (New York: Doubleday, 1996, c1992), 5:281.

228. Eusebuis *Church History* Book III, as quoted by *New Advent*, last accessed December 26, 2011, http://www.newadvent.org/fathers/250103.htm.

229. Ibid.

230. Irenaeus, *Against Heresies* (Book III, Chapter 3.3). While he claims Peter and Paul founded the Church, this has been proven impossible. Linus was the first bishop on the list: http://www.newadvent.org/fathers/0103303.htm

231. John Paul II, "Homily Of His Holiness John Paul Ii For The Inauguration Of His Pontificate" http://www.vatican.va/holy_father/john_paul_ii/homilies/1978/documents/hf_jp-ii_hom_19781022_inizio-pontificato_en.html (accessed 12/02/2011).

232. Charles Hodge, *Systematic Theology* (Oak Harbor, WA: Logos Research Systems, Inc., 1997; originally published 1872), 3:820.

233. Charles E. Powell, "The Identity of the Restrainer in 2 Thessalonians 2:6–7," *Bibliotheca Sacra* 154 (July–September 1997), 329.

234. F. F. Bruce, *Word Biblical Commentary : 1 and 2 Thessalonians, Volume 45*, Word Biblical Commentary (Dallas, TX: Word, Incorporated, 2002), 171.

235. Ibid., 172.

236. Michael Heiser, "Deuteronomy 32:8 and the Sons of God," *Bibliotheca Sacra* 158:629 (January–March 2001), 52–74.

237. Lactantius, *de Mortibus Persecutorum*, Chap. XLIV, as quoted: http://people. ucalgary.ca/~vandersp/Courses/texts/lactant/lactpers.html#XXXX.

238. Eusebius, *The Conversion of Constantine*, public domain (ch. 28–29.) in James Stevenson, *A New Eusebius: Documents Illustrating the History of the Church to AD 337* (London: SPCK, 1987), 283.

239. "A Changing World: House of Constantine Bronzes," *last accessed November 25, 2011,* http://rg.ancients.info/constantine/.

240. Augustine, *Contra Faustum Manichaeum* ("Against Faustus the Manichaean") XIV, 11 (as quoted by: "Augustine: The Writings Against the Manichaeans and Against the Donatists," *Christian Classics Ethereal Library*, last accessed January 17, 2012, http://www.ccel.org/ccel/schaff/npnf104.toc.html#P1575_855688.

241. "The most appropriate form (for the monstrance) is that of the sun emitting its rays to all sides (Instructio Clement., 5). (See: "Altar Vessels: Ostensorium," *Catholic Encyclopedia 1914 Edition*, as quoted by *New Advent*, last accessed December 14, 2011, http://www.newadvent.org/cathen/01357e.htm.

242. Philip Schaff and David Schley Schaff, *History of the Christian Church* (Oak Harbor, WA: Logos Research Systems, Inc., 1997), Vol.3 Chap. 1 Sect. 2.

243. Schaff, *History of the Christian Church*, Vol. 3.10.173.

244. Schaff, *History of the Christian Church*, Vol. 3.1.2.

245. "Christmas," *Catholic Encyclopedia 1908 Edition*, as quoted by *New Advent*, last accessed November, 25, 2011, http://www.newadvent.org/cathen/03724b.htm.

246. Eusebius, *Vita Constantini*, 4.62.4.

247. Eusebius, *Vita Constantini*, 4.64.

248. Philip Schaff and David Schley Schaff, *History of the Christian Church* (Oak Harbor, WA: Logos Research Systems, Inc., 1997), Vol. 4 chap. 9 sect. 89.

249. *Novellae* cxxxi. The Novellae Constitutiones "new constitutions," or Justinian's Novels, are units of Roman law created by Roman Emperor Justinian I in the course of his reign (AD 527–565).

250. Peter De Rosa, *Vicars of Christ: The Dark Side of the Papacy*, 1st American ed. (New York, NY: Crown, 1988), 207.

251. "Donation of Constantine," *Medieval Sourcebook*, as quoted by Fordham University, last accessed January 17, 2012, http://www.fordham.edu/halsall/source/donatconst.asp.

252. Edward Gibbon, *The History of the Decline and Fall of the Roman Empire.*, ed. Henry Hart Milman (Bellingham: Logos Research Systems, Inc., 2004).

253. "In the statements regarding the κόσμος in Johannine theology the concern is with the nature of the world that has fallen away from God and is ruled by the evil one." —Horst Robert Balz and Gerhard Schneider, *Exegetical Dictionary of the New Testament* (Grand Rapids, Michigan: Eerdmans, 1990–c1993), 2:312.

254. Martin Luther, *Luther's Works, Vol. 39: Church and Ministry I*, ed. Jaroslav Jan

Pelikan, Hilton C. Oswald, and Helmut T. Lehmann, *Luther's Works*, 39:65 (Philadelphia: Fortress Press, 1999, c1970).

255. Peter De Rosa, *Vicars of Christ*, 41.

256. Christopher B. Coleman, *The Treatise of Lorenzo Valla on the Donation of Constantine: Text and Translation into English* (Yale University Press, 1971) 61–71.

257. *Vitæ Pontificum Platinæ historici liber de vita Christi ac omnium pontificum qui hactenus ducenti fuere et XX. (Also see: http://vangelisraptopoulos.wordpress. com/english-page/about-his-books-ii/.)*

258. Peter De Rosa, *Vicars of Christ*, 47.

259. "Pope Stephen (VI) VII," *Catholic Encyclopedia (1911)* as quoted by *New Advent*, last accessed December 16, 2011, http://www.newadvent.org/cathen/14289d.htm.

260. Octavian changed his name to John (XII), only the second pope to do so, but with two exceptions, all later popes followed suit. The first pope to change his name, John II (r. 533–535), did so because he felt it unseemly for a pope to be called Mercurius.

261. "Pope John XII," *The Catholic Encyclopedia*, as quoted by *New Advent*, last accessed December 20, 2011, http://www.newadvent.org/cathen/08426b.htm.

262. *Patrologia Latina*, compiled by Dr. Richard Abels, FOR HH315: AGE OF CHIVALRY AND FAITH AT THE UNITED STATES NAVAL ACADEMY, Copyright 2009, used by permission, last accessed January 19, 2012, http://usna.edu/Users/history/abels/hh315/papacy_empire_timeline.htm. (Also cited in Peter De Rosa, *Vicars of Christ*, 51.)

263. E. M. Butler, *The Myth of the Magus* (Cambridge University Press, 1948), 96.

264. "Gerbert Sylvester II," from footnote 1500 in Philip Schaff and David Schley Schaff, *History of the Christian Church* (Oak Harbor, WA: Logos Research Systems, Inc., 1997), 179.

265. Ferdinand Gregorovius, *History of the City of Rome in the Middle Ages* (Cambridge University Press, 1896), 47.

266. "Pope Benedict IX" *Catholic Encyclopedia*, as quoted by *New Advent*, last accessed January 19, 2012, http://www.newadvent.org/cathen/02429a.htm.

267. St. Peter Damian, *Liber Gomorrhianus* as cited in Simon, *Papal Magic: Occult Practices Within the Catholic Church* (New York, NY: Harper Collins, 2007), 42.

268. § 11. The Gregorian Theocracy in Philip Schaff and David Schley Schaff, *History of the Christian Church* (Oak Harbor, WA: Logos Research Systems, Inc., 1997).

269. Johann Joseph Ignaz von Döllinger, *The Pope and the Council* (Boston: Roberts, 1870), 76–77; 79; 115–116.

270. Gregory VII, "Dictatus Papae," *Medieval Sourcebook*, last accessed January 14, 2012, http://www.fordham.edu/halsall/source/g7-dictpap.asp.

271. John Foxe and George Townsend, *The Acts and Monuments of John Foxe: With a Preliminary Dissertation by the Rev. George Townsend, Volume 2* (London: R.B. Seeley and W. Burnside, 1837), 121.

272. Simon, *Papal Magic: Occult Practices Within the Catholic Church* (New York, NY: Harper Collins, 2007), 43.

273. William Webster, *Forgeries and the Papacy: The Historical Influence and Use of Forgeries in Promotion of the Doctrine of the Papacy*, as quoted by *ChristianTruth.com*, last accessed December, 22, 2011, http://www.christiantruth.com/articles/forgeries.html.

274. Jonathan Edwards, *The Works of Jonathan Edwards - Volume 1* (Utgivare), 595.

275. Maitland, *The Apostles' School of Prophetic Interpretation*, 340. (See also Guericke, Kirchengeschichte, 6th edit., Leipzig, 1846, vol. ii. pp. 223–226.) Quoted in Charles Hodge, *Systematic Theology*, (Oak Harbor, WA: Logos Research Systems, Inc., 1997; originally published 1872), Vol. 3, Page 832.

276. Inferno 19; Dante Alighieri, & Eliot, C. W., (1909). *The Harvard Classics 20: The Divine Comedy by Dante* (New York, NY: P. F. Collier & Son), 82.

277. Dante Alighieri, & Eliot, C. W., (1909). *The Harvard Classics 20: The Divine Comedy by Dante* (New York, NY: P. F. Collier & Son), 372.

278. James Brundage, *Law, Sex and Christianity in Medieval Europe* (University of Chicago Press, 1990), 473.

279. Boniface VIII, *Unam Sanctam*, 1302, Medieval Sourcebook, viewable here: last accessed December 22, 2011, http://www.fordham.edu/halsall/source/B8-unam.asp.

280. Dante Alighieri, *De Monarchia* (1559) chapter X: Argument from the donation of Constantine. In *The De Monarchia of Dante Alighieri*, edited with translation and notes by Aurelia Henry (Boston and New York: Houghton, Miflin and Company, 1904). Public Domain.

281. Pius IX, *Quanta Cura*, viewable here: last accessed January 17, 2012, http://www.ewtn.com/library/ENCYC/P9QUANTA.HTM.

282. John Henry Newman, *Essays Critical and Historical* (formerly Fellow of Oriel College, Oxford, London: 1871). *The Protestant Idea of Antichrist*, vol. ii. pp. 173–175.

283. Charles Hodge, *Systematic Theology* (Oak Harbor, WA: Logos Research Systems, Inc., 1997; originally published 1872), 3:819.

284. "Prophecy of the Popes," *Wikipedia*, last modified, December 27, 2011, http://en.wikipedia.org/wiki/Prophecy_of_the_popes.

285. John Hogue, *The Last Pope*, 3.

286. William W. Klein, Craig Blomberg, Robert L. Hubbard, and Kermit Allen Ecklebarger, *Introduction to Biblical Interpretation* (Dallas, TX: Word Pub., 1993), 385.

287. Craig S. Keener and InterVarsity Press, *The IVP Bible Background Commentary: New Testament* (Downers Grove, IL: InterVarsity Press, 1993), Re 17:9.

288. Explained by Woodrow at his site: http://www.ralphwoodrow.org/books/pages/babylon-connection.html.

289. Karl Keating, *Catholicism and Fundamentalism: The Attack On* (San Francisco: Ignatius Press, 1988), 200.

290. Albert J. Nevins , *Answering a Fundamentalist* (*Our Sunday Visitor*, 1990): ISBN 0-87973-433-7 (Library of Congress Catalog Card Number 90-60644), 46.

291. *Pseudepigrapha of the Old Testament*, ed. Robert Henry Charles, 2:400 (Bellingham, WA: Logos Research Systems, Inc., 2004).

292. Viewable here: *SacredTexts.com*, last accessed January 19, 2012, http://www. sacred-texts.com/cla/sib/sib04.htm.

293. Titus Livius (Livy), *The History of Rome*, Vol. 1, book I, last accessed January 13, 2012, http://oll.libertyfund.org/index.php?option=com_staticxt&staticfile= advanced_search.php.

294. Robert James Dr. Utley, Volume 12, *Hope in Hard Times—The Final Curtain: Revelation*, Study Guide Commentary Series (Marshall, Texas: Bible Lessons International, 2001), 119.

295. Dave Hunt, A Woman *Rides the Beast* (Eugene, OR: Harvest House Publishers, 1994), 299.

296. "Sex Crimes and the Vatican" *BBC News*, last accessed January 19, 2012, http:// news.bbc.co.uk/2/hi/programmes/panorama/5389684.stm.

297. "Sex Crimes and the Vatican: Transcript" *Panorama* (recorded from transmission: *BBC One*, Date: 1:10:06), http://news.bbc.co.uk/2/hi/ programmes/panorama/5402928.stm.

298. Ian Traynor, "Tens of Thousands of Children Abused in Dutch Catholic Institutions, Report Says," *The Guardian*, December 16, 2012 (last accessed January 19, 2012), http://www.guardian. co.uk/world/2011/dec/16/children-dutch-catholic-institutions-abused.

299. Chuck Missler, "The Kingdom of Blood Notes," 1996, *Koinonia House Inc.* page 15; http://resources.khouse.org/products/dl040/. For these figures he cites Peter de Rosa, *Vicars of Christ: The Dark Side of the Papacy* (Crown Publishers, 1988), 5; and Will Durant, *The Story of Civilization* (Simon & Schuster, 1950), Vol. IV, 784.

300. Philip Schaff and David Schley Schaff, *History of the Christian Church* (Oak Harbor, WA: Logos Research Systems, Inc., 1997) Volume 8, Chapter XIX, 172; and Chuck Missler "Kingdom of Blood Notes," 22–23.

301. "Rome" Catholic *Encyclopedia*, as quoted by *New Advent*, last accessed January 14, 2012, http://www.newadvent.org/cathen/13164a.htm.

302. Gregory VII, "Dictatus Papae," *Medieval Sourcebook*, last accessed January 14, 2012, http://www.fordham.edu/halsall/source/g7-dictpap.asp.

303. #18. "Deveniendo ad Papae auctoritatem, Papa est quasi Deus in terra unicaus Christifidelium princeps, regum omnium rex maximus, plenitudinem potestatis continens, cui terreni simul, ac coelestis imperii gubernacula ab omnipotenti Deo credita sunt." —Lucius Ferraris, "Papa," art. 2, in *Prompta Bibliotheca Canonica, Juridica, Moralis, Theologica, Ascetica, Polemica, Rubristica, Historica.* Vol. 5, published in Petit-Montrouge (Paris) by J. P. Migne, 1858 edition, column 1823, Latin. Page is scanned online here: http://biblelight.net/1827r. gif.

304. Boniface VIII, "Unam Sanctum" *Medieval Sourcebook*, last accessed January 14, 2012, http://www.fordham.edu/halsall/source/B8-unam.asp.

305. Johann Joseph Ignaz von Döllinger, *Letters from Rome on the Council* (NY: Pott and Amery, 1870), 357.

306. Cardinal Giuseppe Melchior Sarto, "Inaugural Sermon," as quoted in *The Friend, A Religious And Literary Journal, Volume LXIX* (Philadelphia, 1896), 154.

307. Pope Pius XI, "Ad Catholici Sacerdotii," last accessed January 19, 2012, http://www.ewtn.com/library/encyc/p11catho.htm, article 12.

308. Pope John Paul II, *Crossing the Threshold of Hope* (New York: Knopf, 1995), 3.

309. Everett Ferguson, *Church History Volume One: From Christ to Pre-Reformation: The Rise and Growth of the Church in Its Cultural, Intellectual, and Political Context* (Grand Rapids: Zondervan, Kindle Edition, 2009), Kindle Location 5974.

310. "Olivetans" *Catholic Encyclopedia*, as quoted by *New Advent*, last accessed January 18, 2012, http://www.newadvent.org/cathen/11244c.htm.

311. John Hogue, *Last Pope Revisited* (self-published ebook, 2006), 57.

312. Nicholas Kulish and Katrin Bennhold, "Memo to Pope Described Transfer of Pedophile Priest," *New York Times*, March 25, 2010, http://www.nytimes.com/2010/03/26/world/europe/26church.html?pagewanted=all.

313. Jon E. Dougherty, "Malachi Martin: Dispelling the myths," *World Net Daily*, August 2, 1999, http://www.wnd.com/news/article.asp?ARTICLE_ID=15689.

314. Rick Salbato, "Mystery Cloaks Father Malachi Martin's Death," *Unity Publishing*, last accessed October 12, 2011, http://www.unitypublishing.com/Newsletter/Malachi%20Martin.htm.

315. Howard Frederic Vos and Thomas Nelson Publishers, *Exploring Church History* (Nashville, TN: Thomas Nelson Publishers, 1996).

316. Ibid.

317. Martin Luther, Smalcald Articles: II, art. iv, par. 10 in Robert Kolb, Timothy J. Wengert and Charles P. Arand, *The Book of Concord : The Confessions of the Evangelical Lutheran Church* (Minneapolis: Fortress Press, 2000), 309.

318. Pope Boniface VIII, Bull *Unam Sanctam* in Philip Schaff and David Schley Schaff, *History of the Christian Church* (Oak Harbor, WA: Logos Research Systems, Inc., 1997), Vol. 6. Chap., 4 Sect. 1.

319. Millard J. Erickson, *The Concise Dictionary of Christian Theology*, Rev. ed., 1st Crossway ed. (Wheaton, IL: Crossway Books, 2001), 124.

320. John Calvin, *Institutes of the Christian Religion*, Translation of: Institutio Christianae Religionis.; Reprint, With New Introd. Originally Published: Edinburgh: Calvin Translation Society, 1845–1846 (Bellingham, WA: Logos Research Systems, Inc., 1997), IV, vii, 25.

321. Ibid.

322. R. J. VanderMolen, "Francis Turretin," as quoted in *Evangelical Dictionary of Theology: Second Edition,* ed. Walter A. Elwell (Grand Rapids, MI: Baker Academic, 2001), 1221.

323. Ibid.

324. Turretin, *Seventh Disputation: Whether it Can Be Proven the Pope of Rome is the Antichrist,* trans. Kenneth Bubb (Iconbusters.com, ebook location 9.8, last accessed October 01, 2011, http://www.iconbusters.com/iconbusters/htm/catalogue/turretin.pdf.)

325. Ibid., 21.6.

326. Ibid., 24.3.

327. Ibid., 42.6.

328. Ibid., 136.2–136.9.

329. D. A. Carson, *New Bible Commentary: 21st Century Edition* (Leicester, England; Downers Grove, IL: Inter-Varsity Press, 1994), 2 Th 2:4.

330. *Christian History: Thomas Cranmer and the English Reformation.*, electronic ed. (Carol Stream IL: Christianity Today, 1995; Published in electronic form by Logos Research Systems, 1996).

331. John Knox, *The Works of John Knox*, Serial. (Bellingham, WA: Logos Research Systems, Inc., 2003), 4:470.

332. John Wesley, *Antichrist and His Ten Kingdoms* (Public Domain), 110. (See: http://www.whitehorsemedia.com/articles/?d=44.)

333. John Wesley, *Wesley's Notes: Revelation*, electronic ed. Wesley's Notes (Albany, OR: Ages Software, 1999), Re 13:1.

334. Charles H. Spurgeon, *Spurgeon's Sermons: Volume 10*, electronic ed; Spurgeon's Sermons (Albany, OR: Ages Software, 1998).

335. Charles H. Spurgeon, *Sermons: Volume 12*.

336. Charles H. Spurgeon, *Sermons: Volume 50*.

337. Charles Hodge, *Systematic Theology*, Originally Published 1872 (Oak Harbor, WA: Logos Research Systems, Inc., 1997), 3:818.

338. John Henry Newman, *Essays Critical and Historical: The Protestant Idea of Antichrist*, vol. ii., 173–175; as cited in Charles Hodge, *Systematic Theology*, 3:818–819.

339. Le Roy Edwin Froom, *The Prophetic Faith of Our Fathers, Volume 3* (Washington DC: Review and Herald, 1946), 52.

340. George Whitefield, "The Potter and the Clay," as quoted in *George Whitefield's Sermons: Sermon 13* (Logos Research Systems).

341. Clarence Goen, "Jonathan Edwards: A New Departure in Eschatology" (*Church History 28*, 1 Mr 1959), 29. p 25–40.

342. David F. Wells, "The Pope as Antichrist: The Substance of George Tyrrell's Polemic" (*Harvard Theological Review 65*, 2 April 1972) 271–283.

343. Charles Hodge, *Systematic Theology*, 3:815.

344. "The Temple Mount Faithful Movement Held On 'Jerusalem Day" the Most Exciting Event in Israel Since the Destruction of the Holy Temple in 70 CE," *TempleMountFaithful.org*, last accessed October, 11, 2011, http://www.templemountfaithful.org/Events/jerusalemDay2009-2.htm.

345. Charles Hodge, *Systematic Theology*, 3:821.

346. Ibid., 3:822.

347. Ibid.

348. Ibid., 3:825.

349. *The Second Scotch Confession* in Philip Schaff, *The Creeds of Christendom, Volume III* (Joseph Kreifels), 349.

350. Morton H. Smith, *Westminster Confession of Faith* (Greenville SC: Greenville Presbyterian Theological Seminary Press, 1996), 2.

351. James White, "A Review of and Response to 'Evangelicals and Catholics Together: The Christian Mission in the Third Millennium,'" *Alpha and Omega Ministries*, last accessed October 12, 2011, http://vintage.aomin.org/Evangelicals_and_Catholics_Together.html.

352. Susan MacDonald, "Paisley Ejected for Insulting Pope," *The Times*, September 15, 2004, http://www.guardian.co.uk/politics/2004/sep/16/northernireland.northernireland. The actual event was recorded, and is viewable here: "Ian Paisley Heckles the Pope and Makes a Fool of Himself," YouTube video, 1:38, posted by "uptheira99," March 26, 2008, http://www.youtube.com/watch?v=7Fm0QOIw8nQ.

353. "Resolution by the South Atlantic Presbytery of the Bible Presbyterian Church," last accessed October 11, 2011, http://vaam.tripod.com/resolution.html.

354. Personal email to Cris D. Putnam, dated November 14, 2011.

355. "Statement on the Antichrist," *Wisconsin Evangelical Lutheran Synod*, last accessed January 18, 2011, http://www.wels.net/about-wels/doctrinal-statements/antichrist?page=0,1.

356. Ibid.

357. Ibid.

358. Charles P. Arand, "Antichrist: The Lutheran Confessions on the Papacy," *Concordia Journal* (October 2003), 402.

359. Philip Melanchthon, *Apology of the Augsburg Confession* XV,18 in Robert Kolb, Timothy J. Wengert and Charles P. Arand, *The Book of Concord : The Confessions of the Evangelical Lutheran Church* (Minneapolis: Fortress Press, 2000), 225.

360. Ibid.

361. Charles P. Arand "Antichrist: The Lutheran Confessions on the Papacy," 403.

362. Henry Grattan Guinness, *The City of the Seven Hills: A Poem* (London: James Nisbet & Co. 1891), 147.

363. Craig R. Koester, "The Apocalypse: Controversies and Meaning in Western History" *The Great Courses*, (Chantilly, Virginia: The Teaching Company 2011), 102.

364. John F. Walvoord, *The Revelation of Jesus Christ* (Galaxie Software, 2008), 52.

365. Crossway Bibles, *The ESV Study Bible* (Wheaton, IL: Crossway Bibles, 2008), 1581–1582.

366. Leland Ryken, Jim Wilhoit, Tremper Longman, et al., *Dictionary of Biblical Imagery*, electronic ed. (Downers Grove, IL: InterVarsity Press, 2000), 217.

367. Stephen R. Miller, vol. 18, *Daniel*, Includes Indexes., electronic ed., Logos Library System; The New American Commentary (Nashville: Broadman & Holman Publishers, 2001, c1994), 192.

368. Stephen R. Miller, *Daniel*, 196.

369. Henry Allan Ironside, *Lectures on Daniel the Prophet.*, 2d ed. (New York: Loizeaux Bros., 1953), 117.

370. Gleason L. Archer, Jr., "Daniel," *The Expositor's Bible Commentary, Volume 7: Daniel and the Minor Prophets*, ed. Frank E. Gaebelein (Grand Rapids, MI: Zondervan Publishing House, 1986), 85.

371. Gleason L. Archer, "Daniel," *The Expositor's Bible Commentary*, 86

372. John F. Walvoord, *Daniel: The Key To Prophetic Revelation* (Galaxie Software, 2008; 2008), 148.

373. Flavius Josephus and William Whiston, *The Works of Josephus: Complete and Unabridged*, Includes Index (Peabody: Hendrickson, 1996, c1987), Ant 11.337–338.

374. Leland Ryken, Jim Wilhoit, Tremper Longman, et al., *Dictionary of Biblical Imagery*, 368.

375. Stephen R. Miller, *Daniel*, 218.

376. John F. Walvoord, *Daniel*, 151.

377. Henry Grattan Guinness, *The Approaching End of the Age*, 8th edition (London: Hodder and Stoughten, 1882), 94.

378. Charles Spurgeon, "Commenting on Commentaries" *The Spurgeon Archives*, last accessed January 26, 2012, http://www.spurgeon.org/misc/c&c_c11.htm.

379. J. L. Haynes, "What is Futurism? What is Historicism?" *Historicism.com*, last accessed January, 26, 2012, http://www.historicism.com/tour/tour2.htm.

380. G. K. Beale, *The Book of Revelation: A Commentary on the Greek Text* (Grand Rapids, Michigan; Carlisle, Cumbria: W.B. Eerdmans; Paternoster Press, 1999), 46.

381. Larry Richards and Lawrence O. Richards, *The Teacher's Commentary* (Wheaton, IL: Victor Books, 1987), 1067.

382. "Genetic Fallacy," Fallacy Files, http://www.fallacyfiles.org/genefall.html

383. Manuel Lacunza, Edward Irving, *The Coming of Messiah in Glory and Majesty, Volume 1* (Seeley, 1827) pg. 252.

384. The entire set is available for free download here: http://www.archive.org/search.php?query=Horae%20Apocalypticae%20AND%20mediatype%3Atexts.

385. Ibid.

386. Edward Elliot, *Horae Apocalypticae vol 4*, (London: Seeley, Burnside, and Seely, 1847), 233

387. Edward Elliot, *Horae Apocalypticae vol 3*, 229.

388. Edward Elliot, *Horae Apocalypticae vol 4*, 237; viewable here: last accessed February 2, 2012, http://www.archive.org/details/horaeapocaly04elli.

389. Roy Adams, "The Pre-Advent Judgment" *Adventist World*, last accessed January 27, 2012, http://www.adventistworld.org/article.php?id=136.

390. Alexander C. Flick, *The Rise of the Medieval Church* (Manchester, NH: Ayer Publishing, 1964), 148–149.Document2

391. Philip Schaff, *History of the Christian Church*, c1916–1923 by Scribner's Sons., electronic ed. (Garland TX: Galaxie Software, 2000, c1916–1923), vol. 1, ch. XI, section 73.

392. See http://www.great-awakening.com/?page_id=12 for more information.

393. Bruce L. Shelley, *Church History in Plain Language*, Updated 2nd ed. (Dallas, TX: Word Pub., 1995), 175.

394. Clarence Goen, "Jonathan Edwards: A New Departure in Eschatology" (Church History 28, 1 Mr 1959), 29.

395. Jonathan Edwards, *The Works of Jonathan Edwards, Volume 1* (published by Utgivare for Logos Bible Software), 594.

396. Jonathan Edwards, *The Works of Jonathan Edwards, Volume 1*, PUBLIC DOMAIN, (Published by Utgivare for Logos Bible Software), Chapter XV page c.

397. "Christian Herald: Origins and Endings" *Christian Herald*, last accessed February 2, 2012, http://www.christianherald.org.uk/features.htm.

398. Michael M. Baxter, *Forty Prophetic Wonders Predicted in Daniel and Revelation* (New York, NY: The Christian Herald Bible House, 1918), 163.

399. Isaac Newton, *Observations upon the Prophecies of Daniel, and the Apocalypse of St. John* (London: 1733); viewable here: *Newton Project*, last accessed February 2, 2012, http://www.newtonproject.sussex.ac.uk/view/texts/normalized/THEM00204.

400. T. W. Tramm, *2012–2015: The Season of Return* (self-published 2010), 265.

401. Henry Grattan Guinness, *The City of the Seven Hills*, 155-156.

402. Keith Green, "The Catholic Chronicles," *Spiritually Smart*, last accessed January 24, 2012, http://www.spirituallysmart.com/green.html.

403. John MacArthur, "The Pope and the Papacy," *Grace to You*, May 1, 2055, http://www.gty.org/resources/sermons/90-291/the-pope-and-the-papacy.

404. Merriam-Webster, Inc., *Merriam-Webster's Collegiate Dictionary*, Eleventh ed. (Springfield, Mass.: Merriam-Webster, Inc., 2003), "sorcery."

405. Walter A. Elwell and Philip Wesley Comfort, *Tyndale Bible Dictionary*, Tyndale reference library, 844 (Wheaton, Ill.: Tyndale House Publishers, 2001), "Magic."

406. Walter A. Elwell and Philip Wesley Comfort, *Tyndale Bible Dictionary*, Tyndale reference library, 941, "Necromancy."

407. Henry Denzinger, Roy J. Deferrari, and Karl Rahner, *The Sources of Catholic Dogma* (St. Louis, MO: B. Herder Book Co., 1954), 262.

408. Gerald F. Hawthorne, Ralph P. Martin, and Daniel G. Reid, *Dictionary of Paul and His Letters* (Downers Grove, Ill.: InterVarsity Press, 1993), 200.

409. "Scripture," *The Original Catholic Encyclopedia*, last accessed January 24, 2012, http://oce.catholic.com/index.php?title=Scripture, section VI. Latin *"prohibemus, ne libros Veteris et Novi Testamenti laicis permittatur habere"* translated by Putnam.

410. Peter DeRosa, *Vicars of Christ*, 216.

411. Simon, *Papal Magic*, 34.

412. James P. Eckman, *Exploring Church History* (Wheaton, Ill.: Crossway, 2002), 50.

413. Ludwig Ott, *Fundamentals of Catholic Dogma*, (St. Louis: B. Herder Book Company, 1957), 340.

414. Ludwig Ott, *Fundamentals of Catholic Dogma*, 370.

415. Henry Denzinger, Roy J. Deferrari, and Karl Rahner, *The Sources of Catholic Dogma*, 267.

416. "hocus-pocus," *Online Etymology Dictionary*, last accessed January 19, 2012, http://www.etymonline.com/index.php?term=hocus-pocus.

417. St. Thomas, *Summa Theol.,* lib. III in Suppl., q. 40, a4, 5.
418. John A. O'Brien, *The Faith of Millions: The Credentials of the Catholic Religion,* New and rev. ed. (Huntington, Ind.: Our Sunday Visitor, 1974), 255–256.
419. Reviews of this book viewable here: *Amazon.com,* product page, last accessed January 24, 2012, http://www.amazon.com/Faith-Millions-John-Anthony-OBrien/product-reviews/0879738308/ref=cm_cr_dp_synop?ie=UTF8&showViewpoints=0&sortBy=bySubmissionDateDescending#R38Y9EJCVD3E8.
420. Walter A. Elwell and Philip Wesley Comfort, *Tyndale Bible Dictionary,* Tyndale reference library, 844.
421. Confraternity of Christian Doctrine. Board of Trustees, Catholic Church. National Conference of Catholic Bishops and United States Catholic Conference. Administrative Board, *The New American Bible : Translated from the Original Languages With Critical Use of All the Ancient Sources and the Revised New Testament,* Heb 9:24–28 (Confraternity of Christian Doctrine, 1996, c1986).
422. Henry Denzinger, Roy J. Deferrari, and Karl Rahner, *The Sources of Catholic Dogma,* 292.
423. John A. O'Brien, *The Faith of Millions,* 256.
424. Charles H. Spurgeon, "Jesus, the Delight of Heaven," no. 1225, *Spurgeon's Sermons: Volume 21,* electronic ed., Logos Library System; Spurgeon's Sermons (Albany, OR: Ages Software, 1998).
425. Clinton E. Arnold, *Zondervan Illustrated Bible Backgrounds Commentary Volume 3: Romans to Philemon.* (Grand Rapids, MI: Zondervan, 2002) 463.
426. "Council of Illiberi, Cannon 33," as quoted in: Henry Denzinger, Roy J. Deferrari, and Karl Rahner, *The Sources of Catholic Dogma,* 25.
427. John Calvin and Henry Beveridge, *Institutes of the Christian Religion,* electronic ed., IV, xii (Garland, TX: Galaxie Software, 1999). 23.
428. Phil Brennan, "Homosexual Culture Undercuts Priesthood" *News Max,* April 5, 2002, http://archive.newsmax.com/archives/articles/2002/4/4/192430.shtml.
429. Jason Berry, *Render Unto Rome* (NY: Crown, 2011), 225.
430. John-Henry Westen, "German Bishops Caught in Massive Porn Scandal—Why Didn't They Listen to the Faithful?" *Life Site News,* October 31, 2011, http://www.lifesitenews.com/home/print_article/news/32186.
431. Ibid.
432. "Relics of John Paul II Arrive in Columbia," *Catholic News Agency,* January 20, 2012, http://www.catholicnewsagency.com/news/relics-of-john-paul-ii-arrive-in-colombia.
433. Edward McNamara, "Relics in the Altar," *Zenit Daily,* May 3, 2005, http://www.ewtn.com/library/liturgy/zlitur80.htm.
434. "Altar Cavity," *The Catholic Encyclopedia,* as quoted by *New Advent,* last accessed February 2, 2012, http://www.newadvent.org/cathen/01351d.htm.
435. John Barnett, "Romanism, Relics and Purgatory" (he counted based on official church records at 10:25 into the recording he mentions the hand as well as many other impossible duplicates), September 12, 1999, http://www.sermonaudio.com/sermoninfo.asp?SID=122081140324.

436. "Relics," *Gale Encyclopedia of Religion* vol. 11 (Farmington MI: Macmillian Reference USA, 2005), 7686.
437. Ibid, 7689.
438. Carol Glatz, "Hotline to Heaven: How Relics Connect People to Community of Saints," *Catholic News Service*, September 8, 2011, http://www.catholicnews.com/data/stories/cns/1103566.htm.
439. "Necromancy" *Gale Encyclopedia of Religion* vol. 10 (Farmington MI: Macmillian Reference USA, 2005), 6451.
440. Henry Denzinger, Roy J. Deferrari, and Karl Rahner, *The Sources of Catholic Dogma* (St. Louis, MO: B. Herder Book Co., 1954), 264.
441. Millard J. Erickson, *Christian Theology*, 2nd ed. (Grand Rapids, Mich.: Baker Book House, 1998), 1100–11001.
442. Henry Denzinger, Roy J. Deferrari, and Karl Rahner, *The Sources of Catholic Dogma* (St. Louis, MO: B. Herder Book Co., 1954), 247.
443. Pope John Paul II, "Apostolic Exhortation Reconciliation and Penance," December 2, 1984, last accessed January 27, 2012, http://www.vatican.va/holy_father/john_paul_ii/apost_exhortations/documents/hf_jp-ii_exh_02121984_reconciliatio-et-paenitentia_en.html.
444. Matt Slick, "Sorcery in the Roman Catholic Church," *CARM*, last accessed January 20, 2012, http://carm.org/sorcery-roman-catholic.
445. Ibid.
446. Theodore Alois Buckley, *The Canons and Decrees of the Council of Trent* (London: George Routledge and Co., 1851), 43.
447. R.C. Sproul, *Faith Alone: The Evangelical Doctrine of Justification*, electronic ed. (Grand Rapids: Baker Books, 2000, c1995), 179.
448. Theodore Alois Buckley, *The Canons and Decrees of the Council of Trent*, 45.
449. "How to Become a Catholic" Catholic.com, last accessed January 27, 2012, http://www.catholic.com/documents/how-to-become-a-catholic.
450. Eric Svendsen, "How to Obtain Eternal Life," *Real Clear Theology Blog*, April 12, 2009, http://ntrminblog.blogspot.com/.
451. "How to Become a Catholic" *Catholic.com*, last accessed January 27, 2012, http://www.catholic.com/documents/how-to-become-a-catholic.
452. John XXIII, *Address* of 11 October 1962: , In truth, at the present time, it is necessary that Christian doctrine in its entirety, and with nothing taken away from it, is accepted with renewed enthusiasm, and serene and tranquil adherence delivered to the exact words of conceiving and reducing to the form, which especially shines forth from the acts of the Council of Trent and the First Vatican Council." "ALLOCUTIO IOANNIS PP. XXIII IN SOLLEMNI SS. CONCILII INAUGURATIONE" Section 6 final paragraph translated from Latin by CD Putnam http://www.vatican.va/holy_father/john_xxiii/speeches/1962/documents/hf_j-xxiii_spe_19621011_opening-council_lt.html
453. "Catechism of the Catholic Church," 460, viewable here: last accessed January 30, 2012, http://www.vatican.va/archive/ENG0015/__P1J.HTM.
454. "Pope John Paul II Kissing a Copy of the Koran" *Ex Catholics*, last accessed January 24, 2012, http://www.excatholics.org/2010/01/04/pope-john-paul-ii-kissing-a-copy-of-the-koran/.

455. Lorenzo di Cadore, "Pope: Other Christian Denominations Not True Churches," *Fox News*, July 10, 2007, http://www.foxnews.com/printer_friendly_story/0,3566,288841,00.html.

456. "Catechism of the Catholic Church," section 2117, last accessed January 24, 2012, http://www.scborromeo.org/ccc/p3s2c1a1.htm.

457. Carol Glatz, "Hotline to Heaven: How Relics Connect People to Community of Saints."

458. Pope Benedict XVI, "Solemnity of Mary, Mother of God" *The Vatican Today*, January 1, 2012, http://www.news.va/en/news/solemnity-of-mary-mother-of-god-pope-benedicts-hom.

459. Pope Benedict XVI, "Solemnity of the Immaculate of the Blessed Virgin Mary," *Libreria Editrice Vaticana*, December 8, 2011, http://www.vatican.va/holy_father/benedict_xvi/speeches/2011/december/documents/hf_ben-xvi_spe_20111208_immacolata_en.html.

460. Ludwig Ott, *Fundamentals of Catholic Dogma* (St. Louis: B. Herder Book Company, 1957), 203.

461. "Mary 'remained a virgin in conceiving her Son, a virgin in giving birth to him, a virgin in carrying him, a virgin in nursing him at her breast, always a virgin,'" *Catechism of the Catholic Church*, paragraph 510. Viewable here: last accessed January 24, 2012, http://www.vatican.va/archive/ENG0015/__P1K.HTM.

462. Ludwig Ott, *Fundamentals of Catholic Dogma*, 203.

463. Ludwig Ott, *Fundamentals of Catholic Dogma*, 203.

464. John Saward, *Cradle of Redeeming Love: The Theology of the Christmas Mystery* (San Francisco: Ignatius Press, 2002), 206.

465. Johannes P. Louw and Eugene Albert Nida, *Greek-English Lexicon of the New Testament: Based on Semantic Domains, Volume 1*, electronic ed. of the 2nd edition (New York, NY: United Bible Societies, 1996), 352.

466. Johannes P. Louw and Eugene Albert Nida, *Greek-English Lexicon of the New Testament*, 112.

467. *Lunem Gentum 66* Vatican Council II, viewable here: last accessed January 24, 2012, http://www.vatican.va/archive/hist_councils/ii_vatican_council/documents/vat-ii_const_19641121_lumen-gentium_en.html.

468. Pope Pius IX, *The Immaculate Conception*, as quoted in Ludwig Ott, *Fundamentals of Catholic Dogma*, 199.

469. Pope Pius IX, *The Immaculate Conception*, section "The Definition," paragraph 2, viewable here: last accessed January 7, 2012, http://www.papalencyclicals.net/Pius09/p9ineff.htm.

470. Saint Thomas Aquinas and Fathers of the English Dominican Province, *Summa Theologica*, translation of: Summa Theologica.; Includes Index., Complete English ed. (Bellingham, WA: Logos Research Systems, Inc., 2009), STh., III q.27 a.1 obj. 1.

471. Ludwig Ott, *Fundamentals of Catholic Dogma*, 208.

472. Henry Denzinger, Roy J. Deferrari, and Karl Rahner, *The Sources of Catholic Dogma* (St. Louis, MO: B. Herder Book Co., 1954), 647.

473. Michel Esbroeck, "Assumption of the Virgin," as quoted in *The Anchor Bible Dictionary* ed. David Noel Freedman (New York, NY: Doubleday, 1996), 6:856.

474. "The Discourse of Theodosius" as quoted in *The Apocryphal New Testament: Being the Apocryphal Gospels, Acts, Epistles, and Apocalypses* ed. Montague Rhodes James (Bellingham, WA: Logos Research Systems, Inc., 2009), 199. Abbreviated by Cris D. Putnam.

475. Michel Esbroeck, "Assumption of the Virgin" as quoted in *The Anchor Bible Dictionary*, 6:856.

476. Mark A. Pivarunas, "Why Catholics Honor the Blessed Virgin Mary," *The Religious Congregation of Mary Immaculate Queen*, September 8, 1994, http://www.cmri.org/94prog9.htm.

477. James Swanson, *Dictionary of Biblical Languages With Semantic Domains: Greek (New Testament)*, electronic ed. (Oak Harbor: Logos Research Systems, Inc., 1997), 3301.

478. James Swanson, *Dictionary of Biblical Languages With Semantic Domains*, 1525.

479. Scott P. Richert, "Prayer of Pope Pius XII: In Honor of the Immaculate Conception," last accessed January 5, 2012, http://catholicism.about.com/od/tothevirginmary/qt/Honor_Immacula.htm.

480. Alphonse Liquori, "The Glories of Mary: An Explanation of Salve Regina," 1931, *Catholic Tradition*, last accessed January 5, 2012, http://www.catholictradition.org/Mary/glories.htm.

481. Ludwig Ott, *Fundamentals of Catholic Dogma*, 213.

482. Pope Leo XIII, Rosary Encyclical, "Octobri mense" (1891) as quoted in Ludwig Ott, *Fundamentals of Catholic Dogma*, 213.

483. Pope Pius IX, "Ineffabilis Deus," *Papal Encyclicals Online*, December 8, 1854, viewable here: last accessed January 5, 2012, http://www.papalencyclicals.net/Pius09/p9ineff.htm.

484. Ludwig Ott, *Fundamentals of Catholic Dogma*, 213.

485. Ludwig Ott, *Fundamentals of Catholic Dogma*, 213.

486. Walter Martin, *The Roman Catholic Church in History* (Livingston, NJ: Christian Research Institute, 1960), 49.

487. Pope Benedict XV, Apostolic Letter *Inter Soldalica*, AAS 1918, 181.

488. Kenneth L Woodward and Andrew Murr, "Hail Mary," *Newsweek*, Vol. 130 Issue 8, (08/25/97), 48.

489. Amsterdam, "Lady of All Nations," channeled messages by Ida Peerdeman. For more information, see: last accessed, January 24, 2012, http://www.ladyofallnations.org/dogma.htm.

490. M. Eugene Boring, *Revelation, Interpretation: A Bible Commentary for Teaching and Preaching* (Louisville: John Knox, 1989), 151.

491. Epiphanius *Adv. Haereses* LXXIX; PG 42 [1863] 741, 752 cited in C. Houtman "Queen of heaven" in, *Dictionary of Deities and Demons in the Bible DDD*, 2nd extensively rev. ed. edited by K. van der Toorn, Bob Becking and Pieter Willem van der Horst (Leiden; Boston; Grand Rapids, Mich.: Brill; Eerdmans, 1999), 679.

492. John MacArthur, "Exposing the Idolatry of Mary Worship: What the Bible Says," *Grace to You*, April 23, 2006, http://www.gty.org/resources/sermons/90-317/exposing-the-idolatry-of-mary-worship-what-the-bible-says.

493. "How to Pray the Rosary," *Global Catholic Network*, last accessed January 9, 2012, http://www.ewtn.com/devotionals/prayers/rosary/how_to.htm.

494. Charles Dickson, *A Protestant Pastor Looks at Mary* (Huntington, Indiana: Our Sunday Visitor Publishing Division, 1996), 103.

495. Charles Dickson, *A Protestant Pastor Looks at Mary*, 103.

496. Simon Caldwell, "Sex Lies and Apparitions," *The Spectator* (London: Oct 4, 2008).

497. Charles Dickson, *A Protetstant Pastor Looks at Mary*, 104.

498. Jim Tetlow, "Queen of All," *Journal of Biblical Apologetics: Part 2—Modern Roman Catholicism* (Las Vegas, NV: Christian Scholar's Press, Inc., 2001), 69.

499. Ibid.

500. Jim Tetlow, "Queen of All," *Journal of Biblical Apologetics*, 68.

501. James Anderson, "Virgin's Devotees Build Mystical City Complex," *Expositor* (Brantford, Ont: July 31, 1999), A.6.

502. Benjamin Mann, "Wisconsin Chapel Approved as First U.S. Marian Apparition Site," *Catholic News Agency*, December 9, 2010, http://www.catholicnewsagency.com/news/wisconsin-chapel-approved-as-first-us-marian-apparition-site/.

503. Alex Morrell, "Virgin Mary Shrine in Wis. Surprised by Soaring Attendance," last updated July 6, 2011, http://www.usatoday.com/news/religion/2011-07-06-good-help-virgin-mary-shrine-wisconsin_n.htm.

504. Jim Tetlow, "Queen of All," *Journal of Biblical Apologetics*, 68.

505. "About the Grotto," *Mount St. Mary's University*, last accessed Januray 9, 2012, http://www.msmary.edu/grotto/about/. Attendance as cited in: Jim Tetlow, "Queen of All," *Journal of Biblical Apologetics*, 68.

506. Sara Horsfall, "The Experience of Marian Apparitions and the Mary Cult," *The Social Science Journal* (Volume 37, Number 3, 2000), 375–384.

507. Ibid.; summarized by Putnam.

508. Ibid, 384.

509. Richard J. Beyer, *Medjugorje Day By Day* (Notre Dame, IN: Ave Maria Press, 1993, April 6th meditation), as cited in Jim Tetlow, "Queen of All," *Journal of Biblical Apologetics*, 70.

510. Charles Dickson, *A Protestant Pastor Looks at Mary*, 60.

511. Robert Moynihan, "The Vatican Synod on the Middle East Begins," *Spero News*, October 10, 2010, http://www.speroforum.com/a/41366/The-Vatican-Synod-on-the-Middle-East-begins.

512. Chiara Santomiero, "Prelate: Jerusalem Can't Belong to Just One State," *Zenit: The World Seen from Rome*, October 12, 2012, http://www.zenit.org/article-30628?l=english.

513. James Swanson, *Dictionary of Biblical Languages With Semantic Domains: Greek (New Testament)*, electronic ed. (Oak Harbor: Logos Research Systems, Inc., 1997), 948 χρι.

514. P4 is likely the earliest existing copy of Luke's Gospel but his silence on the fall of Jerusalem in AD 70 leads most to conclude it was written prior: see http://en.wikipedia.org/wiki/Papyrus_4.

515. Leon Morris, vol. 20, *Revelation: An Introduction and Commentary*, Originally published: The book of Revelation. 1987., Tyndale New Testament Commentaries, 153 (Downers Grove, IL: InterVarsity Press, 1987).

516. Don Stefano Gobbi, *To The Priests: Our Lady's Beloved Sons*, St. Francis, ME, The National Headquarters of the Marian Movement of Priests in the United States of America, 1998, p. 333. Message given to Father Gobbi who is the head of the Marian Movement of Priests. Message received on December 8, 1982. Text from an article entitled, "The Woman of Revelation 12," *Eternal Productions*, last accessed February 7, 2012, http://www.eternal-productions. org/PDFS/Revelation12Woman.pdf.

517. Benedict XVI, "Solemnity of the Immaculate of the Blessed Virgin Mary," Thursday, 8 December 2011, http://www.vatican.va/holy_father/benedict_xvi/speeches/2011/december/documents/hf_ben-xvi_spe_20111208_immacolata_en.html.

518. Arnold G. Fruchtenbaum, *Israelology: The Missing Link in Systematic Theology*, Previous ed.: 1993., Rev. ed. (Tustin, Calif.: Ariel Ministries, 1994), 837.

519. Ibid., 52.

520. John Chrysostom, *Eight Homilies Against the Jews* (Adversus Judeaus), Homily VI Section II Paragraph 10, *Fordham University*, last accessed February 7, 2012, http://www.fordham.edu/halsall/source/chrysostom-jews6-homily6.asp.

521. Origen, as quoted in *Rome Has Spoken… A Guide to Forgotten Papal Statements and How They Have Changed Through the Centuries*, edited by Maureen Fiedler and Linda Rabben (New York, NY: Crossroad Publishing, 1998), 67.

522. Maureen Fiedler and Linda Rabben, *Rome Has Spoken…*, 200.

523. Everett Ferguson, *Church History Volume One: From Christ to Pre-Reformation: The Rise and Growth of the Church in Its Cultural, Intellectual, and Political Context: 1*, (Zondervan, 2009, Kindle ed.), Kindle location: 6358.

524. Ibid., Kindle locations 7799–7803).

525. Roger of Hoveden, "The Persecution of Jews, 1189," *Medieval Soucebook*, viewable here: last accessed February 7, 2012, http://www.fordham.edu/halsall/source/hoveden1189b.asp.

526. Canons 68, 69: Jews and Moslems shall wear a special dress to enable them to be distinguished from Christians.

527. Maureen Fiedler and Linda Rabben, *Rome Has Spoken…*, 69.

528. Ibid., 69.

529. Cushing B. Hassell, *History of the Church of God* (Middletown NY: Gilbert Beebe's Sons, 1886), 470.

530. Reverend J. A. Wylie, *Genius and Influence of the Papacy*, Book III - Chapter III, viewable here: *JesusIsLord.com*, last accessed February 7, 2012, http://www.jesus-is-lord.com/papacy/03-03.htm.

531. W. C. Brownlee, *Letters in the Roman Catholic controversy* (New York, NY: 1834), 347–348; viewable here: last accessed February 9, 2012, http://www.archive.org/details/lettersinromanca00brow.

532. Translated by Putnam from Latin Text available here: http://www.ariberti.

it/scuola/ebrei/documenti_chiesa_ebrei/cum_nimis_absurdum.htm; also see http://en.wikipedia.org/wiki/Cum_nimis_absurdum.

533. Edward H. Flannery, *The Anguish of the Jews* (New York, NY: Paulist Press, 2004), 146.

534. "Libel Against Luther," *Frontline*, last accessed February 7, 2012, http://www.frontline.org.za/articles/libel_againstluther.htm.

535. Martin Brecht and James L. Schaaf, *Martin Luther the Preservation of the Church Vol. 3 1532–1546* (Minneapolis, MN: Fortress Press, 1999), 349.

536. Ibid., 349.

537. Pope Benedict XIV, *A Quo Primum*, promulgated on June 14, 1751: viewable here, last accessed February 7, 2012, http://www.papalencyclicals.net/Ben14/b14aquo.htm.

538. Adolf Hitler, *Mein Kampf* (New York, NY: Hurst And Blackett Ltd, 1939), 7.

539. Leo H. Lehmann, "The Jesuits and the Protocols of Zion," last accessed February 3, 2012, http://www.historicism.com/misc/protocols.htm.

540. "VATICAN CITY: Pope to Get Jerusalem?" *Time Magazine*, July 8, 1940: viewable here: last accessed February 7, 2012, http://www.time.com/time/magazine/article/0,9171,795047,00.html.

541. Edmond Paris, *The Secret History of the Jesuits,* 1975; republished as an e-book, available here: http://arcticbeacon.com/books/Paris-The_Secret_History_of_Jesuits%281975%29.pdf, 7.

542. Ibid., 48.

543. Arnold G. Fruchtenbaum, *Israelology: The Missing Link in Systematic Theology,* 837.

544. Lewis Sperry Chafer, *Systematic Theology*, Originally published: Dallas, TX: Dallas Seminary Press, 1947–1948., 4:353–354 (Grand Rapids, MI: Kregel Publications, 1993).

545. Giulio Meotti, "Expose: The Vatican Wants to Lay its Hands on Jerusalem," *Israel National News*, December 15, 2011, http://www.israelnationalnews.com/News/News.aspx/150757#.TzV9aORnDmd.

546. See: "Rabbi Kaduri Reveals Name of the Messiah," last accessed February 10, 2012, http://www.cyber-synagogue.com/rabbi_kaduri_reveals_name_of_Messiah.htm.

547. Arnold G. Fruchtenbaum, *Israelology: The Missing Link in Systematic Theology*, Previous ed.: 1993., Rev. ed. (Tustin, Calif.: Ariel Ministries, 1994), 716.

548. Robert Laird Harris, Gleason Leonard Archer, and Bruce K. Waltke, *Theological Wordbook of the Old Testament*, electronic ed. (Chicago: Moody Press, 1999, c1980), 195.

549. See: http://www.joshuaproject.net/.

550. "Fastest-Growing Christian Population," *Worldmag*, last accessed February 10, 2012, http://www.worldmag.com/articles/13748 .

551. Ali Sina,"Islam in Fast Demise: In Africa Alone Everyday, 16,000 Muslims Leave Islam," last accessed February 10, 2012, http://www.faithfreedom.org/oped/sina31103.htm.

552. Brent Kinman, *History, Design, and the End of Time: God's Plan for the World* (Nashville, TN: Broadman & Holman Pub, 2000), 71.

553. Ava Thomas, "Among Israeli Jews, 20,000 Embrace Christ," *Baptist Press*, May 26, 2011, http://www.sbcbaptistpress.org/BPnews.asp?ID=35389 .

554. "United Nations General Assembly Resolution 181," *The Avalon Project at Yale Law School*, November 29, 1947; viewable here: last accessed February 12, 2012, http://www.yale.edu/lawweb/avalon/un/res181.htm#back5\.

555. David Ben-Gurion, "Israel's Proclamation of Independence May 14, 1948," in Bernard Reich, *A Brief History of Israel* (NY: Infobase Publishing, 2008), 47.

556. Daniel Pinner, "Judaism: The Six Day War: Recognizing the Miracle," *Israel National News*, May 16, 2007, http://www.israelnationalnews.com/Articles/Article.aspx/7133#.TzaHB-RnDmc .

557. Minutes from Bilateral and Trilateral US-PAL-ISR Sessions Post Annapolis, Tuesday, 29th July 2008: viewable here: *Al Jazeera*, last accessed February 7, 2012, http://www.aljazeera.com/palestinepapers/.

558. "Vatican Secretary of State Speaks with Condoleezza Rice about Christians in Middle East, Iraq," *Catholic News Agency*, last accessed February 13, 2012, http://www.catholicnewsagency.com/news/vatican_secretary_of_state_speaks_with_condoleezza_rice_about_christians_in_middle_east_iraq/.

559. Thomas Horn, *Apollyon Rising 2012*, 60–61.

560. Levitt Letter 21:2 (Feb 1999), 3 as cited in Randall Price, *The Coming Last Days' Temple* (Eugene, OR: Harvest House Publishers, 1999), 475.

561. Randall Price, *The Coming Last Days' Temple* (Eugene, OR: Harvest House Publishers, 1999), 481.

562. *Nostra Aetate*, last accessed February 9, 2012, http://www.vatican.va/archive/hist_councils/ii_vatican_council/documents/vat-ii_decl_19651028_nostra-aetate_en.html.

563. Ibid.

564. Ibid.

565. Peter Kreeft, *Ecumenical Jihad: Ecumenism and the Culture War* (San Francisco: Ignatius Press, 1996), 103–104.

566. Peter Kreeft, *Ecumenical Jihad*, 86.

567. "Pope Leads World Prayer Day," *BBC News*, January 24, 2004, http://news.bbc.co.uk/2/hi/europe/1779135.stm.

568. *Nostra Aetate*.

569. Jack Bemporad and Michael Shevack, *Our Age: the Historic New Era of Christian-Jewish Understanding* (Hyde Park, NY: New City Press, 1996), 17.

570. "The Vatican Opposes Jewish Home in Palestine," *Jewish Virtual Library*, June 22, 1943, viewable here: last accessed February 9, 2012, http://www.jewishvirtuallibrary.org/jsource/anti-semitism/vatpal.html.

571. As cited by Joel Bainerman, "The Vatican Agenda: How Does the Vatican View the Legitimacy of Israel's Claims to Jerusalem?" last accessed February 13, 2012, http://www.joelbainerman.com/pages/vatican.html.

572. Barry Chamish, *Save Israel* (Israel: Modlin House, 2001), 117.

573. Joel Bainerman, "Secrets of Oslo," last accessed January 10, 2012, http://www. joelbainerman.com/articles/chronology.asp.
574. J. Michael Parker, "PLO Pact Could Bring Israel, Holy See Together," *San Antonio Express-News* (San Antonio, TX: Sep 25, 1993), 11C.
575. See: http://www.mfa.gov.il/MFA/MFAArchive/1990_1999/1993/12/ Fundamental+Agreement+-+Israel-Holy+See.htm.
576. Barry Chamish, *Save Israel,* 117.
577. Joel Bainerman, "The Vatican Agenda."
578. John L. Allen, "Israel Again Delays Negotiations with Holy See," *National Catholic Reporter* (Jan 21, 2005), 10.
579. Robert Bridge, "Vatican Rejects 'Chosen People' Claim, Calls on Israel to End 'Occupation,'" *RT*, October 25, 2010, http://rt.com/politics/vatican-israel-palestinians-catholic/print/.
580. Jonah Mandel, "Israel, Vatican Reach Understanding on Real Estate Taxation in Holy Land," *Jerusalem Post* (Jun 16, 2011), 6.
581. Ibid, 6.
582. Giulio Meotti, "Don't bow to the Vatican Op-ed: State of Israel Should Not be Giving Up its Sovereignty Over Holy Sites in Jerusalem," February 4, 2012, http://www.ynetnews.com/articles/0,7340,L-4185027,00.html.
583. Barry Chamish, "On Top of Mount Zion, All Coveted By Rome," *Rense,* December 17, 2005, http://www.rense.com/general69/topmz.htm.
584. Joel Bainerman, "The Vatican Agenda"; also viewable here: last accessed February 15, 2012, http://www.redmoonrising.com/chamish/vaticanagenda. htm.
585. "The Last Prophecy of St. Malachy Decoded," October 14, 2008, http://www. gradale.com/malachy.htm.
586. Christian J. Pinto on "Noise of Thunder Radio: Vatican Secret Archives," January 4, 2012, (27:55–30:15); reader can access recording here: http://www. noiseofthunder.com/noise-of-thunder-radio-show/2012/1/4/notradio_1412. html.
587. René Thibaut, *La Mystérieuse Prophétie des Papes,* 21–22, translation Putnam.
588. "The Global Ruling Class," *The Economist,* April 24, 2008, http://www. economist.com/books/displaystory.cfm?story_id=11081878.
589. Stanley Monteith, "The Occult Hierarchy: Part 1," *Radio Liberty,* May, 2005, http://www.radioliberty.com/nlmay05.html.
590. Mark Morford, "Is Obama an Enlightened Being?" *San Francisco Gate,* June 6, 2008, http://www.sfgate.com/cgi-bin/article.cgi?f=/g/a/2008/06/06/ notes060608.DTL.
591. Dahleen Glanton, "Some See God's Will in Obama Win," *Chicago Tribune,* November 29, 2008, http://www.chicagotribune.com/news/nationworld/chi-obama-godsend_glantonnov29,0,7660180.story.
592. Dinesh Sharma, "Obama's Satyagraha: Or, Did Obama Swallow the Mahatma?" *OpEdNews,* June 27, 2008, http://www.opednews.com/articles/Obama-s-Satyagraha—Or—Di-by-Dinesh-Sharma-080626-187.html.

593. Steve Davis, "Barack's Appeal Is Actually Messianic," *Journal Gazette*, March 31, 2008, http://www.jg-tc.com/articles/2008/03/31/opinion/letters/doc47f0586a2fflb441328510.txt.

594. Chris Matthews, *MSNBC*, February 12, 2008, http://newsbusters.org/stories/Matthews-obama-speech-caused-thrill-going-my-leg.html?q=blogs/brad-wilmouth/2008/02/13/Matthews-obama-speech-caused-thrill-going-my-leg.

595. *Daily Kos*, April 26, 2008, http://www.dailykos.com/storyonly/2008/4/26/83118/7371/654/503796.

596. Lynn Sweet, *Chicago Sun Times*, March 21, 2008, http://blogs.suntimes.com/sweet/2008/03/sweet_richardson_in_endorsing.html#comments.

597. Gary Hart, *Huffington Post*, February 13, 2008, http://www.huffingtonpost.com/gary-hart/politics-as-transcendence_b_86490.html.

598. Ezra Klein, "Obama's Gift," January 3, 2008, *Prospect.org* (brackets in original *Apollyon Rising 2012*, not in original article), http://www.prospect.org/csnc/blogs/ezraklein_archive?month=01&year=2008&base_name=obamas_gift.

599. Gerald Campbell, "Obama: On Toughness and Success in Politics," *First Things First*, December 22, 2007, http://geraldcampbell.typepad.com/impact/2007/12/recently-on-npr.html.

600. Janny Scott, "In 2000, a Streetwise Veteran Schooled a Bold Young Obama," *New York Times*, September 9, 2007, http://www.nytimes.com/2007/09/09/us/politics/09obama.html?pagewanted=print.

601. Micah Tillman, "Plato, Obama, and Peters on the Question of Mighty Pens," *The Free Liberal*, July 10, 2008, http://www.freeliberal.com/archives/003418.html.

602. Representative Jesse Jackson, Jr., "On Obama's Winning the Democratic Presidential Nomination," *Politico*, June 5, 2008, http://dyn.politico.com/printstory.cfm?uuid=55D13D94-3048-5C12-00E851454E822F1E.

603. Thomas Horn, *Apollyon Rising 2012: The Lost Symbol Found and the Final Mystery of the Great Seal Revealed* (Crane, MO: Defender Publishing, 2009), 93–96.

604. Michelle Boorstein and Jacqueline Salmon, "A Rush of Spiritual Outreach, Spirited Partying," *Washington Post*, January 11, 2009, C04.

605. Bob Unruh, "CNN Likens Inauguration to 'Hajj,'" *WorldNetDaily*, January 24, 2009.

606. Drew Zahn, "Obama Triumphal Entry: Gentle, Riding on a Donkey," *WorldNetDaily*, January 24, 2009.

607. "Doorway Anointed with Oil for Obama," *EURweb*, January 12, 2009, http://www.eurweb.com/story/eur50011.cfm.

608. "Barack Obama Versus Fundamentalism & Religious Sectarianism," YouTube video, 4:57, posted by "thruthem," June 14, 2008, http://uk.youtube.com/watch?v=LXcvbnzNIjg&feature=related.

609. Terry Neal, "A New Faith Needed to Unify Humankind as We March Into Future," *Hamilton Spectator*, February 14, 2009, http://www.thespec.com/Opinions/article/513536.

610. *Catechism of the Catholic Church* (Second Edition) 460: The Word became flesh to make us *"partakers of the divine nature"*:78 "For this is why the Word became man, and the Son of God became the Son of man: so that man, by entering into communion with the Word and thus receiving divine sonship, might become a son of God."79 "For the Son of God became man so that we might become God."80 "The only-begotten Son of God, wanting to make us sharers in his divinity, assumed our nature, so that he, made man, might make men gods"81 (http://www.scborromeo.org/ccc/p122a3p1.htm#I).

611. "Many Have Asked: Is Obama the Anti-Christ? Famed Novelist Michael O'Brien Answers," *LifeSiteNews.com*, November 3, 2008, http://www.lifesitenews.com/ldn/2008/nov/08110307.html.

612. "Is Obama Speech Site Contaminated by Nazi Past?" *Spiegel Online*, July 20, 2008, http://www.spiegel.de/international/germany/0,1518,566920,00.html.

613. Ibid.

614. As quoted by J. R. Church, *Prophecy in the News Magazine* (December, 2008), 36.

615. Ibid.

616. Ibid.

617. Amir Taheri, "Obama and Ahmadinejad," *Forbes*, October 26, 2008, http://www.forbes.com/2008/10/26/obama-iran-ahmadinejad-oped-cx_at_1026taheri_print.html.

618. Ibid.

619. See http://www.youtube.com/watch?v=Zr4VZ8xCzOg&eurl=http%3A%2F%2Fwww%2Eraidersnewsupdate%2Ecom%2F&feature=player_embedded.

620. Manly P. Hall, *The Secret Destiny of America*, (Los Angeles, CA: The Philosophical Research Society, Inc., 1991), 128–131.

621. Ibid., 132–134.

622. Jim Marrs, *Rule by Secrecy*, (New York, NY: HarperCollins, 2000), 249–250.

623. Ibid.

624. "Come Worship with Us," *Liberal Catholic Church International*, last accessed January 19, 2012, http://www.lccireland.com/ourbeliefs.htm.

625. Julia M. H. Smith, *Europe After Rome: A New Cultural History 500–1000* (Oxford: Oxford University Press, 2005), 77.

626. Helena Petrovna Blavatsky, *Star Angel Worship in the Roman Catholic Church* (Whitefish, MT: Kessinger Publishing, 2003), 24. See: http://books.google.com/books?id=0RFeM8WHw5kC&q=The+Archangels+were+now+urging+the+Popes#v=onepage&q&f=false.

627. Manly P. Hall, *Secret Teachings of All Ages: An Encyclopedic Outline of Masonic, Hermetic, Qabbalistic and Rosicrucian Symbolical Philosophy* (Lulu.com, 2005), 589.

628. Ibid.

629. "MASONIC SYMBOLS OF POWER IN THEIR SEAT OF POWER—WASHINGTON, D.C.," *CuttingEdge.org*, last accessed January 19, 2012, http://www.cuttingedge.org/n1040.html.

630. "The Most Approved Plan: The Competition for the Capitol's Design," *Library of Congress*, last accessed January 18, 2011, http://www.loc. gov/exhibits/us.capitol/s2.html.

631. David Ovason, *The Secret Architecture of Our Nation's Capital: The Masons and the Building of Washington DC* (New York, NY: HarperCollins, 2000), 73.

632. Ibid., 71.

633. Ibid., 361.

634. Julie Duin, "Ergo, We're Virgo," October 16, 2000, *Insight on the News*, http://findarticles.com/p/articles/mi_m1571/is_38_16/ai_66241134.

635. David Ovason, *The Secret Architecture of Our Nation's Capitol*, 71.

636. Foster Bailey, *The Spirit of Freemasonry* (New York, NY: Lucis Press, 1957).

637. Albert Pike, *Morals and Dogma of the Ancient and Accepted Scottish Rite of Freemasonry* (Masonic Publishing Company, 1874), 104.

638. Thomas Horn, *Apollyon Rising 2012*, 120–122.

639. President George H. W. Bush, Address before Joint Session of Congress on the State of the Union (January 29, 1991).

640. Henry Kissinger, "The Chance for a New World Order," *Real Clear Politics*, January 13, 2009, http://www.realclearpolitics.com/articles/2009/01/the_chance_for_a_new_world_ord.html.

641. Transcribed from a tape recording made by one of the Swiss delegates.

642. The full text of "Toward Reforming the International Financial and Monetary Systems in the Context of a Global Public Authority" can be read at: *Zenit: The World Seen from Rome*, October 24, 2011, last accessed January 19, 2012, http://www.zenit.org/article-33718?l=english.

643. Carl Teichrib, "The Vatican's Quest for a World Political Authority," *Forcing Change Magazine*, Vol 3, Issue 8, September, 2009.

644. Ibid.

645. Cliff Kincaid, "Who Will Probe the U.N.-Vatican Connection?" *Accuracy in Media*, August 4, 2009, http://www.aim.org/aim-report/who-will-probe-the-u-n-vatican-connection.

646. President George W. Bush, Second Inaugural Address (January 20, 2005).

647. Pat Robertson, *The New World Order* (Dallas, TX: Word, 1991), 5.

648. Barry M. Goldwater, *With No Apologies: The Personal and Political Memoirs of United States Senator Barry M. Goldwater*, 1st ed. (New York, NY: Morrow, 1979), 284.

649. Ibid.

650. "Christian Reconstructionism," *Wikipedia*, last modified December 10, 2011, http://en.wikipedia.org/wiki/Christian_reconstructionism.

651. Michelle Goldberg, "A Christian Plot for Domination?" *The Daily Beast*, August 14, 2011, http://www.thedailybeast.com/articles/2011/08/14/dominionism-michele-bachmann-and-rick-perry-s-dangerous-religious-bond.html.

652. John F. Maxwell, *Slavery and the Catholic Church: The History of Catholic Teaching on the Moral Legitimacy of the Institution of Slavery* (Chichester, U.K. : Antislavery Society, 1975), 20.

653. Dave Hunt, *A Woman Rides the Beast* (Eugene, OR: Harvest House Publishers, 1994), 54.

654. *Brownson's Quarterly Review*, January, 1873, vol. 1, 10.

655. Dave Hunt, *A Woman Rides the Beast*, 54–55.

656. Ronald L. Conte Jr., "The Future and the Popes," *Catholic Planet*, November 14, 2004, http://www.catholicplanet.com/future/future-popes.htm.

657. "Henry Edward Manning," *Wikipedia*, last modified August 28, 2011, http://en.wikipedia.org/wiki/Henry_Edward_Manning.

658. "Ultramontanism" *The Oxford Dictionary of the Christian Church*, 3rd ed. rev. ed. F. L. Cross and Elizabeth A. Livingstone (Oxford; New York: Oxford University Press, 2005), 1667.

659. Cardinal Manning, *The Present Crises of the Holy See Tested by Prophecy*, reprinted in 2007 under the title, "The Pope & the Antichrist" (Tradibooks, Dainte-Croix du Mont, France), 75.

660. Ibid., 79–80.

661. Ibid., 81–82.

662. "PERMANENT INSTRUCTION OF THE ALTA VENDITA," PUBLIC DOMAIN, viewable here: *Catholic Voice*, last accessed January 19, 2012, http://www.catholicvoice.co.uk/dillon/text.htm#14.

663. Rev. Herman Bernard Kramer, *The Book of Destiny* (Belleville, IL: Buechler Publishing Company, 1955), 277.

664. Ronald L. Conte Jr., "The Future and the Popes," *Catholic Planet*, November 14, 2004, http://www.catholicplanet.com/future/future-popes.htm.

665. Ibid., 92.

666. In the Wion manuscript which reads Peregin' apostolic' the raised ' is a common scribal notation for an "us" ending. It looks similar to a fat comma placed after the letter on the median line represented us or os, generally at the end of the word being the Nominative case affix of the second declension sometimes is or simply s. The apostrophe used today originated from various marks in sigla, hence its current use in elision, such as in the Saxon genitive. See: http://en.wikipedia.org/wiki/Scribal_abbreviation#Latin_alphabet.

667. René Thibaut, *La Mystérieuse*, 91.

668. Ketchum, *The Evidence for End Time Prophecy* (Bloomington, IN: iUniverse, 2003), 81.

669. Ibid., 81.

670. "Our Lady of Fátima," *Wikipedia*, endnote 34, last modified January 24, 2012, http://en.wikipedia.org/wiki/Our_Lady_of_F%C3%A1tima#cite_note-33.

671. Catechism of the Catholic Church: Second Edition, Catholic Church (Random House Digital, Inc., 2003), 193–194.

672. John Vennari, "The Fourth Secret of Fátima," *Catholic Family News*, last accessed February 13, 2012, http://www.cfnews.org/Socci-FourthSecret.htm.

673. See: http://www.vatican.va/roman_curia/congregations/cfaith/documents/rc_con_cfaith_doc_20000626_message-fatima_en.html.

674. John Vennari, "The Fourth Secret of Fátima," *Fátima.org*, last accessed February 13, 2012, http://www.fatima.org/news/newsviews/010207fourthsecret.asp.

675. "Cardinal Sodano Reads a Text on the 'Third Secret,'" *Fátima.org,* May 13, 2000, http://www.fatima.org/news/newsviews/thirdsecret01.asp?printer.
676. Ibid.
677. John Vennari "The Fourth Secret of Fátima," *Catholic Family News.*
678. "Joseph Ratzinger as Prefect of the Congregation for the Doctrine of the Faith," *Wikipedia,* last modified November 14, 2011, http://en.wikipedia.org/wiki/Joseph_Ratzinger_as_Prefect_of_the_Congregation_for_the_Doctrine_of_the_Faith.
679. "Published Testimony: Cardinal Ratzinger (November 1984)," *Fátima.org,* last accessed February 13, 2012, http://www.fatima.org/thirdsecret/ratzinger.asp?printer.
680. John Vennari "The Fourth Secret of Fátima," *Catholic Family News.*
681. "Cardinal Oddi on the REAL Third Secret of Fátima: 'The Blessed Virgin was Alerting Us Against the Apostasy in the Church," last accessed February 13, 2012, http://www.tldm.org/news7/thirdsecretcardinaloddi.htm.
682. Published Testimony: Cardinal Alonso (1975–1981)," *Fátima.org,* last accessed February 13, 2012, http://www.fatima.org/thirdsecret/fralonso.asp.
683. "Three Secrets of Fátima," *Wikipedia,* last modified February 6, 2012, http://en.wikipedia.org/wiki/Three_Secrets_of_F%C3%A1tima.
684. Ibid.
685. Erven Park, "'Diabolic Disorientation' in the Church," *New Oxford Review,* October 2006, http://www.newoxfordreview.org/article.jsp?did=1006-park.
686. Antonio Socci, "Dear Cardinal Bertone: Who between You and Me is Deliberately Lying? And Please Don't Mention Freemasonry," last accessed February 13, 2012, http://www.fatimacrusader.com/cr86/cr86pg35.asp.
687. John Vennari, "The Fourth Secret of Fátima," *Catholic Family News,* last accessed February 13, 2012, http://www.cfnews.org/Socci-FourthSecret.htm.
688. Bishop Richard Williamson, "Bishop Fellay of the Society of St. Pius X to Meet Pope August 29," August 15, 2005, http://www.freerepublic.com/focus/f-religion/1464382/posts.
689. "Apparition of the Blessed Virgin on the Mountain of La Sette," last accessed February 13, 2012, http://www.thepopeinred.com/secret.htm.
690. As quoted in "Warnings from Heaven Suppressed," last accessed February 13, 2012, http://www.cardinalsiriandtheplotagainstthepope.com/warnings_from_heaven.htm.
691. Yves Chiron, *Saint Pius X: Restorer of the Church* (Angelus Press, 2002) 122.
692. "Jus Exclusivæ," *Wikipedia,* last modified December 7, 2012, http://en.wikipedia.org/wiki/Jus_exclusivae.
693. "Liber LII: Manifesto of the O.T.O.," last accessed February 13, 2012, http://lib.oto-usa.org/libri/liber0052.html.
694. William Guy Carr, *The Red Fog Over America* (Hollywood, CA: Angriff Press, 1959), 225–226.
695. John L. Allen, "A Triptych on Benedict's Papacy, and Hints of What Lies Beyond," May 13, 2011, http://ncronline.org/blogs/all-things-catholic/triptych-benedict%E2%80%99s-papacy-and-hints-what-lies-beyond.

696. Ibid.

697. Ibid.

698. Edward Pentin, "Naming of New Cardinals Prompts Speculation about New Pope," *Newsmax,* January 10, 2012, http://www.newsmax.com/EdwardPentin/Cardinals-Pope-Benedict-Successor/2012/01/10/id/423629.

699. Ibid.

700. The full text of "Toward Reforming the International Financial and Monetary Systems in the Context of a Global Public Authority" can be read at: *Zenit: The World Seen from Rome,* October 24, 2011, last accessed January 19, 2012, http://www.zenit.org/article-33718?l=english.

701. Richard Owen, "ROME: Black Pope Could Follow Barack Obama's Election, Says US Archbishop," *Virtue Online,* November 6, 2008, http://www.virtueonline.org/portal/modules/news/article.php?storyid=9314.

702. The Associated Press, "Ghanaian Cardinal to Head Vatican's Peace Office," *USA Today,* October 24, 2009, http://www.usatoday.com/news/religion/2009-10-24-vatican-africa_N.htm.

703. John L. Allen, "A Papal Contender Grabs the Spotlight," *National Catholic Reporter,* October 28, 2011, http://ncronline.org/blogs/all-things-catholic/papal-contender-grabs-spotlight.

704. Sandro Magister, "Too Much Confusion. Bertone Puts the Curia Under Lock and Key," *Cheisa,* November 10, 2011, http://chiesa.espresso.repubblica.it/articolo/1350080?eng=y.

705. "Cardinal Bertone Seizes Control of the Curia," November 14, 2011, http://aronbengilad.blogspot.com/2011/11/cardinal-bertone-seizes-control-of.html.

706. Andrea Tornielli, "Cardinal Bertone Turns 77," *Vatican Insider,* December 12, 2011, http://vaticaninsider.lastampa.it/en/homepage/the-vatican/detail/articolo/bertone-cardinale-vaticano-vatican-cardinal-cardenal-10436/.

707. "Monsignors' Mutiny," revealed by Vatican leaks, Philip Pullella | Reuters – Mon, Feb 13, 2012.

708. Francis X. Rocca, "Vatican Downplays Charges of Financial 'Corruption,'" *Catholic News Service,* January 26, 2012, http://www.catholicnews.com/data/stories/cns/1200336.htm.

709. "Monsignors' Mutiny" revealed by Vatican leaks, Philip Pullella | Reuters – Mon, Feb 13, 2012.

710. Ibid.

711. Elisabetta Povoledo, "Transfer of Vatican Official Who Exposed Corruption Hints at Power Struggle," *The New York Times,* January 26, 2012, http://www.nytimes.com/2012/01/27/world/europe/archbishop-viganos-transfer-hints-at-vatican-power-struggle.html.

712. Malachi Martin, *Windswept House,* 7.

713. Malachi Martin, *The Keys of This Blood* (New York, NY: Touchstone, 1991), 607–608.

714. Ibid.

715. *The Siri Thesis,* compiled by. William G. von Peters, Ph.D., 8; viewable here: http://www.cartesio-episteme.net/st/siri-thesis.doc.

716. Ibid., 30.
717. *Works of the Seraphic Father St. Francis of Assisi* (1182–1226), Washbourne, 1882 AD, 248.
718. Rev. Herman Bernard Kramer, *The Book of Destiny*, (Belleville, IL: Buechler Publishing Company, 1955), 277.
719. See: http://www.ilfattoquotidiano. it/2012/02/10/complotto-di-morte-benedetto-xvi/190221/.
720. "'Within Twelve Months, the Pope Will Die'—What Are We to Make of These Alleged Words of Cardinal Paolo Romeo?" February 10, 2012, http:// areluctantsinner.blogspot.com/2012/02/within-twelve-months-pope-will-die-what.html.
721. J. R. Church, e-mail message to Tom Horn, 2009.
722. William J. Reid, *Lectures on the Revelation* (Stevenson, Foster, 1878), 306.

Images

1. Here is a copy of the massive 1595 *Tree of Life* Latin text: http://books.google. com/books?id=a4o8AAAAcAAJ&pg=507#v=onepage&q&f=false.
2. File: Leone 13.jpg, *Wikipedia*, used by permission, last accessed January 30, 2012, http://en.wikipedia.org/wiki/File:Leone_13.jpg.
3. Image as sourced on NoBeliefs.com, viewable here: last accessed February 7, 2012, http://nobeliefs.com/nazis.htm, as taken from: "Pope Pius XII," *Wikipedia*, last modified February 4, 2012, http://en.wikipedia. org/wiki/Pope_Pius_XII.
4. *Pastor Angelicus*, Screen capture, Vatican Film Library, last accessed January 30, 2012, http://www.vaticanstate.va/EN/Other_Institutions/Vatican_Film_ Library.htm.
5. File: Coat of Arms of Pope Paul VI, used by permission, *Wikipedia*, last accessed February 2, 2012, http://en.wikipedia.org/wiki/File: Coat_of_Arms_of_Pope_Paul_VI.svg.
6. Image from: http://vaticaninsider.lastampa.it/en/homepage/news/detail/ articolo/papa-el-papa-pope-dimissioni-resignation-renuncia-8389/.
7. René Thibaut, *La Mystérieuse Prophétie des Papes* (Paris: J. Vrin, 1951), 62.
8. Ibid., 63.
9. Ibid., 64–65.
10. File: CumaeanSibylByMichelangelo.jpg, used by permission, public domain, last accessed January 23, 2012, http://en.wikipedia.org/wiki/File: CumaeanSibylByMichelangelo.jpg.
11. F. Paul Peterson, *Peter's Tomb Recently Discovered In Jerusalem* (4th Edition, 1971). (Copies may be obtained from your local bookstore or from the author and publisher, F. Paul Peterson, P.O. Box 7351, Fort Wayne, Indiana; Price $2.00.) Permission is granted to reproduce any part of this book if title, price, and address where it may be purchased are given. (Cris Putnam obtained this information here: http://biblelight.net/peters-jerusalem-tomb.htm.)
12. Image source: *Vatican Insider*, November 12, 2011, for use in the article, "Turkson: It Was Our Duty to Publish the Memo on the Global Public Authority," by Atoine-Marie Izoard, last accessed February 16, 2012, http://vaticaninsider.lastampa. it/en/homepage/documents/detail/articolo/crisi-crisis-9875/.
13. File: Follis-Constantine-lyons RIC VI 309.jpg, used by permission, last accessed January 17, 2012, http://en.wikipedia.org/wiki/File:Follis-Constantine-lyons_ RIC_VI_309.jpg.

14. File: Silvester II. and the Devil Cod. Pal. germ. 137 f216v.jpg, used by permission, last accessed January 17, 2011 (Illustration from Cod. Pal. germ. 137, Folio 216v Martinus Oppaviensis, Chronicon pontificum et imperatorum PUBLIC DOMAIN), http://en.wikipedia.org/wiki/File:Silvester_II._and_the_Devil_Cod._Pal._germ._137_f216v.jpg.

15. Coin photo viewable here: *ICollector.com*, last accessed January 19, 2012, http://www.icollector.com/Roman-Empire-Vespasian-69-79-Sestertius-71-28-39g_i9258028.

16. File: Gregory XIII medal.jpg, used by permission, public domain, last accessed January 19, 2012, http://en.wikipedia.org/wiki/File:Gregory_XIII_medal.jpg.

17. Public Domain, last accessed January 19, 2012, http://www.valueoftruth.org/rome/church-seated.jpg.

18. Image scanned by Brad Gsell and emailed to Cris D. Putnam, dated November 14, 2011.

19. File: Tiara Benedict XVI.jpg, *Wikipedia*, used by permission, last accessed February 9, 2012, http://en.wikipedia.org/wiki/File:Tiara_Benedict_XVI.JPG.

20. File: Millerite 1843 chart 2.jpg, *Wikipedia*, used by permission in the United States, last accessed February 2, 2012, http://en.wikipedia.org/wiki/File:Millerite_1843_chart_2.jpg.

21. William J. Reid, *Lectures on the Revelation* (Stevenson, Foster, 1878), 306. Download free here: http://books.google.com/books?id=WqgGAAAAQAAJ&printsec=frontcover&source=gbs_ge_summary_r&cad=0#v=onepage&q&f=true.

22. " 'Holy blood' of John Paul II Arrives in Colombia," *News that Matters*, last accessed January 22, 2012, http://ivarfjeld.wordpress.com/2012/01/22/holy-blood-of-john-paul-ii-arrive-in-colombia/.

23. File: Aachen Cathedral North View at Evening.jpg, *Wikipedia*, Image by (Aleph), http://commons.wikimedia.org, used by permission, last accessed February 13, 2012, http://en.wikipedia.org/wiki/File:Aachen_Cathedral_North_View_at_Evening.jpg.

24. File: HagiaMariaSionAbbey052209.jpg, *Wikipedia*, PUBLIC DOMAIN, last accessed February 13, 2012, http://en.wikipedia.org/wiki/File:HagiaMariaSionAbbey052209.JPG.